SECOND EDITION

RECLAIMING OUR SCHOOLS
Teaching Character, Academics, and Discipline

Edward A. Wynne
The University of Illinois at Chicago

Kevin Ryan
Boston University

Merrill, an imprint of Prentice Hall
Upper Saddle River, New Jersey   *Columbus, Ohio*

Library of Congress Cataloging-in-Publication Data

Wynne, Edward.

Reclaiming our schools : teaching character, academics, and discipline / Edward A. Wynne, Kevin Ryan.—2nd ed.

p. cm.

Includes bibliographical references and index.

ISBN 0-13-459041-4

1. Moral education—United States. 2. Classroom management—United States. I. Ryan, Kevin. II. Title.

LC311.W96   1997

370.11'4'0973—dc20   96-6855

CIP

Cover photo: © K. Wyle/H. Armstrong Roberts

Editor: Debra A. Stollenwerk

Production Editor: Julie Anderson Peters

Design Coordinator: Jill E. Bonar

Text Designer: Frankenberry Design

Production Manager: Patricia A. Tonneman

Electronic Text Management: Marilyn Wilson Phelps, Matthew Williams, Karen L. Bretz, Tracey Ward

This book was set in Century Schoolbook by Prentice Hall and was printed and bound by Quebecor Printing/Book Press. The cover was printed by Phoenix Color Corp.

© 1997 by Prentice-Hall, Inc.

Simon & Schuster/A Viacom Company

Upper Saddle River, New Jersey 07458

Earlier edition © 1993 by Macmillan Publishing Company.

Photos by Edward A. Wynne

Printed in the United States of America

10 9 8 7 6 5 4 3 2 1

ISBN: 0-13-459041-4

Prentice-Hall International (UK) Limited, *London*

Prentice-Hall of Australia Pty. Limited, *Sydney*

Prentice-Hall of Canada, Inc., *Toronto*

Prentice-Hall Hispanoamericana, S. A., *Mexico*

Prentice-Hall of India Private Limited, *New Delhi*

Prentice-Hall of Japan, Inc., *Tokyo*

Simon & Schuster Asia Pte. Ltd., *Singapore*

Editora Prentice-Hall do Brasil, Ltda., *Rio de Janeiro*

...some schools have adopted conservative models that tend to emphasize order, discipline, and courage—what Boston University educator Kevin Ryan labels the "stern virtues" as opposed to "soft" or easy virtues like compassion and self-esteem.

[University of Illinois educator Edward] Wynne calls for a return to the "great tradition in education," that is, the transmission of "good doctrine" to the next generation.

—"How to Raise a Moral Child: Let's Hear it for Honesty, Self-Discipline, and Empathy," *U.S. News & World Report*, June 3, 1996, p.56

Foreword

by James S. Coleman
President, American Sociological Association, 1991–1992

The act of educating another is a moral act: Whatever part the concern with their own needs plays in the lives of educators, it shares its place with their concern for those they teach. Thus teaching is itself a part of the moral message transmitted by a teacher to a child. And the school is the social agency that organizes such transmission. That moral message may be strong and clear if the teacher is dedicated to the task of teaching, or distorted if the teacher has largely given up on that task.

But the moral message contained in the act of teaching is only part of the values teachers and schools transmit. Teachers and schools, like parents and families, cannot avoid teaching values. And as schools come to encompass an increasing part of most children's lives, the values transmitted by schools come to be a larger part of the cultural heritage that the younger generation receives from the older. Yet this teaching of schools often goes unnoticed, unintentional and unreflexive.

Sometimes, however, it is not. In recent years, the recognition that schools inevitably teach values has become widespread. As a result, attempts to teach values have arisen, along with controversies about what values are taught. Often the recognition and the controversy have led to a frightened drawing-back, resulting in the teaching that "all values are equally meritorious," a form of moral relativism that undermines the very values inherent in the act of teaching. Sometimes it is teaching of values about what others do, or are doing wrong. This includes teaching about the wrongs that governments do, the wrongs that corporations do, the wrongs that others in authority do. What is taught most broadly is that those in authority or those in power do wrong. This is not all bad. One is never too young to learn the lesson of Lord Acton, that "Power corrupts; absolute power corrupts absolutely." But such values have a serious defect as an aspect of moral education. They provide no guides for one's own action; they are not values about what one should and should not do.

Edward Wynne and Kevin Ryan have responded differently. They are not reticent about what values are to be taught in schools by teachers. Nor do they advocate focusing on the wrongs that others do. They are concerned with each child's personal values, those that will guide the child's own actions. Their unhesitating answer is that it is traditional values that schools should teach. This book is designed to be an aid for those who agree with that answer.

They do not provide an explicit argument to persuade those who do not agree with them or who are uncertain about what values to transmit. Their argument is implicit in much of what they have written, but a few points may be added.

What is most striking about traditional values is their similarity from one culture to another. The values of respect for others, taking responsibility for one's own actions, helping others in need, keeping promises (and not making promises that one cannot keep), honesty, and putting forth one's best efforts are all widely shared among cultures, primitive and modern, on every continent. There is no imposition of these values by one cultural group on another; in every culture, there is an attempt by the adult generation to impose these values on the young.

Why the similarity? The answers, I believe, must lie in the fact of society itself, and the demands that the proper functioning of a society imposes on its members. Every society has its members whose actions do not uphold the traditional values stated in the preceding paragraph. But if the society were largely made up of members who were dishonest, did not keep promises, did not help others in need, and ignored the other traditional values, the society would hardly function well.

Thus it is not accidental that these traditional values are so similar in different cultures. These values are important to the functioning of a society. Yet this leads to the question: Why doesn't the "society of the school itself" (for the school is a small society, with its values, norms, taboos, and heroes) induce this socialization by the very demands it makes on its members? I believe the answer is that the school does so to some degree, but much less than it might if it were a different kind of society. The society of the school is a partial society, a dependent society, a society largely without common goals. A child does not live with the other children in a school, but spends only some hours each day there (and those hours with others of the same age). Therefore, it is easy for children to escape helping others in need, easy to escape the consequences of dishonesty and of breaking promises. The children and youth in school are under the supervision of a staff, like inmates of a prison. As a result, their values can become biased in the direction found in all dependent societies: collusion in cheating, norms against working hard, lack of responsibility for their actions. Because this society of the young has mostly the individualistic goals of individual achievement and few common goals (except interscholastic athletics), the values of helping one another, of contributing to a joint effort, and of respect for others have little means for encouragement.

The typical organizational deficiencies of a school prevent it from being a society in which the values that can sustain a society's functioning are learned in the very process of interaction. Yet if the school is to function well, and if its students are to be fit for the society they will inhabit as adults, these values must be transmitted. How this can come about in a school, how its teachers and principals can bring it about, is the focus of this book. I commend it to your attention.

Preface

This book shows educators and other citizens how morals can be taught in both elementary and secondary schools. They can be applied by individual teachers in the classroom as well as administrators concerned with the entire school. The text clearly identifies appropriate opportunities for such applications. Our writing is based on the research and analytic writings of many recognized authorities, many modern and some ancient, as well as our own research, including numerous interviews with educators and observations in schools.

MORAL INSTRUCTION

In this book we emphasize that moral instruction is fully consistent with students attaining excellent academic results. Many of the book's themes are congruent with the revival of public and professional interest in pupil character as a goal of education. Readers of this book will learn how to conduct moral instruction and gain a better understanding of what teaching morality really means. We also propose and justify a practical definition of moral instruction. Even readers who disagree with elements of that definition should find many of the insights in the book useful.

By *morals*, we mean such long-honored educational concerns as teaching character, academics, and discipline. We will show the many moral ramifications of effective academic teaching and learning. In a sense, the traditional emphasis of education that prevailed through thousands of years encompassed many of these same concerns. And we are unabashed about using the word *traditional* in discussing moral education.

Morality is not a novel concern in education. Many good ideas about how to teach morality have been around for a long time. Indeed, we are not reluctant to recommend education policies and practices that were employed successfully long before our country was founded, such as expecting students to be diligent and work hard at learning. Obviously, not all things that happened in the past were good or desirable. However, we believe that many recently introduced educational practices are unsound. Unfortunately, contemporary education literature typically gives an extraordinary emphasis to what was allegedly invented yesterday. In such an intellectual environment, it is fair to say our perspective is much more sympathetic to tradition than that of many other authorities.

Our collective experiences in research and teaching over forty years assure us that many contemporary educators share our interests in traditional morality. Some of these educators do not even realize the unique nature of their priorities. The book is addressed primarily to such educators. We also hope to engage academics who want to understand these themes more fully or inform their students about an important educational issue. The book's focus is essentially secular. However, many educators in religious schools will find its materials useful.

OUR BELIEFS

We believe too much educational writing during the past three or four decades has been pervaded with sentimentality. Readers accustomed to such sentimentality may find our analysis upsetting. However, we do not propose to take sentiment out of education. Love, dedication, and caring will always be vital components of good teaching. We merely want to mix such sentiments with a moderate dose of prudence. This blending can serve the interests of both students and society.

As for prudence, we do not think that education regularly is, or should be, fun. Nor do we believe that everybody can become an *A* student. However, we do not imply that anyone's moral worth is dependent on attaining that difficult academic goal. Furthermore, we do not believe that fifty percent or more of our young people should aim to obtain a four-year college education. Indeed, there are undoubtedly even a number of young people who should not aim to complete an academic high school program, especially by proceeding straight through school. Many such young people need alternative paths to maturity; America is currently making excessive demands on the adaptability of our schools.

FEATURES OF THE TEXT

The book's contents represent an interweaving of factual information, theoretical discussion, and examination of instances of good and bad classroom and school-wide practices. The thirteen chapters comprise a thematic sequence. The first chapters deal with the larger issues surrounding education and the teaching of values and the state of youth and student conduct and learning in contemporary America. The succeeding chapters focus on particular practices and issues relevant to teachers and administrators, morality in the classroom, character and academics, curriculum, the school as a community, moral leadership in schools, and ceremonies in effective schools. The highly practical School Assessment Checklist in the Introduction of the book allows educators to estimate the quality of the focus on character, academics, and discipline in their school or classroom.

NEW TO THIS EDITION

This second edition has intensified the hands-on emphasis of the first edition. For instance, we have added a list of 100 suggestions to teachers and administrators in the Appendix. These are specific ways that educators can apply the book's principles in their own classrooms and schools. Another hands-on tool is the list of suggested exercises, Practices and Policies, at the end of each chapter. Readers—both students and practitioners—have told us they find such materials provocative and enriching.

Two new chapters have been added to this edition: Chapter 11 addresses sex education and character and Chapter 12 offers portraits of two pro-character public schools in operation.

ACKNOWLEDGMENTS

Any book is built on the shoulders of those who have gone on before it. Certainly, that is the case for this effort. We have freely borrowed from the works of scholars and writers from classical Greece to the present. Much of this work has been drawn from the views of our contemporaries, friends, students, and colleagues, all of whom have been struggling with the problems of American schooling for many years. And, while we have borrowed from them, we must quickly add that we bear the total responsibility for how we interpret and apply these ideas. While we are indebted to many, the blame is ours alone.

We also owe thanks to certain individuals who have read and reacted to various drafts of our manuscript. Specifically, we must acknowledge Thomas Masty, James Grandison, and Judith Wynne for their thoughts and reactions. Marilyn Ryan and Cathleen Kinsella Stutz labored over several drafts of the manuscript and gave us thoughtful and often penetrating criticism. We wish to thank the following academic reviewers for their careful criticism and praise of drafts of our manuscript: Jacques Benninga, California State University—Fresno; R. Lewis Hodge, The University of Tennessee, Knoxville; Mark Holmes, Ontario Institute for Studies in Education; James R. Rest, University of Minnesota; and Robert C. Serow, North Carolina State University. Finally, the authors want to acknowledge one another. Whatever the merits or defects of this book, the task of composition has been intellectually and personally satisfying. Surprisingly, we are better friends at the end of the project than we were at the start. It has been a labor of love.

About the Authors

For more than twenty-five years, Edward A. Wynne has been Professor at the College of Education, The University of Illinois at Chicago. He has published, coauthored, or edited ten books and more than 120 articles and other writings. He has published in journals ranging from *Phi Delta Kappan, Educational Leadership*, and *Educational Evaluation and Policymaking* to *The Wall Street Journal*. In addition to his many personal studies of individual public and private schools, his students, under his supervision and training, have conducted more than 300 school studies. Many of his writings deal with character, and he founded two successive national periodicals, *Character* and *Character II*. He was also principal organizer and editor of *Developing Character, Transmitting Knowledge*, a national statement on the issue of character and education signed by twenty-seven prominent Americans. He is probably the academic most prominently associated with the revival of intellectual interest in the topic of character as a goal of education.

Kevin Ryan is Professor of Education at Boston University, where he is also Director of the Center for the Advancement of Ethics and Character. A former high school English teacher, Ryan has been a university educator since 1963. He has taught on the faculties of Stanford University, the University of Chicago, Harvard University, the University of Lisbon, and The Ohio State University. Ryan has written or edited fifteen books, including *Those Who Can, Teach* and *The Roller Coaster Year: Stories by and for First Year Teachers*, and more than ninety articles. His primary academic foci are character education and teacher education. Ryan has received awards from the University of Helsinki, the Association of Colleges for Teacher Education, and the Association of Teacher Educators. In 1990 he was the recipient of Boston University's Scholar Teacher Award.

Brief Contents

INTRODUCTION

CHAPTER 1   Educators and the Teaching of Values   1

CHAPTER 2   The Multiple Goals of Education   32

CHAPTER 3   How To Teach Character and Academics   58

CHAPTER 4   Teaching Discipline   86

CHAPTER 5   The Moral Nature of the Classroom   106

CHAPTER 6   Teachers as Moral Educators   120

CHAPTER 7   Curriculum as a Moral Educator   142

CHAPTER 8   Fostering Community in Schools and Classrooms   172

CHAPTER 9   Leadership in Moral Schools   188

CHAPTER 10   Using Ceremonies in Moral Schools   208

CHAPTER 11   Sex and Character   218

CHAPTER 12   Pro-Character Schools in Operation   138

CHAPTER 13   A Final Word   254

APPENDIX: 100 Ways Educators Can Help Students Acquire Good Character   260

Contents

Introduction   xvii

The School Assessment Checklist   xxi

CHAPTER 1   Educators and the Teaching of Values   1

The Tension   2

Bridging the Gap   3 ✦ A Shopping Mall Story   4 ✦ Such Dismal
Images Do Not Represent the Only Reality   6

Trends in Youth Conduct   7

Summarizing the Data about Youth Disorder   9 ✦ Thinking about
the Data   10 ✦ Students See the Reality   11 ✦ What the Changes
Mean   13

The Relevance of Philosophy   17

To Be Concrete   18 ✦ Learning About Philosophy   19 ✦
Teacher Diligence   24

The Role of Religion   26

References   29

CHAPTER 2   The Multiple Goals of Education   32

The Great Tradition   34

Old-Fashioned   35 ✦ The Intellectual Rationale for the Great
Tradition   36

Understanding Learning   38

Incentives for Learning   39 ✦ Intensifying Learning   41 ✦
Reconsidering "Learning Is Fun"   42

Who Decides What Values?   45

Profound Learning in Schools   47

Competitive Athletics   48 ✦ Transformational Education   51 ✦
About Education Research   53

References   57

CHAPTER 3   How To Teach Character and Academics   58

Teaching Character   59

Comparing Virtues   60 ✦ What Do We Owe to Beings on Other
Planets?   61 ✦ Prosocial Conduct   63 ✦ Incentives   67 ✦
After-School Paid Employment   68 ✦ Deferred Gratification   69 ✦
Implications for In-School and In-Classroom Practice   72

Teaching Academics   75

Equality: A Critical Issue   76 ✦ Incentives for Academic Learning   78 ✦
Social Promotion   80 ✦ Pupil Grouping   82 ✦ Definitions of Equality   83

References   84

CHAPTER 4   Teaching Discipline   86

Are Rules and Punishments Necessary?   87

Policies that Cause Misconduct   89 ✦ Rules as Teachers   91

Establishing Rules   91

Schoolwide Rules   91 ✦ Classroom Rules   94 ✦ Rules for
Establishing Rules   95 ✦ Rules, Rights, and Responsibilities:
The Current Confusion   95

Punishment   97

Natural Versus Constructed Consequences   99 ✦ Classroom
Punishment   101 ✦ Rules Under Pressure   102 ✦ Collective
Punishment   103 ✦ Enforcement   103 ✦ Some Principles
for Teachers on Administering Punishment   104

References   105

CHAPTER 5   The Moral Nature of the Classroom   106

Ethos   109

Toward Creating a Moral Ethos in the Classroom   112 ✦ Self-Esteem—
A Dead End?   113 ✦ Diligence—The Alternative to Self-Esteem   115

Students' Attitudes About Education   116

References   119

CHAPTER 6   Teachers as Moral Educators   120

The Moral Teacher   121

Characteristics of the Moral Teacher   123 ✦ The Morality of Craft   123

The Teacher as Direct Source of Moral Communication   126

Ineffective Instructors   127 ✦ Preaching—Often Important and
Acceptable   129 ✦ Conducting Moral Education   131 ✦
Hard-Case Morality   131

The Moral Education of the Teacher   133

Where Help Is Needed   134

Making the Moral Domain a Priority   138

References   140

CHAPTER 7   Curriculum as a Moral Educator   142

Types of Curriculum   143

Curriculum as a Social Wager   145 ✦ Knowing the Good   146 ✦
The Moral Facts of Life   146 ✦ Ethical Ideals   147 ✦
The Practical Roots of Shared Morality   149 ✦ If a Consensus
Is Unattainable   152 ✦ Thinking Through the Moral   153

Loving the Good   155

The Curriculum and the Hero   155 ✦ Heroes and Villains   157 ✦
Developing the Moral Imagination   159 ✦ Everyday Heroes   160

Doing the Good   161

Moral Action and the Democratic Schools Movement   162

Cooperative Learning: An Uncertain Remedy   164

The Real Moral Action   169

References   170

CHAPTER 8   Fostering Community in Schools and Classrooms   172

Community and School Spirit   173

A Definition   174

About Boundaries   174 ✦ Conceptual Boundaries   176 ✦ Community
and Charter or Magnet Schools   178 ✦ School Philosophies   178 ✦
Persisting Over Time   179 ✦ Listening to the Past, Speaking to the
Future   180 ✦ Sharing Common Goals   181 ✦ Significant Symbols
and Rites   182 ✦ Cooperating With and Serving One Another   183

The Need for Hierarchy   184

Microcommunities   185

References   187

CHAPTER 9   Leadership in Moral Schools   188

Being Nimmukwallah   190

Identifying Good Teaching   193

Desirable Traits   194 ✦ Causing Pupil Learning   195 ✦
Translating Traits Into Observable Conduct   195 ✦ Translating
Role Modeling into Observable Conduct   196 ✦ Publishing Criteria
and Behaviors   197 ✦ Applying Criteria to Job Applicants   198

Challenges Surrounding Information Collection   199

Collecting Information   201

Fostering a Collegiate Spirit Among Teachers   203

Providing Teachers With Feedback   204

Maintaining Rewards and Sanctions to Affect Teacher Performance   205

The Principal as Role Model   205

References   206

CHAPTER 10   Using Ceremonies in Moral Schools   208

What are Ceremonies?   209
Elements of Ceremonies   210   ✦   A Multiplicity of Purposes   212   ✦
The Heart of Ceremonies   212
Concrete Examples   213
The High School   214   ✦   The Elementary School   214
References   216

CHAPTER 11   Sex and Character   218

The Inevitability of Sex Education   220
Changing Sexual Values   221   ✦   Sex Education in a Moral Void   222   ✦
Comprehensive Sex Education and the Evidence   223   ✦   The Sexual
Behavior of the Young   224
How Did We Get This Way?   225
Our New Sexuality   226   ✦   The New Sexuality and the Schools   226   ✦
The Real Divorce: Sex Education and Character   228   ✦   The Moral
Nature of Sex   228   ✦   Religion, Sex, and the Schools   229   ✦
The Condom Solution   230   ✦   The Traditional Wisdom of Parents   231   ✦
Abstinence: The Dreaded "A" Word   231
Conclusion   233
Basic Principles   233
References   236

CHAPTER 12   For-Character Schools in Operation   238

Background of the Studies   239
The Two Schools   241
Hiring Staff   241
Athletics and Character   242
Pupil Discipline   245
Effective Student Councils   246
Academics   247
Teacher Supervision   248
Creating Collective Identities   249
Ceremonies   250
A Can-Do Attitude   252
References   253

CHAPTER 13   A Final Word   254

Sentiment over Sentimentality   255
The Dangers of Happy-Think   256
From Its Beginnings   258
References   258

APPENDIX   100 Ways Educators Can Help Students Acquire Good Character   260

INDEX   265

Introduction

This book has evolved from the findings of our own research in public and private schools, numerous suggestions we have collected from educators, and our interpretations of extensive contemporary and antecedent literature and research.

Portions of this book will apply to both elementary and secondary school educators. Other materials are suitable for particular grade levels. Some of these differences are noted in the text; in other instances, the level of emphasis is evident. Our discussion will say little about some volatile issues such as AIDS education or drug education. However, in this edition, we have added a chapter on sex education and character because of a growing controversy in schools and the fact that so many educators, presumably with the best of intentions, currently attempt to treat this subject in a moral vacuum.

We are infinitely more concerned, however, with the general prevalence of sound moral instruction in a school or classroom than with systems of problem-oriented instruction in schools that are otherwise moral vacuums. We believe moral schools will comfortably devise ways of handling immediate, topical moral issues. Conversely, schools without sound moral norms may well misapply the most wholesome problem-oriented instruction. Furthermore, this book focuses on day-to-day decisions of typical educators, compared to the presentations of specialists teaching a certain curriculum to successive classes.

Our subject matter is sometimes controversial. However, the book does not aim to inspire grand intellectual conversions among readers.

Instead, its premises are more realistic. It assumes that the values underlying the conduct of most experienced educators have already evolved, whether they are protradition or not. This assumption applies even to many teachers in training. Much of the moral formation of neophyte teachers has already occurred through their parents, communities, schools, and religious organizations, and the motives that caused them to select teaching as a career. As you proceed, we invite you to weigh the numerous implicit practical questions posed throughout the text. Such examination will help you view yourself in an intellectual mirror. It can permit you to better see the connection between certain traditional values and many concrete, common school practices. Some readers of this book will be uncertain of the merits of traditional moral education in schools. Such objectors may discover that many school policies they essentially favor are really rooted in moral perspectives.

From such interpretations, you can learn to identify your own values and apply them more coherently through this book's mix of analysis and concrete examples; your own personal introspection; and carrying out the exercises provided at the end of each chapter.

An able principal once explained the importance of such coherence after being asked, "What is the first thing you look for in hiring a teacher?" The principal's answer: "A well-thought-out philosophy of teaching. It is not crucial that I agree with the applicant's philosophy. However, it is important that its different parts cohere—fit together in a predictable fashion. Without coherent personal philosophies, it is difficult for teachers to maintain classroom control. Their practices and expectations for students will be inconsistent and disrupt their classes."

THE SCHOOL ASSESSMENT CHECKLIST

Practicing educators prefer concise, focused professional literature. At the same time, educators concerned with transmitting traditional morals must sometimes engage in refined analysis. They must identify the connections between immediate acts and relatively remote effects. This book bridges these two contrasting themes. At the beginning of the book is the School Assessment Checklist, which focuses on observable acts and policies in and around schools. In *100 Ways Educators Can Help Students Acquire Good Character* in the Appendix, the book concludes with 100 concrete, character-oriented measures teachers and administrators can apply to the management of their schools and classrooms.

The checklist has undergone extensive development and field testing, allowing educators to use the list immediately to estimate the quality of the focus on character, academics, and discipline in their school or classroom. This estimation process also generates insight into how to improve current school or classroom policies. In other words, groups or individuals can use the list, and the inventory it provides, as a stimulator. It can identify policies that must change to increase moral learning in schools and classrooms. The checklist can also provide readers with a good idea of the perspectives underlying the critical concept of traditional values.

The checklist focuses on everyday, nontechnical school and classroom activities, such as flag-salute practices, the amount of homework regularly completed by pupils, and the policies applied in publicizing written discipline codes. Most educators will recognize that such mundane activities are usually ignored in formal school evaluations. However, we believe, as we emphasize throughout this book, that such bread-and-butter topics are critical to sound moral instruction. From experience, we know many practicing educators share this viewpoint.

The checklist was developed to identify schools applying highly effective moral education practices by a team of fifteen practicing educators and three academics, all sympathetic to such concerns.[1] Over several years it was used in about 300 schools, including public and private, urban and suburban, elementary and secondary schools in a large metropolitan area. They ranged from flagship suburban public high schools to schools in disordered, even dangerous, urban neighborhoods. The checklist has been revised periodically in response to many participants' suggestions.

We do not propose that a school is morally flawed if it fails to satisfy every item in the checklist. Such an approach would be simplistic. Innumerable local and historic factors may ensure that variations in policies prevail even among excellent schools. However, the list's items are not mere speculations. They represent carefully considered and field-tested principles. Educators who find notable variations between their school's policies and a number of the items on the list owe it to themselves and their pupils to reconsider their policies. Perhaps they should even invite qualified evaluators to help them engage in probing introspection.

Busy educators may be properly concerned with knowing how much time it takes to complete the checklist. In an elementary school, the checklist can be completed by an informed staff member in about an hour. It might take three or four hours for the careful examination of a larger high school. If time is a problem, even skimming the checklist can be instructive.

The checklist, in part, asks users to estimate the frequency of certain in-school activities relevant to moral education. Users will see that such questions imply value judgments about what acts are good or bad. Users will also note the list's emphasis on right conduct, or behavior, and on policies that stimulate correct conduct. This emphasis on conduct stresses a critical premise of traditional values: words and acts (or refraining from bad acts) are the essence of day-to-day virtue. Good or bad *character*—the word is derived from the Greek word for "marking"—is visible. It may be that, ultimately, each act of good conduct is inspired from within, founded on a person's internal state of mind. But, as a practical matter, educators must focus on pupils' acts or words; acts are the external measure of invisible internal states. A school or classroom devoid of virtuous acts is not transmitting traditional values, regardless of the refined thoughts that may be passing through pupils' minds.

To derive the benefits from this self-study, educators simply have to ask themselves repeatedly: Are we now doing as much as we can and should to emphasize the good activities that the inventory focuses on? Users will inevitably ask if statistical norms are provided to identify high and low levels of frequency; in other words, what levels are desirable? The answer is that no such norms are available. It is true that our research has disclosed considerable variations among schools in their levels of frequency. Some schools and classrooms are doing better than others. Furthermore, these variations are due in part to deliberate policies adopted by schools. However, the variations are also affected by factors beyond the control of particular educators, such as size of school enrollment, differences among the communities served, and age levels of pupils. These factors mean that an extraordinarily large research project would be necessary to collect and analyze enough data to generate broad statistical norms. Such resources have never been available to us. But the checklist can still be of considerable value.

The 100 Ways in the Appendix complement the checklist by translating the checklist's themes into concrete operating suggestions. Like the checklist, the 100 Ways are not intended to be flatly prescriptive. The applicability depends on the ages of the pupils in the school, the other opportunities and problems now confronting the school, and the skills and interests of the faculty.

After the checklist, our text analyzes the intellectual themes underlying that instrument. The checklist is to the succeeding text as a collection of recipes is to an explication on the theory of cooking. Excellent cooks must know something of both cooking practice and theory. However, we have chosen to put the checklist first, and the 100 Ways—which may be likened to correcting the seasoning of a cooked dish—last. Our experiences have convinced us that adult learners usually proceed from the specific to the general, from examining a list of items to considering its underlying theory. As a form of double-checking, many learners will again return to the specific.

We place some emphasis on analysis because our research, as well as educational literature overall, shows that teachers and principals have made innumerable, profitable adaptations of the themes in the list. These adaptations have been related to local circumstances and challenges. For example, some items on the list emphasize the importance of rich communication among faculty members and between faculty members and administrators to foster moral cohesion. This cohesion is important to produce wholesome effects on students. The moral—and morale—importance of such cohesion is later explicated in the analysis. Some educators, already recognizing the value of faculty cohesion, have worked to establish comfortable faculty rooms in their schools for staff socialization and relaxation. Yet the checklist and the 100 Ways say nothing about faculty social rooms, or about the myriad of other adaptations that might be stimulated by considering the premises of the checklist. Adaptations are discussed only in the analytical chapters of the text. We encourage other educators to engage in similar imaginative innovations. But innovation, whether in cooking or education, should rest on a sound intellectual framework. Thus, our book examines the themes and traditions underlying the checklist and the 100 Ways. That analysis will provide educators with the stimulation and tools to enhance the re-creating of moral education that is now underway in many American schools.

The text will also consider some other methods of teaching character, academics, and discipline, which are bypassed in the checklist. For example, the checklist deliberately does not address using formal curriculum to teach traditional values and stimulate good conduct. There are no references to textbooks, readers, or literature. Despite this silence, there is a persisting recognition that curriculum materials are an important resource for teaching values. There is the important matter of helping pupils to acquire the skills and empathy that often underline moral acts: to be helpful because they have learned to see things from another person's perspective.

It is unsound to settle such subtle matters as curriculum content or the cultivation of empathy by a checklist. But these matters are essential to moral instruction and are therefore considered in the text.

To emphasize our concern with practical suggestions, each chapter concludes with a list of questions or proposals. These identify school or classroom issues consistent with the chapter's themes.

REFERENCES

Wynne, E. A. (1987). *Chicago area award winning schools, 1987.* Chicago: University of Illinois at Chicago.

The School Assessment Checklist

The items in this checklist, as well as those in the "100 Ways Educators Can Help Students Acquire Good Character" list in the Appendix, relate to moral education in a variety of important direct and indirect ways. For some readers, the logic of many of these relationships will be readily evident. Other readers may find such relationships, even after reading the book, less obvious or even problematic. For either type of reader, the list is a good introduction to the opportunities and challenges pervading moral education.

The authors of *Reclaiming Our Schools: Teaching Character, Academics, and Discipline*, Edward A. Wynne and Kevin Ryan, designed the checklist and the "100 Ways" list for use in a variety of schools, public or private, elementary or secondary. We encourage readers to photocopy the checklist and "100 Ways" list and distribute copies to co-workers informally or at staff, department, or association meetings. Many of their elements are easily adaptable to individual classrooms. However, a few items on the list apply only to special categories of schools. Those items are so designated.

The list focuses on what actually happens in the school, rather than what the school's formal policies prescribe. For certain items, you may only be able to answer by making a sincere estimate. For many items, you may want to consult other teachers and even students. Many perspectives can be applied in considering such questions.

I. Interaction Among Staff, Students, and Parents

The following items relate to the nature of the human environment of the school. "Staff members" includes all certified or certifiable personnel.

1. Estimate the average number of hours per year a typical staff member spends in scheduled meetings and conferences with parents, including report card time. ————

2. Estimate the average number of parent contacts (e.g., via phone calls, face-to-face meetings, notes) per week for a typical staff member, apart from scheduled appointments. ————

3. Estimate the percentage of staff members who spend one or more hours per month in out-of-class contacts with students (supervising clubs, chaperoning dances, going to sporting events, tutoring). ————

4. Estimate the number of hours per year a typical staff member spends in scheduled staff, committee, or department meetings conducted for all or part of the staff. _____

5. Estimate the number of hours per year a typical staff member spends informally with other faculty (lunch, parties, coffee break, car pool). _____

6. Does your school have a student council? (Circle) *Yes* *No*

7. If yes, estimate the percentage of pupils (from all of the grade levels eligible for student council) who participate in student council during the year. _____

8. If yes in 6, estimate the number of hours per year a typical council member spends on council activities. _____

9. (For private elementary schools) Estimate what percentage of families provide the school with two or more hours per year of volunteer services. _____

10. (For private elementary schools) Estimate the average number of hours volunteered per family per year for the most active 5% of families who volunteer service to the school. _____

11. Estimate the percentage of pupils who routinely help keep halls, playgrounds, and classrooms neat, without adult supervision. _____

12. Estimate the number of multiclass school assemblies, ceremonies, or other activities (e.g., viewing athletic competitions) the average pupil attends in a typical month. _____

13. (For private, church-related schools) Estimate the number of religious assemblies or other multiclass gatherings an average pupil attends in a typical month. _____

14. (Typically for elementary schools—also relevant for some high schools) Estimate the percentage of pupils in classes who regularly recite the Pledge of Allegiance with the teacher and students standing, hands on hearts, with some degree of seriousness. _____

15. (For middle, junior high, and high schools) Estimate the percentage of graduating pupils who have spent a considerable time as part of a relatively stable group, under the continuous, immediate direction of one or more adults (e.g., four years as part of the same homeroom or athletic team). _____

16. Does your school have a school song? *Yes* *No*

17. If yes, estimate the percentage of pupils who can sing the first verse of that song. _____

18. Treating the school's annual budget as 100%, estimate, as a percentage of that sum, the value of gifts donated to the school by local individuals, excluding parents, or business organizations. ————

19. Treating last year's graduating class as 100%, estimate the percentage of previous graduates who might stop by to responsibly visit the school this year. ————

II. Character Formation

Good character, or citizenship, is much more than having right or profound ideas. It stresses doing right things—engaging in conduct immediately helpful to others. Such conduct is comprised of acts, such as being a math team member, serving as an aide or monitor, participating in sports as a good team member, cleaning up a classroom, tutoring others, helping in fund-raising, or providing entertainment for the school. The good citizen is not only an observer or critic, but also someone who pitches in on a day-to-day basis to make the school or community work.

Proper student conduct is enhanced by a code of conduct that not only prohibits wrongdoing, but also encourages students to do things that immediately help others. Such behavior is fostered by clearly defined policies in classrooms and throughout the school that (a) invite or require students to practice helping conduct; (b) stimulate praise and recognition for such conduct; (c) surround students with appropriate role models, either adults or students, who engage in such conduct; and (d) present a curriculum that sympathetically portrays real and fictional people who have displayed helping conduct.

We can analyze a school's (or classroom's) systems for developing student character by counting how many students are involved in positive conduct, how long they stay engaged in such activities, the types of activities they conduct, the forms of recognition for such activities, and the frequency and elaboration of such recognition.

The following list identifies various activities conducted in many elementary and secondary schools. Estimate what percentage of pupils take part in these activities in a typical month in your school.

1. Academic team competitions in or among schools (e.g., math or spelling bees) ————

2. Band or choir ————

3. Cheerleading ————

4. Classroom or building clean-up (not as part of a detention) ————

5. Class monitors, messengers, hall guards, office assistants _____

6. Crossing guards, patrol duty _____

7. Community service _____

8. Dramatic presentations (outside the classroom) _____

9. Fund-raising in school (e.g., bake sales) _____

10. Fund-raising out of school (e.g., walkathons, selling chances) _____

11. Clubs or other extracurricular activities not specified elsewhere _____

12. Interscholastic sports _____

13. Intramural sports _____

14. School newspaper _____

15. Providing deliberate academic help (e.g., peer tutoring) _____

16. Well-organized academic group projects (see discussion on cooperative learning in Chapter 7) _____

17. Library aides _____

18. Other _____

Listed below are types of recognition that may be awarded to individual pupils for positive conduct. Estimate for each category the percentage of pupils who receive one or more such awards in a typical school year.

1. Athletic or sportsmanship awards _____

2. Certificates _____

3. Mention in school newspaper _____

4. Mention in newsletter or general publication to parents _____

5. Mention over P. A. system _____

6. Mention on report card _____

7. Note home to parents _____

8. Pep rally _____

9. Posting name or photo _____

10. Gold star, sticker _____

11. Other _____

Recognition may also be given to groups of pupils, as members of successful teams, classes, clubs, etc. Estimate for each category the percentage of pupils who are members of one or more groups that attain such recognition pupils who are members of one or more groups that attain such recognition in a typical school year.

1. Athletic or sportsmanship awards ———
2. Certificates ———
3. Mention in the school newspaper ———
4. Mention in newsletter or general publication to parents ———
5. Mention over P. A. system ———
6. Mention on report card ———
7. Note home to parents ———
8. Pep rally ———
9. Posting name or photo ———
10. Special jackets or other garments ———
11. Other ———

III. Academics

The following items assume that academic learning depends on high standards and well-defined expectations of students and staff, with both groups receiving appropriate support and supervision.

1. Does your school have a written policy of not advancing pupils who are regularly not performing at or above grade or class level? *Yes No*
2. Estimate how often wall-space coverings (charts, displays of pupil work, notices, materials on bulletin boards) are changed in a typical classroom. ———
3. Estimate the average amount of homework per night a typical sixth- or seventh-grade pupil (elementary or junior high) has to do away from the school premises. ———
4. If the average is one hour or more, what percentage of students regularly finish and submit their homework each day? ———
5. (For high school) Does the school have any programs that invite—or require—seniors to stay engaged with academic and other purposeful activities through the end of the year? *Yes No*
6. Is there an honor roll for academic achievement that is conspicuously displayed, is changed at least twice a year, and lists between 5% and 25% of pupils in the affected grades? *Yes No*

7. Estimate the number of times per year the principal or another administrator meets with a typical tenured teacher on a one-to-one basis, either formally or informally, to discuss teaching. ———

8. Estimate the number of times per year other professionals (teachers, administrators) enter the typical teacher's classroom while class is in session. ———

9. Are lesson plans for all teachers collected and reviewed on a routine basis with written comments occasionally sent back? *Yes   No*

10. Is there a teacher's handbook that is thorough, has been revised within the past two years, and is distributed to all teachers? *Yes   No*

11. If yes, do teachers and administrators apply the rules and principles in the handbook consistently in dealing with students and other staff? *Yes   No*

12. Estimate the percentage of teachers who are strongly dedicated to stimulating students to attain their maximum potential. ———

IV. Discipline

Preventing misbehavior is part of fostering character development in pupils. Codes of conduct that prohibit foreseeable violations, are widely disseminated, and apply appropriate sanctions are important for preventing misconduct.

1. Does your school have a written code of conduct that clearly specifies desirable and undesirable conduct? *Yes   No*

2. If yes, is there a procedure to ensure that copies of the code are distributed to at least 90% of the parents annually (e.g., parent signs a receipt)? *Yes   No*

3. Do some or all of the school's students ride school busses? *Yes   No*

   If Yes, is there a code explicitly covering bus conduct? *Yes   No*

   Is it distributed as provided in questions 1 and 2? *Yes   No*

4. If you have a districtwide conduct code, does your school also have a local supplement in writing and widely distributed, that deals with the problems and opportunities relevant to your school? *Yes   No*

5. Do prompt, simple consequences, which almost all pupils perceive as unpleasant, routinely result from moderate rule violations? *Yes   No*

6. Does the code specifically prohibit rudeness and abusive or foul language among students? *Yes   No*

7. (More appropriate for older pupils) Are cheating and plagiarism clearly defined in the code? *Yes   No*

   Are clear consequences mandated? *Yes   No*

8. Does the code provide that violations of the criminal law (e.g., possessing drugs in school, bringing in weapons) will automatically be referred to the police? *Yes   No*

9. If a student is referred to the police, does the school regularly monitor the case and student to assist rehabilitation and ensure the case does not get lost? *Yes   No*

10. Estimate what percentage of pupils routinely observe the code almost all of the time. _____

11. (For middle, junior high, and high schools) Does the school regularly attempt some systematic assessment of illegal substance use by pupils (e.g., an anonymous survey)? *Yes   No*

12. Are there effective student organizations that directly promote responsible conduct (e.g., SADD)? *Yes   No*

CHAPTER 1

Educators and the Teaching of Values

Speaking of the testimony of early travelers to the good manners found in Ngoni households, a Ngoni elder said: "Such honoring of each other came to the Ngoni because they liked living together without any scattering as was the custom of other Malawi people. . . . Such honor was not shown by young people for fear of being beaten, but because all children were well taught that this behavior was right and proper for the upbuilding of the land."

—Margaret Read, *Children of Their Fathers*[1]

In this chapter we identify the book's primary audience and explain why we have written it for that audience. We present graphs and other research about trends in youth conduct. These materials show why there is dissatisfaction with current moral education policies. We interpret these data and demonstrate their connection to more traditional education approaches. We show the philosophical implications of our analyses, as well as the relevance of formal religion to the practice of moral education. Finally, we examine the feasibility of providing traditional moral instruction in secular public schools.

The primary audience for this book is the numerous—we estimate hundreds of thousands—teachers and administrators who recognize that

✦ transmitting character, academics, and discipline—essentially, "traditional" moral values—to pupils is a vital educational responsibility.

✦ at this time, there is increasing public and professional interest in improving our schools' capabilities to transmit good character to pupils.[2]

✦ some educational approaches to transmitting morality, such as values clarification or other consensual methods, underestimate the importance of parents and educators in establishing pupils' moral priorities. More effective means of moral education stress goals such as character formation and the importance of day-to-day good conduct in routine situations.

✦ schools should generally hold high academic expectations for pupils.

✦ maintaining good pupil discipline is a critical and sometimes difficult job, but it can and must be done.

✦ teachers must be in charge in their classrooms and provide pupils with positive role models.

✦ schools, like other complex institutions, must be led by principals, i.e., managers. These leaders should listen to and consult with teachers and cooperate with parents but must finally make and monitor the key decisions within the institution themselves.

✦ students have specific responsibilities that are integral to their education and the effective functioning of the school.

✦ all pupils deserve a 100% effort from their teachers. But schools, especially as pupils grow older, are not responsible for attaining 100% success. Insistence on such perfection undermines the coherence of many education programs. Pupils, as they mature, must assume increasing responsibility for their own accomplishments or deficiencies.

✦ many recent steps to "soften up" education have not been helpful for most pupils.

These principles are not novel. In some ways, they represent education themes going as far back as Plato and Aristotle. In our own era, they are congruent with many of the demands made on education by protradition reformers. These reformers include academics such as Ernest Boyer, E. J. Hirsch, Diane Ravitch, and the late Allan Bloom; present and former state and federal officeholders such as Bill Honig, Lamar Alexander, Thomas Kean, and William J. Bennett; practicing educators such as Jaime Escalante; and union officers such as Albert Shanker. Despite such congruence, a distressing tension has developed between many reformers and most practicing educators—school teachers and school administrators.

THE TENSION

A special irony colors this tension between educators and reformers. In fact, the two groups have more congruence than meets the eye. The authors, as researchers and teachers of educators, have worked with hundreds of practicing and potential teachers and administrators. Our experience convinces us that a great many educators—although not all—strongly sympathize with the principles urged by the previously mentioned critics. The opening paragraphs of this chapter echo some of their criticisms. For instance, all the critics have emphasized holding high academic expectations for pupils; educators should assume that most pupils are capable of performing better and working harder than they do currently.

The causes of the problems that critics have identified extend far beyond policies developed and applied by educators. Thoughtful authorities have noted many contributing factors: shifts in popular values; the role of the mass media; the increase in comparative affluence among the young; the growth of families with a single parent or two working parents; and the decline in vigor of many extended families. Still, many educators can do more to moderate the effects of such problems than they are now doing. In this book we identify constructive things educators can do and acknowledge the right things some of them are already doing.

Proposals for educational reform have come from a myriad of directions. Many such demands, even some of the responses we propose, cannot be classified along a right-left political continuum. For example, an item on our School Assessment Checklist is the importance of keeping pupils in relatively stable, coherent, adult-monitored groups through high school. This emphasis on cohesion among high school pupils has been found among both protradition groups favoring smaller, family-based schools and some liberal reformers, such as Theodore Sizer or Deborah Meier. To our mind, however, the protradition criticisms generally represent the more coherent and relevant body of reform proposals. Unfortunately, many academics and "education leaders" are too far removed from the realities of the typical school and classroom. As a result, they are intellectually trapped in a Rousseauian perspective and its naive vision of the innocence of childhood and the natural joys of learning. The harmful effects of such misconceptions are notorious. New teachers holding the same visions are regularly subjected to profound culture shock as they enter their first classroom. The shock results largely from the neophytes' dysfunctional romantic views on the incorruptibility of nature and people, which have been reinforced by their academic training.

Many educators who value character, academics, and discipline do not see themselves as traditionalists. Our studies show that in practice many such educators strongly support traditional values and try to apply those values in their work. Furthermore, we have studied policies applied in many successful public and private schools and classrooms. To a large degree, these schools and classrooms are managed on quite traditional principles—to the benefit of pupils and teachers. In other schools and classrooms, many educators try, with varying competence and success, to apply such principles.

In sum, protradition reformers have many potential allies among practicing educators. However, communication between these two groups has been poor. Too many reformers, on both pro- and antitradition sides, have displayed more arrogance than appreciation toward the real constraints that affect practicing educators. As a result, too many educators reflexively withdraw from anything with a label like "traditional." It is almost as if only new (and inadequately tested?) ideas and approaches deserve defense. Some educators believe that protradition reformers have made educators into scapegoats for deficiencies not of their making. A considerable antipathy has developed between the two camps.

Bridging the Gap

In this book we are trying to bridge the gap created by this antipathy. The book may also be informative to noneducators who have an interest in education reform. But our first audience is educators.

The distressing reality is that many protradition reformers, like adept agitators, have allowed their contentions to generate considerable polarization. In addition, those reformers, despite their vision and courage, have an imperfect knowledge of the typical patterns in elementary and secondary schools. They lack what the anthropologist Clifford Geertz called a fine-grained approach to the complexities of schools.

Furthermore, many reformers lack an appreciation of educational history. Conversely, all mature teachers have had considerable experience with successive waves of widely touted—and relatively transitory—reforms. This knowledge leads practicing educators to approach many reform proposals with suspicion. The teachers feel they will be left to pick up the pieces when the promoters of some expiring innovation skip off to sell another fad. Such experiences have engendered deep cynicism among many educators.

In addition, some reformers have made unrealistic proposals. We hear reiterated demands about what every child *should* know. What such reformers must mean, if they have ever taught a typical group of pupils for any length of time, is "here is what we would *like* every child to know." Unfortunately, the word *should* is interpreted to mean that practicing educators are at fault if only—let's say—87% of all pupils learn the recommended knowledge. Many reformers have also spoken strongly about students' "right" to an education, their right to be taught this and that, and their right to be treated as responsible individuals and participate in "democratic" school governance. Finally, many political leaders make proposals about the "right" of all students "to attain certain competencies." Where such rights come from, what are the "rights" of such students' teachers, and what responsibilities are attendant on being students are too often washed away by a warm bath of rhetoric.

Teachers understandably object to the idea they must attain a 100% success rate. They especially resent it when such proposals come from college professors who teach carefully screened students, often in elective upper-level or graduate classes. (Or from business professionals who can choose whom they employ or keep employed.) No one dares inform college professors they must attain a 100% passing rate for their pupils. Sometimes, too, educators are told, "Well, the Japanese are able to do this or that." Certainly some Japanese practices are ingenious and adaptable in the United States. But it is one thing to adopt particular practices. It is another to expect American schools to be able to apply an integrated body of norms embedded in a 2,000-year-old insular culture.

In this book, we aim to

+ show many educators how their present concerns and even practices are congruent with the proposals of many reformers.

+ help readers appreciate the profound and ancient roots of our proposals (the proposals are essentially not adaptations of yesterday's fads, but based on thousands of years of experience).

+ explain why certain proposed reforms need refinement in light of the realities of school experiences.

+ identify ways that certain proposed reforms are discordant with vital moral principles.

+ identify a variety of measures, many now applied by educators, that can help schools improve pupil character, academic learning, and discipline.

A Shopping Mall Story

Arthur Powell and his fellow researchers coined the vivid term *shopping mall high school*.[3] The term characterizes high schools with strong patterns of work avoidance by many pupils and teachers. The lack of diligence in schools has emerged as a key complaint of the reform movement. The researchers concluded that such shopping mall schools are relatively common in our era. In these schools, some pupils and faculty work hard at constructive learning. Yet many pupils and faculty, as far as education is concerned, only go through the motions. Students and teachers essentially make and carry out mutual pacts to avoid creating trouble for each other. The pupils avoid conspicuous breaches of discipline and don't make trouble for the teachers, and the teachers do not hassle pupils with demanding assignments. Systems of elective courses aggravate the whole pattern. Such systems license disengaged pupils to take "gut" courses—those courses that put little or no learning demands on students. These courses are often taught by teachers who do not take things too seriously. At the same time, some engaged pupils and their teachers are working diligently in the demanding electives or academic programs they have chosen.

As we will emphasize, many of the problems confronting educators are as much philosophical as tangible. A typical story about a shopping mall high school illustrates common patterns of philosophical confusion.

Several high school teachers complained to one of the authors about their school's lax enforcement of a tardiness policy. Some students did not promptly enter their classrooms immediately after class change. Instead, they hung out in the halls, talking and disturbing other classes and students and obviously wasting their own time.

The teachers said, "We believe the principal should more vigorously suppress such hanging around. The students should be identified, reprimanded and, if necessary, punished."

The author replied, "What about the teachers whose classes these pupils are going to? Shouldn't they identify their own tardy students and punish them?"

The teachers answered, "Well, part of the trouble is that some teachers themselves are regularly late for class. It is their students who most frequently hang out, since their teachers are not in their rooms."

The author remarked, "It seems the problem is more tardy teachers, rather than tardy students. If the principal would simply pressure the teachers to be on time, that would do more good than harassing the students."

The teachers mumbled something. Then they dropped the matter.

The teachers were willing to try to mobilize the principal against the unruly students. However, they were unwilling to complain about their equally erring colleagues. That would be impolitic. So things were left as the principal's "fault" or the pupils' "fault."

Of course, this same situation could occur at work sites other than a public school. Norms among many workers discourage them from complaining to the boss about their colleagues' lack of diligence. But we are often told teachers want to be seen as professionals, and such "ain't it awful" perspectives erode teachers' professionalism and responsibility. Unfortunately, the story is typical of the philosophic contradictions that too often pervade education.

The pupils who hung out in the halls were breaching the norms of this shopping mall high school. It was acceptable for students in some teachers' classes to kill time. It was also all right for teachers to be frequently late for class. But, according to the tacit school code, students should not kill time so as to disturb others, and the late-to-class teachers had erred in letting their students drift into the hall. However, it was not proper for teachers to complain about one another's tardiness. While they would have liked to see themselves as dedicated profession-als, they felt no responsibility for monitoring their peers. It was the principal's job to correct such defects.

Due to the general laxity in the school, the complaining teachers did not have to work extremely hard. But the situation frustrated them. They were not pleased to see pupils hanging out in the hall, not just because it disturbed their own classes, but also because it symbolized the triviality of many pupils' school experi-ences. While the general lassitude in the school excused much teacher malinger-ing, it also undermined the work of many other teachers.

The patterns of toleration, or permissiveness, that have evolved in many schools are too often taken as unchangeable, immutable, the way things "should be" or "must be." At the same time, these patterns make many teachers defensive. They do not feel they receive (or deserve?) respect. Further, much of their time is spent dealing with breaches of school convention—like pupils hanging out in the halls—that leave them embarrassed. In their hearts, they know what should be done in many situations, as with the teachers in the shopping mall high school, who really knew the first blame was on the late teachers. But too many tacit com-promises have been made to allow a clear attack on the issues. And so faculty members muddle on, complain about peripheral questions, feel a degree of shared complicity, and grumble about burnout.

Of course, we, the authors, know of many genuine school "horror stories"; situ-ations where the issues are much more dramatic than pupils merely hanging around. However, we deliberately chose to recite the low-key hanging around inci-dent. In reality, as most teachers know, the main discipline problems in most schools are not so much students bringing in guns. Instead, the problems are typ-ically more like the hanging around incident. Too many students do not take their responsibilities very seriously. And, too often, teachers go along with such irre-sponsibility. Furthermore, there is a certain self-correcting quality to real horror stories, e.g., about guns, sexual assault, and other such crimes around schools. Because such episodes make good copy, they usually attract some attention. Then, at least some short-term remedies are applied. Unfortunately, the prescrip-tions for correcting problems like hanging around, as our discussion suggests, are more complex. This is why we have brought the matter up in the first chapter of the book.

Such Dismal Images Do Not Represent the Only Reality

Fortunately, shopping mall patterns are not inevitable in high schools. We have observed many vital public schools that have escaped or corrected this disarray. These schools apply policies that stress character, academics, and discipline. The rest of this book will describe and interpret such policies and identify some of the barriers to their implementation. It is our consistent impression that faculty in vital schools are more diligent than educators in more lax schools. But such dili-gence is tied to purposive patterns of accomplishment. The educators' work is not routinely undermined by trivial discipline problems, such as pupils not being monitored by their assigned teachers. Instead, the teachers' work is typically related to the predictable challenge of providing demanding teaching to reasonably engaged pupils. Such diligence is often associated with understandable teacher (and pupil and parent) pride and sense of accomplishment.

Teachers in these schools also feel they work in highly supportive environments, instead of being largely on their own. Their colleagues and supervisors provide them with advice, encouragement, and constructive criticism. People work together to plan and put into effect sensible, coordinated schoolwide policies.

In a sense, protradition schools are high-demand/high-payoff environments—for faculties, pupils, and their families. All involved find that more is asked of them, and similarly they receive more from others. Conversely, more permissive environments—like the shopping mall high schools—do not make such high demands of their "inhabitants." However, their inhabitants often feel more alone and unsupported, due to the very "freedom" from intrusion and coherence in their school practices.

The matter of diligence also requires some consideration. This concept has strong moral overtones. It relates to the obligations human beings owe to certain other persons. It connotes trying hard, striving to attain a legitimate goal. Teachers have an obligation to parents, pupils, and taxpayers to teach diligently. Pupils owe it to themselves, their families, their teachers, and the taxpayers to work hard at school. Parents should diligently encourage their children to learn and be responsible. In sum, whenever people display nondiligence, it is likely they are simultaneously violating an obligation to others. They are betraying a moral duty.

TRENDS IN YOUTH CONDUCT

All serious discussions about school reform should begin by confronting a body of facts. As Abraham Lincoln said in his House Divided speech, "If we could better know where we have been, and whither we are tending, we could better see how to confront our challenges."[4]

As we will see, a variety of measures show there has been a substantial, long-term decline in the conduct of young Americans. These shifts in conduct have not been especially related to school attendance or in-school incidents. Instead, the measured acts of misconduct are more general, for example, increased rates of death due to suicide and homicide and increases in the rates of illegitimate births. True, there is no explicit tie between these data and school policies. However, it seems reasonable to believe that the widespread and remarkable trends we will examine inevitably affect pupils' conduct in school and are probably partly due to deficient school policies. After all, the school is the main public institution that absorbs the away-from-home time of these increasingly distressed young people.

As one example of such patterns, consider Figure 1.[5] The main graph in Figure 1 shows annual figures for (a) the rate of death by homicide among young White males, ages 15–24, from 1914 to 1994; (b) the rate of death by suicide among young White males, ages 15–24, from 1914 to 1994; (c) the percentage of a sample of high school seniors who admit to having used an illegal drug (not alcohol) at least once in the past thirty days, from 1975 to 1994; and (d) the rate of out-of-wedlock births among unmarried White females, ages 15–19, from 1940 to 1993. The enlargement on the right in Figure 1 provides a detailed picture of the more recent trends in youth disorder for the years 1978 to 1994.

Using rates and percentages in the graph makes allowance for changes in the absolute numbers of persons involved in different years. Each plotted line shows all of the years for which appropriate data breakdowns are available. We obviously lack the space to show misconduct trends affecting all possible classifications of youths, such as White youths from lower-income families. We have thus chosen to present four streams of the most compelling and clearly defined conduct.

The graphs deliberately focus on Whites—our most "advantaged" youths. This avoids the complications affecting minority youth behavior. There, issues of discrimination and poverty may come into play.

The phenomena plotted in Figure 1 are based on relatively reliable criteria. A death is classified as a homicide by an official decision. In the case of suicide, officials make a determination about the cause of death. Such determinations may underestimate suicides, to moderate the sufferings of survivors. However, the sociologist Durkheim observed such undercounting will probably represent a continuing tendency.[6] For example, assume suicide was undercounted by 10% in a

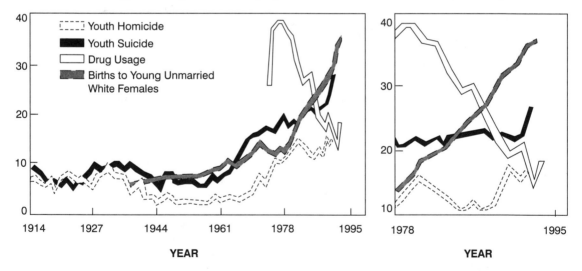

NOTE: Suicide and homicide deaths calculated as rates per 100,000 members of the age group 15–24 years old. Births to young unmarried white females calculated as rates per 1,000 members of the age group 15–19 years old. Drug use calculated as percentage of responding high school seniors admitting illegal drug use in past 30 days. Numbers in left ordinate represent, as appropriate, either percentages or rates per specified number. Homocide and suicide rates, 1914–1991; births to unmarried white females, 1940–1992; and drug use, 1974–1993.

Figure 1
Changes in the Rates of Suicide, Homicide, Drug Use, and Out-of-Wedlock Births

particular year. That same tendency to undercount will presumably prevail in the future. The data will still permit us to accurately estimate the changing rates of death by suicide, even if the absolute numbers are off. Since 1975, the rates of adolescent drug use have been calculated from the results of annual surveys of deliberately chosen samples of each successive senior class. The evidence of out-of-wedlock births is simple: the absence of the signature of a male on a birth certificate affirming he is the mother's husband.

Summarizing the Data about Youth Disorder

The statistics underlying Figure 1 can be easily summarized.

+ In 1994 the rate of young White male homicide deaths was 17.2 per 100,000 members of the age group 15–24 years old. This rate was 1% below the record-high rate of 17.5 in 1992. The difference of 1% is so small as to be statistically insignificant. The 1994 rate was over four times the record low for young White males, observed in 1941.

+ In 1994 the rate for young White male suicide deaths was at its record high of 26.5 per 100,000 members of the age group 15–24 years old. This rate is over four times the national low for young White males, observed in 1923.

+ Readers will note the apparent decline in youth drug use during the 1980s. The implications of this decline will be discussed in some detail in "What the Changes Mean" later in this chapter.

+ In 1992, illegitimate births to young White mothers were at their record rate—33.6 per 1,000 unmarried women in the age group 15–19 years old—and more than ten times their 1940 low.

+ Data on youth alcohol abuse, although not portrayed on the graph, should also be noted. These data have been collected as part of the annual drug use survey cited earlier. According to the survey, levels of youth alcohol use have remained relatively stable. Such stability is not very reassuring, however, in light of other findings. In 1993, for instance, 27% of the respondents reported that "all or almost all" of their friends got drunk at least once a week.[7] Another survey of female college students, in 1993, found that 35% of the students replying said they drank "to get drunk."[8] The comparable figure in 1979 was 10%.

Readers may wonder how these rates of change among youth compare with similar measures of trends among adults. Such relationships can be simply described:

+ The rates of death by homicide and by suicide among young White males have been increasing at a faster rate than comparable rates for adult males.

+ The rates of out-of-wedlock births among young, unmarried White females have been increasing at about the same rate as among adults.

Thinking about the Data

America is a vast country. Each year millions of adolescents and young adults come of age. Such a massive progression ensures that, despite the increasing disorder, there are still many competent young Americans—disciplined, diligent, good-natured, just-beginning citizens. However, the preceding data makes one thing unmistakably clear: this pool of competence is shrinking.

It is also notable that many of the acts counted in Figure 1 represent other problems as well. In the case of homicide, usually both the victim and the murderer are of the same sex, age, and ethnic group. Thus, the increase in youthful victims also represents an increase in the numbers of young murderers. Furthermore, such deaths are often due to aggressive quarreling or heavy drinking or drug abuse, by both the victim and the killer. Of course, no such misconduct excuses murder, but it does increase the size of the pool of disordered conduct. The statistics also undoubtedly subsume many other forms of distressing but uncounted conduct, such as severe emotional depression, assault and battery, attempted murder, and sexual exploitation. In the case of out-of-wedlock births, a male has impregnated an unmarried female typically ill-equipped for motherhood. Both persons have cooperated to cause the birth of an infant under highly unfavorable circumstances. To further complicate the matter, the dramatic increase in out-of-wedlock births has occurred—ironically—during an era marked by increased availability of information about, and means of, contraception and more accessible and safer abortions.

We have already mentioned that some of the measured rates of disorder are at record-high rates. We also believe they are probably at their highest points since the first European settlements in America. That assertion is founded on the following simple analysis:

The deaths by homicide and suicide and the births to unmarried females were probably, in part, aggravated by rising levels of urbanization. In 1990, for example, researchers compared the rates of violent crime in larger cities, with populations of a million or more, to those in smaller communities, with populations of ten thousand or less.[9] Crime rates in the larger cities were ten times higher than in smaller communities. We also recognize that, from the first European settlements to the early 1900s, we find a pattern of steady increases in America's levels of urbanization.

We know that many mature adults believe that the disorder and ambiguity among our adolescents and young adults is greater than in their own youth. This belief may seem simplistic, an unrealistic plea for the "good old days." Simplistic or not, however, the statistics seem to support that opinion.

The internal coherence of the statistics should also be recognized. The data logically fit together. The forms of increasing disorder feed on one another. Both folklore and many thoughtful human observers have frequently made connections between (a) ardent (and heedless) youthful love and jealousy, despair, and violence; or (b) sexual exploitation of one partner, typically the female, by an older, more sophisticated "seducer," leading the victim into extreme alienation and despair. And the connections between drug use and imprudent sex are evident.

As for the effects of premature but sincere love, consider Shakespeare's *Romeo and Juliet*. In the play, such powerful emotions as love and despair led to two killings and two suicides. True, Shakespeare pitied his "star-crossed lovers," but he never implied it was wise for two adolescent members of two feuding families to fall recklessly in love with each other.

Public perceptions about the spread of youth disorder are congruent with all of these distressing data. The public has routinely rated "pupil discipline" as the major problem facing education in the annual Gallup polls on education. If the national data show persisting high levels of youth disorder, it is easy to understand why the public sees schools as troubled with disorder.

Despite frequent public complaints about discipline, some educators regard these concerns as exaggerated. From our own research, we recognize that few schools are affected with conspicuous, gross disorder. It is equally our impression that many schools and teachers tolerate mild, persisting disruptions that would have been prohibited in most earlier eras. The differing lay/educator perspectives may be an instance of the phenomena identified by Senator Daniel Moynihan as "defining deviancy down."[10] In effect, Moynihan says we have lowered our standards for discipline and behavior so that yesterday's serious offense is today's peccadillo. An obvious example is the casual use of expletives and sexual language by students (and sometimes teachers) currently allowed in schools.

The U.S. Department of Education conducted a series of surveys in 1985–1987.[11] One survey of school administrators found that 65% believed pupil discipline in high schools had improved in the past five years. Unfortunately, a similar survey of teachers working in classrooms found that only 34% of them believed there had been improvement. Furthermore, there were striking differences between administrators and teachers about the decay in discipline over those same five years: three times as many teachers (37%) as administrators (12%) thought things had gotten worse. The question is, Who is correct, the pessimistic teachers working in the classroom or the optimistic administrators often away from the classroom working in the office?

There is other evidence, even more striking, of the prevalence of denial. A 1988 national survey examined teachers' and pupils' perceptions about in-school discipline.[12] The students reported far more discipline incidents than did their teachers; 16.6% of all students said "physical conflicts among students" were a "serious" problem. The comparable figure for teachers was 7%. Similarly, 15% of students saw student drug and alcohol use as a serious school problem, compared to 7% of teachers. From the differences in administrator and teacher perspectives already reported, we might also speculate the administrators would have found even fewer disorder problems than the teachers.

Students See the Reality

We believe that students' estimates of the extent of disorder are more accurate than those of teachers and administrators. Students are much closer to the acts of disorder and have no particular reasons for exaggerating the problems. Unfortunately, the further the adults are from such matters, the greater the likelihood they will minimize the problems.

One of the authors used the first edition of this book as a teaching tool with experienced teachers in graduate courses. The experience was instructive to us as well as to our adult students. By the end of the course, many students would easily admit that the book convinced them they had been too tolerant of disorderly acts in their classrooms. They had accepted low- to medium-level pupil disorder—which they instinctively did not like—because they had unconsciously picked up the impression that such disorder was not worth troubling about. After reading, discussing, and reflecting on the book, many decided to change their priorities. They did not intend to become dictators or repressors, but they would insist their students display in the classroom the same manners that might be expected in a moderately serious job or at a normal social occasion.

Our graduate students' previous patterns of inappropriate tolerance can be identified as a form of denial. In the short run, such denial makes administrators' and teachers' lives easier. Many forms of disorder—pupils sitting bombed in class or tense about being pushed around after school—do not directly impinge on the adults' lives. Furthermore, when administrators do make an issue of improving discipline, they will need to initiate new policies. For example, assume they initiate a policy of expelling students sixteen years old or older who use schools as places to hang out away from the cold. Inevitably, the changed policies would attract public attention. As a result, there would be community concern about safety and order in schools. This could lead to bad publicity. In addition, some community groups might object to such get-tough policies. Contradictory messages about discipline pervade our society, implying "get tough, but don't hurt anybody's feelings." These messages undoubtedly provoke many administrators to try and bury discipline problems. So denial—and the victimization of many young people—goes on.

Disturbing changes in youth conduct have been accompanied by concurrent declines in measured pupil learning. There have been long-term declines in pupil scores on standardized tests, such as the Scholastic Aptitude Test (SAT). From 1955 to 1982, the average SAT verbal score declined from 479 to 425. Since 1982, annual test scores have stopped declining, but scores remain at or near the all-time low in that year.[13] Various technical criticisms have been made about the representativeness of such test data. Researchers serving the Congressional Budget Office have examined the SAT as well as a mass of test-score data from different states and school systems.[14] These researchers have concluded that the decline in precollege test scores approximately parallels a similar decline in a variety of test scores. In other words, measured pupil learning in America has declined wherever consistent systems of testing have been applied. In view of the youth disorder that has been occurring, these shifts are not surprising. It is true, however, that no existing research shows a clear and definitive relationship between disorder and the learning declines.

Definitive findings would be hard to derive. The methodological problems involved are extraordinary. Still, there is a common-sense assumption that can be justified: young people who are more prone than in the past to commit homicide or suicide, abuse drugs, and indulge in sexual exploration are also likely to do poorly in schoolwork. Furthermore, the prevalence of disorder in American schools—despite the equanimity of administrators—must have harmful effects on teacher conduct and pupil learning. When the American researcher Benjamin Bloom visited classrooms in America and Japan, he was impressed with how little energy Japanese teachers had to put into maintaining pupil order. He concluded that if Japanese classrooms were given a score of 20 (out of 100) for the amount of teacher time spent keeping order, the average American classroom would rate an 80.[15] Presumably, the ease of maintaining order among Japanese pupils is one reason for their schools' educational excellence.

What the Changes Mean

No one knows definitively why these many unfortunate changes in conduct and learning have occurred in our young. Few thoughtful people suggest it is solely the fault of shifting school policies. There is more general agreement that a vast number of economic and social changes have occurred over many years. In different ways, these changes have helped generate disorder in schools. Exactly how much weight should be attributed to each influence is highly problematic. How much of the change is due to television? the increased stress confronting two-parent families? the spread of the one-parent family? the general increase of affluence? a variety of shifts in popular values? the erosion of authority at all levels from within households to the national government? The list goes on.

Some striking cross-cultural research, summarized by Daniel Goleman, provides a backdrop to such speculations.[16] The research shows that, by a variety of measures, typical contemporary Americans place a higher value on individual fulfillment and personal equality than citizens of any other nation. In one study, Americans working together on group projects were asked to estimate their contribution (in percentages) to their project. When the figures are summed up, they typically total more than 100%. In other words, Americans believe they usually do more than their share. And, in the United States, when people feel they are doing more than others, we know the typical response—a sense of exploitation. Conversely, in other societies, the study found, team members underestimate their individual contributions. The sum of estimates is usually less than 100%. Presumably, these respondents do not believe they are doing enough for the group. Again, in many countries, especially traditional societies, studies show that citizens attribute special talents to their leaders, even if they are democratically elected. On the other hand, American citizens typically believe they know as much as their leaders. A contrary position would be "elitist," currently a pejorative word.

The research demonstrated that individualistic attitudes were more typical of industrial societies than of traditional cultures. Still, Americans consistently displayed the highest levels of such attitudes. The research did not clearly show long-term trends, such as whether contemporary Americans are more individualistic than Americans twenty-five or fifty years ago. But there are undoubtedly popular impressions to that effect.

The research did not study the relationship between these findings and topics such as youth unrest. Still, it is not hard to identify a hypothetical connection between the two phenomena. It is easy to imagine that young people who believe they are as competent as anyone else (objective evidence to the contrary!), or who believe they usually contribute more than their share to joint enterprises, may begin to feel put upon, angry, and impatient with the ordinary circumstances of life. In addition, everyday experience demonstrates that, in many situations, there are people with greater ability than their evident peers or subordinates. These people are often designated as experts, leaders, bosses, supervisors, or teachers and principals. Finally, adults who share with the young opinions about their own "exploited" status are likely to prefer immediate over delayed gratification. They will not provide the young with purposeful care or wholesome role models.

Some considerations about the nature of American individualism are analyzed in a pamphlet prepared for foreign students visiting the United States.[17] The pamphlet was distributed by an international agency that arranged such visits. The pamphlet included the following remarks about friendship among young Americans:

> Historically, many Americans have not been able to enjoy the continuity of long friendships because they have not lived in one community long enough. This mobility is thought to contribute to the open, outwardly friendly style with which Americans meet people. It may also encourage the making of friends quickly, rather than developing complicated relationships with various obligations. . . .
>
> In contrast, in many cultures, a family remains in the same city for generations, friendships between families have long histories, and children go to school with the same group of young people throughout primary and secondary school. Circles of friends are stable and provide an important source for the next generation's friends who have strong ties and obligations to each other throughout life.

It is easy to identify the connection between the relatively fragile friendships of many American pupils and the egocentric patterns described by Goleman. "Complicated relationships" are inconsistent with egocentricity. Such relationships require participants to accept frequent imbalances in obligations and to tolerate external, hierarchal structures that define family and community ties. Unfortunately, the policies in many contemporary American school environments, as we will demonstrate later, place many pupils in structures that foster transitory relationships. It is not surprising that adults raised by such a process learn the distressing attitudes portrayed by Goleman.

Another study of international perspectives on American attitudes is also enlightening.[18] There is a reverse Fulbright program that brings foreign high school teachers to America for a year to teach in American schools. McAdams interviewed a number of foreign teachers who visited the States under the sponsorship of that program. The teachers were asked their observations about American school norms. One observation was common to all members of the group, regardless of their nationality or place of assignment. Occasionally, as in all schools, conflicts arose between pupils and teachers over matters such as grading, homework, or discipline. According to the visiting teachers, American parents were far more prone to back up their children in such conflicts than the parents in the teachers' homelands would be. The pupils and their parents shared a suspicion of authority. This pattern has many distressing implications for pupil-parent-educator relations in American schools.

Readers may have noted that youth drug use apparently declined throughout the 1980s, while other signs of disorder continued to increase. This contrast deserves comment. Between 1980 and 1988, the major federal government antidrug strategy was expressed in the slogan "Just say no."[19] In particular, William Bennett, the Director of the National Office of Drug Enforcement Policy, and Nancy Reagan, the wife of President Reagan, were prominently associated with this strategy. The strategy implied that dramatic (but true) antidrug information and persuasion were critical components of suppressing illegal drug abuse—especially among adolescents. The approach drew much criticism. It was controversial because it stressed scare tactics and moral responsibility, rather than stressing treatment. Treatment was more expensive, and provided grant and contract funds for certain activities.

Some critics of the Just Say No program contended that the strategy was largely a publicity gimmick, an effort to avoid spending more dollars against drugs. With the election of a Democrat, President Clinton, William Bennett and Nancy Reagan and their campaign were put aside. When the most recent figures about youth drug abuse were released, they showed two successive years of increasing use, after the long decline. The researchers who had been tabulating the drug data for many years largely attributed the upturn to the comparative ignorance of young cohorts with the dangers of drug use.[20]

The researchers did not suggest ignorance was the sole cause of drug experimentation. They simply implied that honest, strong antidrug arguments uttered to young people by caring adults should and can have an profound effect. The history of the Just Say No campaign and its outcomes had important implications for many other procharacter activities. Often such activities are deprecated, with charges of "preaching." It is contended that young people will adamantly ignore adult advice and warnings. All caring adults can do is to stand by and try to provide "after the crash" treatment. The apparent course of the Just Say No campaign—and the increased drug use after the campaign ended—suggests that such antipreaching arguments underestimate the wisdom of our young. The young are not immune to serious, strongly stated arguments by caring adults—if the adults have the moral courage to make them. And if someone calls such effective tactics "preaching," so be it.

Mature readers must recognize that during the past ten to fifteen years, the American public has gradually developed more sympathy with traditional values. Perhaps the very spread of youth disorder has been one reason for this shift. Much of the public and many educators concluded that, in practice, the application of relatively permissive values has produced bad effects.

This shift has been evident in a number of ways:

✦ Many political candidates who are more protradition on social issues than previous officeholders have been elected to office. Some of the candidates have emphasized concepts such as diligence and discipline in education.

✦ In both 1994 and 1995, President Clinton hosted a White House Conference on Character Education. The Congress responded by designating a week in October as "Character Counts Week."

✦ Demands on public education have changed. For example, criticisms have been made of social promotions, lax discipline, untracked classes, sex education, and value-free education. A national organization called the Partnership for Character Education has been formed, with a commitment to increasing educators' and citizens' concerns with character and schools.

✦ The judges elected or appointed to our courts are more protradition than their predecessors. As a result, courts have reversed or moderated some decisions (made ten to twenty years ago) hostile to traditional educational practices.

✦ Laws passed and proposed in various jurisdictions have placed greater emphasis on prohibitions and punishments of different forms of misconduct.

✦ There is increased public interest at all levels—local, state and national—in various forms of youth service. Such service is obviously seen as a way to increase sound character formation.

✦ An elaborate intellectual controversy has arisen around issues such as political correctness, multiculturalism, and family values. It is hard to say which "side" is winning such debates—if such disputes can be won or lost at all. Still, it seems safe to say that members of the political right are speaking out more forcefully than they did twenty or so years ago.

Most of these changes have been in protradition directions. The changes have had some effect on the environments around many young Americans. They have even caused some shifts in school policies. Unfortunately, the shifts in values and policies have not notably remedied the situation. A quick fix will not work here. The causes of youth disorder are numerous and deeply embedded in our society. Uplifting speeches and dramatic (and sometimes superficial) reforms can be encouraging. However, more deliberate and persisting changes are still required.

More effective education policies should emphasize the goals of improving pupil character, academics, and discipline. Conversely, the long-term decline in youth conduct, which has recently shown some improvement, offers a telling caution. That decline was associated with innumerable attempts to relax the demands for order in youth environments by

✦ lessening the requirements on the young for academic diligence

✦ providing students with more choices among elective courses

✦ shifting the focus in literary studies to materials stressing the antihero and the absurd

✦ presenting history materials that emphasize revisionism—wrong things our predecessors did—and imply that the pursuit of power and self-interest are the sole aims of purposive action

✦ making schools and classrooms more "democratic," which means more authority for pupils and less for teachers

✦ deemphasizing the importance of character as a goal of education

✦ encouraging teachers to recruit pupils into various problematic value systems, such as values clarification programs that encourage pupils to make their own decisions about sex and drugs

✦ lessening the emphasis on traditional patriotism

✦ restricting the application of discipline

✦ tempering the influence of criminal law

✦ applying measures popularly characterized as "permissive"[21]

✦ lessening the consequences of poor performance in school

✦ placing great emphasis on students' rights but little on their responsibilities

✦ allowing young students to adjudicate the misbehavior of fellow students

THE RELEVANCE OF PHILOSOPHY

Many current education-reform proposals are fraught with controversy. An important intellectual principle underlies many of the controversies: the rights and wrongs of the proposals cannot be clearly settled by some body of facts or research. Facts are not irrelevant. For instance, the data about increasing youth disorder and test-score stagnation and/or decline provide an important foundation for any discussion about school policies. Once we recognize that data, however, we are still left to derive practical principles from them. And that is not a simple task. The problem is that many basic issues are essentially philosophical, not pragmatic. Let us consider an example of such philosophic roots.

Suppose one contends that a reason for the youth disorder was a softening of school policies: schools became too permissive. Assume one also contends that there has been some improvement coincident with certain tightening-up measures. Then, suppose one went to great lengths to identify and measure instances of such permissiveness and tightening-up. We can even imagine that, during the period of tightening-up, measured levels of youth conduct and learning improved. That pattern of events would still not prove tightening-up was better for pupils than permissiveness. After all, perhaps the improvements were due to forces other than the tightening-up. Indeed, maybe pupil conduct and learning would have been even better without the tightening-up. Someone might contend that, but for the tightening-up, the rate of improvement would have been greater.

Furthermore, assume we could prove that tightening-up caused the improvement. In other words, we can only now show that tightening-up and improvement apparently happened at the same time. But that is only correlation. That could be due to coincidence. But suppose we show that the tightening-up made certain things get better—that it caused good things to happen. Even that might not necessarily settle matters. Someone then might say that the long-term repressive effects of tightening-up would eventually become generally deleterious. The democratic quality of our way of life might be undermined. In five or ten years, we might see those bad effects.

Finally, despite any improvement caused by tightening-up, some pupils would still be doing poorly. Indeed, perhaps some pupils—who had previously done satisfactorily—would find themselves doing worse during the tightening-up. In other words, the tightening-up generally raised average performance, but some pupils' performances (among the thousands of pupils who benefited) actually declined. Perhaps the costs of some new policy to a particular group of pupils is so high that it is not worth its benefits for most pupils. Weighing such conflicting and unmeasurable alternatives is the province of philosophy.

To Be Concrete

All of this may sound hypothetical. But the underlying issues are critical to school and classroom management. Imagine a relatively rigorous academic high school, where teachers are distressed about high levels of pupil cheating. This is a problem in many high schools. Some adults might propose the school should develop a detailed list of cheating infractions. That list would identify and define the kinds of cheating the faculty believes are practiced by some students. It might cover matters such as plagiarizing, letting other students observe one's exam, and passing notes around during exams. The list would be publicized to pupils, and significant consequences could also be announced. Some schools do apply such practices.

It is certain that some adults will say that such an approach is a bad idea, since it will

+ give some students ideas for cheating they had not yet considered
+ serve as a challenge and provoke aggravating adolescent bravado
+ overemphasize adult distrust of pupils

Such objections are similar in spirit to many of the complexities we recited in the preceding hypothetical analysis. For example, it might be possible by sophisticated and relatively costly research to prove rates of pupil cheating declined after the promulgation of the prohibition and consequences. Even then, suppose the punished pupils include disproportionate numbers of males, children from poor families, or other identifiable groups. Then the policy, though it inhibits cheating, may still be labelled discriminatory. Some accused cheaters (who really are innocent) may be mistakenly punished. Some cheaters will not get caught, and learn contempt for rules.

The preceding discussion may seem strained. However, it is not irrelevant that only a small proportion of high schools promulgate well-organized and comprehensive rules against cheating. Furthermore, our own college pupils regularly report that cheating was widespread—and the prohibitions weak or poorly enforced—during their high school experience.

The nub of the matter is simple. A major component of one's evaluation of an anticheating rule is one's basic philosophic disposition. How important is it that high school pupils be held individually accountable, regardless of family circumstances or ethnic factors; faced with significant consequences if they fail to observe published rules; and allotted grades that are serious measures of personal learning?

The themes underlying the topic of cheating affect many other important school practices, such as the amount of homework assigned; policies regarding pupil tracking (or class assignment), promotion, enrollment, examinations, and testing; the place of honor rolls and other forms of pupil recognition in school life; and a variety of discipline issues. In all such areas, when difficulties arise, important questions of fact must be considered. What are the ages of the pupils involved? What are the school's previous practices? How are parents likely to respond to any changed policies? Still, in the end, issues of personal philosophy—even wisdom—are the important elements of any sound policy decision.

Learning About Philosophy

Eminent philosophers have often focused on education: Plato, Aristotle, John Locke, Confucius, Buddha, John Dewey, and others. These thinkers have articulated educational insights of enduring value. Until quite recently, the major philosophers concerned with education have stressed the critical role of moral education. They were nearly unanimous in assuming that adults, as either teachers or parents, should bear the central authority and responsibility for shaping character in youth. They also emphasized that such activities should be carried out with love and diligence. Plato, through his whole adult life, expressed his gratitude for the attention he received from Socrates, his mentor. But he had little or no sympathy for teachers surrendering authority to the young until they had attained a relatively late stage of development.

The important insights of most of these philosophers were articulated long before the creation of our present education structures. These authorities typically envisioned situations where parents were their children's principal educators, or where external teachers were family slaves or paid employees of individual families. Furthermore, the philosophers' concerns were often directed at the education of young adult members of elite classes.

These concerns seem far afield from our typical current public education institutions: individual schools and colleges enrolling hundreds and even thousands of pupils from all social classes and ability levels, for periods of twelve to sixteen years. Each institution is staffed by tenured, paid government employees. Each employee may relate to numerous pupils for brief periods of time. Even Dewey's basic educational writings were composed during the early twentieth century—over seventy-five years ago. At that time, perhaps 5%–10% of the youth population completed high school. The current figure is 80%. None of the teachers in Dewey's era had tenure or belonged to a union.

Despite such shifts, many insights of earlier philosophers are still relevant. Ironically, their philosophical comments are often pervaded with a practical wisdom, a realism sometimes unusual in our era. Both Aristotle and Plato made trenchant remarks about the important role of the arts, and music in particular, in shaping the moral life of the young. Plato proposed that young people should be supervised by responsible adults, who would monitor their artistic exposure.

Otherwise, children would be exploited by irresponsible artists. Plato also had considerable suspicion of the motives of many "artists," whom he evidently saw as mischievous and self-interested agitators. Such insights are surely relevant in our own era of MTV and sexually explicit music. Today many adults are urgently concerned—just like Plato—about the effects of popular music on youth values.

Aristotle recommended that intensive training in philosophy be withheld until pupils were over the age of thirty—until they had acquired the wisdom of experience. Otherwise, immature pupils might apply their learned skills at argumentation to unsound ends. This caution is pertinent to some modern education practices. For example, in 1991 the New York State Department of Education appointed a Social Studies Syllabus Review Committee. The committee recommended that elementary and secondary school pupils "must be taught social criticism" and to "promote economic fairness and social justice" and "bring about changes in their communities, the nation, and the world." The historian Arthur Schlesinger, Jr. was a member of the committee and one of the dissenters from the report. He was unsympathetic to the idea that public schools should strive to inspire a new children's crusade. He observed that he would be "satisfied if we can teach children how to read, write, and calculate." Undoubtedly, Aristotle would have agreed with Professor Schlesinger.

Ironically, both Plato and Aristotle had high aspirations for the graduates of their "ideal" school(s). Such graduates should be equipped to help run the world. But there is an important difference between such classic philosophers and our contemporary innovators: the classicists were more conscious of the developmental limitations of children and adolescents. They believed it was unwise to assign excessive critical responsibilities to comparatively immature children and adolescents. Unlike the New York State Report, neither Aristotle or Plato would recommend asking—let us say—twelve-year-olds to

- ✦ recite what mistakes you believe Thomas Jefferson made in drafting the Declaration of Independence.
- ✦ provide a critical analysis of Abraham Lincoln's policies regarding the Emancipation Proclamation.
- ✦ evaluate the decision of certain American leaders during World War II, including President Roosevelt, to choose not to bomb German death camps such as Auschwitz.

True, some American children may, as adults, face questions of equivalent scope. Their schooling should help prepare them for such contingencies. However, this does not mean their education should immediately engage such pupils in confronting such world-class issues. Many earlier philosophic perspectives cannot be applied to contemporary education without considerable intellectual adaptation. Thus, much of our philosophical discussion will involve interpreting traditional perspectives in the light of our immediate, and historically novel, situation. Our efforts at adaptation are congruent with the contributions of contemporary philosophers such as Alasdair MacIntyre and Russell Kirk. Some protradition educators may find this discussion especially helpful; they may be heartened to discover their experiential perspectives about education have far more intellectual legitimacy than they realize.

It is also relevant that many currently popular psychological principles used to justify contemporary educational practices are founded on philosophical premises. For example, the Harvard psychologist Lawrence Kohlberg wrote a lengthy volume on the philosophy of moral education. Such an interdisciplinary approach is quite legitimate, even traditional. But many philosophical approaches to psychology actually fail to appropriately confront the philosophical issues involved. They apply a form of pseudoempiricism to justify what are really philosophical arguments. For example, the prominent psychologist B. F. Skinner was a vigorous opponent of punishment as a means of maintaining order, although the experimental data he cited to prove his point were very limited in scope.[22] Skinner's proposals would have been much more direct if he had simply said, "Let us logically think about the nature and effects of punishment," rather than reflexively reciting, "Research shows . . . " However, such deliberate appeals to logic would probably have undermined his problematic contentions.

Finally, we recognize that most adults' personal philosophies are not due largely to reading books. Instead, they are based on some amalgam of their previous experiences, including their religious commitments, if any. Such personal learnings, quite properly, are deeply rooted. They are not likely to be changed by professional books. But we will be more directly philosophical than many education books in one important way.

We will tacitly and persistently raise the question, "Do you think such-and-such a school or classroom policy is good or bad? Why? Why not?" In particular, our questions will confront important elements of prevailing intellectual norms, such as

- ♦ the sanctity of the doctrine of the classroom as a democracy, rather than a learning environment managed by a responsible and authoritative adult
- ♦ the hostility towards the unapologetic use of appropriate punishment as one tool to maintain order
- ♦ the tendency to emphasize relatively limited goals for education, such as subject matter mastery to be demonstrated by pupil test scores or an almost exclusive focus on emotional development

We will stress the practical implications of particular beliefs. We aim to stimulate readers to clarify the ramifications of their own beliefs.

There is little doubt that beliefs about education can have important effects. For instance, take a philosophical belief that it's not worth the trouble to vigorously suppress adolescent cheating because the pupils may simply respond with counterchallenges. The major effect may only be a sterile confrontation. It is true that adolescents sometimes respond in such a way to mandates. It is also true that many adolescents simply do what people in authority tell them to do. Furthermore, some adolescents do try in different ways to test authority; if they finally perceive the authority means business, they yield and get down to work. There are surely other variants of this hypothetical situation.

In the end, most commentators recognize that almost all adolescents have points at which they will discontinue resistance. Setting aside the clichés prevailing in popular culture, persisting adolescent rebellion—or, at least, successful adolescent rebellion—is not very typical. Successful rebellions, indeed, are probably more a sign of adult weakness rather than of adolescent determination. In the cheating example, the basic philosophical issue is, How important is it for adults to enforce anticheating rules or comparable institutional norms in general?

Some readers may find it beneficial to see the topic of adolescent rebellion, or testing, in such a light. The answers to the issues are not self-evident. Still, the issues invite readers to manipulate or reexamine their principles and test them in alternative perspectives. Helpful practical insights may evolve from such an examination.

Philosophy is also important because it relates to the issue of consistency. Consistency is an element of the virtue of fairness. We all know how pupils, and parents too, stress the importance of fairness in school.

Fairness means treating equally situated persons and equivalent acts of virtue or offense alike. It means being predictable. Consider a general principle that we believe is right, for example, pupils should obey faculty. Teachers should make that principle a classroom goal and regularly apply it in different situations. Teachers can vary the application of the principle, for instance, deciding to make distinctions among pupils of different ages. Mature pupils who have displayed considerable responsibility might have more freedom to question certain teacher directions. Similarly, different principles may apply in private—compared to public—occasions. Or an exception may be possible if the pupils and teacher recognize that the occasion allows for some license, such as when a teacher is chaperoning a student dance or attending a school athletic competition. However, such variations should be internally logical. The exceptions must be plausible, not arbitrary. Neither fairness nor consistency can occur without the analysis of existing or proposed principles. We must consider the ramifications of these principles in diverse real and hypothetical situations. Such an analysis touches on the fields of ethics and philosophy, as well as on the realities of teaching and administration. It is our aim to help readers acquire this valuable intellectual discipline. To conclude the matter, let's examine one other specific instance of practical philosophy and consistency. Some educators and many psychologists, such as Alfie Kohn, believe pupils should learn altruistic motivations for actions.[23] These authorities deprecate school policies that provide pupils with recognition (e.g., gold stars, certificates, conspicuous good-conduct awards) to honor virtuous acts. To these optimistic authorities, altruism means good deeds done without expectation of reward. The idea is akin to John Dewey's concept of intrinsic motivation: pupils should learn because of the innate appeal of the subject matter, rather than from a desire to earn grades, please adults, or otherwise respond to adult pressures. The authorities label as *consequentialism* the contrasting doctrine that proposes pupils should be encouraged to do good or avoid the bad through the application of rewards and punishments.

However, almost all such no-reward prescriptions for encouraging altruism tacitly approve of the innumerable reward structures now typically existing in schools. For example, intrinsic policies regarding good conduct assume each school's academic programs will continue as currently instituted. This means that successful academic learners will still receive their typical awards: getting good grades, receiving certificates, having excellent papers posted for others to see, having their names listed on the honor roll, being considered for scholarships. This generates an anomaly. Should educators conspicuously praise competence in academics yet fail to praise notable helping conduct? Furthermore, do we really mean that teachers should not praise virtuous conduct? Should teachers refrain from sending appreciative notes home to parents, or otherwise expressing gratitude for good conduct? In practice, such reliance on intrinsic rewards and no-reward proposals seems incredible. To sink to the level of pun, this policy of not rewarding virtue seems inconsequential, i.e., without consequences.

The questions just posed about intrinsic motivation may stimulate readers to reconsider their own views about recognizing good conduct in pupils. If we hold consistency as a virtue we want to cultivate, then tensions will be generated by recognition policies that propose to ignore good conduct and only reward academic learning. Again, if we assume that realism is an important element of an effective philosophy, then it seems unlikely most teachers will, in practice, ignore pupils' good acts that occur in their classrooms. Teachers, we hope, will reflexively say "Thank you" or "Isn't that nice." Anyone concerned with promulgating a no-reward policy should anticipate the inconsistencies between the abstract principles underlying that policy and the day-to-day practices of teachers.

Some administrators who believe in ignoring pupil virtue (while some teachers informally praise it) may deliberately intend that such ambiguous policies be applied. They may want teachers to do one thing and administrators to follow contrary policies. We have seen many schools where little or no official recognition was provided for pupil virtue, though many teachers still tried hard to encourage such conduct. As one might expect, such muddled policies generate mixed results. These schools had at best only moderate levels of pupil good conduct, and many teachers and parents felt frustrated. The administration did not support the efforts of teachers and parents to encourage good conduct. Even so, some of the administrators in these schools seemed pleased. They believed they were carrying out the intrinsic-altruism theory, just as certain authorities had recommended. Furthermore, developing schoolwide policies for encouraging pupil virtue requires administrative diligence. Therefore, administrators who did not reward student virtue could also enjoy the satisfaction of applying a philosophy that cut down on their work.

Of course, in the adult world some citizens pursue serious learning or do good deeds without formal stimulation. Despite such occurrences, however, few adults advocate abolishing report cards or honor rolls in schools. For example, how many people would learn to compute their elaborate tax returns if the existing powerful system of rewards and punishments were abolished? Perhaps similar realism should be applied in teaching pupils to practice virtue. This discussion may provoke second thoughts in readers who believe that virtue in children should not be regularly and systematically rewarded; perhaps such adults should consider the ramifications of their beliefs.

Teacher Diligence

Diligence is another important topic that often arises in discussions of protradition reform. The reality is that many protradition reforms involve various sorts of tightening-up. Such measures often require educator diligence.

Again, let's use the example of pupil cheating. Precise, restrictive rules against cheating may or may not be a good idea. We may not even be sure they diminish cheating if they are enforced. We can be certain, however, that enforcing clear rules against cheating causes more work for teachers in the short run than casually applying vague prohibitions. Diligent enforcement requires teachers to design a system of prohibition; carefully monitor exams; maintain the security of exam questions; issue clear warnings to students; probably detect and punish some violations; and often face the angry parents of violators, along with all the tensions of such incidents. Conversely, imagine a more lax school environment. Teachers do not need to work as hard monitoring student conduct, maintaining the security of their exams or confronting students or parents. They can afford to be less diligent.

One essential point underlies most tightening-up reforms: the changes require teachers and administrators to be more diligent in monitoring pupil conduct. That is what tightening-up means. And this requires work. Some of the work is physical, actually expending more time and labor, and much of it is emotional, such as talking to pupils and parents (and teachers) who may be angry and defensive. There is a basic human disposition to avoid unpleasant activities. Some people seek entirely to escape diligence. Others resist new work demands, since such demands will conflict with their existing network of obligations. More dedicated professionals recognize that diligence is a critical element of commitment.

It is also relevant to recognize that the greatest work demands occur at the shift from indifference to greater rigor. At that moment, educators are under the twin stresses of abandoning an old habit, which is usually a frustrating experience, and applying a new mode to pupils who resist the change. When the new mode is firmly in place, things may work better than ever. But the process of transition can be arduous and prolonged.

One of the authors recently faced a simple example of the ramifications of diligence, cheating, and teaching. He volunteered to proctor an exam for a colleague who had to be out of town. When he arrived at class with the sheets of objective questions, he discovered that the classroom was filled with fifty or so closely spaced desks. All the desks were occupied. Obviously, under such circumstances, even well-intentioned students might be tempted to cheat. He was peeved at his colleague for drifting into such a situation. Then he recalled that classroom space was at a premium in the college. Due to the large class, there were legitimate reasons for favoring an objective exam—it made grading more manageable. But it made cheating more tempting. Trying to make the exam more cheating-proof would have been difficult. Furthermore, the administration had given faculty no signal that they considered it important to prevent cheating or that they would provide extra resources, such as a second proctor or temporary assignment to a larger room for the exam, in difficult situations. Indeed, a professor who handled such a vexatious situation without asking for extra resources would be viewed as a good soldier, one who knew how to get along.

The matter of increased adult diligence is quite important in considering teaching morality to pupils. We often see situations where conflicting claims are made for protradition and more permissive approaches. Arguments can be offered for either side. It seems the protradition approach, whatever its ultimate merits, also requires adults to be more diligent. One need not be a cynic to imagine that, for many people, the less-work factor may be the clinching argument for permissive approaches.

Consider, once again, the shopping mall high school. Much philosophy and education research can be amassed to justify such shopping mall patterns, for example, teaching to pupils' interests, making learning fun, having open and relaxed relationships between teachers and pupils. Beneath such rationales lies a profound reality: a shopping mall school also makes some teachers' work easier. Teachers' lives would be harder if they had to diligently assign and insist on homework, give and grade serious exams, fail pupils who did not apply themselves, and justify their rigorous policies to distressed parents. The deeper, more worrisome reality is, of course, that American students are not learning—academically or morally—as well as their counterparts around the globe.

In sum, tradition and diligence usually mean pupils are subject to more demands than in the typical shopping mall school. Maintaining such demands also increases the work of the faculty, who must dedicate more energy and time to class planning, monitoring and counseling students, and grading papers. This prospect is not entirely bleak. Today a great many educators, while they work relatively hard, are frustrated by the disjointed schools they operate. Shopping mall high schools offer mixed benefits for teachers. Some forms of work are avoided, but the schools are pervaded by indifference. Often a moderate level of disorder goes over the edge into turmoil. Furthermore, most teachers decided to become educators partly for moral reasons: to help better the human race. They are often properly offended and discouraged by the moral indifference and mediocrity affecting their schools.

Of course, not all pupil options, like shopping malls, are entirely unpromising. Some students and teachers may use their new flexibility to design or learn approaches that require extreme ingenuity and intense pedagogical work. It may be that more permissive classrooms actually stimulate more work for teachers than do traditional approaches. But Ann Swidler, Jonathan Kozol, and others have looked at the realities of many such experimental schools.[24] They concluded that, despite individual exceptions, the expansion of options for teachers in the recent past did not unleash a vast increase in pupil and teacher creativity. In too many instances, they found that freedom from restraint meant freedom to be slovenly. Diane Ravitch supported these conclusions in *The Troubled Crusade*. Interestingly enough, the historian Lawrence Cremin, describing the progressive education movement of the first half of the twentieth century, made similar observations about the patterns of open pedagogy during that era.[25]

THE ROLE OF RELIGION

Transmitting character, academics, and discipline is critically intermeshed with teaching morality. And many persons consider morality closely related to formal religion. Indeed, most religions have much to say about childrearing. For example, the Old Testament says "Honor thy father and mother," and "Train up a child in the ways he should go; and when he is old. . . ." Undoubtedly, many educators working in public schools consider precepts like these important parts of their own core moral values.

We have a few remarks to make about the role of formal religion in teaching values in public or private schools. Some private schools are religiously affiliated. In these schools, the curriculum can be organized to teach fidelity to that religion and to advance its moral values. The methods of achieving such ends vary widely. They depend on the particular religion, the communities involved, and the judgments of individual educators. The methods may include

- ✦ hiring teachers strongly committed to the expression and transmission of a particular faith. One evangelical Christian school principal told us his first concern is whether teachers acknowledge Jesus Christ as their Lord and Savior. The employment application asked potential teachers to detail this discovery. Theoretically, it was possible for applicants to try to deceive the principal. But the school was small, with comparatively low salaries. It would be difficult and unrewarding for teachers to conduct such an arduous deception. Obviously, teachers satisfying such criteria and employed in a religious school might approach their work with a special religious perspective.

- ✦ asking pupils to witness their faith in daily conduct, e.g., praying publicly, attending religious rites, displaying appropriate virtues

- ✦ using faith doctrines to justify certain policies, e.g., a discipline code based on the Ten Commandments

- ✦ teaching the doctrines of the faith as if they were true, rather than simply saying "this is what we believe"

- ✦ expecting parents to support the school's religiously oriented endeavors, e.g., observing religious holidays in their families and being involved as families in the school's charitable activities

- ✦ being willing to reject or expel students who do not support the values of the religion or school

- ✦ asking families to express their belief by contributing not only money, but also time and energy to the school

Through much of U.S. history, public schools, depending on the communities they served, acted in congruence with many of the preceding themes. Even today, constitutional prohibitions to the contrary, some public schools probably have Bible readings as well as teachers who assume a common body of religious values among their pupils and appeal to those values in their teaching. When the space shuttle *Challenger* exploded before television cameras, with millions of horrified school children watching during class, we know a number of public school teachers who suggested to their students that they might wish to pray.

Actually, interpretations of prohibitions in the Constitution against religion in state schools are relatively recent. They were identified in decisions by a divided U.S. Supreme Court in about 1960. Since that time, those prohibitions have been undergoing continuing redefinition. The decisions have created a wider gap between religion and state-supported schools than exists in any industrial democracy in the world.

For a century and a half before those decisions, such matters were at the discretion of the individual states, where practices and policies varied widely. Technically speaking, the recent prohibitions do not transform educators who violate them, through choice or mistake, into criminals. A citizen who objects to an allegedly religious practice in a public school must bring a civil suit. In the suit, the complainant must persuade a court to issue an injunction—a prohibition—against the objectionable practice. The court may agree with the complainant or with the school and its educators. If the court agrees with the complainant, it will then enjoin, or prohibit, the continuation of the practice. Only if a school or an educator then disobeys the injunction can the school or the educator be punished—for contempt of court.

Most educators do not want to violate the law. Nor do they want to be subjected to a court injunction, with the loss of face that entails. Thus many public educators eschew significant contacts between school activities and expressions of religious belief. Others take mild risks. They may have religious invocations recited at graduations, or they may encourage pupils to sing religious Christmas carols and/or Hanukkah songs. The courts have emphasized that schools may teach about religion. Religion is a notable historic force, like major political movements, and the Bible is a foundational literary resource. Such a license, however, is unlikely to satisfy many religious believers. The license places their religion and sacred book on the same plane as other secular academic subjects, e.g., Nazism, the Democratic or Republican party, or *War and Peace* or *Gone With the Wind*.

Questions about the appropriate role of religion in public schools must finally be considered in light of certain statistics. These data emphasize the role of religion in contemporary American life. American citizens place a higher value on religion than citizens in any other modern industrial country. For instance, one survey asked citizens in a number of countries to characterize the importance of God in their lives. On a scale of 1 to 10, with 10 the highest rating, the average answer for Americans was 8.2.[26] The only higher rating was given by citizens of Malta. Not only are Americans quite religious, their beliefs are also relatively congruent. A 1991 nationwide phone survey found that 86.5% of respondents characterized themselves as Christians.[27] Only 3.7% characterized themselves as religious but not Christian (Jewish, Buddhist, Muslim). Characterizing themselves as nonreligious were 7.3%, and 2.3% gave no response. The data make our current patterns of disaffiliation of religion from public education seem anomalous. Moreover, most textbooks lack any reference to God or religion. It is one thing to protect the young from sectarian evangelizing; it is another for a government agency to tacitly ignore a powerful aspect of world history and culture and the profound beliefs of most of its citizens. It seems almost intolerant to so thoroughly disasso-ciate children's schools from such an important force in many of their lives.

Educators should also be sensitive to the concept of a "tacitly" antireligious curriculum or school environment. Richard Neuhaus raised this issue when he wrote of *The Naked Public Square*. His point was that traditional religions adopted a holistic approach to life. They were concerned not only with the formal moments of worship, but also with the engagement between the religion's values and rites and the ordinary and extraordinary moments of public life. Such engage-ment was expressed via public prayers; the contents of literature, everyday speech, and the media; the demarcation of rites of passage (e.g., graduation); and systems of public symbolism, music, and art.

As the title of Neuhaus's book implies, this holistic tradition has been attacked from many directions in our era, for a variety of reasons. Indeed, the medley of perspectives associated with the tradition of "secular humanism" is deliberately dedicated to keeping religious belief out of the public square. The tensions sur-rounding such philosophical-theological conflicts will continue to trouble public schools as long as they are required to collect pupils from such disparate families under one roof. Teachers concerned with communicating values to pupils must remain sensitive to such issues.

Such secular-religious tensions are moderated in certain settings: where com-munities are relatively homogeneous, where pupils are older (age 16 plus?), or where educators display notable ingenuity and sensitivity.

The matter of teaching or enforcing abstract nonreligious values (e.g., pupils should not lie, or pupils should be kind) must be considered. Is such teaching legally permissible in schools? The question is less a matter of constitutionality than of local policies or priorities. If a school or school board has especially strong feelings about how students dress, what should be taught in sex education, or whether to require community service as a condition of graduation, it has consid-erable local discretion in such matters. Public schools can go quite far in teaching pupils morality, as long as they do not use religious rationales for their assertions.

Undoubtedly, it might be easier to teach certain values by relating them to reli-gious premises. Yet many nonreligious people, and their children, lead morally wholesome lives. It would be defeatist to assume that wholesome nonreligious schools cannot hope to transmit moral values.

Practices and Policies

1. Identify some elementary or secondary school or classroom with which you are familiar. List some ways the school or classroom either (a) holds pupils per-sonally accountable for their good or inadequate conduct or (b) does not maintain such accountability. Do you believe that the level of accountability applied by the school or classroom is appropriate or not?

2. Do you know of any school where the faculty seem to accept second-rate pupil performance partly to avoid the work of insisting on academic learn-

ing and appropriate discipline? What examples of such conduct can you cite? Do you believe the faculty would be better off showing more diligence to attain better pupil learning and conduct?

3. An effective policy against pupil cheating requires the school (and/or teacher) to identify all foreseeable forms of cheating; specify significant punishments; publicize the forms and punishments; and strongly encourage teachers to transmit and enforce such procedures. Does your school have such a policy (appropriate to the ages of the pupils involved)? Cite evidence to support your conclusion.

4. Generally classify the ways a school or classroom you are familiar with formally recognizes individual pupils or groups of pupils who succeed in academic learning, e.g., honor rolls, posting good papers, transmitting report cards, mention in school newsletter, certificates, recognition at awards assembly, oral praise from teachers, etc. Then, similarly classify the systems for recognizing pupil-helping conduct in and around the school or classroom. Finally, compare the intensity of the two systems. Are they equivalent? If not, which is stronger? How great is the disparity? What does such disparity imply about the goals of the school or classroom?

References

1. Read, M. (1968). *Children of their fathers*. New York: Holt, Rinehart, & Winston.

2. Kilpatrick, W. (1993). *Why Johnny can't tell right from wrong*. New York: Simon & Schuster; Linkona, T. (1991). *Educating for character*. New York: Bantam; Whitehead, B. (1995). "The failure of sex education," *The American Educator, 18*(1), 22 et scq.

3. Powell, A. G., Farrar, E., & Cohen, D. (1985). *The shopping mall high school*. New York: Houghton Mifflin.

4. Basler, R. P. (Ed.) (1953). *The Collected Works of Abraham Lincoln, Vol. II*. Rutgers, NJ: Rutgers University Press, p. 461.

5. U.S. Department of Health and Human Services, Public Health Service, Bureau of Vital Statistics, and predecessor agencies. Annual vital statistics reports for appropriate years [homicide and suicide, 1914–1994; drug use, 1975–1994; out-of-wedlock births, 1940–1993]. Washington, DC: U.S. Department of Health and Human Services; Johnston, L., O'Malley, P. M., & Bachman, J. G. (1994). *National survey results on drug use, Vol. 1, Secondary school students, 1993, Monitoring the future survey, 1975-1993*. Washington, DC: U.S. Department of Health and Human Services.

6. Durkheim, E. (1951). *Suicide*. Glencoe, IL: Free Press.

7. Johnston et al., p. 79.

8. Center of Addiction and Substance Abuse. (1995). *Rethinking rites of passage*. New York: Author.

9. Reiss, A. J., & Roth, A. (Eds.). (1993). *Understanding and preventing violence*. Washington, DC: National Academy Press, p. 81.

10. Moynihan, D. P. (1993). Defining deviancy down. *The American Scholar, 62* (Winter), 17–37.

11. Harris, L. (1988). *The American teacher*. New York: Harris Poll.

12. Office of Educational Research and Improvement, Center for Educational Statistics. (1987). *Public school teacher perspectives on school discipline*. Washington, DC: U.S. Department of Education.

13. Ogle, L. T., Alsalam, N., & Rogers, G. T. (1991). *The condition of education 1991* (Vol. 1). Washington, DC: U.S. Department of Education, p. 78.

14. Congressional Budget Office. (1986). *Trends in educational achievement*. Washington, DC: Author.

15. Cummings, W. K. (1980). *Education and inequality in Japan*. Princeton, NJ: Princeton University Press, p. 111.

16. Goleman, D. (1990, December 25). The group and the self. *New York Times*, pp. 13, 15.

17. Youth for Understanding. (1989). *Towards understanding those mystifying Americans*. Washington, DC: Author.

18. McAdams, R. P. (1993). *Lessons from abroad*. Lancaster, PA: Technomics.

19. Johnson, L. D. (1991). "Towards a theory of drug epidemics." In Donohew, L., Sypher, H. E., & Bukoski, W. J. (Eds.), *Persuasive communication and drug abuse prevention*. Hillsdale, NJ: Lawrence Earlbaum, pp. 93–132.

20. University of Michigan, Public Information Office. (1994, December 12). Teenage drug use continues to rise [Press release]. Ann Arbor, MI: Author.

21. For examples of criticisms of permissiveness, see, e.g., Traub, J. (1994, September 19). Class struggle. *New Yorker*, *78*(29), p. 76 et seq.; Bernstein, R. (1995). *The dictatorship of virtue*. New York: Knopf; Himmelfarb, G. (1995). *The de-moralization of society: From Victorian virtues to modern values*. New York: Alfred Knopf; Kilpatrick, ibid.; Whitehead, ibid.

22. Skinner, B. F. (1955). *The behavior of organisms*. New York: Knopf, p. 154.

23. Kohn, A. (1993). *Punished by rewards*. New York: Houghton Mifflin.

24. Swidler, A. (1979). *Organization without authority*. Cambridge: Harvard University Press; Kozol, J. (1972). *Free schools*. Boston: Houghton Mifflin.

25. Cremin, L. (1961). *The transformation of the school*. New York: Vintage, p. 348.

26. Gallup, G., Jr., & Castelli, J. (1989). *The people's religion*. New York: Macmillan, p. 4.

27. Kosmin, B., & Lachman, S. P. (1933). *One nation under God: Religion in contemporary American society*. New York: Harmony.

CHAPTER 2

The Multiple Goals of Education

. . . [my children] at this moment my love for you has increased so much that it seems to me I used not to love you at all. This feeling of mine is produced by your adult manners, adult despite your tender years; by your instincts, trained in noble principles which must be learned; by your pleasant way of speaking, fashioned for clarity; and by your careful weighing of every word. . . . Therefore, most dearly beloved children all, continue to endear yourselves to your father and, by those same accomplishments which make me think I had not loved you before, make me think hereafter (for you can do it) that I do not love you now.

—Letter from Thomas More to his four children, 1517[1]

For most of history, educators have directed their energies toward three related goals: teaching pupils character, academics, and discipline. Pupil academic learning has been only one of several critical learning goals. To our mind, these integrated priorities constitute an important measure of any educator's personal values: Is the educator dedicated to following that tradition of multiple goals? Educators who see their roles in such a light are, by definition, sympathetic to traditional values. They will be interested in seeing how traditional institutions, or modern schools dedicated to tradition, pursued such diverse learning outcomes. In this chapter we will focus on the overall picture, chapter 3 will examine character and academics, and chapter 4 will examine discipline.

It is instructive to look back to the classic writers on education, such as Plato, Aristotle, and Plutarch. These writers "invented" tradition. In their works, one sees a persistent concern with moral learning, as well as technical skill. The Roman author Quintilian (c.35 A.D.–c.95) said in his *Institutes on Oratory*, "No man will ever be thoroughly accomplished in eloquence, who has not gained a deep insight into the impulses of human nature, and formed his moral character on the precepts of others and on his own reflections."[2]

The matter of attaining multiple learning goals even antedates the evolution of historical societies, with their reliance on written records. Many anthropologists study surviving preliterate societies. Their studies provide some idea of how humans lived for the tens of thousands of years preceding urbanization and literacy. It seems that such societies also gave a higher priority to moral instruction than to technical training. In this context, the word *moral* should be construed in a broad light, signifying the sense of propriety or values prevailing in a society. Almost all such values relate to social relationships: how members of a society should treat one another. For example, one of the Ten Commandments articulates children's obligations to their parents. As the anthropologist Yehudi Cohen put it, "No society allows for the random or promiscuous expression of emotions to just anyone. Rather, one may communicate those feelings, either verbally, physically, or materially, to certain people."[3]

THE GREAT TRADITION

The long-term perspectives that have governed education and the conduct of educators can be characterized as the *Great Tradition*. That phrase was first applied by the literary critic F. R. Leavis to a body of writings that supported traditional moral values. The phrase is equally applicable to classical approaches to education.

In education, the Great Tradition emphasized the transmission of good moral values to students. Skills and information were also taught; however, no one imagined these matters were more important than teaching good character. In earlier societies, the institutions we now call schools and families were more intimately intermixed than in our time. Teachers or tutors were often relatives or family friends. Teaching was not so much a matter of conducting formal discourse as it was behaving as a role model, emphasizing politeness, good habits, and other appropriate conduct. Furthermore, family members, especially in rural environments, were usually involved in teaching children significant work skills. It was natural due to such intermixture for these teachers to stress the relationship between formal knowledge and the right conduct appropriate to different situations. In our own era, distancing has frequently occurred between homes and schools; teachers find it difficult to reinforce the moral values of pupils' parents, whom they may not even know.

As David Tyack and Elizabeth Hansot have observed, the tradition of multiple educational goals prevailed in American public education from our founding in the early seventeenth century until well into the twentieth century.[4] However, beginning in the mid-nineteenth century, applying the tradition became complicated. Efforts were made to separate public education from explicitly religious influences.

The shifts occurred partly because of the spread of secular values among intellectuals and opinion-formers. Previously, moral teaching in schools had usually been intertwined with Christian beliefs and doctrine. Until the mid-nineteenth century, this policy was respected by most public figures. Gradually, public life became more secular, and demands for church-state separation intensified. Another cause of the shift was the rising rate of Catholic immigration. These immigrants believed the schools' religious perspectives were too Protestant. Eventually, many schools adopted secular—nonreligious—moral education. These efforts were later described by Yulish as the *Character Education* movement.[5] Although the movement had a nonreligious thrust, it included a strong moral focus. The movement enlisted many public educators and persisted from about 1900 to the mid-1930s. Finally, the movement's intellectual support declined; it lost its appeal—often for poor reasons—to academics and education intellectuals. We will consider some causes for its decline later in this chapter.

Due to this shift, many education leaders abandoned the teaching of traditional values, especially character, in public schools. This does not mean that all practicing educators ignore traditional values. Different public schools and teachers

✦ still, to varying degrees, communicate moral values by way of explicitly religious themes.

✦ try to transmit moral values tied to traditional, but secular, themes.

✦ make no deliberate efforts to transmit moral values.

✦ transmit antitradition values to pupils against the objections of many parents, e.g., provide pupils with free contraceptives without informing individual parents; conduct highly relativistic discussions about value-laden issues such as obedience, sexual experimentation, drug use, and the limits of loyalty to one's country; or make low or no academic demands on pupils.

Today, it is common for some authorities to propose we appraise schools largely or solely on academic outcomes, including pupil test scores. Despite such patterns, the Great Tradition is still important for many educators in our era. The vitality of the Great Tradition is evident to anyone who listens to discussions among teachers about particular pupils. It will quickly become clear that much of their discussion focuses on pupils' moral traits: their kindness, honesty, diligence, and obedience, or their laziness, dishonesty, and unkindness. Most teachers, for a myriad of reasons, are profoundly interested in pupils' characters. One important reason is that teachers spend long periods of time with their pupils. As a result they are inevitably concerned about their conduct and other indices of their moral lives.

Old-Fashioned

Our book's sympathy with some past practices may upset some readers. After all, in a literal sense, past practices are old-fashioned. But does this mean they are automatically out-of-date, obsolete, or invalid? Some things that prevailed in the past are gone and probably will never return. For instance, over the past several centuries, the average human life span throughout the entire world has lengthened by about thirty years—an increase ranging from 50% to 100%, depending on the nation involved. We assume there will continue to be variations in that average. However, we do not imagine a return to the shorter average life spans of several centuries ago, when the average life span was only twenty to thirty years. Similarly, some other long-term developments are probably immutable, such as increases in rates of literacy and the increased speed of communications.

On the other hand, certain changes have been—and will be—mutable. During the Great Depression of the 1930s, the average unemployment rate in the United States approached 25%. Eventually the Depression ended, and the employment rate since that time has ranged from 6% to 12%. Apparently, our country returned to employment patterns that had prevailed before the Depression. Again, during the 1970s, our average rate of inflation was more than 10% per year—double-digit inflation. This was perhaps the highest long-term rate in our history. Circumstances changed, policies shifted, and currently our inflation rate is less than 6%. Finally, the historian Ted Gurr has carefully measured, over several centuries, long-term shifts in crime rates in the United States.[6] He has concluded that, at this time, our crime rates are abnormally high. Presumably, Gurr believes that those rates may decline, as they have from previous high points. The concept of historical cyclicity is ancient. The theme is stressed in Ecclesiastes in the Old Testament: "To every thing there is a season, and a time for every purpose under Heaven."

Again in our own era, the historian Arthur Schlesinger, Jr.[7] has rearticulated the concept of cyclicity. He has written extensively about liberal-conservative cycles in American politics. Evidently, some practices or patterns common in the past have perished and will never return, while others that have declined or expired will revive, sometimes with even greater vitality. It would be nice if we could identify which changes are permanent and which are transitory. But such forecasting is beyond the aims of this book. We emphasize only a simple point: the criticism that certain proposals are old-fashioned, in the sense that they are obsolete and impractical, tells more about the critic's lack of imagination than the virtues of any proposal. Perhaps diligence, honesty, and kindness are also old-fashioned; however, we cannot assume they are extinct and will never be revitalized.

The Intellectual Rationale for the Great Tradition

The emphasis on pupils' right conduct, that is, the moral elements of education, has been undervalued by many observers of contemporary education. In our era, questions about the appropriate goals of education are asked in an ambivalent intellectual environment. Educators adhering to tradition often feel uneasy about publicly declaring their values. Therefore, it is especially important that the roots of education's moral traditions be carefully identified.

As John Dewey observed in *Democracy and Education*, education, broadly speaking, is the process through which society renews and maintains itself. Any particular human being is born with the capability of adjusting—or learning—to live in any one of innumerable forms of societies. All of us, depending on when and where we were born, could have been reared as tenth-century Italians or contemporary Japanese citizens. We could have been fifteenth-century Aztecs, deeply committed to the patterns of human sacrifice that are so embedded in that culture. As we mature, our almost infinite ore of human potential is refined and molded. Finally, we emerge with the limited and focused learnings and dispositions relevant to our society and our roles in it.

Most of us do not remember precisely how we were taught our current roles. Similarly, most of us do not remember exactly how we learned to read or write. Indeed, even while reading this text, we are unconscious of applying the specific learned skill we call reading. Yet, if we are reminded, we recall that an elaborate process of formal and informal instruction underlay our learning to read. Similarly, in learning our roles in society, there has been an elaborate process of formal and informal instruction. Often the instruction worked just because we saw our choices as self-evident: is there any other possible way of doing things?

The most important components of belonging in any society are moral: knowing and accepting the society's standards of right and wrong, what is expected and what is disapproved. There are certain inevitable differences in such standards. Muslims believe polygamy is moral, while Christians do not. The Aztecs believed they were justified in publicly sacrificing thousands of war captives by cutting out their hearts while they were alive, but many cultures despise such practices. Some societies may even explicitly regard one society's morality as their own immorality. Still, when people disagree strongly with what their society calls moral, they may feel like aliens in their own country. Such conditions caused the Pilgrims to leave England a few hundred years ago to found a colony in New England. They went to America to escape a land whose morality they found deeply objectionable.

The centrality of teaching morality is evident when we recognize that all societies apply the most severe sanctions against people who violate their moral codes. All societies want people to be formally competent, to possess appropriate skills. Yet societies direct the greatest opprobrium at *morally* incompetent people. It may be bad to be stupid, but it is far worse to be evil. Societies also generally recognize that a technically skilled person who is seriously immoral poses a special danger to society. Skills minus morality enable immoralists to commit more consequential acts of immorality than unskilled people. Moral teaching is also given the highest priority because right morality is harder to transmit than formal, or technical, skills such as reading or mathematics.

Conceptually, it is easy to motivate people to learn most technical skills. One can usually demonstrate that such skills often bring benefits. For example, because people recognize they are better off knowing how to read, literacy is considered a valuable individual good. Or again, most adolescents, believing that learning how to drive will give them power and freedom, will go to considerable trouble to learn that skill. It is not equally evident that people are better off being moral, even though many philosophers and thoughtful people have made that contention. It may even be that the contention is objectively correct. However, it takes considerable ratiocination to make that point stick.

Conversely, the arguments that selfishness pays or that being polite is often a waste of time contain powerful primitive logic. In the Christian tradition, they are the arguments attributed to Satan, an eloquent advocate. Societies only endure if their citizens learn the morality appropriate to their status. And morality is a very difficult subject to teach. As Freud observed in *Civilization and Its Discontents*, learning morality requires learners to inhibit and redirect many strong emotions, emotions that drive us to pursue raw power, untrammeled self-expression, and reflexive erotic gratification.[8] Perhaps in the long run people are happier because they repress such drives. They have learned to be unselfish or to redirect their gross emotions. However, it is unrealistic to rely solely on such long-range considerations to persuade pupils to be altruistic. That was Freud's basic point: only through pervasive, indirect, artful, and imaginative tactics do societies succeed in teaching altruistic values.

Each such socialization system must be so strong that most successful learners never realize they have had tacit options. They never consider they might have chosen to be polygamous or to use drugs, to survive by being hunter-gatherers or to live solely on meat and fish. This foreclosure of options has some implications for the word *pluralism*, a current catchword in education. Like many other educational catchwords, there is no clear definition of the term. However, pluralism connotes a sympathy with licensing, or even encouraging, divergent values and traditions within particular schools. Sometimes these divergences relate to matters of race, religion, or social class. Some degree of tolerance and diversity is essential to a wholesome community. Whatever the virtues of pluralism, however, there are some patterns, typically associated with social class, that we hope most supporters of diversity would want to suppress. For instance, drug and alcohol abuse are more typical of lower-class (compared to middle- or upper-class) life. Some children are reared in environments where such options are vividly placed before them, and we refer to these children as being *at risk*. We surely do not rejoice about their access to pluralism. Supporters of pluralism are clearly obligated to define what they believe is acceptable and unacceptable diversity.

Protradition educators recognize that American schools and colleges are important components of our country's elaborate, pervasive, and powerful system of teaching morality. Indeed, without the support of our schools, the system cannot meet its essential ends. It will not be sufficiently elaborate, pervasive, and powerful. Furthermore, American education, including schools and colleges, uses 9.3% of our gross national product and enrolls our youth population for long periods of time. If such an enormous institution is not clearly in favor of our basic moral norms, its effects are not merely neutral.

The statistics about youth disorder in chapter 1 bear a special relevance to the topic of moral instruction. Those statistics suggest the moral instruction that young Americans are receiving is less adequate than previously. It seems plausible that one serious deficiency in our current system for moral instruction is the relative disengagement of public education from its traditional role of supporting morality.

UNDERSTANDING LEARNING

All educators have had extensive practice in trying to analyze and apply learning theories. Despite such rich experience and courses in psychology, many educators do not recognize exactly how pupils learn important moral values. Indeed, the bulk of psychological materials taught to education students focuses on cognitive, or academic, learning. Yet, as we have emphasized, moral instruction is an important function of schools. We will directly consider some psychological propositions about learning important and complex values and beliefs, such as personal morality. We will present an intellectual model. Our model is not attributable to one particular authority, but is derived from a variety of sources. This model of how we learn morality is the basis for many practical proposals we make in later chapters.

Before we describe our model, we need to define the term *learning*. Learning means using new information, to the extent possible, to change conduct. A person who has learned to cook, for example, not only knows the elements of certain recipes but also is able to prepare attractive and tasty food. A person who has learned arithmetic can add, subtract, and so on with relative accuracy. Conversely, a person who can write a clear description of swimming but is unable to keep afloat or move about alone in deep water has not learned to swim.

Let's begin by examining a series of levels of learning of increasing profundity and complexity.

First, consider the variety of things an adult might learn in a day: the weather forecast, the day's television news, a daughter's good grade in school, or the manipulation of algebraic equations. All constitute learnings.

Next we can identify things we have learned in the past month: our new coworkers are not too competent; in the future, some foods will be fortified with anticancer agents; I am learning to be an adequate bowler; our last stock investment is not turning out well; or my husband sprained his ankle.

Then we can list things we have learned in the last six months: I have decided to enroll in graduate school; in the future, knowledge of genetic background will reveal much about our current physical and mental makeup; my married sister is pregnant for the first time; my wife is going back to work; and one of my brothers had a heart attack.

Finally, if we make a list of things we have learned over the past five years, we will inevitably touch on profound learnings: deciding to get married to a particular person (or deciding to get divorced); learning to live separated from particular people we love; choosing a career (or leaving one career and going to another); or newly affiliating with a religion.

All these things are *learnings*—changes in our values, dispositions, and conduct. In other words, learning is completed only if we integrate the acquired information into our life. Thus, we do not say someone has "learned to be married" until she regularly conducts herself as if she were actually married to a particular person. This definition of learning is consonant with the ancient concept of *habituation*, an important theme in the writings of Aristotle and others. Habituation stresses that learning must generate desirable habits—routine, reflexive ways of acting. There is a large body of traditional psychological principles about how to foster habituation.

Our varied list of learnings reminds us of a number of truths; for one, many important learnings in our lives have little to do with formal education. By *formal education* we mean learning that focuses on lectures, routine written examinations, classroom recitals, typical homework assignments, and periods of deliberate study and reading—in other words, everyday school instruction. If students were invited to develop a broad list of their learnings, their in-school academics would only be a fraction of that list. Furthermore, a great many of our learnings occur as by-products of the incidents of life. We do not learn most important things (e.g., habits) from going to classes, hearing lectures, or reading texts.

Another truth about learning is that many of the important things we learn are unpleasant, even destructive, such as to accept the death of loved ones, adjust to a divorce, or practice destructive habits like cigarette smoking or drug addiction. People also "learn" to be criminals, sadists, and the like.

Let us now see how the preceding list of trivial and profound learnings helps us understand the principles of learning moral conduct, particularly in schools.

Incentives for Learning

It is easy to derive principles of learning from our list. The more profound—the more important and difficult—a thing is to learn, the more profound the learning pressures that must be applied. As we have noted, learning to prefer right over wrong is perhaps the hardest thing for humans to learn. Obviously, strong learning pressures must be applied to transmit such knowledge. We learn easy things—tomorrow's weather, who won the ball game—simply by casual listening and reading. But the greater effect a particular learning has on our lives, the more substantial the relevant pressures or incentives must be. Some of these principles have been recognized by the researchers Krathwohl, Bloom, and Masia.[9] In their taxonomy, or outline, of affective learning objectives, they said:

> . . . we should point out the high cost in energy, time and commitment in achieving complex objectives in either the cognitive or the affective domain. Such objectives are not to be attained simply by someone expressing the desire that they be attained or by a few sessions of class devoted to the attainment of the objectives . . . educators who wish to achieve these more complex goals *must be willing to pay the rather great price involved.* [emphasis added]

The model of learning we have presented is homeostatic. Because profound learning is difficult and uncomfortable, people will try to avoid it. This avoidance makes for stability. People try to avoid learning, or change, since stability is usually desirable. We believe it is good that profound learning is difficult. As we will explain, such difficulty makes for better mental health. After all, profound learnings bring about important changes in our conduct or way of looking at things. Changes in our perspectives, if they are really important, eventually lead to major shifts in conduct. Important changes in conduct disrupt our relationships with persons or institutions we are close to. If we pursue a dramatic new career, shifting from being a social worker to a bodyguard or a rock band drummer, it may seriously damage our social and family relationships. We may be occasionally amused at someone who moves about from one novel pattern of belief to another—today Buddhism, tomorrow New Age crystals, next day—? However, we usually do not become good friends with such people.

As an example, assume you must adapt to the death of a loved one. You may witness her slow physical decline, stand outside her hospital room, touch her as she is dying, see her in the coffin, go through the wake or other services, and perhaps be present at the burial. Now assume a dear one dies suddenly or while you are away, or the mourning process is otherwise truncated. As a result your adaptation may be disordered. You may continue the habits you applied while the deceased person was alive.

We can also turn to literature to interpret the meaning of *profound*. In Shakespeare's *Hamlet*, a ghost appears to Hamlet. In an extremely dramatic fashion, the ghost tells Hamlet that his uncle, with his mother's help, has murdered Hamlet's father. Much of the play is concerned with whether Hamlet should believe this disturbing message. In effect, *Hamlet* is about profound learning and the ramifications of such learning. The hero tries to decide if this new information is true and, if so, how it should change his values and conduct. Such learning drives Hamlet into deep depression and leads him to contemplate committing suicide or killing his mother and stepfather. It is not surprising that the being who bears this disruptive message to Hamlet is his father's ghost. Information from such a remarkable messenger would not be lightly cast aside.

Finally, it is obvious that many forms of profound learning are objectively bad. Thus, it is good that people are careful about adopting dramatic new habits. In sum, all emotionally healthy people have basic and wholesome patterns of resistance to important learning. They approach such potential occasions with suspicion, just as Hamlet was suspicious about the ghost's plausibility. It is understandable why great pressures or incentives are needed to bring about morally profound learning.

Intensifying Learning

The intensity of the learning situations proposed in the model can be increased by several factors. We now present a list of such factors, along with their brief rationales. Such factors are applicable to all subject areas. If the designers of learning systems are imaginative, they will find ways to apply these factors towards a variety of ends.

1. Time—The longer the learner is exposed to certain influences, the more likely the subject will be learned.

2. Status—The greater the power or prestige (in the eyes of the learner) of the instructor or the institution of learning, the more likely it is the topic will be learned. We know from modeling studies that people tend to want to imitate or satisfy attractive people.

3. Rewards and punishments—The more powerful the rewards and punishments involved, the greater the likelihood of learning. For many effective people, the most significant reward is conspicuous praise and attention (or criticism) from large numbers of people. When such attention is favorable, it is called fame.

4. Insight—The greater the insight and imagination of the instructor or the agency of instruction, the greater the likelihood of learning. It may be insight into a particular person or topic, or some general psychological insight about how effectively to conduct an institution set up for a particular end. For instance, one might propose that U.S. Marine Corps boot camp is designed with considerable insight. Most "graduates" have learned to be Marines, and they are proud of what they have overcome to attain that status. Conversely, many modern prison systems do not have insightful designs. It is notorious that they rarely succeed in improving convicts, for example, teaching most prisoners to become honest. Part of such insight involves the institution's intake system. It may be easier to teach Marine volunteers than condemned criminals. However, the Marines' message is harder to teach. Their recruits are taught to fight and die; all prisons want to do is teach unsuccessful criminals the plausible proposition that honesty pays.

5. Proximity and intensity—The more intense the physical closeness between the instructor and the learner (e.g., a mother hugging a child, a lover caressing a mate, or a bully beating a victim), the more powerful the learnings transmitted.

6. Consistency—The greater the consistency in the environment around the learner during most of the teaching process, the more powerful the learning.

7. Body management—The more the teaching process requires learners to change the way they manage their bodies, the more powerful the process.

Such changes include the imposition of a particular diet; the prescription of particular garments (e.g., uniforms, wedding gowns) or hair styles; requirements that learners assume particular postures, often during public ceremonies or rites (e.g., publicly stand as a group, hold their hands over their hearts, and salute the flag); or, in some cultures, people accepting scars or other conspicuous marks on their bodies.

8. Volition—As learners mature, learning environments will have important elements of discretion or choice. When learners voluntarily and publicly commit themselves to a course, they lose dignity when they fail. Conversely, when they have been forced or drafted in, they maintain dignity by resisting compulsory learning. Boot camp works better than prison partly because people enlist in the Marines ("We're looking for a few good men."). In contrast, prisoners are sentenced to prison. It is often better for learning if adult learners can choose whether to commit themselves to particular patterns of demands, e.g., marrying, joining the Baptist Church, or pursuing a specific career.

Reconsidering "Learning Is Fun"

The preceding discussion implicitly questions the popular educational aphorism, "learning is fun." It is indisputable that many forms of learning—adjusting to death, falling out of love or facing the rejection of a lover, adopting an important and different moral doctrine—are not fun by any definition. *Hamlet* is a tragedy about an intelligent, sympathetic person who could not handle the enormous learning demands thrust on him. Everyone can recall academic materials they are happy to have learned, even though they did not enjoy the process. We all have different lists of difficult subjects we learned, and we all recall situations where we had to struggle (often successfully) to learn particular subjects. Someone might contend that truly brilliant teachers might organize things so that all academic learnings are enjoyable for all students. Maybe. But the prospect seems utopian.

When we consider the evident implausibility of the learning-is-fun doctrine, its intellectual vitality is remarkable. Because of such vitality, we must understand more deeply the history and meaning of this mischievous and seriously flawed doctrine. Fundamentally, the doctrine traces its roots to the French philosopher Jean-Jacques Rousseau (1712–1778). Rousseau, in influential works like *Emile*, argued for letting learning be a by-product of natural development, or the routine incidents of life. He echoed Shakespeare's "Ripeness is all" and urged teachers to adopt noninterventionist postures.[10]

A little more than a century later, John Dewey articulated similar themes in his praise of intrinsic motivation. Popular statements of such ideas were more explicit. In l905, the principal of the University of Chicago Laboratory School (founded less than ten years earlier by Dewey), in a bulletin to parents, remarked, "The School realizes the utter futility of trying to teach anyone anything when he is not in a happy frame of mind."[11] It is not clear that Dewey would have stated this obviously incorrect proposition so baldly. It is evident, though, that the principal believed his proposition was derived from the concept of intrinsic motivation for learning. Furthermore, the bulletin's statement articulates a point of view that has appealed to many twentieth-century educators and education theorists. For instance, we can see elements of such themes in recommendations that children should develop or freely choose their own moral values—rather than adults "imposing" values on them. After all, pupils will obviously be happier learning values they freely choose instead of being directed to learn more demanding values. Such educational approaches are logically rooted in the concept, "learning is fun."

Another flaw is the difficulty of developing a clear, operational definition of fun or happiness. Are people happy when they are drunk? High on drugs? There is also the matter of the time frame applied in testing for happiness. The Greek historian Herodotus contended that no one should call himself happy until he had reached the point of his death. He buttressed his point with tales of prominent persons who died lonely and dishonored and contrasted such disappointments with stories of persons of relatively low status who died surrounded with praise and honor.

The anthropologists Robert Le Vine and Merry White vividly characterized many of the theories and practices about the enjoyability of children's learning. The key word in their discussion was *sentimentality*. Although their remarks focused on the nineteenth century, we could extend their vision backwards a century to include Rousseau. We believe he is one of the foundations of the sentimentality they identify. The two authors said:

> In the nineteenth century, literary and artistic romanticism established an emotional climate on which the struggle for children's rights as a form of political liberation could draw . . . the sentimental idealization of childhood combined with the liberal notion that children had rights to be politically enforced, in such cultural phenomena as the novels of Charles Dickens and the legislative struggles against child labor. Much of the complexity of this history derives from the fact that the debate over freedom versus constraint in childhood has not led to a final revolution, but continues even today, in issues specific to contemporary contexts.[12]

Sentimentalism aside, the fact is that most learning is not fun, but work. Ironically, some of the things we truly enjoy learning—using drugs and alcohol, committing certain crimes—are bad for us. When wholesome learning is fun, it is at about the level of a hobby—something we do not have to do, which has no vital effect on our lives or our relationships with others, and where we can enter or withdraw at will. It is like learning bird watching, fishing, or amateur photography. Conversely, suppose we had to do any of these things for a living, and our income or children's security depended on our success. Then the process of learning would probably be accelerated and require more diligence. And it would be less fun.

This does not mean the diligent pursuit of learning is never enjoyable. We all recall situations where we finally were gratified at the outcomes of certain demanding learning activities. Still, in spite of such gratifications, it is misleading to portray such activities as fun. The word *fun* does not characterize the efforts, discipline, and stress that often underlie such activities.

The doctrine that says learning is fun condemns educators to trivial activities. Why, then, has it gotten so far? There are two attractive arguments for the doctrine.

The *pragmatic argument* contends that if teachers only teach what keeps students happy, they need not be diligent. It is also true that students do not learn many important good things in such permissive environments. As long as fidelity to the doctrine of keeping students happy persists, teachers have a relatively easy time. They are teaching motivated pupils because they keep presenting subjects that win pupil approval. Of course, when in-school learning is designed to be fun, sometimes parents, and even some students and teachers, become upset when they discover that serious learning is being avoided. Many students occasionally become bored with the triviality of the whole process. While the approach is not without practical difficulties, it still has a powerful superficial appeal.

The other case for the learning-is-fun concept is a *philosophical argument*. Unlike the pragmatic argument, which appeals to adult irresponsibility, the philosophical argument has honorable substance. If teachers reject the doctrine that learning is fun, they are obligated to apply their power in an interventionist mode. They must strongly encourage and even coerce pupils to learn things that often do not immediately please them. What should such adults decide to teach, and what forms of significant incentives and punishments should they apply to learners? After all, putting strong pressure on people to learn (partly against their will) is a severe constraint on their liberty. There is no doubt that teachers—especially when compulsion is involved, as it often must be since our society makes education mandatory—may abuse their necessary power. This danger has been recognized for many centuries. Dramatic examples from folklore and literature easily come to mind, such as the Pied Piper or Fagin in *Oliver Twist*. These evildoers led children astray by teaching them bad things.

Despite such potential for abuse, the reality is that adult determination is essential to form good morals in children. Human beings must receive significant and powerful instruction. Otherwise, they cannot acquire sufficiently stable moral identities to meet the identity challenges of adult life. How will they learn to resist the temptations to cheat or abuse drugs? How will they remain loyal to their spouses and children, or apply themselves when confronted with legitimate arduous demands? It is impossible to form strong personalities without a profound molding system. This system must have considerable authority, as well as potential for abuse. In most societies, the systems that teach young people their identities—and identities largely involve moral matters—are principally under the control of their parents. Due to the nature of typical parent-child relations, the conditions for fostering profound learning are generally present in families. Coincidentally, the potential for abuse is also at hand. In our own era, we are familiar with contentions about rising rates of child abuse by parents.

It is hard to say whether such abuse has become more prevalent, or merely more visible or aggressively investigated. The potential for such abuse, whether by parents or other authority figures, is surely an essential, but tragic, concomitant of the power to transmit significant instruction. A world in which the potential for child abuse was eliminated would be a world in which parents were surrounded with enormous constraints. They would be subject to frequent and intrusive inspection and external reviews about problematic and subtle issues. Such pervasive monitoring, if it were possible, would necessarily undermine the intensity of parent-child relations. Relations would become more legalistic and formalistic, less spontaneous and intimate. Families characterized by such relationships would still teach children important things, but most of these learnings would probably be undesirable. None of this discussion is intended to deny the appalling reality of child abuse or to discourage efforts to moderate abuses. But we are engaged in a balancing process. We may be pressing our anti-abuse efforts too hard if we undermine the power of legitimate adults to subject children to strong learning. For instance, the word *punishment* is rarely found in professional literature for educators unless it is used pejoratively to mean punitive.

One would not typically say that "During World II, the Allies had a punitive attitude towards Hitler." Instead, it would usually be phrased, "During World War II, the Allies sought to bring Hitler to justice."

The word *consequences* is usually used as a substitute for punishment. But the two words have notably different connotations. *Punishment* has a more profound moral tone. Arguments against punishment arise from the same misconceptions underlying the oratory against child abuse. Unfortunately, when the moral framework of parenting is eroded, many harmful effects occur.

The authors recently ran across a list of suggestions for parents: rules that parents should make and their children should obey. The suggestions seemed to offer common-sense, obvious ideas. But we quickly noticed the list had no suggestions about the punishments to apply if their children failed to obey particular directions. Presumably, the people transmitting the suggestions felt the main need of contemporary parents was to know what to "command." Our perception is that parents need, just as much, to know how to compel obedience to their demands. Such compulsion often requires sensitive attention to punishment.

Although the family is a child's first and most important source of profound instruction, many other agencies have always been involved. As long as schools have existed, they have been important allies in this process. The recent partial break with the Great Tradition represents a notable historic shift. The shift may not persist. We should also say something about school-family conflicts over the values taught to children. This issue, too, has a long history.

WHO DECIDES WHAT VALUES?

Various theories can be applied to determine what should be taught to children. Later in the book, we will discuss some of these theories. However, there is a related, but separate question: regardless of the rationale applied, what persons or institutions should have the power to make such choices?

There have often been shifts in the location of such authority. In the early Roman Republic, in about the third century B.C., families had life-or-death power over their children. The family—essentially, the father—decided what values children should learn. Gradually, however, the political institutions of the Roman

Republic obtained power to intervene in cases of aggravated abuse by parents of children. Since that era, public institutions, in limited instances, have tried to supplement "teaching deficiencies" in some families. For instance, if children in some families are learning delinquency or otherwise being severely abused, some right of public intervention is recognized. While acknowledging that intervention, it still is extremely difficult for societies to invent sound substitutes for families. Therefore, intervention, or what some consider undermining of parental values, has generally been attempted by schools in very circumspect ways. This is a sound and realistic principle.

We have not finally stated which persons or institutions should decide what morals children should learn and what forms of incentives or pressures can be applied. We have implied that parents and educators should play important roles, with the parents' concerns receiving top priority. Beyond that general remark, however, we have not definitively answered the question. The broader answer to "Who should decide?" is essentially a political issue. In all societies, individual families play a vital role. Beyond the family, external agencies, such as extended families, formal religion, schools, and local and national institutions, also play a part in shaping such policies. The precise roles assumed by these institutions depend on a medley of factors, including the political structure of a society, the nature of its economy, and its technology. In a totalitarian country such as Germany in 1935, the Nazi party was an important factor in deciding how German children should be formed. In the former Soviet Union, the policies of the Communist party carried heavy weight.

Conversely, in the highly decentralized and pluralistic United States, such decision-making power is widely diffused. Significant authority is possessed by local and national legislatures and local school boards. However, this formal authority is also shared with many informal agencies, such as the creators of television cartoons, sitcoms, and soap operas, rock musicians and their promoters, and various religious entities.

Such a listing of forces can be put in another way: America is a complex, multilayered democratic society. In our country, deciding what values should be taught to children is not largely a matter of some group debating and passing a definitive law, although particular laws are not irrelevant. It would be ridiculous to propose that the Supreme Court be given the authority and responsibility for deciding what values should be taught in our public schools, or that some nationwide convention with real authority be created for this purpose, and so on. Possessing the power to decree national homogeneity, except at the most abstract levels, in such an intimate matter as education would be tyranny.

Instead of national decrees, here is what we envisage. At this time, a variety of patterns of childrearing values exist, though some communities and some parts of society have more coherent values than others. Additionally, as circumstances change, childrearing values also shift. Changing circumstances can include matters such as changing public and intellectual perceptions, different technologies, the development of new or different evidence (such as the statistics about youth disorder we outlined in chapter 1), and the formation of new organizations and the decline of existing ones. Such shifts may move in a good or bad direction.

These diffuse networks of authority are implicit in the U.S. Constitution. That document implicitly grants control of critical education policies to states and other local entities. However, in the recent past, more control over moral education policy has shifted toward more remote authorities. Some of these authorities are governmental—the federal courts and Congress. Other authorities are nongovernmental—our national media and national professional and labor organizations. The shift has diminished the authority of local entities, which are more sensitive to the priorities of parents and other protradition forces. What are some examples of the policies stimulated by the shifts? Greater emphasis on simplistic in-school egalitarianism. Lessening ability of educators to apply vital discipline due to actual and potential court decisions. Increased youth interest in immediate gratification and freedom from constraints.

We believe the locus of authority in the system for governing American moral education should shift. The shift should bring about more decentralized, deliberate, discrete, and altruistic adult authority over young persons and youth-serving institutions. The particular names and affiliations of such agencies will vary in different communities. However, at this point we are not concerned with explicit designations of existing or new agencies. We only want to clearly state the parameters of an improved policy. Conversely, we should lessen the influence of some current decision-makers, such as popular musicians, youth marketeers, highly individualistic intellectuals and popular figures, and certain national private associations concerned with education and strongly dedicated to advancing particular adult self-interests. This shift to more local authority will encourage the development of policies that will help the young learn more traditional values. Such a shift will not extinguish all the moral deficiencies in our current situation; this would be utopian. However, our current youth morality situation is perhaps at its worst point in history. In this light, a change that cuts current disorder levels in half would be a notable improvement. Exactly how such a complex change can occur is beyond the scope of our book, except to say that this book, by presenting data and arguments, may provide ammunition to assist that change.

PROFOUND LEARNING IN SCHOOLS

Let us now compare the list of intense learning incentives with typical patterns of learning that occur in most schools. One element becomes immediately apparent: most day-to-day learning in schools is of rather low profundity. Likewise, many of the instructional devices used—lectures, exams, film strips, recitations—are means of comparatively low power. To some degree, these perceptions are correct. We tend to overestimate the significance of most schools' academic curricula. But we should not underestimate the actual and potential power of in-school instruction—if we consider things in a broad light.

Schools usually do meet the criterion of absorbing pupils' time; students typically stay enrolled in formal education (often through college) from twelve to sixteen years. The subject matter at different levels varies, and the formal lessons are often forgotten. How many readers recall how to do trigonometry, or what genetic mixes determine which hereditary patterns? In addition, certain learned subject matter that students often use in later life—reading, arithmetic, perhaps some history and geography—will tend to persist.

But school-taught dispositions may linger even longer than formal knowledge: learning how to keep quiet and at least appear to pay attention; learning impulse control and some patience; and learning that adults believe schools are important. Furthermore, assume pupils are required to work diligently at schoolwork, for example, to do considerable homework or be subjected to demanding grading. Then they will also learn diligence, even if they forget the particular subjects of their work. If the school has a rigorous dress code or uniform requirement, it can also heighten the students' learning about their group identities. They will learn that life is more enjoyable for members of purposeful, well-managed groups. Learning the values of group identity are important for learning morality; to keep our affiliation, we will strive to learn the morality that will ensure our continuing membership.

There are other powerful forms of in-school learning that may be skipped in our classification. In particular, we should study the learning that occurs for members of school athletic teams. Through such study, we can obtain an appreciation of the other learning means sometimes available to schools.

Competitive Athletics

Membership in athletic teams is voluntary. Coaches can expel players who will not conform, and players who cannot "take it" can quit. Many students, even some who are capable athletes, may choose not to join such teams. Because of such volition, coaches can feel comfortable in deciding to make more severe demands on learners than is typical in classrooms. Team members, due to their choosing to join, learn about commitment and loyalty. Team practices are often very intense and make little pretense of being fun. Team members wear special uniforms. Teams sometimes perform before audiences and occasionally even are encouraged by cheerleaders. Sometimes, the audience pays to see them perform—pretty heady stuff for an adolescent! Team members see that their activities are similar to the much-publicized feats of adult professional athletic heroes. The team's record is often displayed in various ways, including in the community newspapers. The achievements and deficiencies of individual players are carefully and publicly enumerated by elaborate tabulation systems, e.g., times at bat, hits, strikeouts, walks, batting average, runs batted in, runs scored, home runs. The school may hold pep rallies. Coaches are often selected for their ability to motivate team members to make intense efforts and usually have considerable prestige in players' eyes. There is great emphasis on improving team performance. Coaches are licensed to make contact with players' bodies. They often pat players on the back, use their hands to set players' bodies or hands in correct positions, and otherwise engage in legitimate touches. Finally, students on teams are usually in vital social systems, and their competitive commitment is supplemented by horseplay, easy give-and-take, and the assurance of continuing lively social relations.

Athletic teams constitute very powerful learning systems. It is well known that many pupils work infinitely harder to learn athletic skills—to tolerate exhaustion and ignore pain, hold their temper in the face of provocation, control their weight, and do other difficult things—than they do at academics. The learning systems surrounding athletics are very intense.

One of the authors interviewed a twelve-year-old player on a grade-school basketball team. The boy told a story nicely illustrating some of the kinds of learning that can arise around competitive teams. The boy, for his age, had considerable athletic ability and common sense. So he was team captain in seventh grade. One day the coach, dissatisfied with the team's performance in some exercise, told all team members to do fifty pushups each. Some players thought the punishment was unfair, and talked of some form of "rebellion." The twelve-year-old captain persuaded them to "cool it" and take the punishment. The next day the captain went to the coach and politely and privately questioned the justice of the punishment. The coach listened to him and agreed his protest was justified. Later in the day, the coach apologized to the whole team for his previous mistake. The whole incident showed people—the team captain, the players, the coach—practicing considerable wisdom.

The discussion about competitive athletics suggests a variety of ways the principles of profound learning can be, and are, employed in many school programs. Particularly with high school students, such principles can deal with diverse learning goals, including character, academics, or good discipline. Without specifying the particulars of such programs, which will be considered later, let us generally sketch some examples. We can:

1. intensify rewards for successful learning: public attention and praise; publicity; conspicuous symbols to be worn by or given to successful learners (similar to athletic letters and trophies); public audiences watching contests among learners.

2. increase the opportunities for voluntary enrollment: pupils and their families can be invited to enroll in high-pressure, prestigious programs or schools, where they choose to accept strong learning demands.

3. increase the status and power of teachers: give them prestige and simultaneously ask them to hold to high standards, working very hard like dedicated coaches; be rated by the success or failure of their pupils; permit them to expel pupils from their classes to lower-status classes.

4. increase the punishments for poor performance, lack of effort, and disorder: more or less conspicuous public humiliation; being sent to various forms of "exile"; being kept out of enjoyable activities; being sent to lower-status "reform schools" where highly repressive policies are applied to students; being required to display their inadequate learning before some audience by looking bad in a public competition.

5. increase the role of ritual, art, and ceremony in emphasizing incentives for learning: the articulation and attainment of learning goals can be ceremonially demarcated; colorful posters and other art work can emphasize the importance of particular goals; and assemblies, pledges, musical performances, and speeches can intensify commitment to learning.

6. increase students' learning obligations to particular groups (their "teams"): use uniforms and other identity-creating symbols and forms of group grading and grouping to heighten collective identity; provide students with occasions for friendly but work-centered socialization; publicize the successful and unsuccessful groups, as well as the names of group members.

7. increase the learning demands on pupils: teachers should show that they know pupils usually can do much more than they have been doing, just as coaches make rigorous demands on athletes.

8. clearly identify learning goals related to character, academics, and discipline and provide students with precise and dramatic feedback about their progress: students will know what is expected and can tell when they are nearing success, like participants in an athletic contest.

9. encourage whole schools or whole programs consistently to press towards common learning aims: pupils will receive uniform reinforcement in pursuing difficult goals.

10. increase the diversity of learning demands on pupils, just as different athletic teams use various forms of talent, from beefy weight-lifters to slender long-distance runners: more pupils will have an activity that allows them to shine.

11. provide incentives for pupils to graduate from programs more quickly: pupils who do not like school do not have to be "kept in jail their full term." They can earn "early release" if they learn to work hard. It is better they apply themselves than become resigned.

12. emphasize pride, rather than novelty and fun, as the objective: pride suggests effort and accomplishment.

It is well known that interscholastic athletics is sometimes affected with many dishonorable acts.[13] Sometimes the players engage in such practices, but more often they are done by coaches. Such practices are much more frequent in college than in high school athletics because much greater temptations are involved at the college level. Some coaches receive large salaries, and television contracts and similar activities also involve large amounts of money. However, to a lesser degree, some misconduct spills over into high school athletics. Readers may naturally ask, "Shouldn't such misconduct serve to sharply moderate any praise of high school athletics?"

To our mind, a major cause for such misconduct is the high-stakes nature of interscholastic competitive athletics. The moment the desire for some team to win is shared by both the athletes and other community members—their in-school peers, their families—pressures inevitably arise to increase the likelihood of team success. Most of these pressures are healthy and even natural, e.g., people want the school to employ an able coach, athletes are urged to work hard at practice and play, and more attention is paid to their victories and defeats. Of course, sometimes these pressures become unwisely intense, or particular players or coaches succumb to temptations the pressure generates. Such acts of misconduct must be prohibited, monitored, and punished. However, it would be unwise, except in the most aggravated situations, to simply suppress interscholastic athletics. Part of its learning value is precisely the strong emotions it engenders in players, coaches, and the audience. Such emotions can greatly increase the constructive power of the learning experiences involved. Pupils are learning how to control their emotions under considerable pressure, which is a notable act of learning. Furthermore, as far as the pressures on players goes, the pupils have volunteered to enlist in such environments and have the right to leave at any time. Most of us are familiar with pupils who have begun to play sports and later dropped out, even when they possess the necessary skills. Such volition is a valuable characteristic of team sports. It licenses the sports system to subject players to somewhat greater stress than would be appropriate for regular students, who are often drafted into and "imprisoned" in their academic activities.

None of this is to say that dishonorable conduct in athletics should be ignored or licensed. Rigorous attention is quite appropriate. However, the monitors should also understand the special virtues of athletic competition.

Transformational Education

Our discussion should conclude with some harsh words about the "transformational" aspirations some authorities have for education: the idea that certain unique forms of education, almost on their own, can form (or transform) significant segments of society into human beings possessing novel virtues and talents. Such aspirations are often a dangerous fallacy. Educators who apply diligence and imagination and are supported by informed and insightful parents *can* form many pupils into persons who are relatively unusual compared to typical Americans. Our research has identified various institutions that have attained such effects. Typically, such institutions have served traditional ethnic and religious groups, for example, Lithuanian-American Catholics and Orthodox Jews. A few of the institutions have been secular and served highly literate, liberal, and individualistic families. To call the goals of all of these schools *novel* is problematic. The schools have only succeeded to the extent their novel values are strongly supported by the pupils' families.

One Lithuanian Saturday school we studied succeeded in forming second- and probably third-generation bilingual Lithuanian-American children into adults who saw themselves as Americans deeply identified with traditional Lithuanian values. From age six to sixteen, students attended the school all day every Saturday and learned Lithuanian language and traditions. The school's curriculum assumed that its pupils' parents: spoke only Lithuanian at home, while they and their children spoke English at work and during regular school and college attendance; sent their children to a Lithuanian-American summer camp; participated in the life of Lithuanian-American Catholic churches; and otherwise evinced a deep commitment to supporting Lithuanian traditions. If the parents failed to meet such expectations, their children would eventually feel quite out-of-place in the school. In a certain sense this school attained its goal—to create bicultural Lithuanian-Americans. But we should also be conscious of the limits (and costs) of such success. Many other Lithuanian-Americans chose not to accept such significant constraints on themselves and their children. Still others started their children in this program but found it too rigorous and withdrew them. Our study provided no estimate of the proportion who refused to join or who dropped out. All of these powerful schools expect their graduates to marry persons from the same group. Orthodox Jews will marry Orthodox Jews. Or very liberal people graduated from "liberal" schools will marry other liberal people. Without such in-group marriages, the unique values that the schools aspire to transmit will be dissipated by the exigencies of adult life. Furthermore, one measure of a school's strength is its pupils' determination to carry forward its peculiar values focus, or if one chooses, its parochialism. Students choosing to marry someone who shares values learned in the school are simply another example of the school's shaping power.

It is also theoretically possible for schools to form new or unusual personalities without the support of pupils' families. But such unsupported schools will not work effectively unless:

1. the pupils are completely separated from immediate community and family values, e.g., set off in the country. Then, the schools can deliver a simple, clear message. The political scientist James Q. Wilson has proposed such systems of separation for the education of seriously delinquent urban children and adolescents.[14]

2. the school and community are closely aligned, and the child's parents are evident deviants. As children mature, they may prefer school and community values to those of their parents. Such a shift might occur when one child abandons delinquent parents in favor of an ordered school and community, or when another abandons moral parents for the attractions of an immoral school and community. As for the latter instance, both the Communists in the Soviet Union and the Nazis in Germany foresaw that some children might grow up pro-state while their parents were not. In one example, schools in the communist Soviet Union taught pupils to honor as a "martyr" a thirteen-year-old boy who informed police about his parents' anti-state conduct. Students were taught that the "hero" was killed by a local antigovernment mob and that his anticommunist parents were sent to jail. Statues of this "heroic" youth were prominently displayed near many Soviet schools.

3. the "schools" are powerful institutions that informed adults deliberately choose to join to shape their personalities into different forms, e.g., Marine Corps boot camp, Catholic religious orders. Much of the power of such institutions depends on the learners' voluntary enlistment. Volition provides the institution with a deliberately selected group of learners and licenses the institution to apply powerful techniques that might be inappropriate for "drafted" pupils. In general, transformational powers are inappropriate for institutions that draft their members. However, even typical public schools should increase their power *somewhat*.

Schools with transformational powers *can* be created. However, such schools are potent medicine. Their powerful effects are often unpredictable, and the risks of abuse and error and the costs involved are often unjustified. The general school norm should be to reinforce parents' values. Of all the complex values surrounding children, those of parents are usually the most realistic and helpful. However, suppose circumstances compel us to conduct schools that must conflict with many parents' values in certain communities. Then we must recognize the complexities involved and proceed only with realism, caution, and determination.

About Education Research

The relationship between the findings of education research, particularly psychology, and moral education must be particularly considered. The topic is complex, and the existing research far from definitive. Still, a general survey is justified.

Humans have a long history of reflecting about moral growth, of puzzling over what helps individuals live a good life and learn habits that enable them to live in harmony with neighbors. We have evidence of the centrality of these questions for many ancient peoples even before the Greeks, who were deeply concerned with these issues. The cardinal question for ancient Greeks about education, "What is most worth knowing?" was, in turn, driven by the question, "What type of mind and character are worth possessing, and how can they be acquired?" Central to our education at all levels, then, is a probing of what leads to—and away from—ethical development and character.

A story told by the Greek writer and political figure Xenophon (c.430–355 B.C.) nicely illustrates the sophistication of such ancient concerns. Xenophon wrote *The Education of Cyrus*.[15] Cyrus was a successful and prominent Persian king, and Xenophon had actually traveled in Persia. Supposedly, *The Education* portrayed the forms of education applied to train the male children of upper-class Persians, who were expected, as adults, to rule that state. But it still seems the story was only partly fact. The other "part" was Xenophon's imaginative attempt to publicize certain educational theories that he favored.

Xenophon said the Persian parents stressed that their children had to be scrupulously honest to adults—even to the slaves and tutors who took direct care of them. Then, as the children matured, they were gradually introduced into the adult world of deception, as applied in war and diplomacy.

Eventually, as adults, the "graduates" could distinguish between the truthfulness owed to family members and the like—at all costs—and the deception that was justified towards enemies and foreigners.

Xenophon's exposition was a sensitive application of the principles of developmental psychology. It is possible that some readers may regard Xenophon's prescription as too Machiavellian—too manipulative. Other readers may see the story as simply a realistic reflection of how the world must work. However, the very fact that there may be differing opinions about the moral content of Xenophon's story makes a point. The story identifies, in a realistic and sophisticated manner, an important and persisting issue confronting education: what facts and concepts should be taught to what children at what ages? Xenophon's story provokes readers to think carefully about that issue. And Xenophon, some 2400 years ago, wrote the story precisely to stimulate readers' minds. He obviously knew his business as a writer and thinker.

In the recent past, the discipline of psychology has been most prominent in trying to answer the inevitable questions about moral education. Psychiatrists and psychologists from Sigmund Freud to Jean Piaget to Lawrence Kohlberg have offered theories to explain how we develop moral consciousness and identify the stages that our ethical thinking is capable of passing through. But antedating even the formal development of psychology, other thinkers, such as Plato, Aristotle, and Rousseau, have enriched the "science of the mind." Less prominent among the sciences aiding educators are anthropology and sociology. Their concerns focus on people in communities. This emphasis makes them ideally suited to address the moral realm. In fact, though, much contemporary sociology and anthropology are relatively critical of traditional values. Too often, such disciplines display the sentimental and romantic focus decried by Le Vine and White.

One major exception is the French scholar Émile Durkheim, considered by many the father of sociology.[16] During much of his life, Durkheim was a rector of a teachers college, conducting classes for aspiring teachers. He gave serious attention to the role of school in helping children acquire the community's best values. In particular, Durkheim advocated the development of a strong school spirit and ethos; the necessity for forging self-discipline; and the school's commitment to moving children toward moral maturity. Indeed, much of what we have written in this book has been strongly influenced by Durkheim's views. We have also been influenced by the sociologist Orrin Klapp, who has written extensively about the role of institutions in shaping individual identity and values.[17]

Some contemporary research on education has demonstrated many differences among public schools in the priorities they allocate to learning objectives such as character, academics, and discipline. Not every public, or private, school gives the same emphasis to each of these different goals. Other research has indicated that schools that deliberately define such goals and treat them as serious priorities are more likely to attain those goals than less committed institutions. Furthermore, some research has indicated that the three goals of character, academics, and discipline are not inherently contradictory; instead, they are complementary. A school that gives priority to both character and academics may do better in academics than a school that emphasizes academics only.

For most of Western history, the development of proper habits, or habituation, was the basic mode of teaching good conduct. That approach was founded on what came to be called *trait*, or faculty, *psychology*. Aristotle was one of the early promoters of this doctrine, which assumed that each person was a bundle of latent traits, such as honesty, diligence, and good humor. Education's task was to encourage the shaping of those traits in the right direction. Eventually an adult would develop with a collection of good dispositions. To give a common-sense example, believers in trait psychology were not surprised when they learned that a disproportionately high number of early American astronauts had earned the prestigious Eagle Scout status while in the Boy Scouts. Dedicated Boy Scouts who reached this status were likely to display the traits required in adult astronauts: discipline, determination, independence, and high capability for learning.

The doctrines of trait psychology provided a ready foundation for the practices of the Great Tradition. But in the late 1920s, a series of elaborate studies by psychologists Hartschorne, May, and Shuttleworth questioned the rationale for trait psychology.[18] Their research concluded that the relationship between students being "taught" any trait and their later good conduct in a somewhat different moral situation was quite slight. The ability to generalize about moral learning was not great. A pupil who was honest in the classroom might later steal from a cash register as a store employee. These research findings had a considerable negative impact on intellectual sympathy for the Great Tradition in general and the Character Education movement (discussed earlier) in particular. As Kohlberg later derisively remarked, the tradition was merely a "bag of virtues" approach.[19]

To a great degree, in education the concepts of trait psychology were replaced by concepts allied with developmental psychology. Those new concepts were relatively congruent with the values identified by Rousseau. They emphasized letting the "natural virtues" of the child emerge. At best, the teacher would act as a facilitator. More intrusive intervention would be ineffectual, immoral, and distorting.

Despite the rise of the new concepts, it is evident that many practicing educators still apply the doctrines of trait psychology. Presumably, these teachers cannot condone cheating or other misconduct, even if research allegedly shows that teaching a child to be honest in exams has little generalizability. In other words, responsible educators are inevitably concerned with their pupils' moral formation.

Furthermore, regardless of the research, any observer can see that much teaching throughout education, including the offering of graduate degrees, relies on tacit forms of the discredited trait psychology. The major purpose of most doctorate programs is to teach modes of thought. These programs assume that one can be taught to think like a researcher, just as one can be taught to be honest or diligent. In sum, many of the diverse attitudes that educators at all levels try to impart to students are still founded implicitly on trait psychology. Trait psychology is the "underground psychology" of most education and is probably applied to graduate students by the very researchers who decry any school emphasis on trait psychology.

Since the sixty-year-old studies of Hartschorne, May, and Shuttleworth innumerable other studies have affected the significance of their findings, refining some of the original calculations. The corrections undermined their anti-trait psychology findings. Later studies, summarized by Philip Rushton and his colleagues, have gone even further.[20] They have generally found higher correlations than did Hartschorne, May, and Shuttleworth between the teaching of virtues and the subjects' later virtuous conduct. Actually, such muddled findings about the ways of teaching virtue were consistent with the important themes of the Great Tradition. All earlier authorities recognized there was no perfect system for teaching virtue. Even the best approaches would occasionally produce imperfect products. Indeed, in the area of cognitive instruction, imperfect success is also the norm in teaching demanding subjects to randomly chosen audiences. Human beings are too complex to be stamped out like widgets.

Some systems of moral instruction work better than others, and the issues involved require persistent intellectual analysis. In practice, even elaborate programs of transmitting virtue do not ensure later virtuous conduct by all participants. The generalizability of such efforts is moderate. Yet this applies to many types of instruction. The factual knowledge or skills we learn in one environment often do not transfer to other situations. All such efforts are only probabilistic: it is more probable that we will display particular conduct or values if we have received earlier instruction. Perhaps the correct way to interpret the findings of Hartschorne, May, and Shuttleworth, as well as the later research, is to conclude that Americans had exaggerated expectations for their prevailing systems of moral instruction—not that the approaches were bad, but the expectations were unrealistic. But Americans usually have unrealistic expectations for education innovations, regardless of whether the basic ideas are good or bad. It is likely that, whatever the flaws of trait psychology, this approach to moral instruction is more efficacious than all other alternatives we have tried. Indeed, as we have stated, those opposed to trait psychology actually apply this psychological theory when they train their own students. It seems protradition educators who choose to stick with trait psychology make a sound decision.

Practices and Policies

1. Does your school have a written statement of philosophy? Can teachers easily derive coherent operating policies from its text? In conducting your examination, pay special attention to concepts such as "learning is fun," or any references to ideas such as diligence, voluntary commitment to learning, the importance of the school as a social institution, and the recognition of different sorts of excellence.

2. If no such statement exists, or the statement is obscure or ambiguous, does this lack signify (a) there is coherence among the views of the school's professional staff, but the statement fails to reflect it; or (b) the views of the staff are too disparate to permit drafting a coherent statement?

3. Draft or update a statement of school philosophy (either real or hypothetical), reflecting the issues posed in this chapter. It might stress concepts such as diligence, commitment, institutional pride, and high aspirations. If possible, ask other faculty members to take part in the process. In drafting or revising the statement, try to ensure the prose is precise enough so readers can identify practices that are congruent with the statement. Compare the statement to the practices that prevail in the school.

4. If you are a classroom teacher, draft a written statement of the philosophy of your particular classes.

5. Does your school or classroom have a pledge or other brief statement of principles that students can memorize and recite periodically? The following is an example of a daily school pledge that students recited publicly in one Chicago public elementary school.

I pledge, as a student of Schiller School, to strive toward excellence in my scholastic performance, my school attendance, and my behavior. I will work diligently each day toward reaching my goals. I deserve and will only accept from myself and others the very best education possible. Excellence is my goal.

References

1. Marius, R. (1985). *Thomas More, a biography*. New York: Knopf, p. 225.

2. Bowen, J. (1971). *A history of western education* (Vol. 1: The ancient world). New York: St. Martins Press, p. 153.

3. Cohen, Y. (1964). *The transition from childhood to adulthood*. Chicago: Aldine, p. 47.

4. Tyack, D., & Hansot, E. (1982). *Managers of virtue*. New York: Basic Books.

5. Yulish, S. M. (1980). *The search for a civic religion*. Landover, MD: University Press of America.

6. Gurr, T. R., & Graham, H. N. (Eds.). (1979). *Violence in America* (Vol. 1). Beverly Hills, CA: Sage, introduction, pp. 13–15.

7. Schlesinger, A., Jr. (1986). *The cycles in American history*. Boston: Norton.

8. Freud, S. (1938). *Civilization and its discontents*. London: Hogarth.

9. Krathwol, D., Bloom, B., & Masia, B. (1964). *Taxonomy of educational objectives, handbook II: Affective domain*. New York: David McKay, p. 79.

10. Rousseau, J. J. (1974). *Emile*. New York: Dutton, p. 56.

11. De Pencier, I. B. (1967). *The history of the laboratory schools*. Chicago: Quadrangle Press, p. 59.

12. Le Vine, R. A., & White, M. (1986). *Human conditions*. New York: Routledge & Kegan Paul, p. 69.

13. Wynne, E. A. (1987, March). Competitive sports—inevitably controversial. *Journal of Physical Education, Recreation and Health, 58*, 80–86.

14. Wilson, J. Q. (1991). Human nature and social progress. Bradley Lecture, American Enterprise Institute, May 9.

15. Xenophon. (1915). *The education of Cyrus*. New York: E. P. Dutton, p. 63.

16. Durkheim, E. (1961). *Moral education*. New York: Free Press.

17. For an example supporting this point, see Klapp, O. (1969). *The collective search for identity*. New York: Holt, Rinehart, & Winston.

18. Hartschorne, H., May, M. A., & Shuttleworth, F. K. (1930). *Studies in the organization of character*. New York: Macmillan.

19. Kohlberg, L. (1981). *Essays on moral development* (Vol. I: The philosophy of moral development). New York: Harper & Row, p. 31.

20. Rushton, J. P., Brainerd, C. J., & Preisley, M. (1983). Behavioral development and construct validity. *Psychological Bulletin, 94*, 18–38.

CHAPTER 3

How To Teach Character
and Academics

. . . the implication of the most recent concept [of equality] is that the responsibility to create achievement lies with the educational institution, not the child. . . . This is a notable shift, and one which should have strong consequences for the practice of education in future years.

—James S. Coleman[1]

Certain traditional principles of instruction apply to teaching morality, or, more particularly, teaching character and academics (we will address the topic of discipline in chapter 4). The principles are:

1. Decide the information, values, and skills you want pupils to learn.
2. Provide pupils with occasions to absorb and apply the information, values, and skills.
3. Make the learning demands consonant with the pupils' developmental limitations. As pupils mature, give them increasing elements of choice about such learning situations. Compulsion is not always appropriate.
4. Establish strong incentives for pupils to learn.
5. Strive to keep anti-learning forces and persons out of the learning environment.
6. Measure, by informal and formal techniques, pupils' levels of learning.
7. Examine the results of such measurements to see who has done better or worse.
8. Reward success and rebuke failure.
9. Analyze the overall instructional process (steps 1–8), make appropriate changes, and resume instructing the learner.

Educators should carry out these activities in a framework that stresses the necessity of aiming for objective, identifiable goals, such as acts of good conduct, higher levels of pupil diligence, and measured academic learning. We will separately structure our recommendations on teaching (a) character and (b) academics. These recommendations, unlike some contemporary systems of moral education, do not give top priority to changing pupils' states of mind or reasoning abilities about moral issues. Approaches that claim such results may sometimes be justified. However, the key issue is improving pupil conduct—their words and acts in social situations.

TEACHING CHARACTER

Character centers on conduct. It focuses on the regular display of desirable traits by pupils. The good traits we want pupils to learn must be identified. As an example, we can look at the secular components of the traditional Scout law: A scout is trustworthy, loyal, helpful, friendly, courteous, kind, obedient, cheerful, thrifty, brave, and clean.

This listing of virtues helps us make two points. First, any list is relatively arbitrary. What about diligence, patriotism, or charity? Second, any list of more than six or eight virtues will have some overlap. For example, are not the terms *helpful, friendly, courteous,* and *kind* very nearly about the same thing?

Comparing Virtues

Listing virtues can be a useful intellectual stimulant. For example, Aristotle proposed that *character* involves habituating students to routinely display certain specified virtues. And *habituation* simply means to learn something so deeply that it becomes a habit—like brushing your teeth daily, locking the door when you leave the house, or counting your change in a store. Obviously, the ranking of particular virtues, such as kindness or bravery, can help focus the process of habituation.

However, one should not overemphasize the idea of a perfect list. The Maryland State Commission on Values Education proposed a list of 23 values to be taught in that state's schools.[2] Most of them are quite admirable. Still, one cannot imagine a teacher keeping all 23 in mind during curriculum planning, or any pupil remembering the whole list. On the other hand, the Scout list was designed to be memorized. The process of memorization is one element of the tradition of habituation: have the learners memorize certain key words, concepts, or slogans. And, apparently, adults who previously taught traditional values consciously created lists that were easy to memorize.

Listing virtues brings to mind the issue of competing priorities. Is kindness more important than bravery? What about diligence versus loyalty? One contemporary authority, Nel Noddings, proposes that compassion should be the central virtue.[3] Such concern over ranking virtues has sometimes led moral education down the slippery path of relativism and ambivalence, or of tendentious attempts to compare different virtues. But the whole matter of lists should be examined with some degree of realism. After all, we are focusing on students, mainly from age six to seventeen. Weighing comparative virtues is not, and should not be, a vital activity for most people in that age group. Everyday experience shows that the typical moral problems for young people do not arise from subtle moral conflicts. Instead, problems occur when young people fail to observe even rudimentary rules. Many do not obey legitimate authority, meet appropriate responsibilities, or even maintain simple politeness. These are among the reasons there are a disproportionate number of auto accidents involving young drivers, many of whom have been illegally drinking. If more young people simply obeyed the prohibitions against drinking, we would probably save as many lives as would the greater diffusion of caring.

Many literary works about morality focus on more problematic and novel conflicts than issues such as young people deciding whether to drive drunk. To return to the instance of Hamlet, should Hamlet kill his uncle and perhaps his mother to avenge his father? Such complex and novel questions are touched with glamour. They engage reader interest. However, educators with moral concerns should not let such precedents mask the typical situation. The first moral need of the young is to learn to avoid ratiocination. Instead, they must accept the centrality of doing the hard thing without thinking about it; they must delay their gratification.

What Do We Owe to Beings on Other Planets?

One of our friends told us a story along these lines: His daughter—age twelve—had been talking to him about the moral obligations we owe to "outsiders." He proposed to her that we owed a somewhat lesser obligation to such people than to those who are immediately proximate, for example, our parents, siblings, friends, and neighbors. She was distressed by this apparently selfish proposition. Then, our friend said to his daughter:

> Suppose we traveled by rocket for several weeks to one of the more remote planets in the solar system. On that planet, we found human-like inhabitants suffering some apparent form of injustice. What would be the moral obligation—if any—of people on earth to correct that injustice? Should we deliberately build a fleet of rockets to fly to this planet to correct this matter? Or should we act only if we accidentally happened to land on the planet? In other words—like knights-errant—should we go around looking for "injustices" to correct, going out of our way to intervene? Or should we only attack those who incidentally come to our attention? Suppose the planet was one day's flight from earth? Six weeks? Two years? How much difference would it make if the inhabitants were more or less like human beings? Suppose they spoke English? Suppose we could not interpret their language? Or suppose the injustice was on earth, and carried out in a small, weak country, immediately adjacent to the United States? What if the country of injustice was in the remote Himalayas, between Tibet and India?

We recognized our friend was trying to teach his twelve-year-old about another critical virtue—prudence. We will always live in a world of limited resources, uncertain knowledge, and conflicting needs. In such circumstances, important moral decisions involve weighing different virtues and living with the inevitable discomfort. Furthermore, we must learn to control the anxiety that ambiguity often generates—or, like Hamlet, we can end up makings things objectively worse. All of this means that we have to learn how much emotional discomfort different external circumstances generate in our psyches. For instance, what do we learn from "living through" the deaths of people we love—our parents, our spouse or child? We learn how much terrible emotional pain can exist and how much we can tolerate. After such awful incidents, some adults find themselves giving a higher priority to protecting the lives of their immediate family—including their children—than to other persons suffering tens of thousands of miles away. But, too often, it takes loss to teach us the great values of what we possess. After such losses, we realize why most of us—unlike the twelve-year-old—see life as concentric circles of declining caring and responsibility.

Coincidentally, at this time, many television series focus on space ships traveling many years away from their home bases. Often, the plots in such stories involve conflicts between the travelers and nonhuman, but intelligent, inhabitants of remote planetary systems. Typically, the space travelers from Earth display great tolerance for such remote foreigners and their cultures. The travelers are models of caring. And usually, the conflicts are either resolved, or at least all the important Earth travelers end up safe. If key people are injured, they get better in a day or two. As for death, the important people on our side are immortal. The good guys always win. The stories portray a world unlike the world of Shakespeare, which includes the pain, passion, and horror that pervade Hamlet, Othello, and Macbeth. In the space stories, tolerance and forbearance always lead to happy endings. The world of the future sounds like a fantastic place.

The real question underlying the twelve-year-old's query was, "Assume the United States should only intervene in foreign civil conflicts if its 'national interests' are affected. How should we define the national interests of the United States?" That is a hard question to answer. It has perplexed many persons far more than twelve years old.

Hopefully, as pupils mature, or consistently display wholesome conduct, their ability to handle emotionally complex issues increases. More problematic topics can be discussed in literature classes, or conflicts over practical values can be considered in small-group or one-to-one teacher-pupil meetings. But all such explorations must be grounded on obedience and diligence. The formal priorities among traditional virtues that schools transmit are far less important than the depth of their pupils' commitment to these demanding ends.

In practice, the virtues that educators teach are not so much determined by the refined analysis of competing values. Instead, such priorities are shaped by the practical exigencies of school life. This is precisely why authorities like Durkheim and even Dewey have regularly characterized schools as microcosms of society. Healthy schools and societies should both be shaped by important moral norms. Pupils and teachers live and work in the community of the school. They learn character by carrying out planned and incidental activities in that environment. The activities invite pupils to absorb and practice virtues. Part of that process involves the ordinary curriculum presented to students in literature, reading, and social studies. Those materials traditionally have provided pupils with historic and fictional role models. Such models stimulate pupils to healthy emulation and also identify cautionary instances of heinous misconduct, such as Benedict Arnold, Adolf Hitler, or Jack in *Lord of the Flies*. The matter of using these materials to teach character is important and will be separately considered later. But virtues should be applied, as well as studied, in schools.

They can be applied in activities in individual classrooms, typically in elementary school or preschool, or in schoolwide activities, which can occur in schools at all levels through high school. Some intraclass activities can be under the direction of individual teachers on their own initiative. Most schoolwide activities require administrative support. Essentially, all such activities involve pupils engaging in prosocial conduct: words or actions of immediate, evident help to others or to the common good of a larger group. Providing such help usually requires the helpers to make some sacrifice, such as practicing self-control, providing certain services, or abandoning or postponing personal projects in progress, which cause the pupils some trouble. It is helpful to use the formal term *prosocial*, which implies taking affirmative steps to do good, as opposed to "being good," which sometimes simply means being quiet. To our mind, the important but passive process of not making trouble is better encompassed under the topic of discipline.

Prosocial Conduct

The emphasis on prosocial conduct as part of good character has ancient roots. In the first century B.C., the Roman moralist Cicero wrote that people should be generous by giving personal help rather than donating money. Providing such help "is nobler, more impressive, and worthier of a strong and generous man . . . generosity that consists of service and hard work is more honest, has wider application, and can be useful to more people."[4]

From our research we know a vast number of prosocial activities are carried out by pupils in schools at all levels. Educators encourage such conduct so that pupils can practice virtues and learn character.

School service organizations are one form of prosocial activities. Such organizations are formed to allow students to provide service to the school itself or to its surrounding community. Service organizations and individual volunteers have had an important place in American life for many generations. Recently, however, a number of social forces have eroded this important aspect of our community life. For one thing, we have institutionalized a number of functions formerly performed by individuals or local groups. Care for the elderly and infirm has been assumed by institutions for the elderly and nursing homes. The needs of our poor neighbors have been assumed in large part by welfare. The family's care for the retarded or physically disabled has been augmented substantially by state agencies. As a result, many states, having taken on responsibilities previously handled by the family, are staggering with the costs and are being forced to cut back on such services. At a more profound level, many persons have asked whether the quality of our lives has been undermined by transferring these responsibilities to paid employees, rather than keeping them with our relatives, friends, neighbors, and fellow students.

It is in the nature of being human that we both give and receive. We are all born into the world helpless and dependent on others. If we live until old age, we will end our lives helpless and dependent on others. Most of us will experience other moments in our lives when we will be vulnerable and need to rely on others. It is imperative, therefore, that people learn how to come to the aid of others, to take on the responsibilities that others cannot, or are unable to, assume. We must learn to help, to serve others.

Some recognize in this need for effective helpers a sociological and biological fact of life, while others see it as a religious fact of fulfillment. The saints and other holy people found themselves in helping others. Albert Schweitzer, the great doctor, churchman, and musician, once said, "There is no higher religion than human service. To work for the common good is the greatest creed." Whatever the motivation—secular concern for the common good, spiritual fulfillment, or both—people need to be taught how to be of service. Caring attitudes and skills do not just happen.

In considering service, we should recognize the current public and political interest in government programs for stimulating and sponsoring youth service.

Such interest has generated a variety of proposals to encourage youth service activities. The proposals have been uttered at national, state, and local levels. They have even encompassed suggestions to make service completion a requirement for school graduation. Such concerns are only one of the many signs of the spreading of interest in youth character in our country.

Schools can and should teach students how to serve others. Ideally, a school's service program should have a number of characteristics:

1. *Training.* Students may fail when they first try to provide service. Many students, with little experience helping others, lack the skills to be effective. Before being put in a helping situation, a student should be trained in the necessary skills, often by a more seasoned student.

2. *Supervision.* Students normally find performing service very satisfying. However, initially they often experience conflicting reactions. They present themselves to help another and can be met with ambivalence or tension. For example, a high school volunteer may read to a blind person, who peevishly complains about the student's performance. Service programs do not always work out the way they were planned on paper. Therefore, it is critical that the school provide some overall supervision for service volunteers, especially in the beginning phases. Helping the student adjust to the situation and develop new skills, as well as providing feedback and encouragement, are necessary components of a service program.

3. *Ongoing support.* Once service-givers are settled into their work, they should not be abandoned. Students should regularly come together to discuss their work. The focus of these sessions is primarily to solve problems the students are having in their work and to receive additional training. However, the sessions should also encourage reflection. Teachers should help pupils recognize the value of what they are doing. They should be continually reminded that they are both doing important work and forging important habits.

In addition to formal, schoolwide service programs, many other forms of prosocial conduct can be encouraged, either in individual classrooms or on a schoolwide basis. In individual classrooms, the activities include:

1. Directly helping teachers as aides, messengers, monitors, and during clean-up.

2. Directly helping other pupils as tutors, homework contacts, or participants in well-conceived cooperative learning projects, team games, dramatic performances, or singing (where the pupil's engagement assists the group activity).

Schoolwide activities can include:

1. taking part in competitive sports, interscholastic or intramural, especially those involving teamwork.

2. becoming members in performing groups—band, choir, dramatics, forensics. When students perform as group members, they inevitably accept certain demands and make sacrifices on behalf of the whole group. Thus, they are engaged in a prosocial activity.

3. joining student service groups that serve either the school or the community.

4. accepting diverse responsibilities to assist, or even simply participate, in classes or other activities with special education pupils with varied disabilities.

5. participating in fund-raising for worthy causes.

6. engaging in miscellaneous extracurricular activities, e.g., clubs, school newspaper, tutoring students in other grades, student council. (Some educators have objected that activities like student council often involve mere popularity contests, compared to legitimate service activities. From our research, we conclude that well-managed schools can shape such activities to ensure that character, and not mere conviviality, is the measure of council officership.)

7. representing the school, class, or team in academic competitions.

Such activities are common. However, our research discloses there are important variations in the frequency and quality of the activities. Schools with high levels of activities, almost by definition, are doing a better job in developing student character. Of course, individual students participate in these activities for a wide mix of motives, sometimes including deliberate character development. As for the adults in these "activist" schools, we believe from our studies that most are quite conscious of the connection between such activities and the formation of pupil character. For example, the following quote from a student handbook is similar to many statements broadcast in high schools with an elaborate variety of activities:

> Clubs, teams, and other such activities are an important part of a student's life. They not only provide each member with a lot of fun and friends, but help members to learn the necessary skills of working together with others in an organization. Organizing ideas, making decisions, learning to compromise, and working towards a common goal are all part of every activity.[5]

We must also consider the traits and skills that teachers should possess as supervisors of prosocial activities. A high level of energy and a liking for children and adolescents are obviously valuable. Foresight is important; such prosocial activities often move at a more unpredictable pace than typical patterns of classroom life. Insight—or empathy—should be coupled with foresight: prosocial activities often excite emotional tensions in students. Responsible adults must identify and interpret such tension so they can moderate it. Imagination is also precious, since the challenges that arise are not exactly the same as those in classroom teaching. Many of the foregoing qualifications can also be subsumed under the generic term *leadership*—the ability and willingness to get others to follow your direction, even in somewhat unstructured situations.

In an elementary school we studied, one special education teacher and an adult aide worked in a small classroom with about eight pupils with severe emotional disabilities. The teacher had a special talent for bringing "normal" pupils into the classroom to work as student aides with the pupils. She believed such activities were good for both the pupils and the student aides. But such valuable arrangements took some organization. The special education teacher had to enlist the cooperation of the regular classroom teachers whose pupils she might recruit. The teachers had to decide how these student aides could be absent from their classrooms without seriously disrupting their own learning. Another task was to design constructive roles for the proposed student aides. The special education teacher had to arrange a system of parent notification and signed consent for the student aides and give the aides some simple training. The teacher also had to involve the adult aide in the class. Once the activity was in progress, it had to be monitored, and some adjustments were inevitably necessary. The teacher also developed some forms of recognition for the student aides, including certificates, "Thank You" remarks in the school bulletin, and a sign on the outside of the special education classroom door listing their names.

As for the value of prosocial conduct, a number of long-term studies have measured the effects of college and high school activities on pupils.[6] The studies asked: if pupils received the same number of years of education, was it better for later-life success to get good grades or be heavily involved in activities? The studies found that involvement in extracurricular activities is a better predictor of later-life success than good grades. "Later-life success" was measured by a variety of means, including level of income, expressed self-gratification, and a stable marriage. In retrospect, the findings are not too remarkable. Very few adult roles require people to spend most of their time doing reading assignments, or homework, or listening to lectures. Many adult roles require people to work closely with and get along with others, compromise, and display both initiative and obedience—the sorts of behaviors involved in prosocial conduct.

The School Assessment Checklist at the beginning of this book can help educators estimate the richness of their prosocial learning programs. You may want to apply its questions to your own classroom or school.

Supervising students engaged in prosocial conduct is a challenging and rewarding responsibility for many educators. The supervision often requires a subtle mix of inspiration, direction, and even moral counseling. Some educators became teachers precisely because they wanted to carry out such responsibilities. Organizing prosocial activities requires imagination, commitment, planning, and insight. Adult monitors must recognize the developmental limitations of their charges and tread the fine line between unrealistic delegation and stifling intrusion. The monitors can increase pupil learning if they identify the parallels between student services and the conduct of many adults. Like the students, many adults contribute time and energy to community activities. Furthermore, most paid employment involves assuming various helping roles with coworkers, customers, clients, or subordinates. Students practicing prosocial conduct are partly being trained for such later roles in everyday work.

Something should also be said about courage as an outcome of prosocial conduct. Courage reveals itself in a variety of situations. Among children, it often is tested in a child's willingness to carry out unpleasant duties, resist the tyranny of the peer group, dare to seek adult counsel, or confront wrongdoers. As a pupil approaches adulthood, courage can be displayed in the willingness to admit error and accept difficult responsibilities. Finally, in adulthood, courage may even be displayed when a reflective adult resists the wrongful imposition of authority. But assume that such adult resisters never had the courage, when students, to support the rightful assertion of authority against peer-group abuses. Then, one can wonder whether their adult "courage" is little more than persisting adolescent rebellion. Courage without obedience and discipline can lead to acts of willful malfeasance.

Incentives

We have already emphasized the worth of explicit incentives to stimulate pupils to develop good character. Undoubtedly, as adults, these same pupils may (and probably should) often display good conduct for altruistic reasons, without concern for evident rewards. But similar principles apply to cognitive learning; we expect adults to read without receiving praise or formal rewards. However, whatever our adult reading expectations are, we usually are willing to reward reading competency among students. We assume that children need special support, or incentives, to learn literacy. It seems reasonable to apply similar principles to stimulate moral learning.

What incentive structures should educators establish to foster learning? How profound should incentives be? Profundity is especially important since we are trying to teach values that we hope will last a lifetime. Very powerful incentive systems sometimes surround athletic activities. We can look for similar incentives to encourage nonathletic prosocial conduct:

1. *Conspicuous praise*: notes or phone calls to parents; announcements over the school public-address system; names listed on the blackboard or the class or school bulletin board; photographs prominently displayed; mention in the school paper; notations on report cards; certificates on award occasions; bumper stickers for parents ("My child is a character-award winner at the _____ school"); invitations to a special party; names on a plaque or poster placed on the school wall.

2. *Symbolic recognition* (like athletic letters): pins, ribbons, badges, jackets, medals, trophies.

3. *Publicly recognized titles*: school president, team captain, member of the honor society (where character is one requirement for membership).

4. *Contacts with prominent people*: breakfast with the principal.

Most of these forms of praise may be awarded to either individuals or groups. Both types of recognition are important, especially for fostering prosocial conduct. Such conduct almost always occurs in a social context and usually must be encouraged by other group members. When groups win awards for displaying prosocial excellence in a particular endeavor, solidarity is enhanced.

If vital awards are offered, criteria for excellence in various activities must be established. Once again, we find a useful model in athletics. Team members who meet certain basic criteria—"make the team"—receive uniforms, are entitled to wear team jackets and go to games, and are listed on the program. If members play well, they will play regularly. They can then earn athletic letters to wear on team jackets. If the team plays well and wins games, the whole team is recognized as successful. Individual players then enjoy the prestige earned by the whole team. If the team wins a championship, everyone gets a special jacket. There are also specific awards, such as Most Valuable Player.

Clear criteria of successful performance are very important. These standards tell students what they should try to achieve. Sometimes, even in nonathletic activities, we can apply quantitative criteria, for example, the group who raised the most money in the fund-raising campaign or the student who won the election for class officer. In other activities, the matter of defining what conduct deserves recognition is more subtle. Teachers sometimes face similar challenges in framing criteria of successful learning in academic areas—consider the criteria for grading math exams and prose compositions. We all realize learning is better when we use grading systems more refined than Pass/Fail. It is also good to list criteria so students who are not "stars," but who do improve, can, with a little introspection, identify their areas of success.

After-School Paid Employment

The prosocial activities we endorse, if aggressively fostered, may cause some high school pupils to feel tensions between their school responsibilities and the part-time after-school jobs students often hold. Such patterns of youth employment are common in America. For instance, in one high school in a middle-class neighborhood where we conducted a survey, 25% of the pupils worked twenty hours a week or more during the school year. Such notable away-from-school commitments can undermine in-school efforts to encourage prosocial activities. This matter deserves direct consideration.

A school should have several levels of prosocial activities:

1. Certain activities that are required for all students, e.g., all students must help in clean-up.
2. A list of activities from which all students must choose a certain number of options, e.g., pupils may select from among certain chores.
3. Some options that are only available to students who pursue them and are admitted, e.g., membership on an athletic team.
4. Some activities that are open only to invited students.

This arrangement permits many students to opt for less than full involvement and even to hold somewhat demanding paid jobs while attending school. It somewhat moderates the tensions on pupils who have other commitments. At the same time, it establishes minimum criteria for all student-citizens. These requirements are based on an important proposition: a student attending a publicly supported school should be expected to work hard at education. Otherwise, taxpayers' money is not well spent, and the student is learning a bad lesson in civics. Probably a few pupils work part-time to earn money to support their families or to meet other desperate needs. But many students work to earn pocket money to buy audio equipment, run their cars, and otherwise participate in the youth consumer culture. Such participation is their right, but it does not license them to avoid education demands. Furthermore, from the data about youth television watching, which we will present shortly, it is evident that most youths, despite their paid work, usually manage to find ample time for amusement. When students would rather hold paid work than become invested in school, schools should say to such youths: either increase your investment or face certain consequences—you might be dropped from our school or receive a lower-status diploma or a certificate of attendance.

Deferred Gratification

A powerful theme running through the subject of character formation is the concept of deferred gratification—as well as the converse, immediate gratification. We have already alluded to the concept incidentally several times. It is important that educators understand the concept. Its implications affect all elements of character formation, from day-to-day pupil-teacher classroom interaction to the work of school districts or whole states establishing broad parameters for topics such as sex education and drug abuse.

Deferred gratification refers to the frequent necessity of postponing complete human enjoyment until certain preliminary steps are taken. Sometimes the preliminary steps are simple and easy; sometimes they are prolonged and elaborate. The following statements of advice are examples of this concept:

Don't go for a drive unless there's enough gas in the car. Don't start cooking a complex recipe before you check to see if all of the ingredients are available. Don't expect a substantial income as an adult unless you are prepared to probably spend many years in school and college or in other forms of demanding preparation. If you feel impatient or angry with some other person, count to ten before speaking out. Don't get involved in a sexually charged relationship unless you've carefully weighed the potential consequences.

Putting the whole matter in a more positive light, educators and other adults should recognize that young people in particular, and human beings in general, often overvalue the immediate gratification of their emotions and underrate the risks that immediacy entails.

Almost all cultures recognize that young people, as a class, are peculiarly prone to pursue immediate gratification. For instance, Aristotle observed about 2,300 years ago:

> A young man is not a proper hearer of lectures on political science; for he is inexperienced in the actions that occur in life; . . . and, further, since he tends to follow his passions, his study will be vain and unprofitable; because the end [he aims] at is not knowledge but action.[7]

In contemporary America, the disposition of young people to "action" shows itself most notably in the prevalence of violent crime among adolescents.[8] Such crimes substantially endanger both the criminal and the victim. We properly wince with horror when we hear of someone being killed for a pittance during a robbery. But we can also reflect on the foolishness of a criminal randomly holding up some stranger with a gun. In perhaps one of every ten such instances, "something will go wrong." The victim may have a concealed weapon or reflexively decide to resist, or the criminal—under extreme tension—may misinterpret the victim's erratic actions. The tendency toward urgent action may also be associated with the young because young people have not yet made the commitments to family and work; such commitments tend to inspire stability and prudence. Probably, this tendency of many young persons to recklessly pursue speedy gratification—"I want money fast, and so I will steal yours, even at great risk to myself"—serves certain cultural and biological needs. In most societies, such tendencies are shaped, or sublimated, by mature adults and their institutions; this sublimation provides societies with warriors, hunters, explorers, and immigrants.

Even in our era, persons attracted to high-risk activities are sometimes still needed. The autobiography of David Hackworth, a retired Army veteran and bona fide hero, provides a typical instance of properly sublimated aggression.[9] At the age of fifteen Hackworth left a "broken" family to join the U.S. Army in 1944. At that time, he was on the edge of serious delinquency. He ultimately retired as a highly honored and heavily decorated colonel. During his career he was wounded on seven separate occasions, while fighting in Korea and later in Vietnam. His autobiography is a long recital of his zest for military life, especially war and war-like maneuvers—and of the costs such zest generated for himself, his wife, and their children. Presumably, Hackworth's aggressive drives—statistically speaking—were in the upper limits of the 99th percentile. Hopefully, in our time, we will have a diminished need for such extremely aggressive people. Unfortunately, our inherent genetic patterns probably will keep producing such persons for the next ten centuries. Furthermore, there is almost nothing the United States can do to affect the policies other societies apply to persuade their youths to sublimate their drives for immediate gratification.

The concept of deferred gratification relates to a number of traditional virtues, some of which we have already mentioned, such as prudence, thrift, and foresight. Essentially, to become effective adults, young people must gradually learn to contain their drives for immediate gratification. They must focus their energies on more long-term goals. As the economist Milton Friedman put it in another context, "There are no free lunches." Seemingly low-cost activities that generate fast, strong gratifications usually have substantial hidden costs. Sometimes these hidden costs can be economic, for example, in advertisements that offer "merely twelve convenient payments" or invite you to "enjoy the benefits of a credit card now." Or the costs can be emotional, resulting in disappointment, rage, anxiety, or fear. One step towards attaining good character is for young people to acquire the self-control needed to pursue delayed gratification.

Wise adults and old institutions assist in this important process through establishing systems of control and prohibition. Such systems try to prevent young people from heedlessly pursuing immediate gratification. The systems may use devices such as dramatic warnings or establish prohibitions, discipline, constraints, and punishments for the young. The systems keep the young from situations that tempt or release their desires for immediate gratification. Thus, until they attain a certain age, young people are often prohibited from drinking alcoholic beverages, required to attend school and be directly subject to adult control, and prevented from having prolonged private contacts with members of the opposite sex.

They surround youths with cautions against the dangers of alcohol, drugs, and premature sex and/or shield them from exposure to tempting literature.

One high school we studied provided an imaginative example of encouraging deferred gratification. The school had a chapter of Students Against Drunk Driving (SADD). A particular school day had been designated for that chapter to carry out a special program publicized by the national office of SADD. The program's theme was simple: every twenty minutes, somewhere in the United States, someone dies due to drunk driving. And so, every twenty minutes through the day, the names of two students, who had been recruited to take part in the drama, were read off over the school loudspeaker. Everyone in the school heard the announcement. The students whose names were announced quietly left their classes and went to the school office. In the office they were each garbed in white and had their faces made up white to represent corpses. They returned to their classes, and spent the rest of the school day quietly going through their regular routines—in their special garb. One teacher observed to us that, as the school day proceeded, she could see the regular students—who simply observed the "walking dead"—becoming increasingly reflective. The program was a striking example of collective social invention. We say collective because obviously a number of persons and agencies were involved in perfecting the activity. For instance, an important contribution of the school's SADD chapter was its ingenuity in wisely choosing the most appropriate students to act as corpses. One of the first to be announced was a popular student-athlete. Another was a student widely perceived as invested in drug use—perhaps this public involvement symbolized the student's desire to publicly "take the pledge."

Discouragement and prohibition occur in a variety of ways. Some prohibition systems punish adults who exploit the young by pandering to their vulnerability to immediate gratification. For example, a bar can lose its liquor license if it sells liquor to the young. An adult male who has sex with a female below a specified age—even a consenting female—commits the crime of statutory rape. Debts owed by persons below a certain age are legally unenforceable.

Certain obvious philosophic problems arise around such restraints and prohibitions. Is it fair to constrain the young in the ways we have suggested? Don't such constraints amount to unfair discrimination? How severe should we make the punishments established to enforce such constraints? How much should the rights of adults be restricted to "protect" the young? Since most people agree that the restrictions should be lifted at some time, how should such points of relaxation be identified?

In discussing the pros and cons of restraining the young, we also have to look beyond the abstractions of philosophy. It is not irrelevant to recognize that monitoring the young takes adult work. And perhaps some allegedly philosophic arguments against constraints may ultimately be founded on the widespread human disposition to use philosophic propositions to avoid the stress of hard work.

Many cultures establish more profound restrictions for their young than we apply in contemporary America. One common area of restraint in other cultures involves contacts between young, postpubescent, unmarried males and females. Essentially, the restrictions lessen the privacy available to such males and females. The culture either severely constrains contacts among couples or ensures that contacts are monitored by chaperones and equivalent persons. Obviously, the restrictions rest on a basic assumption: young males and females, without strong constraints, would be unlikely to prudently handle the powerful attractions of sex. Even America, with its more individualistic traditions, applied many such constraints until relatively recently. For example, a certain proportion of our colleges and high schools were single sex, student housing arrangements in residential colleges were closely restrained, and contacts between male and female students were often monitored.

Adults and adult institutions also use "carrots," as well as "sticks," to moderate the typical adolescent drive for immediate gratification. The sticks are the prohibitions that we have mentioned previously. The carrots stress the positive benefits promised to those who pursue deferred gratification. The carrots include: the security and safety that surround nonalcoholic driving; the benefits that often flow from advanced education; and the stability, intimacy, and affection usually associated with committed conjugal sex.

At this time, readers must recognize signs of the evident unpopularity of deferred gratification among many young Americans. Chapter 1 presents a great deal of data about youth disorder. All such data essentially counts various acts in pursuit of immediate gratification. If someone angers or humiliates you, kill him. If you are seventeen years old, and your girl friend is threatening to leave, or you're lonely and over-involved with illegal drugs and quarrelling with your parents, do not recognize that such problems can often be solved if you pursue help—be impatient with incremental solutions, and kill yourself. Or, suppose you are trying to quickly give significance to your relatively sterile life. If you are a female, you can get pregnant or, if you are a male, you can try to cause some female to become pregnant. Chapter 1 cites other telling data beyond the numbers about homicide, suicide, and illegitimate births. For instance, the notable increase in the percentage of college women reporting they drink to get drunk is very disturbing. Such data are clear indicators these students are pursuing immediate gratification and trying to use alcohol to extinguish their concern for the future. Obviously, this invites risky sexual experimentation.

Implications for In-School and In-Classroom Practice

Anyone with the least experience in working with children recognizes their general problems in handling certain forms of deferred gratification. Ironically, in many ways the problems become more complex as children mature. As time passes, children's and adolescents' verbal, physical, and intellectual facilities increase. For instance, if they attain puberty at the age of thirteen or fourteen, adolescents can respond to sexual stimulation, participate in sexual intercourse, and help create new life—even though such young people are rarely prepared to rear children. Furthermore, such capabilities are surely affected by different innate capacities and previous experiential learning. After such qualifications are uttered, some general principles about education and deferred gratification can still be recited:

- ✦ Contemporary American culture places unrealistic demands on our adolescents to display delayed gratification. To put it another way, those considerable demands are surrounded by weaker supports than are typical in other cultures. Educators should generally support efforts to increase youth self-control and shield the young from unrealistic demands.

- ✦ Students should be recurrently reminded of the important role deferred gratification plays in the lives of competent adults, as well as the severe risks generated by the pursuit of immediate gratification.

- ✦ The enemies of deferred gratification should be frequently delineated for students, e.g., alcohol, illegal drugs, sex, crime, circles of problematic acquaintances, money mismanagement. Adults should not be reluctant to make and enforce deliberate rules diminishing the temptations around the young, and/or punishing persons supplying such temptations.

One of the authors conducted an extended in-school research project. During this study, he was able to follow one teacher's—let us call her Ms. Leon—successful handling of a student having difficulty with deferred gratification. The very ordinariness of the story justifies its recitation. The student's difficulties—we will call him Joe—were displayed on the first day of class. Ms. Leon presented some problem to the class and invited them to raise their hands to respond. Joe quickly raised his hand, and then, while waiting for Ms. Leon to call on him, began to hop up and down in his seat. Finally, his patience exhausted, Joe began to shout out the reply. Ms. Leon's back was toward the class, as she wrote some items on the board. She abruptly turned around, and loudly shouted at Joe, "Be quiet, until *I* call on you!" She returned to writing on the board. Joe's face flushed, and he was silent for a while. As days went by, it became evident that sitting reasonably still and keeping quiet were severe challenges for Joe. He was bright, but he had definite problems. Ms. Leon deliberately adopted a multistage strategy: keep Joe under tight rein, let him know conspicuous public impatience was intolerable, and help him learn to extend his wait time. For example, when Joe raised his hand to answer a question, she would never call on him first. Instead she would help him learn to wait until three or four other volunteers had a turn. When the school held its annual science fair, Joe brought in a commendably ambitious project. Ms. Leon concluded that Joe had displayed appropriate commitment and foresight, and she volunteered to work with him to perfect his project. By the end of the school year, Joe had raised his reading score by two years and had generally improved his self-control.

Adult-sponsored policies and activities that signify surrender to, or tolerance of, the pursuit of immediate gratification should be viewed with extreme suspicion. A teacher or other responsible adult with authority may mimic some form of pop culture conduct to catch pupils' attention, such as sympathetically referring to some rock musician or television celebrity. True, matters of "tactics" may occasionally license some tempering of position, to facilitate "packaging." However, so far the overall record of such tempering—acting like one of the gang—has been miserable. The authority of schools and colleges to constrain student sexuality under the doctrine of *locus parentis* has steadily declined. At the same time, the level of youth sexual disorder has steadily increased. Furthermore, more and more in-class time has been dedicated to formal sex education. Simultaneously, sexual experimentation among the young has increased. It would be ridiculous to largely blame education for such disheartening developments. But, surely, it would be equally naive to ignore the fact that our schools and classrooms have become increasingly "sexualized." This sexuality reveals itself not only in the subject matter taught in sex education, but in other forms of sexual expression—in dress, words, and conduct—pervading too many schools.

There is a sex education establishment on the political left, and it is now being countered by one on the right.[10] Readers should at least be conscious of the key contrasts between the two establishments.

The older establishment of the left stresses: youth choice about sexual matters; the withholding of adult judgment of such choice; the assignment of presentations largely to sex education specialists; the amoral nature of the discussion presented; the critical importance of modern technology; the irrelevance of religion; the principle of presenting sexual instruction to coed audiences; the tacit assumption that youth patterns of sexual activity are immune from adult intervention; the comparative tendency to perceive youth sexual activities as separate from the students' overall life and career goals; and relative indifference to youth-family ties.

The emerging establishment of the right stresses: certain constraints on youth choice regarding sexual matters; the consideration of adult judgments in such matters; a principal role in presentations allotted to teachers known to pupils in classes away from sex education; a stress on the moral and religious elements of the situation, rather than emphasis on technology or science; the principle of presenting more emotional components of sex education to single-sex audiences; the tacit assumption that youth patterns of sexual activity are largely shaped by the activities and values of some or all parts of adult society; an attempt to integrate each youth's sex education with other family and life concerns; and a strong sensitivity to youth-family ties.

A separate incentive for moral learning is the *rite of passage*. Such occasions are ceremonies that publicly demarcate moments when the subject of the ceremony moves to a new status, for example, weddings, which mark the passage from single to married status, and graduations, which mark the movement from the status of student to that of graduate. The rites are a form of instruction and incentive. They stimulate and license the participants to learn and carry out new roles, which usually have important moral elements. The rites also instruct observers how they should act toward the participants—cry, laugh, offer congratulations, display deference.

Vital in-school ceremonies in general, and rites of passage in particular, are complex activities. The organization of these occasions is discussed in chapter 9. Many school activities provide natural occasions for more or less elaborate rites of passage: graduations, end-of-year promotions, enrollment of new students, the beginning of the school year, retirements or other leave-takings of employees. Different schools handle such activities with varying degrees of style. Well-designed rites can notably increase pupil learning of important values.

TEACHING ACADEMICS

This discussion of academic learning will focus solely on the themes of academic diligence (or "press"), schoolwide learning incentives, and pupil grouping. Some other elements of academic learning are covered elsewhere in this book.

The data show that, in general, American pupils do not work very hard at learning. Academically, they are not pressed. For instance, the U.S. Department of Education reported that a 1988 survey of twelfth-graders by the National Assessment of Educational Progress found that on a single night, 19% of the respondents had no assignment or did not do it, and 53% had assigned work that took less than an hour.[11] The Department of Education also reported that another survey of eleventh-graders in 1983–84 found nearly equivalent data: 33% of the respondents either had no homework assigned or did not do it, and 26% had less than an hour's work assigned. Meanwhile, 43% of the sample spent three or more hours each day watching television. School simply is not very rigorous.

The data about homework reiterate the point we made in chapter 1 about shopping mall high schools: faculty members and students at many schools (at all levels) have entered into implicit compacts to reduce the emphasis on learning and teaching. It is fine to talk about well-planned curriculums and imaginative teaching. However, to our minds, student and teacher diligence are the heart of successful instruction. Protradition educators favor a strong academic press for two reasons: it fosters academic learning, and it teaches pupils to persevere at hard tasks—a precious virtue.

There are a number of measures educators can take to increase pupils' diligence in learning. They can organize schools and classrooms so students receive significant assignments, which teachers promptly monitor, grade, and return to students. They can establish incentives to encourage students to work hard. They should take all possible steps to stimulate parent cooperation with such activities, such as having parents sign their child's completed homework, promptly calling parents to inform them of their child's significant successes and insufficiencies, and inviting parents to sign explicit pledges of support.

The authors heard of one elementary school teacher's imaginative approach to win such cooperation. On the second day of school, her fifth-graders were to bring in their first homework. As might be expected, a number of students had not completed the assignment. The teacher had arranged for an aide to cover the class. She went to the office with some of the offending pupils. With the pupils beside her, she immediately called their parents, many of whom were at their work sites. She told the parents she was sure they wanted to cooperate with the school policy that homework was very important, and she asked their help in correcting the situation. She returned the first group of students to class and went to the office with the next group. It was hard for the parents to object to her direct approach, and the students speedily got the word.

The subject of levels of homework leads to a basic issue affecting instruction: the legitimacy of setting learning demands and rewards that inherently divide students on the basis of innate talent, commitment, or levels of family support. In other words, assume we recognize, or honor, students who diligently do homework, earn good grades, or otherwise demonstrate academic excellence. It is likely that students from certain situations, for instance, nonsupportive homes, will do more poorly than others. If certain patterns appear among the groups of pupils who do and do not earn recognition, the school may be charged with engaging in some form of invidious discrimination. The school may be viewed as acting against equality, a sacred American principle. All efforts to establish and maintain public incentives for learning are closely tied to the topic of equality. Therefore, a careful analysis of the implications of equality is critical to examining academic learning.

Equality: A Critical Issue

The almost unqualified pursuit of egalitarianism is a root cause for the recent declines in pupil learning. From our own research, we know that many educators are reluctant to require pupils to work hard. They are reluctant because they observe that pupils' willingness to work at academics is not an equally distributed characteristic. The educators believe, quite logically, that if they establish strong demands for pupils to work, an identified group of poorer learners will gradually appear.

Furthermore, to some degree, such willingness indirectly reflects the skills and priorities transmitted by pupils' parents. Assume that educators are asked or required to produce learning results unrelated to pupils' home background. This is often the case. Many educators, in self-defense, tend to simply lower demands on all pupils. Everyone receives good grades, measured learning slacks off some, and no pupil's feelings are especially hurt. In such situations, the only pupils who work very hard are those who want to. They feel only moderate pressure, since they are doing what they and their parents want.

Most Americans believe in equality. But to most of us, equality does not mean everyone learning the same amount of facts and skills or attaining the same level of education, or having equally happy marriages, equal incomes, equal athletic talents, equal wisdom, or equal levels of diligence. We believe equality largely relates to formal political matters: everyone has one vote, can serve on juries, is equal before the law, and so on. Furthermore, for religious believers, it is common to hold that all persons are equal in the eyes of God. Moral virtue is not measured by external factors. However, it is simply utopian and chimerical to extend the principle of equality further into political and economic life. Such an extension denies the everyday realities that confront us. It is true that certain contemporary Americans favor more expanded definitions of the term *equality*.

But their propositions have shallow roots and have not been applied anywhere for any length of time.

Jefferson's Position. Thomas Jefferson crafted the phrase "created equal" in the Declaration of Independence. He strongly supported the principle through his long and active life. He was also a proponent of public education to foster equality. We know precisely what educational equality meant to Jefferson. He drafted a plan to establish public education in Virginia.[12] In his plan, he proposed that three or four years of grade-school education, at public expense, should be made available to all children. At the end of this time, a test would be administered. The pupils who excelled—perhaps the top 5%?—would go to the next education level at public expense. After several years, the second-level pupils would take another rigorous test. The survivors would go to the University of Virginia, again at public expense. Students who failed the test at any level would have to pay the full costs if they decided to pursue further education.

To Jefferson, equality meant that all people who demonstrated equal achievements—regardless of their "defects" of birth—should be treated equally. He never conceived of lowering standards to ensure that certain patterns of results were attained.

The Jeffersonian definition of equality is not historically novel. It has been applied by other societies determined to encourage excellence. In France immediately after the French Revolution, an era dramatically committed to equality, an elaborate and "open" system of higher education was created. According to the historian James Bowen, the "main theoretical foundation for the new system was the interpretation of equality as equality of opportunity."[13] Higher education should be open to persons of all social classes who demonstrated academic aptitude.

Earlier, in the Turkish Empire during the sixteenth century, highly egalitarian approaches were applied in recruiting and selecting the members of the state's upper-level bureaucracy. As very young children, these leaders, the Janissaries, had been drafted from the families of the empire's Christian slaves. Essentially, the state kidnapped them. They were raised under state guardianship apart from their families and provided with elaborate training. As it were, the Turks applied the proposals in Plato's *Republic*.

Finally, the most able trainees were assigned important positions in the state bureaucracy and army. The Janissaries were selected leaders who were unconstrained by family or regional loyalties. The sultan was the only person holding hereditary power, and most of such power was delegated to agencies managed by Janissaries. A foreign observer, after witnessing one Turkish state meeting, remarked:

> There was not in all that great assembly a single man who owed his position to aught save his valor and merit. No distinction is attached to birth among the Turks; the deference paid a man is measured by the position he holds in the public service. There is no fighting for precedence; a man's place is marked by the duties he discharges. On making his assignments, the Sultan pays no regard to any pretensions on the score of wealth or rank; he considers each case solely on its own merits, and examines carefully into the character, ability and disposition of the man whose promotion is in question. It is on merit that men rise in the service . . . [14]

We can identify many historic efforts throughout the world to encourage equality through creating opportunities for persons from all classes and groups who show notable competence. These efforts have often been successful. In thousands of years of history, we cannot identify any successful efforts to foster equality by insisting that educators routinely disregard the traditional tests of ability— diligence, acuity, and prudence.

Incentives for Academic Learning

Schools and teachers must establish strong incentives to encourage pupils' academic learning. We have already presented extended lists of such devices.

Regarding recognition of academic excellence, we recall a conversation with one educator about the effects of the Buckley amendment on recognition efforts. This conversation illustrates the complex forces that sometimes inhibit efforts to improve schools. The amendment is a federal law passed to protect pupils' privacy. The educator said the law might prohibit schools from displaying the excellent papers of identified students because the display might violate the pupils' right to privacy. We confess we did not take the trouble to research this arguable interpretation. Whether valid or not, however, the educator's objections are a sensitive index of the climate of opinion in which academic excellence is pursued. Still, we know that many schools do ignore this potential interpretation of the law and post pupils' excellent papers. However, other schools that do not post such papers may be partly motivated by such inhibiting interpretations or by the equally erroneous view that political equality precludes academic excellence. Beyond the matter of legal interpretations, we have to look at the reality of the situation.

Recall that our suggestion was to post excellent papers. Despite the educator's concern, it is obvious that very, very few parents would complain because their children's teachers post their excellent papers in school. Indeed, if a school foresaw such difficulties arising, it could easily settle the matter. Administrators could invite all parents, on enrolling their children in school, to voluntarily sign a simple legal waiver. This waiver would permit the school to post such papers. If the parents choose not to sign, their wishes would be respected. Any future excellent work by their child would be kept secret. Does anyone doubt that the school would get 99% or more signatures? The point is, too many educators are not strongly in favor of pupil recognition in any form. So when moderate barriers to recognition arise, such as arguable interpretations of laws, the barriers are treated as insurmountable. Where there is not much will, there is often not a way.

Wherever possible, the relevance of academic learning to pupils' adult life success should be stressed. Elsewhere, we will discuss the importance of cooperative learning to pupil character development. We see nothing inconsistent with a school or classroom providing students with a well-planned mix of individual and cooperative academic assignments. As our later discussion notes, the grades provided in appropriate cooperative assignments can be integrated into each pupil's individual academic grades.

The allocation of praise or other forms of recognition has always been a critical issue in education. This sensitivity applies to recognition for either academics or prosocial conduct, as well as to individuals or groups. One nineteenth-century study on education made the following enlightening comparison between two different recognition systems:

> As for recognition, no educators have used it so elaborately as the Jesuits. On the other hand, in most English schools the prizes for academics have no effect whatever except on the first three or four boys, and marking is so arranged by teachers that those who take the lead in the first few lessons can keep their position without much effort. This clumsy system would not suit the Jesuits. They often, for prize giving, divide a class into a number of small groups, the boys in each group being approximately equal [in ability], and a prize is offered for each group. The contests between competing classes, too, stimulate the weak students even more than the strong.[15]

We should also mention the form of grading, such as letter grades versus percentages. These two forms provide different incentives. Two-digit, or percentage, grades mean that even moderate improvement in a pupil's performance can lead to higher grades, and a little slacking off can cause a decline. Thus, two-digit grades stimulate at least moderately improved performance. Almost every student can raise a two-digit grade to some extent, for example, from 83% to 85%. Letter grades, in contrast, recognize neither moderate increases nor declines in performance.

Students will try harder to improve or stay in place with two-digit grades. Of course, two-digit grades also make demands on teachers to justify fine distinctions in grading: "Why did she get 78%, and I get 75%?" But making and explaining such distinctions is part of excellent teaching. When one succeeds in teaching a pupil to recognize the difference between 75% and 78%, one has really taught. Admittedly, not every subject area lends itself to such precise evaluation; two-digit grading systems are not always appropriate. However, we must still keep in mind that deliberate and precise grading, where feasible, is an important component of stimulating excellence.

One other caution about the application of rigorous grading is that teachers should make some allowance for the developmental level of the pupils involved. In particular, younger pupils probably should be subjected to less academic pressure. Exactly how and where to draw the line is a subtle question, but the concept of such a line is widely recognized in American education. Still, it is interesting to note that some evidently successful foreign education systems operate on different premises. An American who taught Chinese pupils in public schools in Taiwan reported that, according to school policy, her first-grade pupils received two-digit grades, and all individual pupils' names and grades were posted outside the classroom. The teacher was distressed at the academic press in the school, while being enthralled at her pupils' application to learning. True, there were a variety of modes used to sustain academic press on the students. For example, the parents applied strong pressures on children to stimulate their application. But many of the modes, like the two-digit grades, assumed the students could and should be subjected to demanding pressures.

What do we think about the Taiwan story? Are such pressures justified? Frankly, we are uncomfortable judging, in a vacuum, one such practice woven into the fabric of a complex, long-persisting, and relatively vigorous culture. The only clear point is that children, without being absolutely destroyed, are apparently capable of far greater learning efforts than American schools ask of them.

Another comparison is also relevant. Researchers report that Japanese elementary schools maintain stronger, more uniform academic pressures than is the case in America. The Japanese see learning as the outcome of work more than of natural endowment or luck. And it is assumed that all pupils are capable of hard work. This egalitarian assumption is relatively successful, at least at the elementary school level. But "fractured" families and two-working-parent families with children in elementary schools are far more common in America than in Japan. Furthermore, the order pervading Japanese society makes pupils and parents more disposed to carry out the school's directives. Japanese children are surrounded with more powerful learning support systems at home than are most American pupils. And their schools get pupils to work hard.

Social Promotion

Social promotion is a policy of moving pupils to the next grade, or graduating them, even when they have not learned the appropriate academic material. The policy has important implications for the organization of academic learning. Social promotion is usually a poor idea. Because the topic is complex, and our general premises have already been made clear, our discussion will be somewhat summary.

First, we will discuss rationale. There is a body of research critical of retention, as well as relevant research of another perspective. In addition to the research, we should also recognize that different observers see the problem from understandably contrasting viewpoints. Often, opponents of retention emphasize the immediate situation of the retained child. Undoubtedly, many children are unhappy at being retained. Supporters of retention, on the other hand, look beyond the individual child at a particular moment and focus on the overall policies involved.

For example, the most supportive research on retention is not directly about that topic, but about an analogous issue. In the early 1980s, several states adopted minimum competency tests as criteria for high school graduation. Charges were made that such tests would discriminate against students from low-income backgrounds, especially African-Americans. A considerable controversy arose, involving several federal court cases. Barbara Lerner, one researcher on this topic, reported that, when some of the programs were put into operation, high proportions of African-American students actually did fail. They were provided with appropriate instruction and a chance to retake the test.[16] Of those who had failed on the first wave, about 95% eventually passed. Today, in the states involved, the proportion of students who pass the test before their scheduled graduation date is almost 100%. Putting it simply, the process of pretest instruction has improved. Pupils now graduate knowing more, as well as learning more relevant skills.

The reality is that the adoption of the minimum standards test, and the demonstration that the schools meant business, eventually achieved the desired effect.

The adult opponents of the tests, many with undoubtedly good intentions, were actually fostering an unsound policy.

The tests were not extremely difficult. Many students were able to pass them in the ninth or tenth grade. Thus, the high proportion of passers did not signify that the students concerned had attained notable competency. However, before the test was initiated, about 10% of graduates received diplomas without possessing even minimal skills. Lerner proposed that gradually enlarging the reach and rigor of such minimum requirements was very desirable. The enlargement would continue the process of improvement that had begun.

Other interesting data also emphasize the evident connection between social promotion and general student inefficacy.[17] Across America, social promotion was apparently at its zenith in 1977. In that year, 24% of all male eighth-grade pupils were one year or less behind their age group. This was the smallest percentage of eighth-grade boys behind their group between 1970 to 1988. Presumably, in 1977, the slogan was "pass them along." At the same time, this was a period of relatively poor national test scores. Conversely, since the 1977 low, the percentage of eighth-grade boys behind schedule steadily increased to 33% in 1988. Evidently, things have been tightened-up. Perhaps not coincidentally, the turnaround in national test scores began in about 1983—just as tightening-up got under way.

Of course, there is a time gap for pupils from eighth grade to taking the national college exams several years later. The more basic point is that stringency is an across-the-board principle. If schools pass inept pupils in the lower grades, we should not expect them to suddenly demand academic competence of older pupils in high school. The slogan "pass them along" helps create and sustain an environment that is generally subversive to academic excellence.

Important benefits would flow from the adoption, in individual schools and districts, of uniform, carefully monitored, written prohibitions against social promotions or graduation for students with evidently normal intellectual abilities. The prohibitions could be enforced in the following manner:

1. Schools should have written policies, instructing teachers how to handle pupils achieving significantly below their peers, i.e., those who may be candidates for social promotion.

2. The policies should provide for the (a) identification of such at-risk pupils early during the academic year; (b) written notification of the problem to parents and the principal or other appropriate supervisor; and (c) the development and implementation of remedial plans for such students.

3. Every effort should be made to obtain the support of affected parents for their child's remediation under the plan, e.g., the parent should enforce the school's homework and study procedure.

4. If, despite the plan, the student fails to significantly improve, efforts should be made to solicit parental support for grade retention or makeup summer work.

5. Unless a special case can be made for an exception, the retention should be carried out.

6. If a student regularly falls behind, his or her capabilities should be examined via a careful special education staffing. Perhaps a different school or program placement is needed.

A moderate number of schools and districts already have such programs in operation. Generally, the reports are satisfactory.

Pupil Grouping

The topic of grouping, or tracking academic learners by apparent ability, is an important and sensitive subject. The issue has strong implications for the management of academic learning. Diverse concepts can be applied to implement such grouping. Pupils can be grouped on evident ability, demonstrated commitment, completion of appropriate academic prerequisites, or parental support for a particular program. Such techniques have always been widespread in education; they permit teachers to focus their instruction on certain defined classes of learners. The techniques were implicit in Jefferson's education proposal for Virginia: before the pupils advanced to the next level, they passed a rigorous test. The teachers at the next level would undoubtedly plan their instruction on the assumption that the students had acquired certain knowledge. Today, such selective practices are applied by many public and private colleges and universities, most independent or private high schools, and some public high schools. Diverse adaptations are applied in many elementary schools, especially in higher grades.

Even in nonselective, or open-enrollment, schools, there are often selective programs that require students who want to be enrolled to show notable levels of commitment or competence: Great Books courses, accelerated math, advanced placement courses, honors programs, gifted programs, and innumerable other forms of tracking and academic groupings. Frequently, scores on objective tests are used to determine eligibility for these activities. Such selective programs are often criticized because they foster inequality. Of course, legitimate criticisms can sometimes be made about certain selective criteria. Not all tests are fair. Pupils assigned to one program, typically a less desirable one, should be shifted up, or even down, if their capabilities change. The key criticisms of such programs are not really about flaws in their mechanics. Instead, they are about the truisms that meritocratic programs emphasize: human abilities are not evenly distributed. Pupils from supportive homes tend to benefit especially from such selectivity. Many forms of learning can be more efficiently transmitted if learners have uniform levels of ability or knowledge.

Another question related to definition often affects allegedly antitracking programs. Exactly what happens if students of diverse abilities are placed in the same classroom? Suppose the formerly tracked class typically read and analyzed six novels. Now that things are "untracked," do all students—both weak and strong—read and analyze the same number of the novels as did the previous tracked class? From our experience, this is not the case. Either there are two or more different basic assignments given in such classes, or other drastic adaptations are made. Such devious—or realistic—adaptations leave one very uncertain of how to interpret the generalized research on the processes of untracking.

Definitions of Equality

It is poor policy to apply definitions of equality (or inequality) that discourage schools from making special demands on able pupils or pupils from supportive families. Nondemanding schools prevent pupils from learning critical truths: human attributes, such as mathematics ability or hand-eye coordination, are not equally distributed among individuals; attributes can often be dramatically improved through learning and diligence; and one of the great challenges of life is to optimize the mix of attributes and limitations we possess.

Schools can only provide pupils with differentiated demands if some system of pupil grouping is applied. This is what happens at Harvard College, the Bronx High School of Science, and in the fifth-grade math honors class in your local public elementary school. In the learning area of character, an equivalent system is applied by educators who manage competitive athletic teams or the elementary school student council.

It is sometimes argued that grouping pupils by ability is bad because it undermines academic learning, or, at least, does not help it. But the research findings are not especially hostile to the concept of grouping. For instance, two studies that appear to be critical of ability grouping do not stand up under careful reading. Thus, Robert Slavin conducted an exhaustive review of elementary school grouping, covering only up to the sixth grade.[18] Slavin said his findings applied only to small and medium-sized schools with relatively homogeneous student bodies. He concluded that strict grouping was not effective in such schools. However, he found that a practice called the *Joplin Plan* was useful. Under this plan, pupils were kept in the same homeroom, but for reading and math moved to separate classrooms in groups by ability. Incidentally, the tone of his findings implied that grouping might well be appropriate above the sixth grade. Obviously, whether Slavin's finding is pro- or anti-ability grouping depends on how one chooses to classify the successful Joplin Plan. To our minds, the plan is simply ability grouping under a different name. A second careful review of the research by Drebeen and Barr is also cited to show that ability grouping is unnecessary.[19] And those authors did conclude that ability grouping is unnecessary—if a school enrolls a relatively homogeneous population. But many schools do not have relatively homogeneous populations; indeed, it makes no sense to apply ability grouping in homogeneous schools. Thus, that study, far from criticizing ability grouping, actually supports the practice as it is typically applied.

It seems from such research that tracking and grouping, even at lower grade levels, are usually justified to permit demanding instruction when pupils' abilities vary widely. The real challenge to grouping and tracking lies in its implementation:

1. The curriculum presented to such grouped students must be appropriate to their alleged competencies.

2. Assignments to groups must be based on sound criteria and a variety of observations, e.g., test scores, grades, and teacher recommendations.

3. Educators should monitor pupils' learning and be prepared to shift pupils up or down if their performance changes or the initial assignment seems in error.

4. Parents should be informed about the nature of the assignment process, and consulted often about their child's assignment.

5. Grouping should aim, as much as possible, to maximize the opportunities for all students.

Practices and Policies

1. Complete the sections of the School Assessment Checklist at the beginning of this book that deal with learning academics and good character. Try to persuade other schools, or teachers in individual classrooms, in approximately similar situations to complete the checklist. Share your data.

2. After a school has completed the checklist, ask an appropriate faculty committee to come up with suggestions for how the school can improve its showing on the checklist. What new policies or practices should be developed?

3. Ask a faculty committee, perhaps with student input, to develop ways to enrich the school's extracurricular program.

4. Solicit expert help from an academic or district staff member on how to improve the school's use of test scores to monitor pupil progress.

5. Ask the school's PTA or equivalent organization to help raise funds to increase the school's ability to provide prizes and other incentives for individual and group pupil excellence in character and academics.

6. If you are a classroom teacher, carry out the counterparts of each of these activities for your individual classrooms.

References

1. Coleman, J. S. (1968). The concept of equal educational opportunity. *Harvard Educational Review, 38*(1), 22.

2. Maryland State Commission on Values Education. (1979). *Statement of purpose*. Annapolis, MD: Maryland State Department of Education.

3. Noddings, N. (1992). *The challenge to caring schools*. New York: Teachers College Press.

4. Cicero. (1974). *De officia* [On duties] (H. Edinger, Trans.). New York: Bobbs-Merrill, p. 105.

5. Oak Forest High School. (1992). *Student handbook, 1992*. Oak Forest, IL: Author, p. 2.

6. Mullis, I. V. S., Owen, E. H., & Phillips, G. W. (1990). *Accelerating academic achievement*. Washington, DC: Office of Educational Research and Improvement, U.S. Department of Education, p. 75.

7. Aristotle. (1941). Nicomachean ethics. In Richard McKeon (Ed.), *The basic works of Aristotle* (W. D. Ross, Trans.). New York: Random House, p. 936.

8. Snyder, H., & Strickland, M. (1995). *Juvenile offenders and victims: A national report*. Washington, DC: Office of Juvenile Justice and Delinquency Prevention.

9. Hackworth, D. (1989). *About face*. New York: Simon & Schuster.

10. Whitehead, B. (1994–95). The failure of sex education. *American Educator, 18*(4), 22–29.

11. Office of Education Research and Improvement (1988). *Youth indicators, 1988*. Washington, DC: Government Printing Office, p. 70.

12. Honeywell, R. J. (1964). *The educational works of Thomas Jefferson*. New York: Russell & Russell, p. 26.

13. Bowen, J. (1981). *A history of world education* (Vol. 3: The modern world). New York: St. Martins, p. 250.

14. Parry, V. J. (1969). Elite elements in the Ottoman empire. In Wilkinson, R. (Ed.), *Governing elites* (p. 72). New York: Oxford University Press.

15. Quick, R. H. (1896). *Essays on educational reformers*. New York: Appleton, p. 43.

16. Lerner, B. (1991, March). Good news about American education. *Commentary, 91*, 19–25.

17. Ogle, L. T., Alsalam, N., & Rogers, G. T. (1991). *The condition of education, 1991* (Vol. 1). Washington, DC: U.S. Department of Education, p. 24.

18. Slavin, R. E. (1988, Spring). Synthesis of research on grouping in elementary and secondary schools. *Educational Leadership, 46*, 67–77.

19. Drebeen, R., & Barr, R. (1988, November). The formation and instruction of ability groups. *American Journal of Education, 97*(1), 34–64.

CHAPTER 4

Teaching Discipline

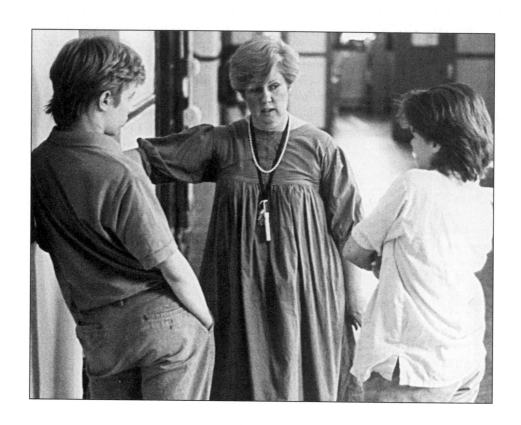

A boy's spirit is increased by freedom and depressed by slavery: it rises when praised, and is led to conceive great expectations of itself; yet this same treatment produces arrogance and quickness of temper. We must, therefore, guide him between these two extremes, using the curb at one time and the spur at another. He must undergo no servile or degrading treatment; he never must beg abjectly for anything, nor must he gain anything by begging. Let him receive it for his own sake, for his past good behavior, or for his promises of future good conduct.

—Seneca (c. 4 B.C.–65 A.D.), *On the Education of Children*

Education would be a good deal easier if it were not for human nature. If students were all intellect and desire to know, teaching would be a snap. We all know this is not true. Students, even with well-organized teaching, sometimes get bored and restless. They can become jealous and resentful of other students. Some resist the authority of the teacher. Some have little self-control. Some are lazy and self-indulgent. Some do not know how to cooperate. Some are deceitful. The list can go on. Furthermore, as children and adolescents, students are highly changeable. Their habits and attitudes fluctuate, occasionally changing from day to day or hour to hour.

These tendencies lead to behaviors that interfere enormously with students' learning and the teacher's efforts to conduct a productive class. To prevent such interference, students must be taught discipline.

To complicate the matter for some teachers, the movement for the inclusion of special education pupils in standard classrooms has attained strong momentum. The push for inclusion means that many regular education teachers have increasing needs to refine their skills in maintaining discipline in order to work with certain emotionally disturbed pupils.

ARE RULES AND PUNISHMENTS NECESSARY?

One of the most famous American quotes is Thomas Jefferson's "That government is best which governs the least." In fact, though, the quote is incomplete and its essence is distorted. Jefferson said, "That government is best which governs the least, because its people discipline themselves." Jefferson knew what was needed for the social experiment on which he and his co-conspirators were embarking to succeed. The people, most of whom were uneducated and many of whom were unruly and undisciplined, would need to be educated about the responsibilities of citizenship. This is why Jefferson was such a strong advocate for education. He assumed education would teach pupils how to display discipline.

Discipline is different from prosocial conduct. Prosocial conduct means doing good deeds or saying helpful words. *Discipline* means not doing or saying wrong things. To teach discipline is to have students learn to obey adult directions not to do wrong things: not to strike another child in school or ruin the environment of the classroom through disruptive behavior or make rude remarks.

Discipline problems are a major concern for most teachers. They are particularly vexing for beginning teachers. We have already mentioned the annual Gallup Poll of the public's views on public education, sponsored by Phi Delta Kappa. For the last twenty years, this poll has shown the public's belief that this is the core problem confronting our schools. Poor discipline in our schools not only interferes with student learning but also erodes teachers' morale and undercuts the public's confidence in our schools. In addition, poor school and classroom discipline subvert the proper moral growth and development of students.

While not often acknowledged by educational theorists and writers, students are quite human; they have vices and failures just as adults do. It is impossible to imagine any large society without some system, formal or informal, of prohibition, adjudication, and punishment. Rules exist because people are tempted to harm others. Anyone skimming a daily newspaper will see it is replete with examples of such misconduct. For instance, one of the authors resides in a relatively tranquil suburban village. The village has a weekly paper, which has a regular column describing the village's reported crimes and arrests. There are usually twenty to thirty items in each issue. That's 1,000 to 1,500 incidents a year. While it is true there are only two or three murders a year in the town, most of the regularly reported misconduct—petty theft, burglary, assault, car theft—would be extremely disruptive in any school or classroom. Similar principles about victims and victimization apply to pupils enrolled in schools.

In classrooms, some students find manifold ways to disobey their teachers. Some pupils, disengaged from academics, focus their intellectual energies on antisocial activities. In some schools, groups of students gang up on pupils who are likely victims, those who are unprotected and vulnerable. Misbehaving students also drive good teachers out of teaching either purposefully or as a by-product of their bad behavior. Some do very evil things that emotionally, and even physically, scar their fellow students. Recently, one student in a disorderly Chicago public high school became the first student from that school to win a National Merit scholarship. According to the newspaper report, in his final year in the school, the faculty allowed the student to eat lunch in the teachers' lunchroom to shield him from the jealous ragging he received in the pupils' lunchroom for his success with academics.

Undoubtedly, some disorder can be moderated by improved instruction techniques. There may even come a day when all disorder is extinguished by a different and dynamic pedagogy. Meanwhile, adults have a solemn responsibility to promulgate and enforce rules and laws on behalf of pupils trying to pursue knowledge.

After all, we should recognize that children display some patterns common to adult taxpayers and automobile drivers. They often adopt lawful behavior for fear of punishment. Some students do their homework, not always because they find the workbooks intrinsically fascinating, but because they fear the consequences of not doing homework. Again, there are students who would rather curl up and go to sleep in a corner of the classroom than attend to the lesson. Fear of punishment, and in some circumstances, fear of minor physical punishment, often works. It keeps many students on track. As a result, these students do things that in the future will be to their benefit, such as learning to calculate percentages and gaining some control over aggressive tendencies. Even if such threats do not permanently change some students, and they resume their misconduct as soon as the threat is removed, achieving even temporary order is valuable. It allows teachers to focus the whole class's energy on instruction and suppresses the distractions caused by pupils conspicuously and successfully modeling disorder.

Readers will recall that the previous chapter focused on pupils learning character and academics in classrooms or in the whole school. These activities have tremendous implications for the suppression of pupil indiscipline. The activities strongly encourage pupils to direct their energies and emotions into constructive affairs, instead of drifting towards disorder. Still, even in the most highly organized schools, teachers and administrators will have to continue suppressing misconduct.

Apropos of the prevalence of misconduct, one of the authors periodically queries his graduate classes as to how many of these mature adults have ever been bosses, directing a number of other employees in some purposeful activity. Typically, about a quarter of the class will respond "Yes" to the question.

After a brief in-class discussion, the former bosses will agree about the most difficult element of being a boss: monitoring and correcting the occasional, and inevitable, employee who, for inadequate reasons, refuses to accept the norms existing at the work site. It is not that all employees are irresponsible. But there are usually enough of such employees to make being a boss quite demanding work. Similar principles affect teachers.

Policies that Cause Misconduct

Besides our flawed human nature, the causes of discipline problems are many:

- ✦ Classroom work that is too easy or too difficult
- ✦ Boring instruction
- ✦ Confusing instruction
- ✦ Unclear pupil expectations (not knowing how to do what the teacher expects)
- ✦ Poor school- or classroom-management techniques (e.g., uneven enforcement of lateness rules or chaos every time something has to be passed out to pupils in class)
- ✦ Ineffectual or unenforced punishments

Many of these problems are caused by the teacher not knowing enough content or having poor instructional skills. Such important deficiencies are beyond the scope of this book. Other deficiencies, though, are quite germane to our focus.

One cause of a breakdown in discipline is a problem of differences in perception between teachers and pupils. Students often behave in ways they fail to perceive as problems. They may perceive the impact of their misconduct as a very marginal problem. They may be reluctant to admit the harmful effects of their misbehavior, hoping to talk themselves out of punishment. Being tardy to class or continually talking in class may seem minor to some students, and even to their parents ("That school with their middle-class hang-ups is driving me crazy!"). However, tardiness means children are coming in after instruction has begun. Talking in class means students are chattering about unrelated social concerns.

Consider, for instance, the instructional effects of frequent tardiness among students, perhaps in a departmentalized school. If some students are regularly late, the teacher may hold up instruction to wait for them. Students who are usually on time may begin to think, "Why should I hurry to class? It will start late anyway." The proportion of late-comers increases. Suppose the teacher now starts the class promptly. Some of the late-comers may now begin to hurry, and make class on time. However, others will still come in late. Since they have missed the beginning of the class, they will find the lesson hard to understand and have even less motivation for being on time for the next class. In a technical sense, these late-comers may eventually "learn their lesson" by failing the course—or even dropping out of school—due to their poor grades. This seems unfortunate, and it may even generate criticisms against teachers who start class on time. A better solution is for the school and the teachers to establish a simple, unpleasant, and prompt system of consequences for tardy students. The system will be far more effective if students feel the consequences within 24 hours of the incident, rather than after a student fails at the end of the term.

A second cause of discipline problems is a lack of incentives, or rewards and punishments, to encourage pupils to behave correctly. In this case we are referring to students who know what they should do, but they see no strong reason to do it. This is a widespread problem, occurring in varying degrees throughout the grades. Some examples are not doing homework assignments because there is no apparent consequence; cheating because the benefits of cheating outweigh the risk of negative consequences; ganging up on another student, perceiving that teachers don't notice; or quietly drifting along during the school day, consciously not making the effort required to engage the work at hand, knowing that teachers and parents expect little.

In all instances of indiscipline, there are two sets of potential incentives and consequences. One set is immediate and relates to the here-and-now world of the teacher and the student. "If I do (or don't do) X, the teacher will do (or not do) Y to me." This is the immediate world of the school, involving detentions, praise, and notes home to parents.

The other set of potential consequences and incentives are more long range. It concerns pupils developing habits of study and self-control. It has to do with students' sense of what they can accomplish in life. It has to do with what others—friends, teachers, college admissions officers, and potential employers—think of them and how others evaluate them as individuals. For some students, these long-range incentives are firmly in focus and affect their daily decisions. For others, they are part of a hazy, disconnected world of the future and have little meaning or power in their lives. Psychologists describe children in the latter category as lacking a vision of the future. Many of the most self-destructive members of urban youth gangs fall into this category.

An awareness of incentives for action and the consequences of our actions, then, are major ingredients in becoming an educated and civilized person. This awareness goes to the heart of the school's intellectual and moral goals. For a small percentage of young students, a simple discussion of incentives and consequences and of short-term goals versus long-term goals, is the best way to incorporate these concepts into their daily lives at home and in school. However, most young people need that most vivid and immediate source of learning, rules.

Rules as Teachers

Rules are guides to behavior. They tell the individual what is acceptable behavior and what is unacceptable. *We don't run in the halls. In our classroom, we don't allow students to use rude words. At our school, our fans don't boo the referees no matter how bad the call.* Rules teach.

Rules, by the very fact of their existence, help children learn the skills and attitudes needed to live in harmony with others. The aim of civility that underlies a good set of rules affects not only the behavior of students, but also their social expectations and attitudes. Much of what is written about the hidden curriculum is about the unseen rule structure and expectations below the surface of school life. On the other hand, much of what teachers actually do is explain the rules, instructing students about the "why" behind the rules: "The reason we don't allow running in the hall is because someone might get hurt. A child could get pushed at the drinking fountain and break a tooth. So, out of consideration for others, we want you to walk." Many teachers find it draining to constantly explain rules. But explaining is an essential task of schooling.

ESTABLISHING RULES

Rules exist on two levels in schools. There are schoolwide rules and classroom rules. This duality parallels our system of federal and state or local laws. Ideally, the schoolwide and classroom systems should work together, each addressing different arenas and activities. Here we will consider both.

Schoolwide Rules

The first operating step in developing a set of rules or a schoolwide disciplinary policy is to list the kinds of misconduct that might occur at the particular school. For example, we probably do not need to worry about pupil alcohol use in a K–6 school in a stable neighborhood. But after recognizing such considerations, there will still be a number of problematic issues. Let us be explicit. Should a school prohibit

✦ different forms of cheating, defined with some precision?

✦ overt acts of affection, such as kissing, holding hands, or hugging?

✦ getting in fights in or near the school, even defensively?

✦ any particular kind of clothing? Should there be a dress code, and should it be defined with considerable precision, e.g., no torn jeans, no miniskirts?

✦ tardiness? How many times should a student be allowed to be late or miss class per semester or year? And how should such incidents be defined?

✦ bringing gum or cigarettes to school?

✦ male pupils wearing earrings or female pupils wearing nose rings in school?

✦ loud talking in the lunchroom?

✦ disobedience or disrespect to any adult in the school?

✦ vulgar language or gestures addressed to other students?

✦ wearing T-shirts or other clothes with vulgar or provocative remarks written on them?

✦ pupil misconduct at school-related activities away from school, e.g., while attending athletic meets at other schools?

✦ failing to report to school authorities serious breaches of school discipline by other students (with the understanding that adults will try to keep the sources of information confidential), such as bringing weapons or drugs into school, committing theft, or making threats to commit suicide or run away from home?

A clear, comprehensive set of schoolwide written rules or codes of student discipline must be developed, aimed at acts of misconduct that can be reasonably foreseen around the school. Conversely, if certain undesirable acts are nonexistent or rare, prohibition may be unnecessary.

As a general principle, elaborate codes of discipline are less necessary in smaller schools, schools with high levels of staff and pupil stability, schools with younger pupils, schools serving specially selected or recruited pupils and families, and schools serving more orderly communities. But, in deciding what to prohibit, educators should recognize the danger of self-deception. That danger was evinced by data that we introduced earlier, which showed that students perceive more serious discipline breaches than do teachers or administrators. Often the school's adults are among the last ones to become aware of serious new troubles.

Still, almost every school should have a set of schoolwide written prohibitions. Obviously, developing and drafting a list of schoolwide prohibitions takes reflection. It is a classic committee responsibility. As one high school principal told us, he solicits advice from faculty, students, and parents to develop the list and draft the text. But the principal recognizes that the buck stops with him. If he strongly disagrees with some faculty recommendations and can't change things by persuasion, he finally decides what's in or out. After all, the public cannot really hold a committee accountable for failing to draft an obvious rule. For example, some members of the committee may have disagreed with the group's conclusion. Only individuals can be fired or reprimanded. Student input can be an important contribution, but it should be identified for what it is—advisory.

The code of discipline must be published and distributed to students and parents. Parents should be asked to pledge that they will cooperate with the school in supporting the code and will discuss the code with their child. The parent and child should sign a receipt to that effect and return the receipt to the school, to be kept with the student's records. Individual classroom teachers should explain the schoolwide code, and the school should hold a general assembly early in the school year to go over special points.

In addition, the code should be reviewed and updated annually, and the whole process of publication, distribution, and discussion repeated on a regular basis. One principal we know throws away the student code of discipline every year and repeats the process to create a new one. She is convinced that having everyone rethink and re-discuss the rules is fundamentally important to the goal of helping the students reach moral maturity.

A code without enforcement, or with uneven enforcement, is worse than nothing. It breeds resentment among teachers and cynicism among students and presents to all a condition of social confusion and paralysis. It is imperative, then, for teachers to uniformly and justly enforce the school's rules. Teachers should not simply leave it up to administrators to sanction other teachers who do not enforce the code. As professionals, teachers must take the responsibility of compliance with agreed-upon rules and, in effect, police their own ranks.

Exactly what should or should not be prohibited? We have not said what rules to establish. In some other parts of this book, we will identify and analyze certain value-laden issues, but we will not provide definitive answers as to what we believe is right or wrong.

We believe it is evident that many schools have discipline codes that are not sufficiently restrictive. However, for several reasons, we will not make specific recommendations about exactly what should be prohibited. As we have noted, there are some causes for legitimate differences among prohibitions, e.g., the varying ages of pupils or contrasts in levels of disorder that make certain prohibitions superfluous in some communities and essential in others. Beyond such matters, there are surely differences in values regarding discipline among thoughtful persons of goodwill. Exactly how severe should the restrictions be on pupils' clothes, such as torn jeans, greasy shirts, see-through blouses, short skirts, hats, sunglasses, or stencilled slogans on clothing?

It would unduly prolong this book to articulate and justify restrictions or licenses regarding these matters. We simply stress that prohibitions in the discipline code should be carefully drafted. The prohibitions should unapologetically reflect mainstream adult values; enable teachers and pupils to concentrate on the business of learning academics and self-discipline; and give maximum weight to the recommendations of educators, pupils' families, and responsible pupils. If these recommendations are followed and the prohibitions enforced, we expect 90% of the controversy about what to restrict will expire.

Classroom Rules

By almost any standard, classrooms are crowded places. They are crowded with children and adolescents full of energy and vitality. For young people, spending six or seven hours of the day sitting and working quietly with symbolic material— reading, writing, manipulating—is not their first choice of how to spend their time. In fact, for many young people, spending long hours in classrooms is a real strain. So, in addition to the individual student's need for rules to provide structure and guidance to activities, rules are needed to channel the pent-up student energy that exists in a classroom. Classroom teachers, especially in elementary schools, must supplement the school's rules and discipline code with their own classroom rules and procedures. In secondary schools, such procedures may relate more to academic expectations than in-class conduct, for example, penalties for late homework. The classroom rules, however, should take into account the circumstances of the particular class and the pupils' developmental level.

Few teachers decide to become teachers because they want to impose rules and regulations on children. Few teachers enjoy being disciplinarians. Many faculty members in colleges of education are prone to give potential teachers unrealistic ideas about the docility of their future pupils. Many teachers do not give much thought to rules and discipline until their first classroom teaching experience. As a result, one common mistake of new teachers is failing to establish a clear set of classroom rules.[1]

For many reasons, inexperienced teachers tend to ignore setting rules and making sure the students really understand them. Some beginners are very anxious to start teaching. In their haste, they neglect to attend to the matter of rules. Or they forget them altogether. Some new teachers are uncomfortable being an authority figure and a disciplinarian. They hope either that the class will know how to behave or that going over the rules once will suffice. A few new teachers ideologically oppose rules they view as oppressive. However, most beginning teachers change their attitude toward rules during the first year. Some change dramatically. Often, they change too dramatically.

The practices of effective teachers differ considerably from typical beginner patterns.[2] Research shows that effective teachers spend a significant amount of time during the first two weeks of school establishing rules and procedures. They also carefully monitor students' adherence to the rules. Such veterans seemingly sacrifice a great deal of time on drilling or grooming students on classroom procedures in the early weeks. Indeed, they are quite fussy and insistent that the students obey the rules. Clearly, though, this pays off in less disruptive classrooms, both in the short run and in the long run.

Many students struggle against rules, testing teachers to see if they are really serious. We know a first-year teacher who patiently explained to his fifth-grade students that they were not to talk in the hall on their way to the gym. He soon discovered that the message did not get through. Instead of letting it go on or displaying aimless anger, he had them come back. He explained again and gave them another chance. They talked. He called them back again. Having missed twenty minutes of precious gym time, his fifth-graders made it on the fifth try. There was no more talking in the halls, and many later messages got through with greater speed and accuracy.

Rules for Establishing Rules

It is important for teachers not to simply issue the rules, but to teach and model the rules. The following are some suggestions for using rules to teach values.

1. Do not confuse preparing children for their future roles as citizens of a democracy with the teacher's responsibility to make and enforce rules in the classroom. Never allow students to think they are responsible for monitoring and maintaining classroom order. This is the teacher's job. Students should learn about democracy and practice democratic living, but schools and classrooms are not democracies.

2. Depending on their age and sophistication, students should be involved in the formation of classroom rules. They should come to appreciate that rules are important and they have a role in developing rules. Their sincere input should be considered. Again, though, allowing children's input should not compromise the teacher's authority.

3. Rules must be seen as contributing to moral stability by encouraging pro-social conduct. Therefore, the teacher needs to point out or demonstrate the positive contribution rules make to the classroom environment.

4. Once established, rules should be written down and kept visible in the classroom. In some situations, it is helpful to have students take home copies of the rules for parents to read, sign, and return.

5. Rules need to be applied. Teachers must be ready to stand behind their rules and be willing to go to the trouble of enforcing them.

Rules, Rights, and Responsibilities: The Current Confusion

We will have more to say about the consequences of violating a code of behavior. Before returning to that topic, however, we address briefly something that has replaced the code of discipline in many schools—the student handbook. Many student handbooks are undoubtedly documents that have a positive tone and contribute to the growth and development of students. Still, some handbooks written in recent years are more part of the problem than part of the solution. This issue is best captured in an account reported by sociologist Gerald Grant.[3]

In the early 1980s, Grant was studying a particularly troubled and disorderly high school in Brooklyn. One day in the school hall he encountered a young female teacher in tears. Eventually, she got herself under control and told how she had just been sexually fondled by three high school boys. Grant urged her to go to the principal's office and report the boys, but the teacher despairingly claimed that wouldn't do any good. She reported bitterly that there were no witnesses. The testimony on the incident would be three pupils against one teacher, she explained, and a teacher's word had no special meaning in that school.

Grant was puzzled how such a flagrant situation could go unpunished. Then he came across the school's student handbook, a booklet twenty-six pages long. All but one page was devoted to a detailed account of students' rights: for example, when and under what circumstances their lockers could be searched; under what conditions teachers could give exams and quizzes; and what were a student's rights if accused of cheating. The remaining page was devoted to the students' responsibilities.

This is a particularly egregious case. Still, it demonstrates one of the worst legacies of the recent past: a massive shift from emphasis on a student's responsibility to be a good student and good member of the school community toward a heightened sense of the student as a consumer of educational services and an institutionalized underling with legal rights. Grant's example also illustrates a loss of nerve on the part of too many educators, an excessive willingness to yield in the face of actual or potential legal demands instead of vigorously striving to protect important educational concerns.

Other considerations also affect policies regarding rules, rights, and responsibilities. Schools are under great pressures from parents and social agencies to keep troubled children in their classrooms. On the other hand, society is reluctant to establish alternative institutions for disorderly students, whose behavior clearly demonstrates that they cannot handle a typical school environment. The result of such inconsistent policies is evident: the unprecedented high levels of disruption that exist in our schools today. Teachers are asked to tolerate habitual conduct that, in an earlier period, would mean swift separation of the offending student from the school or severe punishment. The policymakers and opinion-shapers responsible for this condition—legislators, judges, and academics—have fundamentally changed the American classroom. They have forced classroom teachers to tolerate unequaled levels of offensive behavior, ranging from incivility and intimidation to physical abuse. A major premise of this book is that educators must resist the tendency of some schools, particularly our high schools, to become warehouses for surly, academically disengaged youth. This is an unreasonable extension of the school's responsibility.

Today, all students, not just the offending students, realize that they have to work quite hard to be removed from school. All students know that school is something the adult community compels them to attend. Many see school as continually placing intellectual demands, sometimes arduous ones, on them. It is clear to many students that there is nothing noteworthy about being part of their school community. Many might say, "There is nothing special about being a student in this school." Belonging makes only limited affective demands on them, for example, they need not show loyalty or practice courtesy. In a well-known old gag, comedian Groucho Marx said he would not join any club that would have him as a member. The gag captures the attitudes of many students today.

Too many students think twelve or thirteen years of education is a natural right. They fail to treat it as a privilege or, to use an almost archaic word, a blessing. They have this perception because schooling is forced on them. They know they have to go out of their way—through severe misbehavior—to lose the right.

Adults must change this destructive student attitude. The authority of educators to apply sanctions in the name of the community and to separate offending students from the classroom—from brief (fifteen minutes) to prolonged (days or even expulsion) periods—must be conveniently available. Adult speculations to the contrary, separation from school is typically quite painful for many students. It means not being able to see their friends. It means having to explain why they are being separated from the school to adults, most notably their parents. It means facing up to their own sense of failing at their most important task— getting an education.

On the positive side, the entire school community should transmit the message that education is a privilege and an opportunity. Most important, it is something for which the community must have a sense of responsibility. One clear way for the community to send this message is to emphasize that the privilege can be lost and that the consequences of not going to school are unpleasant.

PUNISHMENT

The themes of prohibition and punishment are closely related. Certain conduct is prohibited in schools and classrooms precisely because it is attractive to some students. If it were not attractive, prohibition would be unnecessary. But prohibition must be coupled with appropriate and significant punishments. Otherwise, the prohibitions will be ineffectual. We will not be able to overcome the inherent attractiveness of the misconduct. Once prohibitions are developed, a system of consequences, or punishments, must be devised. This can be complicated. Obviously, punishment is a two-edged sword. A sword can be used to protect hearth and home, as well as to commit barbarous acts against the weak. There is occasional misuse of punishment in classrooms. Sometimes it is the weapon of weak or ineffectual teachers, an expression of frustration at their own failure to cause students to perform academic tasks. Not knowing how to find appropriate lessons to engage pupils, a teacher might begin a regime of punishment: "If I hear one complaint about this assignment, or see anyone's eyes roll, it's detention for the whole class. And I'm not kidding!"

Sometimes, too, punishment is overemphasized when both punishment and treatment are necessary. Students might find themselves unable to do the work or keep up with others. They become embarrassed and angry and act up. Such students might fake sleeping at their desk, swear aloud at the teacher, or throw paper on the floor. They have earned some punishment because they have violated the code of conduct. But they need both academic help and punishment to encourage self-control. In some cases, students are suspended from school. Such punishments can be excessive and may make it much more difficult for the students to get back on track. In effect, then, punishment can be an easy out for teachers, a quick fix for much deeper instructional problems. Still, in the end, punishment, or at least the realistic threat of it, is essential. The reason is simple: the human nature of children has not suddenly changed in this generation.

Effective punishments, or consequences, share certain characteristics:

1. They must be clearly disliked by students—they must deter.
2. They must not absorb large amounts of school resources, e.g., schools cannot afford to assign a full-time paid adult monitor for each disobedient pupil.
3. They must be capable of being applied in "doses" of increasing severity.
4. They must not be perceived as cruel.
5. In public schools, they often must be applicable without strong cooperation from the parent of the pupil involved.
6. They must be able to be applied quickly—the same day or even within a minute of the infraction, instead of the following week.

Very little is written in educators' textbooks about prohibition and punishment. What does exist is surrounded with warnings about the dangers of punishment. Teachers are cautioned about the ill effects of even mild sarcasm toward students, raising their voices in anger, and simply pointing at a misbehaving student. They are admonished that publicly embarrassing students is not to be tolerated under any circumstances.

Given such common counsel, it is understandable why many teachers, especially beginners, find the matter of prohibition and punishment extremely complex. It seems very difficult to simultaneously punish pupils, not hurt their feelings but make their conduct change, and continue to teach a class effectively.

We do not impugn the motives of those who advocate such popular positions. However, we believe this advice is misleading and can be destructive. It generates unrealistic responsibilities for teachers and underrates the resilience of most young people. Such problematic advice is an instance of a widespread error in educational literature. Practices that may be appropriate for younger pupils are endorsed for all students, without the recognition that different techniques may be needed with certain groups of students, such as those in upper-level high school or those with consistent records of misbehavior.

One of the authors recently read an essay that offered advice to parents and illustrates the matter of underemphasizing punishment. The advice was generally sound, but not very notable. For example, the author wrote, "When you eat with your child in a restaurant, do not let him tyrannize you by having a tantrum at the table if he objects to your demands." Who is in favor of public tantrums? Yet we all know such tantrums sometimes happen—or that parents surrender to such threats. The problem with restaurant tantrums is not that parents want them to happen. The problem is how to punish a child at such a time, with half the people in the restaurant watching and probably judging your parental efficacy. What effective discipline is feasible and wise on such occasions? The advice-to-parents essay did not take up that issue.

Our tentative response to this hypothetical situation involves several steps. First, before leaving the house, consider whether you can foresee any difficulties. If not, then sail on. But assume difficulties are possible, but you still want to go on with the family expedition. Inform the children, in advance, about the proposed adventure. Portray the whole thing favorably, but emphasize that their cooperation—being good—is necessary. Define exactly what you mean by cooperation. If there is some simple, clear, unpleasant consequence that is easily available—withholding a favorite dessert or future restaurant meals—then warn the child that bad behavior means no dessert or no future restaurant meals. If no clear consequence is evident and the meal must go on, then warn the children that very serious—even if unspecified—consequences will result if they act up. That threat must be sincere. The vast majority of such problems are settled by planning. For example, parents should describe the desired conduct and the planned unpleasant, serious punishments in advance; give children the option of not going on the trip; or avoid such a trip if discipline is very uncertain.

Natural versus Constructed Consequences

Many educators stress the concept of natural consequences as the essence of punishment. This implies that natural effects are better than artificial, deliberate, or even hostile punishments. Of course, some natural consequences very properly have punitive effects. If students put graffiti on the wall, they have to wash it off. But the natural consequences of much wrongdoing are obscure and ambiguous and sometimes even reinforce offending behavior. For instance, if bullies beat up small children, the bullies may find such hurting conduct enjoyable. If children swear, they may be pleased to discover such language upsets listeners. Children who steal may enjoy their stolen goods. Drug users in the short run may feel exuberant; in the adult world, many drug lords attain economic success. Meanwhile, innocent children suffer as the victims of bullies, thieves, and coarse belittlement. As a practical matter, educators cannot usually rely on natural consequences to correct misconduct. Teachers often must apply analysis, reflection, and determination to invent, construct, and enforce effective artificial consequences.

First, we will list consequences that we have seen in schools and consider ineffective:

1. Sending pupils alone into the hall, where they can hang around and bother others.
2. Giving pupils tasks as punishment without following up on them.
3. Mailing notices of pupil misconduct home to parents, when pupils can intercept the mail before their parents get home.
4. Frequent and/or unconsidered shouting at unruly individual pupils or groups.
5. Sending pupils to a detention room where they can engage in chitchat, read comic books, or catch up on homework.
6. Sending pupils to the principal's office, where they act as messengers (a welcome novelty) or are entertained by the passing scene or by the secretary.
7. Calling or sending notes or letters to parents of unruly pupils, when it is evident the parents either support their children or cannot exercise effective authority.
8. Scheduling before- or after-school detention at the student's convenience.

9. Sending pupils to deans of discipline or guidance counselors who lack the power to punish or dislike the idea of punishing students for misbehavior.

10. Simply rebuking or suspending pupils who commit criminal acts around the school (e.g., use drugs, bring in weapons), instead of reporting such crimes to the police.

11. Suspending pupils from school if they will not be monitored by the family during suspension, but can instead enjoy themselves at home or out on the streets.

On the other hand, some effective punishments or consequences to misbehavior are:

1. Subjecting pupils to before- or after-school detention within 24 hours of their violation, or, as one school found, scheduling detention on Saturdays for more serious offenses, since they interrupted students' Saturday games and jobs.

2. Providing an in-school suspension in a designated room, supervised by a stern monitor, with chitchat prohibited and students assigned to do their missed class work.

3. Depriving pupils of their regular daily recess time.

4. Promptly phoning parents, even at work, the moment certain violations occur, or at least collecting a signed receipt from pupils that their parents have read the punishment notice.

5. Granting teachers the power to issue detention immediately to wrongdoers, without having to wait for a review of the penalties (although such authority should be subject to long-term review).

6. Sharply and suddenly (and sometimes publicly and in an urgent tone) criticizing individual pupils for particular immediate acts of misconduct, such as treating another student harshly. (Usually, such rebukes are deliberate, though they seem spontaneous.)

7. Having erring pupils write notes to their parents explaining their misconduct, and having them promptly return the notes with their parents' signature.

8. Sending unruly pupils from the class to another class for a short period (e.g., thirty minutes) under prearrangement with a cooperating teacher. The receiving class is usually three or four grades higher or lower than the sending one.

9. Calling the police immediately whenever any student conduct violates criminal law.

10. Assigning punished pupils to do school clean-up at inconvenient times (e.g., Saturday morning) under serious supervision.

11. When parents are uncooperative, insisting they come to school and meet with concerned faculty and their child. At the meeting, teachers should strongly and directly describe the child's misconduct. The child may be present at this meeting. The aim is to provoke parents to become involved in the discipline of their child.

12. When a student continually interferes with the work of the class, using shame. For example, have the child stand at the back of the class face to the wall for a period of time, or have the student stand and immediately make a public apology to the class.

13. In certain cases with older children, judiciously applying moderate corporal punishment, when authorized by local laws and school policy.

14. Having specified high school pupils (who are essentially on probation) carry cards, which are annotated by each of their separate teachers throughout the day regarding their promptness and conduct. At the end of each day, designated adult monitors examine the cards.

15. Suspending and ultimately expelling pupils when other measures have not proved effective. It is important to remind parents that (under most state laws) they are legally responsible for supervising their child while out of school. An attendance officer may even drop by the student's home to monitor this important responsibility.

It is easy to tell if a particular consequence works. Just ask pupils who have been subjected to it, "Would you like to experience that again?"

Classroom Punishment

We have already addressed the role of punishment as a matter of school policy, much of which reaches into the life of the classroom. The existence of clear schoolwide rules will surely spill over into a particular classroom. However, beyond such general policies, issues will arise regarding the punishments individual teachers apply in their particular class. Each classroom is a small community with its own work demands and dynamics.

Teachers, then, must each have an array of punishments appropriate to their classrooms. The punishments should range from mild public or private rebukes for poor work or uncivil behavior to the authority to recommend that the principal temporarily separate the child from the classroom or school, with a high probability of the recommendation being accepted. In situations where students do not clearly understand what the punishment will be, the teacher should transmit, orally and in writing, potential punishments to all students at the beginning of the school year. The penalties should be explicitly linked to the infractions. Most of all, everybody in the classroom should understand the rules as part of the teacher's attempt to establish and maintain a place that is friendly, productive, and happy.

Of course, rules alone will not ensure a disciplined, civil, and productive class. Power is a basic fact of human life, and some people have more of it than others. Power has a moral use and misuse. Much power is legitimate, such as the power a parent has over a child. Some power, such as that of a bully on the playground, is illegitimate. The classroom is a prime setting for learning about power. Teachers have it and legitimately need it. The issue, though, is how they use it. The great potential for misuse of power does not mean that it should be extinguished or surrendered to students. It means, however, that power should be exercised with fairness. This may be the most important message a teacher can give to a child. To achieve fairness, punishment should

+ be applied with consistency and, where there are variations in application, those variations should be based on plausible principles, e.g., a dean of discipline might excuse certain misbehavior by a pupil who had just learned of the death of a parent.
+ in the case of serious punishment (e.g., expulsion), have some system of review or appeal.
+ be the outcome of violating clear or implicit prohibitions.

Rules Under Pressure

Throughout this book we have stressed that, at this moment in our history, too many public schools are overly permissive. They fail to instill in our young the self-discipline needed for citizenship and full adult development. We believe strict schools (certainly by today's standards) are happy schools and, more important, schools that serve children and society well. We must add, though, that discipline must be the servant of the total educative mission of the school. Often the terrain here becomes tricky and messy.

It seems that every fall we see a news report of another town up in arms over a severe punishment meted out by a football coach. The details may vary, but these stories have a common theme. The school has a written and well-publicized rule against drinking alcohol, and this rule is explicitly part of the athlete's code of conduct. Then key players are discovered drinking to celebrate a victory. Often these players have worked hard for years to get where they are. But the coach kicks them off the team and the school board backs him up. Several of the boys claim they had only a single beer. The players and their parents are brokenhearted. The student body and the town cannot understand how the punishment could befall not only the boys, but also the whole school.

Such occasions are painful and difficult for all involved, but it is at times like these that life's most important messages are learned: *Our actions have consequences. Rules have meaning. Not everything can be explained away, or eventually worked out, or made whole again.*

But there are other cases, although not as well publicized. A senior with a spotty academic record in a private school turns in her senior thesis, a requirement for all students in the college track. The school rules prohibit cheating but do not clearly define all possible offenses. The school also has a strong prohibition against directly lying to a teacher. This misconduct is punishable by expulsion. The student's teacher, correcting the paper, is at first pleased and then suspicious. The teacher confronts the student and accuses her of cheating, or, more specifically, plagiarism.

The girl angrily denies the charge. But the teacher goes on to identify whole paragraphs lifted from various sources. Since the student has committed two offenses punishable by expulsion—lying and plagiarism—she is expelled.

On final analysis, we should recognize that (a) the student apparently had never received a clear understanding of the relationship of plagiarism to cheating—the rule was ambiguous; and (b) the student's untruthful denial to the teacher was partly due to misunderstanding the real nature of her offense.

Fairness and mercy require educators to carefully examine both the principles underlying their discipline codes and their everyday application.

Collective Punishment

We will now consider the question of individual versus collective punishment. Should a whole class or other group ever receive group punishment, such as being kept after school or deprived of recess, for certain group misbehavior? Such tactics are sometimes warranted, as when the teacher has made it clear that the group as a whole is liable to be held responsible. Here the aim is to stimulate the innocent students to apply vigorous pressure on the wrongdoers. If punishment occurs, the wrongdoers are punished because of their direct misconduct, and the innocent students are punished because they did not vigorously suppress their erring peers. But to satisfy the important criterion of fairness, the innocent students must have a realistic chance of suppressing the behavior. If there are twenty wrongdoers and two innocent students, for example, the chances are slim that the two students can do much suppressing.

Group responsibility is a facet of the concept of group achievement, either in prosocial conduct or academics. We have already emphasized that groups of students can win praise or other benefits for achievements. It is equally appropriate to hold groups liable for collective misconduct. Of course, each member of an erring group may not commit the same "amount" of wrong as each other member. But each group member who receives praise probably did not do the same amount of "good" as every other member. Moderate inequalities in rewards and punishments are inevitable in group life.

Enforcement

After prohibitions and consequences have been established and published, they must also be enforced by the adults in the school. All adults would like to work in a school with good discipline. Not all adults, however, whether administrators or teachers, are equally willing to enforce discipline. Enforcing discipline is hard work. However, without across-the-board enforcement, pupils will violate rules, testing to see if they are in the presence of a teacher who is an enforcer. Furthermore, pupils will feel emboldened to resist enforcers, argue with them, and criticize them. The pupils will correctly contend that the enforcers are inconsistent with the policies of other teachers. Nonenforcers complicate the work of enforcers, while enjoying the full benefits of the enforcers' responsible conduct.

Principals should emphasize to faculty members that the school code, which they have all helped to develop, must be routinely enforced by all staff. This responsibility is part of everyone's job description. In addition, maintaining a disciplined, civil, and productive educational environment should be a major concern of the school's teachers association. Nothing contributes more to teacher burnout than spending great amounts of energy dealing with poorly behaved students who continually "push the envelope" of permissible behavior or even go beyond those limits. Building-level professional association activities should spend much time on forming a staff consensus on discipline enforcement.

Some Principles for Teachers on Administering Punishment

Punishment can be strong stuff. It makes a deep impression on students. It can arouse long-lasting emotions of anger and resentment. We offer the following principles regarding punishment by individual teachers:

1. The reasons for the punishment should always be clear to the student.

2. A specific punishment should always be administered in a moral framework understood by the student. "I am keeping you after school because you repeatedly bothered your seat-mate today, even after I warned you. That kind of behavior shows little respect for others or for what we are trying to accomplish in this classroom."

3. Never punish (apart from giving a low grade) a student for inept performance. Poor academic performance alone is no reason for retribution. However, failure to try is another matter. "You did not do your homework" *can* be a cause for punishment.

4. Focus on the behavior of the student, not on the student's person. A teacher might say, "I had you stand in the hall because you were wandering around the room again, bothering other students. I know you can do better than this." Or, "You are being denied recess, not because you failed the test, but because you didn't do the homework that might have enabled you to pass the test."

5. Sometimes engage students in the punishment process. Give them practice at judging their own mistakes ("What do you think is a good punishment for being late four days this week?").

6. Don't use positive things as punishment. For instance, don't punish students by having them write a story or read a book. Don't give them what is usually volunteer work or community service as punishment.

7. In all significant cases, quickly involve parents in the adjudication and punishment process. Except in trivial cases, ensure that parents are informed of the violations involved and the consequences generated. Have parents sign to ensure that they have received notes, or phone them at home or work. In some cases, the parents' punishment of a child will be more effective than any the teacher can generate. In other instances, parental permissiveness is part of the cause of the problem, and the teacher may not receive proper support. But even with permissive parents, persistent contacts can often prod them to change their currently ineffective policies. All of this takes teacher engagement, tact, and courage.

8. Have several intermediate steps between the relatively mild punishments of the classroom and the severe penalty of suspension from school. Some teachers use a "time out" for misbehaving students, where the student is sent to another part of the classroom and temporarily separated from the class activity. Many schools have designed in-school suspension, where students are sent to special no-idling, work-oriented rooms. If offending students do not respond to these intermediate punishments, separation from school is called for. This should be a last resort, but a real possibility.

Practices and Policies

1. Can you identify an example of an actual classroom or schoolwide rule you knew of as either a teacher or student that was poorly conceived or drafted? What was it, and what were the effects of its inefficiency?

2. Can you identify a similar instance of a poorly conceived punishment? What was it, and what were the effects of its inefficiency?

3. Provide examples of effective rules or punishments. Why were they effective?

4. Do you know or recall a teacher whom you believe was a poor disciplinarian? What instances of ineptitude come to mind?

5. Describe a teacher whom you believe was a good disciplinarian.

6. Identify and describe a real discipline problem, existing in either the present or past, in a school or classroom, that you are familiar with. What change or new rule or system of punishment would be useful to correct the situation? Draft an appropriate rule or punishment policy to correct the situation.

7. Find an actual set of published school rules and punishment policies. Critique them in light of this chapter.

References

1. Ryan, K. (Ed.). (1991). *The roller coaster year: The stories for first year teachers*. New York: Harper Collins.

2. Ryan, *The roller coaster year*.

3. Grant, G. (1982, January/February). The character of education, and the education of character. *American Educator, 18*, 37–45.

CHAPTER 5

The Moral Nature of the Classroom

In modern times there are opposing views about the practice of education. There is not general agreement about what the young should learn either in relation to virtue or in relation to the best in life: nor is it clear whether their education ought to be directed more towards the intellect than towards the character of the soul. The problem has been complicated by what we see happening before our eyes, and it is not certain whether training should be directed at things useful in life, or at those conducive to virtue, or at nonessentials. All these answers have been given. And there is no agreement as to what, in fact, does tend toward virtue. Men do not all prize most highly the same virtue, so naturally they differ also about the proper training for it.

—Aristotle, 4th century B.C.

A handful of educational theorists think that children are naturally good and would ripen into fully realized people if only the adult world would get out of the way. We wonder if the advocates of theories of natural goodness have ever raised children of their own. Rousseau, for instance, placed all his children in an orphanage. In general, children do not automatically grow up to be good.

Children are born helpless, and they need help from the adults around them well into their teens and beyond. Besides learning how to fill their basic needs for food and shelter, stay out of the mouths of furry beasts, and avoid fast-moving machines, children need to learn how to live in society. They must learn how things are done in their "tribe" and how people work together and settle disputes peacefully. They must learn how to contribute to the survival of the community and how to balance what they need and want with the needs and wants of the people around them.

The primary teacher of this knowledge is the family. Parents, brothers and sisters, aunts and uncles, and grandparents may all work together to civilize the child, to enable the child to exist among people with some degree of comfort and harmony. The task is long-lasting and consumes a great deal of time and energy (more so with some children than others), but it is among the most important functions of the family. However, at this moment in our history, the American family is not a very strong teaching entity. One sociologist, Amitai Etzioni, presented his view.

> [Many] of our youngsters grow up in families that are not viable from an education viewpoint. Frequent divorces, a bewildering rotation of boyfriends [sic] and parents who come home from work exhausted both physically and mentally, have left many homes with tremendous parenting deficits. Instead of providing a stable home environment and the kind of close, loving supervision good character formation requires, many child care facilities, grannies, and baby sitters simply ensure that children stay out of harm's way.[1]

This condition has had a number of effects. For one thing, the current education norm of twelve-plus years of nearly universal schooling is a relatively recent social invention. The role of this invention has been greatly expanded to make up for the lacks and gaps in many families. Since a child cannot get along without the rules of social life and an internalized sense of what is right and wrong, the school is an obvious choice to provide them.

Schools, while accepting broader responsibilities, must continue to play their traditional role as a strong secondary source of moral education and character formation. Further, the individual classroom is the inner arena of this learning. Children spend the bulk of their school days there. Children do not come to school as morally blank slates or without interest and experience in the issues of right and wrong, of good and bad. They bubble over with moral views and concerns. Describing the conversations of children, Robert Fullinwider wrote:

> They complain about parents or teachers; they make fun of the weird-looking kid down the block; they tell tales about people in the neighborhood, spread rumors about their teachers, divulge secrets they had sworn never to reveal, and speculate about the dark sides of their friends. They confide in one another, sharing their fears, hopes, disappointments, and grudges. They make plans for getting even with their enemies and imagine the most fiendish ways they could revenge themselves on the teachers they hate. They rate and they rank: who's the prettiest, who's the best; who's a jerk and who's a snob; who's a good guy and who's a reliable friend; who's nice and who's not.[2]

These are some of the moral concerns and ideas children bring with them into their classrooms. These imported perspectives are further agitated by the cauldron of moral matter that lies bubbling below the surface of the typical classroom. The cauldron is seething with issues about the rightness and wrongness of things. Individual children, be they second-graders or high school seniors, are up to their necks in moral tensions, issues, and ideas.

"Should I do my best on this assignment or dash it off so I can have some free time?"

"I can't do this work. Should I cheat?"

"I can't stand that girl. Why do I have to sit next to her?"

"If I just keep quiet, watch the teacher, and stay out of trouble, I can float right through this course."

"Why should I help him with his homework? If I help him, he could end up getting a better grade than me."

The moral is woven into the very fabric of classroom life.

There is an old saying that claims, "If scientists were fish, the last thing they would discover is water." The same is true for many educators. The environment of the classroom is so morally rich and dense that teachers often do not see it. Like fish and water, we have become habituated to it. We stop seeing how certain children pointedly ignore or even intimidate others. We let troublesome or lazy students, whom we believe can do much better work, simply slide by doing the minimum. We use our own power as teachers in an arbitrary manner. We carefully teach works, such as *Julius Caesar*, emphasizing historical background, language, characterization, and structure, but fail to ask the students critical questions: Was Brutus right to join in the assassination of Caesar? Is killing ever the right thing to do? When is it right to turn against legitimate authority? We go to great trouble developing a final test on arithmetic, but through laxity we let some children cheat. For these teachers, habituated by the everyday quality of school, the bedrock moral mission of education goes unacknowledged and unaddressed. As Aristotle's quote at the beginning of the chapter discloses, confusion and uncertainty about the goals of education are not novel. Still, despite such uncertainty, there is a basic reality: the classroom is a moral environment. Ignoring this dimension of classroom life does not make the issue disappear.

This chapter concentrates on the moral life of the classroom and the classroom teacher. The next two chapters examine the moral dimensions of the teacher's role and the classroom's curriculum. In all three chapters our discussion deals with issues that are relevant to both elementary and secondary teachers. Some matters inevitably will be more important to one group than the other. Some distinctions between the two groups of teachers are due to developmental contrasts among different age groups of pupils, for example, the differing capabilities of children and adolescents. Other distinctions result from various forms of school processes, particularly the differences generated by the contrasts between self-contained classrooms and those with departmentalized instruction.

The issues we will look at specifically in this chapter are two abstractions, two elements of classroom life that fundamentally affect the moral quality and impact of classroom learnings: the ethos of the classroom and the attitudes of students.

ETHOS

Ethos refers to the shared attitudes, beliefs, and values of a community. The term also refers to the spirit of a group or community of people. While not directly observable, the ethos of a classroom or a school can be a formidable force in shaping the minds and hearts of students.

In *Horace's Compromise*, Theodore Sizer describes the ethos of an all-too-typical high school classroom, in which the ethos is one of divided expectations.[3] Horace, a middle-aged teacher, has struck an unstated but clearly understood bargain with those students who, for a variety of reasons, have little interest in doing the work of the classroom. Horace will work hard to teach those who choose to learn. He will let the others slip by with passing grades if they do not hassle him, if they do not bother the serious students and his efforts to teach them. Everyone passes, but only some learn.

In another recent book, Tracy Kidder's *Among School Children*, we see a very different ethos.[4] This book is an account of one year in the life of a classroom, the fifth grade of a school serving the poor in a small western Massachusetts city. The teacher, Chris Zajac, is a fiercely dedicated woman who is in many ways the opposite of Horace. She is all over the classroom, challenging, probing, and encouraging her students. Each of her students is more than known by her; each seems to become a project for her. She will not ease up, even on the weakest, most distracted, and most unconcerned students. Even in the poorest and most hostile students, she will not let the light go out.

From her opening speech to the class to the hugs on the last day of the school year, Chris Zajac works on the ethos of her class, an environment of attitudes and expectations, rules and procedures, ideas and sentiments. At first her students just passively observe her or seem unaffected. But gradually she and the ethos she has created begin to affect them. It does not affect all of them right away or to the same degree. But Chris Zajac generates a set of expectations, a serious work outlook, and a transforming spirit that reaches and changes her students.

The ethos Chris creates in her classroom, while clearly having academic outcomes, is a moral ethos. She demands respect from her students—respect for her, for one another, and for themselves. She expects them to keep promises, to do their work, and to do it well. If they break their promises, there are consequences, for example, no recess, staying after school, a call to their parents. The same is true of incivility and other breaches of good discipline. She expects them to act with respect toward other students. She rewards her students' academic successes and improved behavior. She wins some battles and loses others. There are good days, and there are bad weeks. At the end of her year with them, her 180 days of harassing, praising, confronting, surprising, and challenging them, many of her students are strikingly changed. Some are not. There have been no dramatic turning points, no critical incidents where the scales fell from her students' eyes. The demands and expectations she has imposed have been accepted and taken to heart.

Teachers like Chris Zajac, however, are rare. The majority of teachers do not share her sense of empowerment. They do not believe they have the authority to be so large a force in their students' lives. In fairness, we should note that Chris taught in an elementary school where she monitored only 27 or 28 pupils throughout a whole day. On the other hand, Sizer's Horace taught in a departmentalized high school and was responsible for 100 to 150 pupils per day. His pupils were also older, and, presumably, less impressionable, than Chris's. We cannot make direct comparisons between the two situations.

In a significant study of one high school math teacher, Jaime Escalante, Jay Matthews demonstrates that many high school teachers are prone to underestimate the educational possibilities around them.[5] Escalante was also the subject of the biographical film *Stand And Deliver*. Matthews shows how Escalante's intense caring and demand for high performance from students paid off in their achievements and renewed self-confidence.

Some teachers in departmentalized schools use another tactic to gratify their aspirations for more morally founded student-adult contacts by advising clubs or other student activities or coaching athletic teams. These organizations share many of the characteristics of the self-contained classroom. Many of our suggestions that might seem to be aimed at elementary school teachers can easily be adapted to junior high and high school clubs, teams, and similar activities.

Educational sociologist Gerald Grant has written penetratingly about the transformation of the American teacher in *The World We Created at Hamilton*

High.[6] Grant's research shows how a high school was changed from 1953 to 1985. More to the point, he shows how the experience of being a teacher or a student in high school differed from one five-year period to the next. What Grant has captured in his study is the modification of some American schools. At the beginning of the period involved, many high schools were relatively intimate institutions, infused with local values—positive and negative, functional and dysfunctional. Gradually, they became increasingly bureaucratized and centralized institutions. Most recently, they have been infused with national, even global, values that too frequently reflect the will of highly vocal special-interest groups.

Grant points out in particular how the existential experience of being a teacher, especially in a high school, was fundamentally different at various times during the period he studied. Many teachers and administrators have changed from believing they were special people—enriching, civilizing, humanizing, and continuing the work of parents and the community—to feeling like professionals merely fulfilling certain prescribed tasks in a contractual exchange of services. Teaching once seemed an honored profession, motivated by interest in helping others. Now it is a career that treats term papers, tests, and students as a modern equivalent of piecework. In this transformation from teacher to educational technician, the teacher's moral role has been obscured.

This new legalistic and bureaucratic ethos has altered the relationship between student and teacher in a basic way. The change has engendered an emphasis on established procedures, grievance systems, student rights, and contractual obligations. One example is the tone that resembles a labor-management relationship among teachers, administrators, and school boards, which has been a by-product of the rise of activist teachers' associations and unions. Another example is the prevalence of rights-oriented student handbooks, as discussed in chapter 4, that erode the authority of the teacher and encourage an adversarial relationship between student and teacher. Often, these teacher contracts and student handbooks are silent on the responsibilities of people— children and adults—as members of a community, a shared space of common purpose. They say little about the members' moral responsibilities to the community of which they are all part. All too often, little is asked in terms of a moral obligation, so little is given.

What we need is to revitalize or re-create the moral ethos of classrooms. All teachers must be infused with the sense of moral authority possessed by Chris Zajac and Jaime Escalante. We need to reinvigorate teachers with the idealism and compassion that originally led so many to enter the profession but has gradually eroded over the years. This is the task of teacher education, of the school board, of parents, of the administrators, and of senior teachers. Recognizing and acting on one's moral authority is also the responsibility of each individual teacher.

Of course, many teachers now possess moral authority. However, many others have grown up within our contemporary contractual-legalistic ethos. Such teachers often lack understanding about their moral authority and ethical responsibilities. They do not appreciate that they are selected representatives of the community and share with parents the responsibility for the proper formation of their students' habits and moral values. While this larger sense of their role is missing, it is not far from the surface. Indeed, it is built into the very nature of being an effective teacher. The teacher's sense of moral authority and role of creator of a moral ethos in the classroom are inherent in the job. They come with the territory.

Toward Creating a Moral Ethos in the Classroom

Much of this book is about establishing a stronger, more wholesome ethos, one that contrasts with the loose, low standards and self-oriented tone currently permeating many of our classrooms. Making allowances for the developmental level of students and the specific school situation, we suggest that classroom teachers—or in high schools, the sponsors of pupils' clubs and teams—should

1. continually remind all pupils, parents, and colleagues, through mottos, memos, meetings, posters, and the like, that education is fundamentally a moral enterprise and encourage that attitude to penetrate all aspects of classroom and personal life.

2. encourage each student to develop or adopt a personal motto and strive to live up to it. For example, "Don't wait to be a great adult. Be a great student—today!"

3. from the first classes early in the year establish a spirit of high standards and serious purpose. "You are going to accomplish great things this year. We are going to make this class something truly special!"

4. design your classroom environment to reflect the high purpose and moral goals of the class. Put up pictures and other reminders of those goals and ideals.

5. give individual students and the class clear academic and moral goals to achieve. Regularly keep them aware of their progress towards those goals. Publicly and privately celebrate their achievements and identify instances when there is a failure to make sufficient progress or fulfill commitments.

6. help the class earn a sense of being special. Find something they can take pride in, something that makes them stand out from the crowd. Help them to see themselves as a family, as a tight community. For instance, have the class take on an out-of-school project, such as regular assistance to an elderly couple who need help with getting groceries, house chores, raking leaves, and simple repairs. Or have them plant trees to help the environment, volunteer to clean up part of the school grounds, or hold a car wash and donate their earnings to a charity.

7. develop a sense of connection among the individual students. Make them feel special ties to their classmates, ties that develop from coming to the aid of one another and working together on shared goals in both academics and sports.

8. place pictures of outstanding people on the walls of the classroom and read aloud to students about their achievements, so these portraits teach more fully.

The ethos of a classroom directs much of this action. It is an intangible spirit that tells students what is important and what is not. Ethos is driven by certain ideas, and these ideas structure how teachers and students behave. Two concepts, one rather new and the other quite old, illustrate ethos-in-action: self-esteem and diligence.

Self-Esteem—A Dead End?

Not too long ago our schools reflected the widespread cultural and religious belief that self-love was a perversion and humility was a prized virtue. The social critic Allan Bloom wrote about a man who had recently been released from prison, where through psychotherapy he had "found his identify and learned to like himself." Bloom said of this man, "a generation earlier he would have found God and learned to despise himself."[7] Our schools are permeated with a term that is only a slight variation of self-love: self-esteem. *Self-esteem* is such a slippery concept that it is hard to identify any generally acceptable and clear definition. Perhaps it is fair to say the term connotes a strong sense of self-worth or pride, without such regard being conditioned on any noteworthy achievement.

Too many educators treat the pursuit of pupil self-esteem as self-evidently meritorious. Its current legitimacy is partly due to the efforts of the American psychologist Abraham Maslow. From the 1950s through the 1980s Maslow labored to convince social scientists and educators of the importance of gaining self-esteem.[8] He has surely succeeded beyond his wildest dreams with educators.

Rita Kramer described interviews she conducted at twenty schools of education around the country.[9] She found that the cultivation of pupils' self-esteem was the dominant educational theory she encountered. Whether Maslow's ideas and the adoption of self-esteem as a goal have actually helped children acquire a healthy attitude toward themselves, however, is the issue.

Some psychologists have argued that young people who think little of themselves and do not see themselves advancing in life are also students who have not done well in school and are not currently performing well. In other words, low self-esteem relates in some way to poor performance. These authorities have urged all of us, young and old alike, to learn to like ourselves more and to be our own best friend. Educational psychologists have made the building of self-concept and self-esteem an essential pillar of teacher education. For instance, William W. Purkey, author of *Inviting School Success*, urges teachers to learn the teaching skills of invitational learning in order to encourage students to experience feelings of positive self-worth.[10] Purkey defines an invitation as "a summary description of messages—verbal and nonverbal, formal and informal—continuously transmitted to students with the intention of informing them that they are responsible, able, and valuable." Purkey's writings echo the ideas of Maslow: real learning cannot occur if a student has a poor self-concept. Equivalent positions are also held by some other psychologists, such as Arthur Combs (the teacher as facilitator), Carl Rogers (learner-centered teaching), and Thomas Gordon (Teacher Effectiveness Training).

Ironically, this appealing theory lacks serious research support. For instance, in January 1990 a mathematics test was administered by Educational Testing Services to a sample of fifth-graders from six countries, including the United States. The Americans' test scores were the lowest of the six countries. The Koreans were first. The test also asked pupils to say whether they felt they would be "good at mathematics in high school." Of the Americans, 68% said "Yes," while only 26% of the high-scoring Koreans gave that reply.[11]

Another international study compared parents' opinions with their children's academic performance.[12] Of American mothers, 91% thought their children's schools were doing an "excellent" or "good" job educating their children. We assume this means they felt their children were doing a fine job of learning. This was more than double the rates of satisfaction among Chinese (42%) and Japanese (39%) mothers. Yet the average measured academic performance of the Chinese and Japanese children greatly exceeded that of the Americans. Another research report was developed for the California State Commission on Self-Esteem. The commission was chosen by state legislators sympathetic to the self-esteem movement. The commission concluded that no notable proven connection has been found between self-esteem—however the term is defined—and other desirable personal characteristics goals, such as improved academic learning.[13] Finally, a narrative written by a friend of both Maslow and Rogers discloses that, later in life, both became very disillusioned with their earlier pronouncements and the popularized by-products. The founders felt that their premises had been unduly optimistic and were typically applied in exaggerated fashions.[14]

Despite such impressive data, many teachers have increasingly seen the raising of students' self-esteem as a primary responsibility. It is also evident that many parents have been infected with this perspective—witness the simplistic optimism many American parents have about their children's mediocre academic performance. Undoubtedly, many children are plagued by self-doubt and a poor opinion of themselves. The reasons for this condition are multiple. Poor performance has many causes, few of which yield to simplistic solutions. Nevertheless, many in the self-esteem movement tell us the answer to this problem is to attack head-on to try to give self-esteem to students. Such an attack usually involves removing all elements of school and classroom life that are in some way related to poor self-esteem, such as tests, grades, and demanding assignments. Unfortunately, by removing these elements, we also remove the tools that provide students with both realistic feedback about their efficacy and the knowledge necessary to improve their performance.

We must recognize that all wholesome human life is ultimately social. Social life inevitably subjects us to certain stress; we have aspirations, disappointments, and rebuffs. Sociologist Robert Everhart and his colleagues studied several schools that gave priority to directly enhancing pupil self-esteem. Pupils were given a broad choice among school activities so that they could avoid disappointment and low self-esteem. The levels of academic learning in the schools were quite low. However, the pupils found their undemanding schools relatively satisfying—a good place to spend time. Ultimately, the researchers were critical of the schools' efficacy:

[The schools] gave minimum consideration to the social context in which individuals live—the competing beliefs, actions and ideologies individuals must confront. This created various degrees of doubt and insecurity among the graduating students. . . . Without some complementary belief about social cohesion and the place of the individual in society, a focus on individual attributes is necessarily incomplete.[15]

In effect, Everhart and his colleagues found that the schools fostered a corrosive form of pupil narcissism—surely a fragile basis for self-esteem.

The self-esteem movement puts a false and infectious pressure on teachers. They are more and more expected to keep students feeling good about themselves. In other eras, teachers were expected to provide pupils with an environment and an educational opportunity to grow and achieve. As a result of that growth and achievement, pupils will be entitled to earn self-esteem.

Diligence—The Alternative to Self-Esteem

The idea of requiring diligence from pupils puts the teeth of many on edge. It has an old-fashioned ring about it. It conjures up visions of small boys clutching quill pens, huddled over large desks assiduously copying in their notebooks. On the other hand, it is a much more worthy and achievable educational goal than self-esteem. If we were to use one word to summarize the reasons for the superior academic performance of so many Asian-American students, that word would be *diligence*.

Creating a classroom where diligence is taught and prized means teaching students how to accomplish challenging tasks. It means instructing them how to focus their attention and energies to accomplish goals. It means setting a great variety of tasks for students in which they can practice perseverance, even when they desire to be doing more immediately satisfying activities. It means, in essence, acquiring the habits traditionally associated with achievement in all fields, whether in school, family life, the arts, sports, business, or the professions. For instance, imagine a student who is careless and casual about academic assignments but willing to spend hours honing a basketball jump shot. That student needs to appreciate how diligence can pay off in the nonathletic spheres of life. This insight may be the most important contribution a teacher could make to such a student.

Many reasons exist why students should learn the habit or virtue of diligence at their school tasks. For one thing, learning how to attack an assignment and see it through makes homework, recitations, and tests less stressful and much more rewarding activities. When students leave school, diligence will lead to certain benefits. Finally, acquiring the virtue of diligence is the royal road to developing true self-esteem.

The mistake of the self-esteem movement is putting the cart before the horse. In a paradoxical way, self-esteem does not yield to a direct assault, that is, efforts to directly ensure students they are valuable. Instead, true self-worth and self-esteem are by-products that come to a student as the secret benefit of working to achieve a goal. In life, true self-esteem is never given; it is earned.

Self-esteem and feeling good about oneself ordinarily follow from the effort of working toward a goal and the achievements, large and small, that result from that effort. The knowledge that we have worked hard and accomplished a task brings a sense of personal satisfaction as a by-product. People who habitually accomplish the tasks presented in life gain a sense of personal effectiveness or worth. Those who regularly fail—or worse, make only a meager effort—receive instead important, life-correcting messages from their environment, corrective messages such as the old naval adage, "Shape up or ship out." Our lack of personal satisfaction and self-esteem is, as often as not, nature's way of trying to get us back on course. Teachers can help students get back on course by giving them advice, offering corrective feedback, restructuring assignments, and helping them acquire the habit of diligence.

STUDENTS' ATTITUDES ABOUT EDUCATION

A fundamental component to being a good and effective student is developing an attitude, a way of envisioning what you are doing and why you are doing it. Attitudes about popular education have changed markedly in recent decades. Historically, extended schooling lasting more than three or four years was possible only for those who could afford it—almost exclusively the sons of royalty and of the relatively wealthy class. As societies gained more security and prosperity, they in turn invested more of that wealth in the education and development of the young.

In the nineteenth and twentieth centuries, the concept of universal education, or education for all citizens, seized the public imagination. This occurred particularly in countries moving toward more democratic forms of government. Among these same countries, one after another began making the spread of schooling a national priority. While there was much social altruism in this expansion of education, there was also a good deal of enlightened self-interest on the part of various nations. In a democracy, a literate and skilled populace made self-government more efficacious.

Over the decades policymakers have become more insistent that children be sent from their homes to local schools earlier in their lives and kept there for longer periods. The starting age for attending school has become lower and lower, with some advocating that all children begin attending some form of school by their third birthday. At the same time, leaving school has been extended during recent decades from age ten to twelve to age sixteen. Some communities now require children to stay in school until their nineteenth birthday or high school graduation. The school day and school year have also gotten longer in duration, taking up more of children's waking hours. Today some educators and lay people are calling for a year-round school calendar. This insistence on students spending more time in school may, at first, have had a salutary effect on the gross national product, in that there has been an increase in the job skills of those educated in our school systems. However, there may have been greater costs, such as the corrosive effect on the classroom as a place of learning.

Consider the attitude of a nineteenth-century ten-year-old, who is able to leave the arduous and boring tasks of the family farm and go to a warm schoolroom with other children of the same age and hear about a larger world over the horizon. That child's attitude is sharply different than that of most modern ten-year-old students.

Perhaps the point can be made by analogy. A generation ago, parents sent children to their room as a form of punishment, especially when they added, "And don't you dare turn on the radio!" Today, those same parents would have to add, "And don't you dare turn on the television set, or the VCR, or your CD player. And you can't use your Walkman or your other tape player. And that means no Nintendo! None of those little hand-held games either. And you can't take the cordless phone into your room. And you can't eat or drink anything from your small refrigerator. No sunbathing, either, and stay out of the Jacuzzi. The only thing you are allowed to turn on is your electric typewriter. And if you use your computer, you have to use it for schoolwork and not those video games! And, yes, you can read. What do you mean, you don't have a book?"

Exaggerated? Yes—but accurate for many and partially true for most students. Being sent to one's room today is a release from close supervision.

For many modern children, going to school means leaving their comfortable home with food and drink at the touch, with electronic media to feed them information and entertainment, and with few, if any, chores to perform. And what do they go to when they enter school?

At school students find the stimulation of friends, but the school environment, relative to home or the street, makes real demands on them. Students are compelled to stay in a particular classroom, and sometimes a particular desk. They are required to follow rules about when and how and to whom they speak. They are expected to cooperate with, listen carefully to, and do the tasks assigned by their teachers—teachers who are a good deal less entertaining than the adults who host their television programs. In addition, they are told to be courteous to fellow students and, in particular, toward their teachers. They are supposed to do this for seven hours a day for half the days of their young lives. Compared with home, school no longer seems the chance for an exciting escape that it offered to the nineteenth-century child. As a result, the attitudes of students have tended to shift. Once a rich opportunity for stimulation, school has become more of an institution that interrupts their pleasure and places demands and constraints on them.

The most frequent criticism of schools by students—and one that continually saps the energies and creative juices of teachers—is the whine, "This is boring." Objectively, the complaint may be accurate. Compared to the cornucopia of diversions and delights that our consumer society offers the young, life in school is boring. When Marshall McLuhan, the media guru of the 1960s, wrote about the information-saturated environment, he quipped that children interrupted their education when they came to school. This was well before the explosion of youth-oriented media marketing efforts. Certainly, modern children interrupt their entertainment when they go to school.

From this pattern, another change in attitude has come. School is no longer something for which students have a sense of responsibility. The prevailing attitude now is, "If you are going to force school on me, I must have my rights!" Regrettably, this attitude is often echoed by the child's parents—and by some educators.

Trying to change this resentful, show-me attitude to one of viewing education as something to live up to is no easy task. However, such changes are crucial for the educative process to take root. It is decisive, too, for the child's development as a mature adult. Teachers can rarely change students' attitudes by making only verbal assaults such as, "Education is a privilege. You ought to be thankful you are in school!" The teacher needs stronger and more multifarious medicine than this.

In the same way that different medicines work with different patients, so, too, with teachers and students. Some students respond to gentle prodding, others to positive attention in the form of pep talks, and still others to punishment. Changing pupil attitudes is usually much more difficult than changing behavior. Indeed, since an attitude is an internal state of mind, it is technically invisible. What teachers actually observe are student behaviors, which reflect attitudes. We essentially change bad attitudes by changing the behaviors through which they are typically revealed. In fact, the most efficient way to change attitudes is to change behavior. The attitudes will catch up.

We suggest that teachers

1. teach students about attitudes, how they affect behavior, and how they can be changed and modified.

2. make it clear to students that their attitudes count. Tell them that while teachers cannot literally see an uncooperative or negative attitude, they can see antipathetic behavior—words, tone of voice, gestures, postures, modes of dress. Tell students that such behavior will not be tolerated.

3. recognize and reward individual and group behaviors that reflect positive attitudes. Give verbal support and group rewards, such as a popcorn party, for the display of appropriate behaviors, for example, when the class shows excellent conduct or when attendance is perfect.

4. practice empathy. Teach students to understand and interpret the conduct and attitudes of others and appreciate others' hardships and disadvantages. Use literature and the pupils' own experiences to deepen this compassion.

The great bulk of what is written about schools and teaching has to do with the intellectual domain—so-called book learning. Next is the physical domain—the physical vigor, well-being, and development of our students. Schools formally address this aspect of our human nature through the physical education curriculum, through which the school addresses the requirements students have to grow well and develop soundly. Furthermore, concern for the child's physical nature permeates the school. Temperatures are set and maintained for the students' comfort. The lighting is arranged so they see well and their eyes are preserved. Desks are designed with their physical characteristics in mind and are adjusted as they grow. Schools have fire and tornado drills. The need to attend to the students' physical safety and well-being has caused many schools to disallow smoking anywhere in the building, including the teachers' lounge. Finally, there is the moral domain: learning about right and wrong. Unfortunately, in recent years, we have been less conscious of and less direct in dealing with the ethical nature of children and their need for moral safety.

The teachers' conceptions of their own multidomain responsibilities are critical in this matter. All of us must reemphasize the moral nature of the classroom.

Practices and Policies

1. Informally discuss the topic of moral authority, perhaps using the examples of Zajac and Escalante, with several colleagues or teachers in training. To what extent do the teachers they have known possess this moral authority?

2. Part of the chapter discusses student diligence. To what degree do you think you emphasize effective work/study habits in your students? What habits do you emphasize when you teach your students how to work or study? Do you publicly praise students and the class when they have been diligent in completing a task?

3. With several teachers in the same grade level, department, or physical area of the school, compile a list of feasible projects for your students that would contribute to their sense of feeling special.

4. Encourage faculty members to share ideas with their colleagues on improving the moral ethos in the classroom and school. On the bulletin board in the faculty room, post teachers' suggestions for improving the ethos in school. Implement suggestions that are feasible, giving credit to the teachers who suggest the ideas. During faculty meetings, allow five minutes or more for teachers to present a proposal for improving school ethos or to share what has worked for them in the classroom.

References

1. Etzioni, A. (1989, December 17). Fixing the schools is not enough. *New York Times*.

2. Fullinwider, R. F. (1990). The ends of political and moral education. Unpublished manuscript. Cambridge, MA: Harvard University.

3. Sizer, T. (1985). *Horace's compromise*. Boston: Houghton Mifflin.

4. Kidder, T. (1989). *Among school children*. Boston: Houghton Mifflin.

5. Matthews, J. (1988). *Escalante, the best teacher in America*. New York: Holt.

6. Grant, G. (1988). *The world we created at Hamilton High School*. Cambridge, MA: Harvard University Press.

7. Bloom, A. (1987). *The closing of the American mind*. New York: Simon & Schuster.

8. Maslow, A. H. (1970). *Motivation and personality* (2nd ed.). New York: Harper & Row.

9. Kramer, R. (1991). *Ed school follies: The miseducation of the American teacher*. New York: Collier/Free Press.

10. Purkey, W. W. (1978). *Inviting school success*. Belmont, CA: Wadsworth, p. 3.

11. Stevenson, H. W. (1987, October). America's math problems. *Educational Leadership, 45*(2), 5–6.

12. Stevenson, H. W. (1987, Summer). The Asian advantage: The case of mathematics. *American Educator, 11*, p. 30.

13. Mecca, A., Smelser, N., & Vasconcellos, J. (Eds.). (1989). *The social importance of self-esteem*. Berkeley, CA: University of California Press.

14. Coulson, W. (1991, January). Pop psychology of the sixties. *Religious Life*, pp. 3–5.

15. Everhard, R. (1985). Feeling good about oneself. *Sociology of Education, 58*(4), 158.

CHAPTER 6

Teachers as Moral Educators

Example is the school of mankind, and they will learn at no other.

—Edmund Burke

The great English parliamentarian and philosopher Edmund Burke wrote often about the importance of moral models for the young. He also anticipated many of the findings of contemporary psychologists and researchers, particularly learning theorists like Albert Bandura[1] and Robert Biehler.[2] Much of what we learn is by imitation or modeling. The younger we are, the stronger the impact of models on our personalities.

Children have one primary aim, one that operates both consciously and unconsciously. That aim is to be an adult, to grow up. This is their project, their work in life. The adults who are near and dear to them are the ones they will emulate. If these adults are respectful and caring, the children will try to be respectful and caring. If the adults are self-serving and lazy, the children will be self-serving and lazy. This principle explains why an overwhelming number of states require evidence of good character in individuals who apply for teaching licenses.

THE MORAL TEACHER

Teachers have always been expected to be good examples to the young. Special circumstances of modern life make this aspect of the teacher's work all the more crucial. The comments of sociologist James S. Coleman on changes in the American family clearly indicate these circumstances.[3] Coleman observed that two generations ago the father left the home to work, and that one generation ago the mother, too, left. His point is that, until well into the twentieth century, the majority of parents worked within sight of their children.

A century ago the father of a family was generally a farmer, who worked, ate, and lived in the midst of his family. And even as the proportions of farming families gradually declined, many urban families centered their lives around family-based businesses, such as retail stores. The mother was also working in the family unit, performing farm chores, housework, and food preparation. But that changed with our modern economy, when fathers began to work at factories or in offices. Gradually, the same trend afflicted mothers. In 1970, 33% of women with school-age children worked outside the home full- or part-time. In 1980, the percentage had increased to 51% and by 1990, to 67%. By 1995, according to estimates, women will make up 50% of the American work force. By the year 2000, 80% of American women with children will be working outside the home.[4]

With children rarely contributing to family income and parents working outside the home and busy and tired when they are home, parent-child contacts are different than in earlier periods. Related to this is the fact that parents do not have as much to teach their children as in the past. Many of the skills important to previous generations—how to care for animals, sew a dress, keep a fire going through the night—have little meaning to children who will compete for a livelihood in a high-tech culture. Further, most children live in small nuclear families with few siblings, and these small families are increasingly mobile. Children often grow up without strong ties to relatives in their extended family: grandparents, uncles, aunts, and cousins who have traditionally held great interest in the development of their family members.

All of this increases the prominence of the teacher's role in the lives of young people. For some students, their teachers are a major source of stability. As mentioned in the previous chapter, children are starting school earlier, spending more time in the classroom, and staying in school longer through their teens. Young Americans are in the presence of teachers for more time than ever before.

Apart from the simple matter of presence, there are many other reasons why teachers have a powerful impact as models. Teachers are the designated leaders of their students. This heightens their potential for moral impact, whether positive or negative. Teachers have immediate control over the lives of children. They give out rewards and punishments. They assign tasks in school and tasks to be performed at home. They give grades to evaluate the students' tangible work as well as their effort. They decide who goes to recess and who goes to the next grade. They have power over the lives of children. This power focuses the attention of students on the teacher in a very direct way, but it also has another effect. Students examine the power as an entity in itself. Few parents or teachers have failed to hear emotional complaints and sometimes tearful sobs about real or imagined misbehavior of teachers:

"She's unfair!"

"My teacher gave a surprise test that really counts!"

"He is always playing favorites."

This is not to say that children's complaints are always justified. However, whether the complaints are justified or not, teachers must have the perspective to confront, if not moderate, such objections. All of us are called to escape from what the late novelist Walker Percy called the "great suck of self" to learn to be generous, engaged citizens. Educators, though, have a special responsibility to display such maturity: their unique relationship to children. They must be moral models. However, we cannot simply say, "You are to be a moral model, a moral exemplar." This is too unsettling for most of us. For some teachers, the responsibility is paralyzing. For others, it conjures up a vision of some sort of sainthood, secular or religious. They fear this vision must commit them to a role of complete concern for others and total self-denial. Still others worry about being instant fountains of ethical wisdom, a sort of moral Delphic oracle. Such a vision may explain the uneasiness and suspicion that many teachers feel about this topic. In reality, however, the matter is much simpler, more fundamental, and closer to the ground.

Characteristics of the Moral Teacher

Teachers need to be, first of all, people who are clearly concerned with the good of others, particularly their students. This does not necessarily mean they must be sweet and obliging to students. Some excellent teachers are hard-driving task-masters. They come to class every day "loaded for bear" and expect students to come the same way. These teachers may never gush over how much they love their students. However, the students recognize their love; if not immediately, they know it after some distance on the experience.

Second, teachers need to show their morality by their actions, especially seemingly small actions such as

+ presenting well-planned, enthusiastically taught classes.

+ getting homework and test papers corrected and back to students promptly.

+ not discussing the conduct of students or fellow teachers in a petty fashion, i.e., gossiping.

+ carrying out small acts of consideration for others, such as cleaning the board for the next teacher coming into the room or taking a wad of used chewing gum out of the water fountain.

+ planning a surprise birthday party for a fellow teacher, the principal, or the secretary.

+ going the extra mile for a student who is lost or struggling.

Teachers, like everyone else, are called to humility. Still, it is important that students recognize moral gestures and civic actions in their teachers. It is good for students to know that a teacher volunteers time at a homeless shelter or is a fund-raiser for the church.

Being a moral model is not waiting for a great dilemma to come along: "Should I go out on strike or not?" or "Should I threaten to resign my position because the superintendent is letting go an outstanding teacher?" Such grand gestures have their place. Indeed, many of our greatest teachers have taught us by their ultimate sacrifices, for instance, Socrates taking the hemlock or Christ accepting the cross. However, the good example we are speaking of is much more an everyday matter. It is giving one's diligent attention to teaching and to the small demands of our professional life by those around us—students, other teachers, administrators, parents, and staff.

The Morality of Craft

In the novel *The Way of All Flesh*, Samuel Butler wrote, "Every man's work, whether it be literature or music or pictures or architecture or anything else, is always a portrait of himself." The primary moral responsibility of any workers is to strive to be good at their craft—in effect, to be diligent about their principal life responsibility. Surgeons are morally bound to be as proficient at their craft as possible. Shoemakers have a moral duty to repair shoes as well as they can. Auto workers are ethically bound to make the very best car of which they are capable. Students are morally bound to live up to the demands of parents, community, and school. This principle is particularly binding on teachers. Their work is integral to the growth of children and the progress of society. First and foremost, teachers must do their work well. In a later chapter, we will discuss the expectations that administrators, typically principals, should have for teachers. In the following points, however, we describe expectations that teachers should have for themselves. There is obviously some overlap between these two perspectives. But truly dedicated teachers should often engage themselves beyond the expectations of their supervisors.

The Hard Worker. Educators who are moral work hard at their job. They know that they teach students diligence by example. They always come to class prepared, their materials are the best they can find, and their classes represent the best possible mix of application and imagination. They give students demanding assignments that stretch them and get them more involved in the subject. Moral educators think about where their students are, where they ought to be going, and what they need to get them there. As much as possible, such teachers try to be conscious of the individual needs, potentials, and learning styles of students. There is little wasted time in such task-oriented classrooms. Students feel their teacher's concern that they grow and excel. They recognize the teacher has high standards, and they believe they can, and will, acquire these high standards too. They feel the teacher's insistent but concerned pressure to do their best. Moral teachers never work harder than when they sense students are slipping away, drifting, or thinking of themselves as nonstudents.

Skilled artisan teachers are highly involved in, and identified with, their work. How well they teach and how they are developing as teachers is never far from their minds.

The Continuous Learner. Skilled artisan teachers demonstrate their devotion to their craft through their commitment to improvement. They continuously strive to improve, to learn new competencies, and to gain greater understanding of what they teach. They talk about the craft of teaching with other teachers, read professional journals, and seize on opportunities to advance their own professional training. They regularly take refresher courses. They try to stimulate professional development courses and workshops for themselves and fellow teachers. When training is unavailable, they form study groups with other educators. They see themselves on a journey to be as good as they can become, knowing all the time that they can only approach mastery of the craft. The motivation for their drive for mastery comes from many sources, but one is their sense of responsibility to try to excel. They live out the slogan of the teacher as continuous learner.

Dedication to the Outcome. Like fine artisans, moral teachers are attentive to the final product: student learning. It is critical that students show significant change in the right direction. Moral teachers recognize that learning is often difficult and that it takes great effort for some students, effort that many are reluctant to give. These teachers are not distracted by the need to win popularity or keep all the children feeling good all the time. They will risk the students' displeasure in the short term, because they have in mind larger stakes with longer time lines.

They are attentive to the emotional climate in the classroom, but are not captives to it. They make the class into a community, not primarily a pleasant social community or simply a place for students to pass time, but a community of learners, a community with a purpose. Their students feel special because of what they have accomplished. They are proud to be among their teacher's products.

Talking about the morality of craft runs counter to the spirit of our age of feel-good psychology and the relaxed attitudes too evident in many parts of the American workplace. But this fierce sense of craft is exactly what is demanded of teachers. Think back to the teachers we described in chapter 5: Chris Zajac, the teacher in Tracey Kidder's *Among School Children*, and Jaime Escalante, the subject of Jay Matthews' portrayal.

All teachers need to be good at their craft to fulfill the social requirements of the work and realize themselves as fully developed adults. However, there is an even more important reason for stressing excellence: the impact of their example on students.

Membership in a Guild. Artisan teachers are not solitary workers, plying their trade in isolation from others. They are connected to others, and not only to students. They maintain a special connection with the teachers in their immediate group—the teachers in the building, particularly those at the same grade level or department. They share a responsibility to carefully structure the curriculum and its implementation. They are members of a school faculty, and they take their responsibilities as faculty members seriously. They work under the supervision of administrators and imbue those relationships with high ethical standards, rather than an antagonistic labor-management spirit. For instance, they do not view their allotment of sick days as days of rest that are owed to them.

Further, teachers as artisans see themselves as part of a professional group, whether or not they are members of a teachers association or union. If they do belong to such a group, they work actively to help the group reach its highest goals. They feel obligated to improve and enhance the quality of the profession. They are interested in teacher education, taking on student teachers and others learning how to teach. They participate in the activities of their professional group, taking their turn representing fellow teachers in professional endeavors. In all these guild-like activities, though, they are inspired by professional ideals rather than by the narrow, self-serving issue of the moment. They believe that the best interests of the teaching profession are those that advance the quality of education for children, and they act on that belief.

Some may be troubled with the concept of teachers as craftspeople. Like a craft, teaching involves doing: taking responsibility and control for a process and fashioning something that was not there before. Teaching is a craft because it entails skills, knowledge, and an understanding of the materials—the students—being fashioned. But along with this sense of craft teachers must be especially conscientious. The philosopher, Thomas Green, describes this commitment:

> To possess a conscience of craft is to have cultivated the capacity for self-congratulation or deep satisfaction at something well done, shame at slovenly work, and even embarrassment at carelessness. . . . It is what impels us to lay aside slovenly and sloppy work simply because of what it is—slovenly and sloppy.[5]

THE TEACHER AS DIRECT SOURCE
OF MORAL COMMUNICATION

Children and young adults often lose their moral way. They steal someone's property, cheat on a test, or spread a lie about another student. On such occasions, they need direct guidance about what to do. By *direct guidance*, we simply mean that some authoritative person should remind students what is right, and, in a firm but kindly manner, tell them to go and do it—and to stop doing wrong. Much of our important moral learning does and should proceed at this simple level. One need not apply psychotherapy. Ideally, the young will get quick and sound direction from their parents, who are their primary moral educators. But for a variety of reasons, this is not always possible. They might need help right away and their parents are not available, or the facts of the incident might be unknown to their parents. Being available for this kind of help has traditionally been part of the teacher's work.

One of the authors recalls an incident when he was in high school and got into trouble at home. He found himself in an ugly quarrel with his older sister. He lost his temper (because, he recalls, he was losing the argument) and struck her. Having broken two important family rules, he knew he was in trouble. He fled the house and, after stewing for an hour or so, sought help from a teacher. It was a teacher he did not even like very much, but a teacher who was available at the moment of need. The teacher gave him very calming and sane advice: "You already know you made a big mistake. Go home, say you are sorry, and face the music."

One reason for telling this story is because of its ordinariness just a few decades ago. The teacher was not surprised when he was asked for counsel. No one thought it was unusual. Whether we knew Latin or not, we all knew about *in loco parentis*. As students we knew that in a special way, we belonged to our teachers and, equally important, they belonged to us. We expected them to be concerned about our behavior in and out of school. We expected them to be attentive to the deficiencies of our character, angry at lapses in honesty, and nagging about our laziness. We knew that this was part of their work. And, whenever we thought about it seriously, we were glad they cared.

There are still many teachers who communicate this attitude of "you belong to me and I to you." One of the authors recently heard a teacher say to the class about a forthcoming assembly, "I don't care if the rest of the school raises the roof. You will sit there quietly!" And they did.

Unfortunately, such "you belong to me" teachers are not as common as they used to be. Many teachers simply do not feel they have the support of administrators and parents to feel secure in being moral educators, particularly in such a direct way. Some teachers feel rebuffed and rebuked and cannot rise to this responsibility. A few believe there is no consensus on values or even any basic virtues, so they avoid direct moral education.

Other teachers say this direct response to requests for moral advice is the job of guidance counselors. However, our field work convinces us that many counselors believe they have no special training for this work. Furthermore, in the current intellectual climate, they want to avoid involvement in students' moral problems. They are willing to help students adjust (whatever this means), minus morality. They will help with scheduling courses of study or selecting work or college goals. They are not willing, however, to respond to a student's requests for help with a moral problem, such as helping untangle a family feud, or involvement with alcohol, drugs, or promiscuous sexuality. For many educators, the role of moral counselor has simply slipped off the screen.

In 1990 Harvard psychologist Robert Coles released an extensive study of the moral character of children.[6] His research team interviewed students in grades 4 through 12 across the United States. They posed more than 90 serious questions (e.g., Do you believe in God? How do you decide what is right and what is wrong?) to over 5,000 young people. Among the many findings, the study revealed that children think about issues of right and wrong in very different ways. Coles' team identified five basic orientations. To an important degree, differences in values were related to the different ages of the respondents. However, there were also some notable differences among children in the same age group. Also, children from economically poor families reported greater pressure than other children to engage in immoral behavior, such as taking drugs, disobeying authority, or joining a gang. Coles characterized the typical American student as lacking a moral compass, a clear and firm way to deal with moral issues.

One of the most troubling aspects of the study dealt with where students would turn for advice on a moral problem. Of the high school students in the study, 58% reported that, when confronted with a personal moral problem, they would be most likely to seek advice from another teen-ager. This is additional evidence for what sociologists have been describing for years: the powerful influence of the peer group in the lives of teenagers and the corresponding decline in the influence of traditional forces, such as parents, community leaders, and others. Only 7% said they would consult a teacher for moral advice, and only 3% would seek advice from members of the clergy. The researchers referred to this as the *wallpaper factor*. The term suggests that teachers and clergy play a peripheral role in teenagers' moral lives. These findings are especially disturbing since teenagers must cope with the moral problems connected to their new independence. Although independence is an important part of their progress toward maturity, they should not make decisions about issues such as drinking, drugs, sexuality, and life goals without adult counsel. We do not suggest that teachers become the primary moral counselors of the young. We simply propose that teachers should be more ready and able to respond to students' calls for help. Administrators and parents should encourage and support this involvement, and teachers should solicit their advice in complex situations.

Ineffective Instructors

There are innumerable reasons why so many teachers are so unimportant as sources of moral guidance to so many teenagers. One simple reason is that many teachers are ill-prepared to provide pupils with moral instruction. This deficiency, in turn, has a number of causes. Let us consider some of these.

In recent decades, the teacher's role has been defined as an essentially technical activity. This emphasis has led to the erosion of the teacher's moral authority. Educators must take substantial responsibility for this development. It is often stressed in educational literature that the effective teacher uses "wait time" and brings about high rates of student "time on task."[7] The teacher should be largely concerned with conveying information and skills. The dominant professional literature of the 1970s and 1980s dealt with "effective schools" and "effective teachers."[8] In this influential corpus of research and writing, "effectiveness" seems unrelated to fostering moral and character education. Teachers regularly report going through years of teacher education and inservice education without ever being told, first, that they have moral responsibilities, or, second, how to fulfill them. In a recent study of thirty middle school and junior high school teachers, Alice Lanckton found that not a single teacher recalled being told about the teacher's role or responsibility as a moral educator or developer of good character.[9]

This lack of support has been aggravated by the typical portraits of teachers on television. The medium relentlessly presents teachers in an unsympathetic light: weak, disorganized individuals putting on false fronts for students. Such inept people can barely handle the problems of life themselves, let alone give ethical guidance to others. On the other hand, such distorted stereotypes are similar to the picture of most adults communicated to the young through the popular media.

On some occasions, authorities have licensed teachers to conduct moral education. But these teachers often receive ambiguous how-to advice, which undercuts their efficacy.

For instance, there are the advocates of values clarification, an approach to moral education that we believe has serious flaws. These advocates, particularly Sidney Simon, see the teacher's efforts to inculcate ethical principles and habits as wrongheaded and failing. In their place, Simon maintains, teachers should use morally neutral methods. Children should discover moral truths through natural interactions with other children. Whether its advocates realize it or not, this approach separates students from collective human wisdom about the moral realm. Among other losses, students would lose the moral and ethical principles necessary to maintain a democratic state. The approach compels students ethically to swim for themselves before coming to know the Great Tradition.

Another source of ambivalence comes from the proponents of the dilemmas approach to moral education.[10] These theorists urge subjecting pupils to a heavy diet of moral dilemmas so they can rise to what the proponents call "higher levels of moral reasoning." In their view, the purpose of moral education is mainly to teach students how to deal with hard and improbable cases. For example, if your wife is dying, is it right to steal drugs to help save her? If you are on an overloaded lifeboat, who should be forced to leave first? The dilemma proponents recommend confronting pupils with hypothetical issues that we believe might have troubled Socrates or the Supreme Court. The proponents almost seem affected with a form of hubris. They believe they can teach pupils to solve problems that perplexed the wisest authorities of earlier societies. But the same proponents call it "indoctrination" to stress everyday concerns such as civility, duty, and other basic virtues.

Proponents of the dilemmas approach also undermine the great tradition by their hostility to the concept of direct moral education. They believe teachers should be moral bystanders. They object to the idea of a teacher vigorously promoting honesty and demanding it from students or directly teaching the necessity of tolerance for minority views or that each of us has a duty to our country. Such positions are labeled "miseducative." They are derisively dismissed as the "bag-of-virtues approach." The formal research relating to such specious contentions has been considered in earlier chapters. At this point, however, the logic of the contentions invites direct examination.

Opponents of direct moral education or indoctrination do accept the view that teachers can be authorities in certain areas of knowledge. For instance, such opponents may agree that teachers can make definitive statements about poetry, the composition of matter, irregular French verbs, or algebraic factoring. However, these critics balk at giving teachers authority regarding basic moral and ethical matters. They contend that the teacher and the school must shed their authority and pretend that adults have no acquired moral knowledge. They apparently believe that the institutions of our society have no moral wisdom or moral truth to pass on to the young. Further, the critics do not distinguish between being an authority and behaving in an authoritarian manner.

Preaching—Often Important and Acceptable

The topic of direct moral instruction by teachers naturally leads to the question of preaching. For many readers, the word *preaching* may have strong negative connotations. It may transmit the image of people in authority repetitiously and unimaginatively badgering subordinates with arbitrary opinions. Such tactics are usually self-defeating. However, it is important to recognize that the word *preaching* has far broader significance. As we will see, there is both good and bad preaching, and we should carefully examine the distinction. Without such an examination, we will be unable to engage in good preaching. As teachers, having constraints against good preaching will seriously disarm our arsenal for moral instruction.

It is true that adolescents sometimes talk derisively about preaching: "Don't preach to me." Adults, however, should display more sophistication. They should realize that adolescent remarks sometimes amount to just that: casual, uninformed remarks by young people who have a lot to learn. Adults themselves should be held to more rigorous intellectual standards. Preaching is one form of oratory, a mode of communication. There is a long tradition of complex and profound preaching. It has always been, and always will be, one of several important ways of communicating moral ideas. The Gettysburg Address was a form of preaching. So were the Declaration of Independence, the preamble to the United States Constitution, and Martin Luther King, Jr.'s *I Have a Dream* speech. The list includes innumerable other powerful and noble statements of principle and aspiration. As in all fields of communication, there are adept and inept examples of preaching, just as there are clever and sterile jokes or good and poor Socratic dialogues. Ironically, people who deliver blanket condemnations of preaching often are inspired by what they hear in church, at political rallies, or in school classrooms. However, current educational orthodoxy, perhaps influenced by TV evangelists, has given the idea of preaching extremely negative connotations of fanaticism. Granted, preaching should be done sparingly. But this is not the same thing as banning strong, sincere statements of opinion or well-presented arguments.

One of the authors conducted a simple survey with important implications for the issue of preaching morality. A sample of pupils from several high schools were asked which type of faculty member they would consult if they had a serious personal problem. Both boys and girls overwhelmingly preferred a gym teacher or an athletic coach. Because gym teachers usually also serve as coaches, we assume that the students were expressing support for a "coachlike" style of interaction. Of course, some pupils will prefer different advisors than coaches. Still, the patterns of preference are striking, especially when coaches are sometimes portrayed as insensitive and crude.

Some ideas of what it means to be "coachlike" are indicated in the following remarks—which we might view as preaching—by Bobby Knight about college basketball players and drug use. Knight is the basketball coach at Indiana University and has one of the most successful records of wins in American college basketball. His team members also have notably high rates of college graduation. He made these remarks to a group of college basketball players at a training camp. For background, readers should know that Lenny Bias was a college basketball star who, on the edge of a brilliant pro career, died from an overdose of cocaine. Michael Jordan is considered the best basketball player in the world.

> I don't feel sorry for Lenny Bias, not in the slightest. He had his own mind and his own body to take care of and just wasn't smart enough to do it. Those of you who have been popping pills and smoking dope are doing the same thing Lenny Bias did. Those are serious shots you are taking, boys, serious poor judgments that you're using with your body and your mind. Lenny Bias was better than anyone here. . . . The only college player I've seen in the past few years as good as Bias was Michael Jordan, and I'm not sure if he was as good as Bias was in college, and Bias is dead.
>
> He's dead because he just wasn't strong enough to take care of himself. Somewhere along the way, he wanted to be one of the boys. He wanted to be cool. Well, he was so cool that he's cold right now. . . . That's how cool he was.
>
> You boys will be in all types of situations where there are temptations and all kinds of opportunities to do something detrimental to yourself, and when it comes right down to it, there's only one person who can take care of you, and that's you. Your buddy doesn't really give a damn about you, particularly if he's popping pills or smoking dope.
>
> You know what he wants? He wants you right down where he is because he can't handle the fact that you're tougher than he is. [At this point, Knight suggests a profane street phrase to tell the dealer to beat it.]
>
> Take care of yourselves, boys.[11]

These remarks show that Knight is an extremely able preacher. Good coaches have to know how to emotionally reach and motivate players, to stimulate them to go the last mile, and beyond. That is no small talent. And pupils who prefer receiving moral advice from such persons are showing their appreciation of skillful preaching. We do not contend that all—or most—teachers can approach Bobby Knight's level of delivery. Furthermore, Knight's talent as a motivator is due to many factors beyond his considerable skills at oratory. Still, most teachers can improve their current preaching. But they must feel licensed to do so. And they must practice.

Conducting Moral Education

Obviously, we are critical of nondirectional moral education, such as values clarification. Children should not be invited to reinvent the moral world and will surely fail if they try to. Too many teachers are afflicted by the misguided fear of imposing the wisdom of our culture on students. This affliction has been stimulated by values clarification and the relaxed ethical standards of our time. These teachers have succumbed to *cultural relativism*: the belief that a culture can only be judged relative to the values inherent in that culture. This means there is no supracultural standard against which we can evaluate Nazism, communism, the Holocaust, or the Soviet slave-labor camps.

Unfortunately, too many current teachers, who have taken courses such as Western civilization and are themselves culturally literate, still hesitate to provide students with their cultural knowledge. The ascendancy of relativism has deprived them of the security necessary to assert and defend their own heritage.

During the last twenty-five years teachers have heard the message of these nonjudgmental approaches. They have tried to become, or have been coerced into being, nonauthorities in the moral realm. Furthermore, in both values clarification and the cognitive developmental moral education of Lawrence Kohlberg, mentioned earlier—the formerly dominant approaches to moral education, or those most frequently cited by educational experts and textbook writers—the task of the teacher is to implement a process. That process is supposed to have morally therapeutic benefits down the road. Too often, the popular literature has neglected to report that (a) both these approaches have been shown to be ineffective; and (b) many of the advocates of the approaches have abandoned their claims of efficacy or are currently even recommending more traditional moral education approaches. Nevertheless, these two possibly obsolete approaches still dominate the materials presented to teachers about their responsibilities as moral educators. We have seen few teachers who are actually skilled and active in using these approaches. However, the message of moral neutrality in these approaches has been enormously influential in delegitimizing traditional approaches such as direct moral instruction.

Hard-Case Morality

We believe that a valid concern about direct moral education is whether some teachers will abuse their responsibilities as direct moral educators. Undoubtedly, there is a potential for misuse. In our culturally and religiously pluralistic nation, there is no strong moral consensus in some communities about certain ethical issues. Some of these issues are abortion, the justification for entering particular wars, the death penalty, and certain issues of sexuality, such as homosexuality. These unresolved areas of ethical life comprise what we call *hard-case morality*. It seems that many academics have become fascinated with the intellectual complexities inherent in these topics. They have been excessively engaged with the question, "Can we teach children to solve these complex questions?" In effect, they are urging schools to conduct moral education and character formation by posing hard cases to students. Such concerns reveal a form of arrogance.

Obviously, the unrealistic aspirations of the proponents of moral dilemmas have not threatened the achievements of Socrates. However, such aspirations have had other deleterious effects. The intellectual focus on hard-case morality has had a paralyzing effect on our schools' efforts to transmit "simpler," traditional morality. The hard-case issues actually involve a small fraction of potential moral topics. Because we lack consensus on this fraction, many teachers have been warned off all moral issues. For instance, because there is no local resolution about abortion, teachers have been puzzled about what generally to say to students about sexuality, promiscuity, and, by extension, an entire moral domain. Teachers' uncertainty over the hard cases affects their certainty in teaching about everyday issues, like prohibiting sexually provocative clothes or observing legal prohibitions against drug use. Again, teachers have been unsure of what to do or tell students about classroom cheating, gossiping, vulgar language, and lack of effort. Such withdrawal from everyday morality is not just sloppy thinking; it generates a pernicious spirit, one that undermines the possibility of having a learning classroom and a true school. It not only turns education into a mere exchange of information—if that—but even corrodes the concept of teacher.

However, there are still occasional dramatic situations when a student asks a teacher for advice, and the teacher is drawn into hard-case morality. Taking one of the most inflamed issues, consider a high school girl who becomes pregnant. She asks her teacher about having an abortion. In our view, the teacher should urge the student to share the matter with her parents or religious advisor. If the student will not seek help from them, the teacher should suggest the student seek the counsel of some other wise faculty member, school counselor, or social worker. The teacher should also solicit the counsel of a colleague, ideally the principal, or a school counselor. Such referrals may not be the most satisfying or most dramatic thing for the teacher to do. Still, they are the correct thing. While the student may prefer not to talk to such persons, that preference may be unwise. One reason people ask other's advice is to possibly be told the course they are following is unsound.

In hard cases, as in other parts of our lives, there is no substitute for good judgment. And a hard case, by definition, is one where we doubt our own judgment. Therefore, we should advise students, when they are unsure what to do, to solicit counsel from wise people around them. When it comes to this narrow band of controversial issues, then, we are urging two principles. First, students should seek advice from their primary moral educators, parents and religious leaders, and, failing that, they should seek out truly wise people for advice. Second, they must think independently. Children need to develop their own powers of reasoned thought. The sophistication and level of that thought varies, of course, as children grow up. However, we must prepare them for independent moral thought. These two principles, seeking wise advice and thinking independently, are not in opposition. We should urge students, in thinking through a hard case and coming to their own conclusions, to gather as much information and wisdom as they can.

There are, then, limits on the role of teachers as direct moral educators. However, we believe that for the overwhelming majority of teachers, reflection and good judgment are adequate guides. On the other hand, for teachers to withdraw from their responsibilities to be moral leaders of children and become moral eunuchs is a perversion of their calling.

THE MORAL EDUCATION OF THE TEACHER

A perennial question in education is the definition of a good teacher. The most recent form of that question, as we indicated earlier, is, "What is an effective teacher?" Our view is that there is probably a small percentage of natural teachers, people who come to teaching already possessing the social and organizational skills needed to be a success. However, most aspiring and beginning teachers have a good deal to learn about being a teacher.

Trying to identify the candidates with typical needs, and organizing an instructional program to meet those needs, has been the pervading quandary of teacher education. In recent years there has been great ferment in this field. Numerous alternative approaches to teacher education have been promoted and tried. Most of these new approaches have been based on the idea of the teacher as a transmitter of information and skills. They have focused on equipping teachers with the technical know-how to promote certain intellectual and, to a lesser extent, psychomotor changes in students. This search for the ingredients of an effective teacher has been a vexing challenge. While there have been some improvements, there have also been some big losses.

One of the major losses in teacher education in recent decades is in the moral domain. Teachers in the past learned Socrates' views of the teacher's work: the role of education is to make people both smart and good. Now teacher education focuses overwhelmingly on the first: what can the teacher do to make students smart? Ironically, teachers reduce their chances of making students smart when they neglect teaching how to become good. The undisciplined student and the undisciplined classroom are resistant to acquiring knowledge and intellectual skills.

Regarding pupil discipline, one of the authors attended a meeting of practicing educators. At the meeting, various proposals to improve pupil character were being considered. One of the educators remarked, "All of this is to the good, but I hope we are not simply striving to create docile pupils." There were nods of assent among the group members. Later, the author looked up the precise meaning of *docile*. It means capable of being taught, as compared to a wild animal, which lacks docility. Admittedly, we do not know what meaning the speaker and his associates attributed to the word docility. But the fact is that, apart from docility, it is hard to identify another word in the educational lexicon that means capable of being taught.

From our numerable contacts with educators, we believe the speaker's misunderstanding is symptomatic of a widespread problem. Since the word docile is unacceptable, we can no longer express the concept of "capable of being taught." If an important concept is indescribable in everyday terms, it has effectively expired: no word is readily available to convey the concept that discipline is a prerequisite to instruction. The death of a concept may be one source of many of the deficiencies affecting academic instruction.

One must inevitably reflect on why teacher education turned away from the moral domain and the teacher's role in character formation. The answer to the question is wrapped up with much of the intellectual and cultural history of the United States in the last three decades. During this era, the nation's public morality was questioned on all sides. Our racial policies were revealed to be deeply unjust. Our involvement in the Vietnam War generated, for many Americans, an ethical quagmire. Illegal recreational drugs became widely available and quite acceptable in certain circles.

The moral consensus around our traditional values seemed to be crumbling. Because of this erosion of the consensus, words and phrases like *traditional values*, *character*, *the common good*, and *moral principles and habits* became unpopular with some of our leaders and opinion formers. Teacher education, in effect, dropped its focus on these words and their underlying concepts. Instead, it focused on other, supposedly more scientific and noncontroversial words such as *behavioral objectives*, *advanced organizers*, and *interaction analysis*. Due to these changes, contemporary teacher education rarely addresses the explicit moral dimension of a teacher's role. But while many teachers define themselves in this teacher-as-technician way, many do not. Large numbers of teachers are called to teaching primarily out of concern that children grow up to be good people of principle and strong moral character. Some teachers conceive of their work in a religious framework (e.g., providing an occasion to satisfy one of the Ten Commandments—to love your neighbor—and also helping children to do good), others in a secular context (e.g., helping to form good citizens), and others as a combination of religious and secular missions. But to the degree that these teachers are effective in responding to the moral dimension of their work, they are self-taught. Teacher education has had little effect on these teachers, since it does not often address the moral domain. In fact, when education courses do address moral issues, their effects are often mischievous. They warn prospective teachers that deliberately encouraging traditional moral values can become indoctrination of the innocent. Many professors decry such moral advocacy as elitist, ethnocentric, and narrow. On the other hand, one experienced teacher reported, "My best sources of information and insight into teaching, particularly about right and wrong, values, and discipline, have been my mother and grandmother. They have that good common sense you need with difficult children."

Where Help Is Needed

Throughout the 1980s and 1990s, there has been a drumbeat of concern about the moral health of our young. Many parents, and members of the public in general, have indicated clearly that they want our schools to take a more direct role in children's moral education. While schools in the 1990s are distracted by many other problems, the message, nevertheless, is getting through to administrators and classroom teachers. It is now time for the teacher education community in universities and in school districts to refocus their energies on helping teachers become better moral educators. Teachers need to gain the confidence, perspective, and skills they need to take back this fundamental aspect of their work. Four areas emerge where teachers would need help. These are

+ understanding our moral heritage.
+ acquiring the skills needed to aid children toward moral maturity.
+ knowing the leading theories of ethical development and character formation.
+ placing the moral dimensions of their work in proper perspective.

We will now elaborate on each of these four areas.

Our Moral Heritage. In the mid-1980s, E. D. Hirsch, a professor of English literature, exposed the great deficit of cultural literacy among our students. Too many students lacked a recognition of the basic events and features of Western culture.[12] He described cultural literacy as a code that enables those who possess it to function and rise in the society and that blocks those who lack it—the culturally illiterate. The same principle holds for the moral domain.

Moral literacy means knowledge of our culture's moral wisdom. It means knowing the enduring habits or traits needed for good character. We learn much of this moral literacy through the curriculum, particularly literature and history. For instance, we learn about courage from the little Dutch boy who put his finger in the dike, from Joan of Arc, from Horatio at the bridge, and from Harriet Tubman on the Underground Railroad to freedom. We learn loyalty to our country from Nathan Hale, and its opposite from Benedict Arnold and, more recently, from John Walker, who sold military secrets to the Soviets. We learn the importance of persistence from the little engine that could, from Booker T. Washington's efforts to learn to read, from Lincoln's struggle to hold the Union together, and from Alexander Solzhenitsyn's endurance in the Soviet gulag.

Teachers must be masters of our moral heritage. It is especially important, then, that they receive a solid liberal arts education. They must not only know this important knowledge, but also reflect on its significance. For instance, they should not only know what a democracy is, how it functions, and how it differs from other systems of government, but know especially how and why it is a moral idea. They should have an understanding of the history of Western ethics so that they are well-grounded philosophically. Moral literacy, then, should be a basic expectation of teachers, one gained from their general and liberal arts education, their continuing study of the culture, and their own personal growth.

Having the Skills Needed to Teach Morality. The difference between knowing a skill and knowing how to teach it is well known to every veteran teacher. Knowing how to read does not mean being able to teach someone else to read.

Knowing the theory of supply and demand does not mean knowing how to get it into the heads of two dozen students with different levels of interest, learning styles, and intellectual backgrounds. Teachers, then, must not only be morally literate, but they must also know how to teach this moral legacy to students. Teachers need to learn

1. how to focus students' attention on the ethical dimension of a story. "When you read this short story tonight, I want you to ask yourself, What is the moral of this story? What are we to learn about treating strangers from this story?"

2. how to lead students to thoughtfully consider ethical principles. "Before we study the principle of radioactivity, I want to read you a short account of the lives of two great pioneers of the field, Pierre and Marie Curie. They contributed immensely to our knowledge of paramagnetic substances and radioactivity, but I want you to listen and tell me what was it about how they lived their lives that enabled them to make such contributions?"

3. how to focus students' attention on the moral aspects of an historical event and how to analyze and discuss it. For high school students: "We have been studying how the founding fathers declared independence and built a new nation. I want you to pause here and think about this from the other side. Many people at the time thought they were doing a morally incorrect thing. What is the argument on the side of these objectors? Write down your thoughts and we'll discuss them in a few minutes."

4. how to engage students in the moral of a story and see how it may apply to their own lives. "I am going to read you a famous story about Daedalus and his son Icarus. As you will see, Icarus makes a terrible mistake. After the story, tell me what that mistake is, but most of all I want you to think of examples of how second-graders, like yourselves, could possibly make mistakes like Icarus made."

5. how to build among students the skills of moral discourse, which is not just casual argumentation but serious thinking about what is correct and about the "oughtness of life." "What is the correct thing to do?" "As most of you know, last night the school board accepted the new dress code proposed by the Parent Teachers Association, and the new rules will go into effect in a month. I know that some of you are upset about this issue, and I think we need to take some homeroom time to talk about it. But if we are going to talk about it we must have a rational discussion. First of all, we ought to find out what the new code actually says. We ought to find out the reasons given for the change in dress codes. Could there be other reasons? Who, if anyone, is hurt by this decision? Are they moral reasons, or is this matter just fashion? If we are going to discuss this, our discussion should be driven by the questions, What are the facts? What is the right thing to do? and Why?"

Part of knowing how to be an adept teacher of moral literacy is developing a reservoir of materials and techniques that are effective with different students.

For example, the middle school teacher needs to learn ways to get thirteen-year-old boys interested in the life of a young Jewish girl in *The Diary of Anne Frank* and appreciate her courage. The primary teacher must learn how to create activities that enable second-graders to see beyond the story about King Midas and his golden touch to its universal truth about the dangers of human greed. It is this type of knowledge of craft that separates the culturally literate knower from the culturally literate teacher. It is at this level that much of preservice and inservice education should be concentrating.

Theories of Moral Growth.   Our discussion in chapter 2 covered topics such as faculty psychology, motivations for learning, and the doctrine of learning as fun. That discourse also identified a variety of pertinent authors, works, and theories in psychology and sociology. Materials of this sort should be an important part of the curriculum in any institution helping to teach teachers how to conduct moral education.

In addition to such materials, theology and philosophy are two major disciplines that traditionally have provided much theoretical support for moral education. Both disciplines are preoccupied with questions of human nature and how it can improve, and both have been closely associated with the purpose of school. In colonial America, schools were typically begun out of religious motivation. In seventeenth-century Massachusetts, theology inspired the famous Old Deluder Satan Act. The act directed towns to start schools. The purpose of these schools was hardly to have children learn "salable skills" or to "reach their full human potential." Instead, their pupils were to learn to read and memorize the Scriptures, which in turn would lead to their moral development. As we have discussed elsewhere in this book, Americans are a churchgoing people, and theology is for many Americans an important "meaning maker," particularly in the moral realm. Concepts such as sin and redemption should be understood, not only for cultural literacy, but to allow a teacher to more fully understand the moral orientations of students and their families.

Philosophy, too, represented more than an important repository of human wisdom for earlier Americans. The methods of philosophy were tools necessary to guide one's life, in particular, ethics, the branch of philosophy that deals with rationally discovering what is the right thing to do. Philosophy, because it deals strictly with reason, is less controversial than theology, which includes sacred and revealed truths. At present, though, these two disciplines are somewhat out of favor in certain universities. Still, they include many of the most important theories of moral development and constitute valuable resources for revitalizing teacher education.

It takes some reflection to see the connection between abstract theories and concrete problems. This is why instruction of teachers in the disciplines must be carefully managed. But such connections can be made evident. Different theological views of human nature help us reflect on the premises underlying different policies of prohibition and punishment. For example, if we believe humans are free to choose to do right or wrong, then punishment for wrong choices appears justified. Behavioral psychology helps sensitize teachers so they can analyze the implicit rewards and punishment for good and bad character in their classes and schools. Anthropology can help sensitize us to the important role that ceremonies and symbols can have in transmitting moral values. In sum, appropriate theories enrich teachers' understanding of a problem and enable them to weigh alternative solutions. The disciplines and their theories become lenses for us to examine practical situations. They can open the door for the teacher to construct the solution. And this is precisely why teaching is a profession, rather than a trade. It lacks formulaic answers to be memorized and applied.

MAKING THE MORAL DOMAIN A PRIORITY

Making moral education a priority means a personal decision by individual educators to take this domain of their work more seriously. They must focus more of their time and professional energy on it. This means devoting more time to the issues of moral literacy and how best to teach them to students. While making this domain a higher priority is partly an individual act, educators work within institutions. One part of their professionalism is to take responsibility for the functioning of the whole. Teachers, whether teaching classes or leading extracurricular activities or teams, cannot be concerned simply with the morality of their own units. They need to feel responsibility for the entire school and raise moral questions such as:

✦ What is my policy about character formation and teaching moral values?

✦ What habits am I trying to promote in my students?

✦ Is there a relationship between the way I am treating students and the way they treat one another?

✦ Does my class celebrate any heroes? Are these heroes people of character?

✦ Have I given the same kind of attention to the moral aspects of my curriculum that I do to, say, the language arts curriculum?

✦ Am I contributing to the wallpaper factor (from Coles' research)? When was the last time a student came to me with an ethical problem?

✦ Do children consider my class as a place where they are learning to be good? Are they good students who are learning to be good people and good citizens?

✦ What can I do to foster greater solidarity between my students' parents and me on issues of conduct and values?

✦ What can we do to get the students to take more responsibility for one another?

✦ Does my class discipline policy fit with our goals of promoting responsibility, courtesy, and dignity?

✦ Do I let parents "cover" or "bail out" children, or do I insist that students live with the consequences of their actions?

✦ Do I show that I care about all my students, even when they get in trouble? Or do I abandon them at the point when there is police involvement?

✦ Am I as a faculty member giving students a consistent set of messages about discipline?

✦ Does the entire staff—bus drivers, cafeteria workers, custodians, administrators, and teachers—take on moral development and character formation as a priority?

✦ How can I do a better job of this?

John Adams, our country's second president, once stated, "A teacher affects eternity." We realize he was partly considering the transmission of intellectual matter, such as mathematical and verbal skills. However, we also know from his many other writings that his primary focus was on the moral mission of the teacher and the impact the teacher has on the character of students. As we have suggested, *character* and other words such as *virtue* and *diligence* are making a comeback. Americans are recoiling from the more relaxed child-raising and educational ideas of the last few decades.

The word *character* goes to the heart of the teacher's moral responsibilities. The root of *character* is from a Greek word meaning "to engrave." A character is a sign or a distinctive mark. Engravers mark their work with characters. People with character have worked day after day to shape their own being. As a result, they have a distinctive pattern of behavior or personality, so that we expect them to exhibit moral strength and self-discipline. People of character are "marked" people. Of course, such marks can be either good or bad; there is such a thing as notoriously bad character too. But character usually refers to good character, unless a negative modifier is used. "She is a woman of character" means that life has left certain enduring marks on her so that we can expect a certain pattern of good behavior from her.

Teachers leave their stamp on us. One teacher confronts our carelessness. Another demands self-criticism and attention to details. Another gives us much-needed humility. Yet another inspires in us a passionate concern for justice. Students, whether three years old or nineteen, have a certain waxlike character, and teachers, consciously and unconsciously, leave enduring marks on their students. This is both the grandeur and the terror of teaching. But for good or ill, as Adams said, teachers "affect eternity."

Practices and Policies

1. When teachers are together (in the workroom, faculty lounge, or lunch room), approximately how much time is spent gossiping about or criticizing students, parents, or administrators in a petty and unconstructive way? What are some subtle ways a teacher could constructively and tactfully direct the conversation elsewhere?

2. If your school does not have one already, consider starting a Sunshine Club, or similar organization. Obtain a copy of the bylaws of an existing successful club. A Sunshine Club periodically collects small donations from faculty and staff members and administrators and then uses the money to recognize important events in people's lives. For example, these clubs usually send a card and flowers for the birth of a child, send flowers or memorial donations for the death of a loved one, or organize farewell parties for departing staff members. Your club could also acknowledge birthdays with a card or an announcement over the P. A. system or announce important days in students' lives.

3. Do teachers have input in suggesting particular inservice programs or in presenting inservice programs themselves? Perhaps teachers in your school could volunteer to research and suggest inservice programs that would especially benefit teachers in your building. Or, teachers with knowledge on a specific topic or with a certain talent could present their own inservice to the school faculty.

4. How comfortable do teachers in your school feel being direct moral educators? If they feel comfortable, why do they feel that way? If not, what are their concerns, obstacles, or reservations?

5. Is it accurate to say that your school's community has relatively homogeneous moral standards? How well do teachers know the moral standards of the community? Do they feel comfortable with the moral values of the community? Why or why not?

6. How often are teachers in your school confronted with "hard-case" morality, for example, students asking about contraception or abortion? Generally, how do teachers handle these cases? To what extent do teachers become invested in the hard moral cases of the students?

References

1. Bandura, A. (1977). *Social learning theory*. Upper Saddle River, NJ: Prentice Hall.

2. Biehler, R. F., & Snowman, J. (1986). *Psychology applied to teaching* (5th ed.). Boston: Houghton Mifflin.

3. Coleman, J. S. (1974). *Youth: Transition to adulthood*. Chicago: University of Chicago Press.

4. *The Boston Parents' Paper* (January, 1990), p. 5.

5. Green, T. F. (1984). *The formation of conscience in an age of technology* (John Dewey Lecture, 1984). Syracuse, NY: Syracuse University Printing Service, p. 4.

6. Coles, R., & Genevie, L. (1990, March). The moral life of America's school children. *Teacher Magazine*, pp. 42–49.

7. Walberg, H. J. (1988, March). Synthesis of research on time and learning. *Educational Leadership*, p. 76–81.

8. e.g., see Wittrock, M. C. (Ed.). (1986). *The handbook of research on teaching* (3rd ed.). New York: Macmillan; and Ornstein, A. C., & Levine, D. U. (1989). *Foundations of education* (4th ed.). Boston: Houghton Mifflin.

9. Lanckton, A. (1992). How seventh- and eighth-grade teachers perceive their role as moral educators. Unpublished doctoral dissertation, Boston University.

10. Simon, S. B. (1971, December). Values clarification vs. indoctrination. *Social Education*, 902–905.

11. Berkow, I. (1990, August 20). Sports in the Times. *The New York Times*, section C, p. 9.

12. Hirsch, E. D., Jr. (1985, Summer). Cultural literacy and the schools. *American Educator*, *9*(2), pp. 8–15.

CHAPTER 7

Curriculum as a Moral Educator

As Aristotle taught, people do not naturally or spontaneously grow up to be morally excellent or practically wise. They become so, if at all, only as the result of a lifelong personal and community effort.

—Jon Moline[1]

The curriculum of a school or classroom should be the community's reply to the prime educational question, "What is most worth knowing?" Children are born into an endless universe of facts and figures, theories and opinions, current events and classic stories. This is particularly true in our media-saturated world of television, radio, computers, CDs, and tapes—all fiercely competing for our attention and that of our young people. Given this flood of information and noise coming to children, the curriculum plays the essential role of identifying what, of this mass of choices, educators should select and teach to children in school. The curriculum has always had the function of literally bringing order out of chaos, and today the task is even more important.

Planning a curriculum requires that we recognize and resolve a variety of questions. What does a child need to live a good life? To be a contributing citizen? To be a productive worker? To be a good spouse and parent? To be a fulfilled human being? Furthermore, we must confront these vexing questions in a period of finite time. Students do not, and should not, stay in school forever. Of necessity, much important learning is left to sources outside of school, such as the family, the media, religious institutions, employers, and the personal initiative of the student or ex-student. Thus, we still face the question of which learning should be saved for a later time or left up to other agencies. There are also questions about which knowledge can be understood by pupils of what ages, and in what forms it should be presented to the young. These questions should guide our selection of what we teach students.

TYPES OF CURRICULUM

Curriculum is one of the biggest, sloppiest, and slipperiest concepts in education. We use the term here in its broadest sense: *curriculum* includes all the events and activities experienced by the students—as students—during their school years. One way to make the discussion of curriculum more manageable is to make some distinctions. One obvious distinction is between the formal curriculum and the hidden curriculum.

In contemporary usage, the *formal curriculum* covers the academic experiences that schools deliberately provide for students. These experiences include the knowledge and skills the school or class will teach. Usually, this curriculum is written and available for examination by concerned people. It is also called the overt curriculum, since it is out in the open for public inspection.

The *hidden curriculum* is what pupils learn in and around schools in addition to the formal curriculum. It is all the incidental, typically unplanned, learnings—personal and social, intellectual and physical—that the student gains from being in a particular school and classroom. It is called hidden because it is usually not deliberately observed. Furthermore, it is often unplanned, unwritten, and not subject to evaluation. However, the hidden curriculum is very real. It can have a major impact on the lives of students. As a result of being in a particular classroom, students think of themselves as winners or losers, as community members or aliens. They define themselves in a distinctive manner and relate to teachers and fellow students in particular ways.

The hidden curriculum is intertwined with the ethos of the school and classroom. If bullying is the rule on the playground, it is part of the school's hidden curriculum. If civility reigns on the playground, it becomes a major result of schooling. If teachers ridicule students who, as a result, lose confidence in themselves or interest in their academic work, this is an outcome of the hidden curriculum.

We have been unable to fully trace the history of the phrase *hidden curriculum,* but we believe it became popular during the latter half of the twentieth century. Before that time, the hidden curriculum encompassed the school's efforts to raise children up to the community's highest standards. These activities were the main task of formal education. The hidden curriculum was quite conspicuous, and usually still is. In fact, there is nothing especially hidden about it. It is often easier to tell whether a school's students are learning obedience or politeness than whether they are learning arithmetic. Levels of politeness and obedience in a school can be simply assessed. Just walk into the pupils' lunchroom, observe the playground, or watch pupils during an all-school assembly. But whether pupils really learn arithmetic is a complex question. We may see teaching in progress or examine textbooks. We can say whether arithmetic is being taught. But learning is more than exposure to teaching. In the end, we can only assess cognitive learning by applying relatively subtle measures.

Much of what is written about the hidden curriculum has a negative tone. Even the word *hidden* suggests an attempt to shape children's behavior in illicit ways. This view is a distortion, however, and also extremely naive. Such misconceptions are an outcome of the antischool writings of the 1960s and 1970s, for example, those of Kozol, Holt, and Silberman.[2] The hidden curriculum, just like the open curriculum, can contain much that is either good or bad. The hidden curriculum can stress a spirit of intellectual curiosity, or a strong but unseen bond of affection between teacher and students. Such qualities cannot be captured in the formal curriculum, but they can be core learnings of a school.

Another term that aids our understanding of curriculum is the *null curriculum,* which refers to all that is left out of a curriculum. Think about what a vast concept this is: the hundreds of languages that exist, and the literature and tales of each; most of the immense recorded history of humanity; almost all of our numeracy, only a tiny fraction of which is taught in schools; and most of our physical and social sciences. The curriculum of our schools is—and must be, since life is finite and knowledge, infinite—a thin layer from the surface of the known.

The concept of null curriculum reveals, though, another important feature: the dynamic quality of our curriculum. What is a part of the curriculum in one era or one community is in the null curriculum in another time or locale. For example, our first public schools were founded three and a half centuries ago. Essentially, they were created to teach religion, a subject that is now typically part of the null curriculum. On the other hand, in the same era sexuality, as an area of human experience, was left to the family, church, and the course of life to teach. Now sexuality is very much in our formal curriculum. We believe it one of the ironies of education in the 1990s that some public schools will require a teacher to teach elementary students the proper way to apply a condom using cucumbers, but would reprimand—and possibly dismiss, in the event of a lawsuit—the same teacher for suggesting to students that promiscuity might be sinful. In any event, what is in and out of the null curriculum says a great deal about a culture.

Curriculum as a Social Wager

Many animals have some capacities for learning. Unlike our relations in the animal kingdom, however, human beings face a special challenge in organizing learning. Humans must choose from the universe of knowledge that which is most worth knowing. Even for the higher animals, what they need to learn is programmed by nature. As the most complex learning species, however, humans must consciously seek answers to the core question about what should be learned. Otherwise, we face stagnation or decadence.

The ash heap of history is littered with societies that chose incorrect learning priorities and ended up miseducating their young. This may be one way of interpreting the tensions now afflicting the former Soviet Union. There, the current adult generation was educated in a totalitarian society. The curriculum was designed to perpetuate that society. Now, the adult generation is invited to participate in a shift towards more democratic modes of government. It is unlikely, though, that either the open or hidden curricula formerly presented to Soviet pupils prepared them to participate in democratic government and capitalistic life. Because of this, many observers are concerned about the evolution of democracy in the states of the former Soviet Union, despite popular hostility to past governmental norms. It takes more than a simple desire or a governmental decree to create a democratic citizenry.

Deciding what is most worth knowing has high stakes. Although the question may sound simple, the answer involves a complicated process in which we must peer into the future and simultaneously draw on what we currently know. We must design education experiences to help our children to live well, to be strong individuals living in a good society. Building such a curriculum is a huge social gamble.

An even greater risk, however, is not to wrestle with the question. We could just go along with our current curriculum. But as theologian Harvey Cox is fond of saying, "Not to decide is to decide." Any school community that has not asked the question has still answered it. The answer is what students are now being taught.

Many of the questions underlying decisions about the curriculum have strong moral components, such as "How can people live in harmony with one another?"

and "What is a good way to spend one's life?" The answers to these questions quickly move us into the realm of ethics, morals, and character formation. By its very nature, then, a school's curriculum is its answer to some of our most important human questions. Although this may appear obvious, there is little evidence that the moral mission of our school's curriculum is currently the subject of public discussion or scholarly debate, with the possible exceptions of sex- and drug-education curricula.

Knowing the Good

Moral education and character formation in schools aim to transmit to pupils the community's best values and ethical ideals. An anthropologist might describe this effort as socializing the young into tribal morality. It seems an innate reflex for adults to try to instill the moral values and habits they believe children will need to sustain themselves, to live a good life. Likewise, the larger community wants to instill in the young the values the members believe will sustain the community. To do less is beyond being foolish. It is irresponsible.

From where should the content of ethical and character education come? Where can we turn for this most critical curricular material? What do we as Americans, part of a relatively new society, possess that nearly all of us share and are ready to have the school pass on to young people? And how can schools serving the racial, ethnic, and religious mix that is America find core materials to fit the needs of children from all these backgrounds? Our answer has three parts.

1. We must treat the forging of core materials as a high priority, or our future as a nation is at peril. We need to define our standards of moral literacy if we are to stay a coherent nation.
2. Our schools should return to the source of much of our school content: the moral facts of life and the moral ideals derived from our history and culture.
3. It is possible that some communities or political jurisdictions cannot develop consensus around such matters. In those places, parents and educators must be prepared to develop freestanding schools, either public or private, that appeal to parents who favor certain coherent values.

The Moral Facts of Life

The late C. S. Lewis provides a useful point of focus for any discussion of traditional American ideals. Lewis spent years searching the writings of past civilizations and seeking their core ideas. Gradually, he saw patterns of thought connecting the great civilizations. These ideas and precepts connect civilizations, but they may also act as a common core. Lewis called what he found the Tao, borrowing from the Chinese concept of Tao. In *The Abolition of Man*, he wrote:

> It is the Nature, it is the Way, the Road. It is the Way in which the universe goes on, the Way in which things everlastingly emerge, stilly and tranquilly, into space and time. It is also the Way which everyman should tread in imitation of that cosmic and supercosmic

progression, conforming all activities to that great exemplar. . . . This conception in all its forms, Platonic, Aristotelian, Stoic, Christian, and Oriental alike, I shall thenceforth refer to for brevity simply as 'the Tao.'[3]

Lewis further explains that the Tao is not something we can take or leave as we choose. It is simply there in the nature of reality. At the end of the book, Lewis provides readers with several pages of examples of the ancient writings which reflect the Tao. He claims the Tao is present in and reflected through Babylonian, ancient Egyptian, old Norse, Greek, Roman, Chinese, ancient Indian, Christian, Hebrew, Anglo-Saxon, and American writings, to mention only some of the cultures.

Many different lists of ideas and precepts might guide the development of curriculum for the moral domain. Lewis's approach, with its truly multicultural emphasis, seems particularly appropriate for our schools. Drawing on Lewis's illustrations of the Tao and other materials, we have identified the following list of moral facts of life:

- Human kindness is essential to a fully functioning society.
- We owe a special love, loyalty, and support to our parents and our families.
- We have a special responsibility to posterity, especially our own children.
- Married people have certain demands on each other that extend to specific rights and responsibilities.
- Some degree of honesty is needed for a society to function.
- We are obliged to help the poor, sick, and less fortunate.
- Basic property rights must exist in any organized society.
- Some things exist that are worse than death, for instance, treachery, extreme ingratitude, betrayal, and torturing another person.
- Our own inevitable death colors how we view life and, coupled with the nature of our posterity, gives the continuum of life its meaning.

We should add to this list a warning: we cannot assume these precepts will be reflexively applied by all members of any society, especially the young. Still, these moral facts of life appear to be crucial in order to live in harmony with ourselves and those around us. But they are not enough in themselves. They represent what the wisdom of our species tells us we ought to do to be in consonance with the realities of life. There are other things humanity has learned that go beyond these facts of life and lead us to excellence. These we call *ethical ideals*.

Ethical Ideals

In an earlier chapter we noted that the United States, at present, is overwhelmingly composed of people explicitly committed to Judeo-Christian values. Even the majority of recent Asian immigrants share such traditional beliefs along with already established Americans, such as German-Americans and Irish-Americans. In addition, African-Americans are an ethnic group deeply invested in the Christian tradition.

Relying on this cohesion, we have selected eight ethical ideals tied to (a) this heritage and (b) the antecedent Greco-Roman tradition that enriched the Judeo-Christian tradition. The ideals can serve as a basis for analysis of our formal or hidden curriculum. They represent what some of our great thinkers believe are the proper goals of humanity.[4] The first four ideals come from the Greeks: prudence, justice, temperance, and fortitude. They are called the *cardinal virtues* because they are like hinges (the Latin root meaning of the word *cardinal*) on which our hopes to reach a higher moral state depend.

We would like to acknowledge the help of Thomas Masty, an associate, in formulating this discussion of ideals.

Prudence is the habit of acting with discretion and deliberation. It is human wisdom applied to the practical. George Washington said, "It would be the point of prudence to defer the forming of one's ultimate irrevocable decision so long as new data might be offered."

Justice is the quality of being righteous and fair. One who possesses justice is honest, impartial, and even-handed. Jose Garcia Oliver has written, "Justice is so subtle a thing, to interpret it one has only need of a heart." While injustice will always be with us, it is important that we thirst for justice.

Temperance is the state of being self-restrained in conduct, being under one's own control. It is having in check one's appetites for life's pleasures. Benjamin Franklin wrote, "Temperance puts wood on the fire, meal in the barrel, flour in the tub, money in the purse, credit in the country, contentment in the house, clothes on the children, vigor in the body, intelligence in the brain, and spirit in the whole constitution." It should be noted that temperance does not necessarily mean abstinence from alcohol.

Fortitude is the capacity to withstand misfortune with bravery. It is an ability to endure pain without breaking or to persist patiently in the face of hardship. Of fortitude, Joseph Addison wrote, "In itself an essential virtue, it is a guard to every other virtue."

The next three moral ideals—the virtues of faith, hope, and charity—are found in many of the world's religions.

Faith has two meanings. The original is the capacity to put trust and reliance in God and the confidence that comes from that trust. Faith can also mean the trust and confidence we put in another person or institution. The Bible says, "Now faith is the substance of things to be hoped for" (Hebrews 11:1).

Hope is the habit of desiring the good, but with, at least, a slight expectation of obtaining it, or the belief that it is indeed obtainable. It is confidence in the future. An old Irish proverb goes, "Hope is the physician of each misery." Alexander Pope penned the famous lines, "Hope springs eternal in the human breast; Man ever is, but always to be blest".[5]

Charity is a habit of the heart, a disposition to think favorably of other people. It is the habit of acting, too, with affection and goodwill toward others. Roger Bacon wrote, "In charity there is not excess."

The eighth ideal we have selected is *duty*, which is a disposition to be loyal to those to whom we have an obligation, whether they are above or below us in authority. It involves our sense of responsibility to something outside ourselves. William Corbett stated, "From a very early age, I had imbibed the opinion, that it was everyman's duty to do all that lay in his power to leave his country as good as he had found it." Duty does not mean blind obedience. It means, though, giving what is expected to those who have a just claim on us. It sometimes means helping those in authority, such as government officials, live up to their obligations.

These, then, are a selection of ethical ideals. The moral facts of life, as identified by Lewis, seem to reside in the human condition and are universal. However, ethical ideals exist in a different form. Philosophers would claim that ethical ideals, such as these eight, are part of the very nature of humans. In individual people, these ethical ideals exist in varied forms, from shadowy potential to guiding lights for everyday behavior.

Philosophers and others, of course, may express different preferences regarding the moral facts of life and moral ideals. In this connection, readers are reminded of our earlier remarks about enumerations of moral traits. We stressed that perfect lists are neither essential nor realistic goals. In the preceding inventory, we did not include certain virtues, such as forbearance and humility, which are considered essential to some people. Other virtues we have included, such as hope, are not considered fundamental by some individuals. The aim of our selection is to focus on these facts of life and ideals as examples of our moral heritage, a heritage our society ignores at great risk.

The Practical Roots of Shared Morality

Sociologists, in contrast to many philosophers, usually perceive ethical ideals as partially determined by culture. This implies that different cultures highlight or value particular ideals and that some important ideals are not shared by all peoples. Often, a group, tribe, or nation would apply one set of values among tribe members and another set to outsiders or people who have been cast out from the group. Morality, to the extent it signified good conduct, is often applied solely to group members. For example, all, or almost all, countries regard it as honorable for spies, acting for their side, to deceive enemy states or forces.

Some authorities argue that there are important contrasts among cultures in the matter of morals. Despite such contrasts, one principle still prevails. Societies— long-persisting groups of people acting for certain common purposes—must be bound by powerful, shared beliefs. Such beliefs should motivate citizens to make great personal sacrifices for the general good. Citizens' goals must extend past the pursuit of simple, immediate self-interest. Not all group-cohesion activities are wholesome. Group cohesion has stimulated not only admirable activities such as the American civil rights movement and the crusade against child labor, but also actions as reprehensible as the Nazification of Germany, the public tortures of enemies by Aztec Indians, and the European witch-burners in the late Middle Ages. But any nation that fails to transmit a common morality to its citizens is extremely vulnerable. It can be disrupted or destroyed by the appeals of internal demagogues or external aggression.

We should also recognize that any body of principles or morals that binds a society can never be applied or invented all at once. Such broad codes must develop through a cumulative, incremental process. We believe that any proposal to change American values dramatically and deliberately amounts to demagoguery. Moderate shifts in values are always possible. However, the idea of a total revolution in values is a solecism, unless our society experiences some cataclysmic disaster, such as the crushing defeats suffered by Japan and Germany in World War II.

It is easy to identify instances of such values persistence in America. Some readers will recall dramatic pleas for community living articulated in America during the 1960s and 1970s, often voiced by people who wanted to form "communes." At the same time there were many attempts to create new institutions. However, almost all attempts at living in communes expired fairly quickly. Typically, they foundered on the strong commitments of members to individualism, a vital, traditional American value. The individualism made the communes' members unable or unwilling to make the sacrifices necessary to succeed at intimate communal life. In a more remote instance, during the American Revolution, some patriots saw the war as a prelude to a worldwide shift towards democracy. However, shortly after our revolution, the French Revolution occurred and was succeeded by the Reign of Terror and the Napoleonic Empire. During these climactic events, many Americans discovered important contrasts between the essentially incremental nature of the events leading to our revolution and the more Manichean visions that inspired many French revolutionary leaders.

Absent some total and horrible disaster, America's prevailing values must always carry forward important elements of previous patterns. Thus, serious efforts largely to remake a country through inventing fundamentally different values will merely lead to distortion and disorder. For example, many revolutions throughout the world in the twentieth century have merely established more profound dictatorships than those they succeeded. Consider the revolution in China led by Mao, the revolution in Cuba led by Castro, or the revolution in Russia led by Lenin. All of these allegedly represented dramatic efforts to shift national values towards democracy; instead the efforts led to regimes even more repressive than those of their predecessors. The revolutionaries carried forward many of the errors and few of the virtues of the old regimes. And they coupled their urgency with an arrogant and ruthless faith in their own virtue. The American Revolution occurred in a society that was already relatively open, and the Revolution's development was far more gradual than that of many other, less successful revolutions that occurred over the following centuries. It would be foolish for our schools to resist teaching and promoting traditional American values. If such resistance should succeed in any notable way, the end effect will be to endanger the Republic.

In an imperfect world, we believe American mainstream traditions and achievements are valuable per se, a precious resource for all people. Such universal treasures, however, are not properly cherished in the public schools in their homeland. It is true that efforts to identify or evolve common moral principles to guide the curriculum will be stressful and involve a complex pattern of negotiation and compromise. But this process of development has too long been deadlocked by insensitivity and lack of charity. Relatively small, articulate, aggressive minorities—usually secularly oriented and/or stressing highly individualistic values—have exercised too much influence in this elaborate negotiation. Their energies have been mobilized through court cases, restrictive legislation and regulatory rules, and the constraints created by many interest groups.

For instance, a number of intermediate-level federal court decisions have supported the right of elementary and high school pupils to refuse to participate in the in-class Pledge of Allegiance, if they believe the pledge constitutes a significant constraint on their personal beliefs. The students are not obligated to relate their objections to any significant, external patterns of belief, such as being members of some established religion. In some classrooms, this principle has led to distressing scenes: the teacher and a few pupils awkwardly participate in the pledge, while perhaps twenty indifferent adolescents sit sullenly at their desks, supposedly expressing their deep personal beliefs. Undoubtedly, the few pupils willing to express their patriotism feel like deviates. The extreme individualism of those who refuse to salute has often been supported by our national media and certain intellectual and academic groups.

The inhibitions on the articulation of a protradition curriculum should be removed or, at least, moderated. Schools, and their immediate constituencies, should formulate more coherent statements of moral principles and ideals from which educators can develop morally vital curricula. For Americans about to enter the twenty-first century, the moral facts of life and ethical ideals we discussed are the framework we recommend for this purpose. Schools should be given freedom to put these principles into effect in their programs and activities. The principles should appear early in kindergarten, in stories and games, and be developed and elaborated as the child grows. If these are our Tao and our moral ideals, it is imperative that we teach them thoroughly.

One concrete and successful instance of deliberately changing American values may be instructive. It shows us how and why success in such matters is rare.

Over the past thirty to forty years, American attitudes about cigarette smoking have conspicuously changed, and education has been one notable cause for this shift. The process of change relied on (a) gradual changes—no one seriously proposed a national law prohibiting smoking—and persuasion; (b) enormous persistence by the antismoking camp; (c) powerful, persuasive antismoking evidence that was gradually developed and disseminated; and (d) subjecting the pro-and-con evidence about smoking to a searching and conspicuous public debate. Only a moderate degree of compulsion was applied—until very late in the game. The collection and analysis of supporting, objectively verified data was a high priority. The overall aim of suppressing smoking was consistent with the American tradition of prohibiting harmful substances, for example, prohibiting alcohol in the early twentieth century. Ultimately, the actual changes generated by antismokers were not extraordinary. Only a moderate proportion of people permanently quit smoking. What was more typical is that succeeding age cohorts grew up more disposed to dislike smoking. We should also recognize that rearing an increasing proportion of nonsmokers does not necessarily amount to some vast change in national values. While this development may prolong the typical life span, it does not signify the spread of a lifestyle dramatically different from that which prevailed in the past.

We recognize that, at this time, there are signs of moderate increases in the levels of teenage smoking. Such increases are surely distressing. However, there are simultaneous signs of serious adult concern over such increases. We cannot absolutely predict the outcomes of these developments. However, it is quite possible that rising adult concern will eventually lead to additional new and more effective antismoking measures being devised. For instance, at this time, elaborate civil court actions are being initiated against cigarette companies for deceptive advertising. Antismoking juries may levy large amounts of damages in such cases.

The special circumstances surrounding the successful campaign against smoking have ironic significance. These circumstances emphasize the narrow parameters limiting the role of education in dramatically shifting human values. Only in extraordinary occasions can such efforts to foster change generate large-scale success. On other occasions, the results of such efforts may range from simply wasted energy and resources to aggravated disorder. While it can be realistic to have a campaign to encourage schools to reaffirm traditional values that have evolved over hundreds of years, it is probably naive to campaign to establish dramatic new ones.

If a Consensus Is Unattainable

For many reasons that readers might appreciate, a consensus on principles to guide curriculum development may not be feasible in particular communities, even given notable leadership by local educators. There are also situations where such a consensus may be feasible, but where inadequate leadership has failed to bring this possibility to fruition. In any event, it is important to consider situations where purposeful, good-faith efforts still fail to establish a community consensus on basic education principles. Essentially, three alternative—and possibly overlapping—policies can evolve. One is relatively popular, and quite wrong. The other two are sometimes applied, and make more sense.

The wrong policy is to try to develop a body of curriculum and related educational policies that simultaneously apply a variety of conflicting principles in each affected school. In effect, this results in something for everyone, but no coherent whole.

For example, in one school or even in the same classroom students may: participate in the Pledge of Allegiance to stress patriotism; be taught a body of history or social studies denigrating many national traditions in order to foster pluralism (e.g., being taught how the framers of the U.S. Constitution were largely motivated by selfish considerations); regularly practice values-clarification exercises to decide how they individually feel about ethical issues; be shielded from serious academic learning demands to moderate their stress; and be told they are uniquely gifted in order to raise their self-esteem. We can easily imagine other absurd mixes. Widely divergent materials do not make good sense, either psychologically or pedagogically. Many pupils may be able to survive such incoherent fare. Even at best, however, these policies waste a considerable amount of time, as they dissipate the energies of faculty members and pupils in different directions.

A second, sometimes sound, tactic when a community lacks consensus is for the majority simply to compel the minority to follow its dictates. In other words, assume the majority has a clear vision of its values and believes certain issues are properly urgent priorities in education. Some of our nation's school desegregation court cases provide an example. In those situations, the courts—in effect, representing the majority of the country—forced the majorities in certain school districts to carry out nationally determined policies. Those policies usually did not deal with formal school curriculum. Still, the underlying principles are applicable to curriculum issues. In some instances, the state representing the majority is justified in suppressing certain local curriculum priorities favored by a recalcitrant minority. Indeed, compulsion may even be justified if the minority view is held by a majority in some particular district or other jurisdiction.

Sometimes majority compulsion can be morally justified in curriculum policy; however, it is a desperate alternative. As a practical matter, in most situations parents are and must remain their children's primary educators. This reality is one reason for America's longstanding support of local control of education. It is awkward and impractical to compel all parents in a large, heterogeneous society to submit their children to a relatively uniform curriculum. The fact is that there is no historic instance of any culture—except perhaps the ancient Spartans—inventing a large-scale effective substitute for the family as a child-rearing agency. Of course, there are cases of schools adopting important policies contrasting with the values of a substantial minority of their pupils' parents. In such instances, it is safe to forecast troubling times for educators as well as pupils.

Again we can look to mandatory desegregation of public schools for an instance of such parent-school conflict, particularly in cases involving compulsory busing. In fact, there is considerable evidence that busing often failed to encourage desegregation. It failed due to so-called "White flight"—the refusal of White parents to move into, or continue to live in, communities subject to busing. In many cases, it seems these mandatory policies actually inspired greater segregation than existed previously. In a democracy, one can only push large numbers of people so far before other options for such malcontents begin to arise.

A third, and usually optimum, policy can be applied when a community lacks a values consensus. The state can allow families the freedom to choose schools that reflect, within certain parameters, their own values. Such schools of choice can be fostered by diverse means. Some examples are schools by parent vouchers (essentially subsidized by the government); parents opting to use privately supported schools; or public schools providing families with choices among various genuine alternatives, such as magnet schools. In chapter 9, we will discuss the merits of these approaches in greater detail.

Thinking Through the Moral

We have written much here of adults establishing rules and procedures with the clear expectation that the young will follow these rules. By doing so, students will acquire self-discipline and cultivate virtuous habits. We have stressed the duty of the older generation to indoctrinate the young with what they are convinced are the essential moral realities and ethical truths the young will need to live well. Such measures are important. But they hardly represent all of moral education or character development. With equal vigor and skill, we need to teach the young to think about issues of right and wrong, good and bad. It is essential for the school continually to engage the child in reflection about moral principles.

Teachers should not aim to produce students who are solely rule-followers. Instead, teachers should help students toward moral autonomy appropriate to their age level. By moral autonomy, we are not suggesting the typical twentieth-century antihero, a moral Lone Ranger, a solitary person who either knows nothing of our ethical heritage or rejects it outright. Rather, we are talking about students first knowing and understanding our moral heritage and then being capable of applying that tradition to various situations. For instance, we want students who know how to respond to the common classroom situation of several students picking on a classmate. Moral students should have learned certain principles: it is unfair to gang up on weaker individuals; we must be tolerant of the new and the different; and good people protect innocent people when they are threatened by others. We derive these principles directly from our moral facts of life, which should be firmly set in each student's memory. The moral curriculum for students should be their total experience in school—the rules of the classroom, the events in the lunchroom, stories read for homework. Students must be able to think through these issues.

Philosopher Edwin Delattre, writing in *Education and the Public Trust*, addressed the intellectual role of schools:

> Schools should teach our children the three Rs. We want students to learn to use words and numbers well, to read, write, and translate with understanding, to do calculations, and to conduct experiments. We want them to learn how the past is related to the present, and to be able to look at a painting or listen to a symphony intelligently. Many of us expect our children to study English, mathematics, languages, science, literature, history, and the fine arts. We want our children to achieve reliable study habits and self-discipline through the curriculum, the classroom, homework, and extracurricular activities. When we successfully teach, learning is no longer drudgery. Education cannot be neutral to the difference between good and bad habits. The work of schoolchildren is to become good learners. Teachers must design their courses and assignments so that good habits of learning and success—even the appearance of success—are not separated. A good learner can learn things on purpose, rather than by accident or luck. Working hard is not enough, because the student must know how to work, what to concentrate on, and which skills to use. Good learning depends on one value above all others: the value of intellectual honesty. Children who never learn this have slim chance of significant benefit from school.[6]

An important part of education, then, is regularly posing to students the question, "What is the right thing to do?" This is a central question in any society, and asking it should begin early and continue up to graduation. When people lose the habit and the capacity to ask the question, in the words of Yeats, "things fall apart." Specifically, students need to learn the skills of ethical thinking. Students can learn and apply these skills, just as they can learn and apply the scientific method or a mathematical formula. In particular, students should acquire the following seven skills.

1. Students must be able to identify behavior that is good and contributes to the general good.

2. Students must be able to identify behavior that is wrong, violates social and moral norms, and unjustifiably harms others.

3. Students must know how to think through the question, "What is the right thing to do about this issue going on right now in my class, or in this story?"

4. Students must be able to sort out the facts of what is going on and discover who is doing what to whom, and why. They must learn what evidence is, how to get it, and how to apply it.

5. Students must be able to recall similar incidents or principles that apply to a situation they currently face.

6. Students must be able to think through various solutions to a problem or an issue presented to them.

7. Students must be able to select the best—the most ethical—of the solutions they came up with.

Learning the good is not enough—we must strive to live it. It is the bedrock of a school's responsibility.

LOVING THE GOOD

We know much about the concept of knowing the good, as presented earlier in this chapter, and about doing the good, as we shall see later in this chapter. We seem to know much less, however, about loving the good. Love is like fire, a consuming energy—dangerous, vital, and difficult to contain. But life without love is shrunken and impoverished. Love out of control endangers life. Thus, like fire, love must be harnessed.

Learning to love the right things is the work of a lifetime. As parents we know how important it is for our children to love good people and good ideas. We feel anguish if they choose self-indulgent friends. We fret over the way they want to spend their free time and pay attention to the things they love to do. We worry most about the idealized image they construct of themselves—the self they are trying to become.

The Curriculum and the Hero

The educational response to the perceived values crisis in the 1960s and 1970s was often to create and adopt a new moral curriculum. Materials for that curriculum typically were permeated with the moral neutrality of two seriously deficient approaches: values clarification and cognitive developmental moral education. These two approaches differed somewhat in their emphasis; however, many differences were subtle and required considerable scrutiny to identify. Many practicing teachers, and most lay people, treated the approaches as interchangeable. This greatly enhanced the short-term effects of each approach. It seemed as if all serious concerns about moral education were to be treated with one uniform prescription: "Let the children decide for themselves."

These novel approaches dramatically contrasted with our schools' traditional moral curriculum. That curriculum aimed to engage the young in the most important ideas and content of our mainstream culture. Underlying the traditional curriculum was the question we referred to earlier: "What is most worth knowing?" Out of this quest came the content of schooling: the mathematical and scientific material students must master; the knowledge of their world that future citizens must possess; and our great narratives, the stories and histories that carry within them the moral facts of life and ideals that the young need to know to order their own lives and participate in civic life.

But any broad and noteworthy curriculum must also touch the heart. To be morally educated and ethically disposed to life involves more than just our minds. As Warren Nord has recently written, "The relationship between feeling and reason in ethics is complex and controversial, but certainly morality is grounded to some considerable extent in the moral feeling—compassion, guilt, hope, despair, dignity, mercy, and love, for example. When ethics is stripped of its emotional dimension, it becomes artificial, abstract, and lifeless."[7]

Our great narratives and literature fulfill an important need here. Through encounters with these materials, students learn

- ✦ to have both an intellectual and emotional understanding of the lives of good and evil people and what drove them to do what they did.

- ✦ to acquire an innate sense of justice and compassion and of greed and cruelty, learned through the study of the narrative's characters.

- ✦ to be touched emotionally by some characters' lives, attracted by some and repelled by others.

- ✦ to continually deepen their understanding of and feeling for moral facts of life and ideals by seeing them lived out in the narrative's heroes and villains.

- ✦ to enhance their moral imagination and moral sensibility as they vicariously experience the lives of characters.

- ✦ to have greater insight into the lives and stories depicted in literature and history.

- ✦ to have a storehouse of moral models to guide them when they act.

As students encounter the story of civilization in history and literature, they come to know Julius Caesar and Marc Antony, Henry the Eighth and Macbeth, Joan of Arc and Elizabeth Bennett, Adolf Hitler and Willie Stark, Martin Luther King, Jr., and Atticus Finch, Thomas Edison and Huck Finn, Walter Reuther and Hester Prynne. In these characters, they see abstractions, such as loyalty, compassion, and betrayal, come alive. For younger pupils, the message will also be transmitted by mythology and stories in readers. From Aesop's "The Hare and the Tortoise," they see the dangers of self-indulgence and the importance of staying the course. Patriotic tales, like "Horatio at the Bridge," tell the young that life was not always the way they are experiencing it and that others before them made great sacrifices so that we can live well. Further, these tales should alert them that they, too, may need to make extraordinary sacrifices for their neighbors, fellow Americans, and others in need. Our pupils live the experiences of real and imaginary people from our past. They measure themselves against the motives and accomplishments of these characters, challenge themselves to reach the levels of excellence they read about, and warn themselves against the weaknesses and mistakes they find in these stories. These figures become their models or their caution signs. Or so it ought to be.

Heroes and Villains

Twentieth-century philosopher Alfred North Whitehead argued strongly for the place of heroes in our education. He wrote, "A sense of greatness is the groundwork of morals." Whitehead believed it is impossible to have a moral order apart from "the habitual vision of greatness." Young people, therefore, need to be enveloped by heroic individuals and images.

William Bennett, the former U.S. Secretary of Education, grew up in Brooklyn in the 1940s and 1950s. He has written engagingly about his boyhood heroes. There were people like Gary Cooper as Marshall Will Kane in *High Noon* and ballplayers Lou Gehrig and Roy Campanella. But he also had heroes like Sir Edmund Hillary, Esther, Odysseus, and Abraham Lincoln. These latter heroes were consciously presented to him by parents and teachers. Referring to the heroes of his youth, Bennett writes:

> In all of them, it is fair to say that there was a certain nobility, a largeness of soul, a hitching up of one's own purposes beyond the self, to something that demanded endurance or sacrifice or courage or resolution or compassion; it was to nurture something because one had a sense of what deserved to be loved and preserved.[8]

But who are our children's current heroes? From 1980 to 1989, the *World Atlas* conducted a large-scale study of students from eighth to twelfth grade.[9] The question was simple: "Who is your hero or heroine?" Among the thirty heroes designated by respondents, there is no Jefferson, Washington, or Lincoln; no Eleanor Roosevelt, Jane Addams or Mother Teresa; no Edison or Jonas Salk or Madame Curie; no Henry Ford or Lee Iaccoca; no Abigail Adams or Annie Sullivan; no sign of General Eisenhower or General Colin Powell. Instead they listed celebrities: Eddie Murphy, Arnold Schwarzenneger, Prince, Michael Jackson, Burt Reynolds, and a smattering of sports stars. Individual parents were frequently mentioned. What emerges from these survey results is a picture of children confusing celebrity with the virtue and enduring fame that accompany heroism.

At intermittent occasions since the mid-1980s, one of the authors surveyed his undergraduate and graduate students. All were preparing for careers in teaching. They were asked two questions: "Who is your hero?" and "Who (other than Hitler) do you consider evil?" Some students had difficulty identifying a hero. Of each group, approximately 15% listed their parents or grandparents. A smaller percentage (usually 5% or 6%) designated Jesus Christ. Close behind were Martin Luther King, Jr., and Mother Teresa. At that point the list of heroes breaks down and becomes quite particular (e.g., my fifth-grade teacher, Mr. McCarthy; my high school English teacher, Miss Bohlin). However, 55% to 60% of these young adults named popular and contemporary personalities, the type of "heroes" who fill the pages of *People* magazine.

These same students had even more trouble with the question about whom they considered evil. Many answered, "No one is evil." The most frequently mentioned evildoers were people receiving prominent coverage in news stories at the time of the survey. As a result, during the period of the period of the Gulf War, 20% of respondents in one class identified Saddam Hussein as an evil person. In earlier years, Libyan leader Khaddafi and the Ayatollah Khomeini of Iran had received the highest mention. More recently, Susan Smith, O. J. Simpson, and the Menendez brothers have garnered solid percentages. Television serials were the source of imaginary evil individuals for some, even though the question asked respondents to name real people.

These two preceding separate surveys, one of high-school-age youth and one of future teachers, have relatively consistent themes. They provide serious food for thought. Suffice it to say that our traditional heroes and heroines, our Jeffersons and Jane Addamses, are not large in the minds and hearts of our young people or tomorrow's teachers. The findings are more than simply a curious artifact of contemporary life. The inability of our culture to project its best and brightest as models—or its worst and most heinous as villains—should be a source of alarm.

Paul Vitz discovered another pattern of denigrating heroism in his research.[10] He surveyed innumerable school readers, literature anthologies, and history and social science texts used in American schools during the late 1970s and early 1980s. As educators know, such books often contain stories and portraits aimed at identifying role models for pupils. For example, there were essentially ten different social studies texts used in fifth- and sixth-grade classrooms at that time. Vitz demonstrated that the portrait materials in the ten texts was almost exclusively comprised of recent liberal politicians and important female personalities. Some of these figures undoubtedly could be characterized as bona fide heroes, such as Martin Luther King, Jr. But, more often, it is evident they were presented simply as important representatives of particular groups. However, while they were prominent and successful members of such groups, it was not clear they had really "risked their lives, their fortunes, or their sacred honor." Three-quarters of the persons on the lists might be found in *People* magazine. The figures included no businesspeople, or male White political figures, or notable conservatives. The lists were, in many ways, both unheroic and comparably unrepresentative of America at large. These deficiencies provide a partial explanation for the limited and shallow perspectives displayed in the student surveys conducted by *World Atlas*. The students' curriculum, riddled with transparent and naive ideology, also failed to supply most of them with vital, relevant heroes. And so they turned to rock stars and television, movie, and sports personalities.

Some people might complain that in a democracy there is no need for heroes, that such concerns are elitist. The German playwright Bertolt Brecht said, "Unhappy is the land that needs heroes." Another line of reasoning states that heroes feed elitism, and elitism is contrary to the egalitarian spirit of democracy. In fact, nothing could be further from the truth. Democracy requires heroes and heroines. Thomas Jefferson spoke of democracy's need for a natural aristocracy, a class of persons who would lead the nation and inspire others to think about and work for the common good. Society, through the appeal of heroic models, must arouse in the young a vision of the worthy life and a love for the ideals of democracy. The British poet Stephen Spender has written:

> *I think continually of those who were truly great*
> *The names of those who in their lives fought for life,*
> *Who wore at their hearts the fire's centre.*

Sophie Barat, the founder of a religious community of teachers, once said, "Youth is not built for pleasure, but for heroism." To call out the best in an individual usually takes strong stuff. It involves teachers making powerful demands on themselves in order to make such demands on others. Even what seem to be our individual best efforts may not be enough for life's challenges. The poet May Sarton has written, "One must think like a hero / in order to behave like a merely human being"—another justification for surrounding our students with our best.

Developing the Moral Imagination

Psychologist William Kirk Kilpatrick wrote:

> Moral development is not simply a matter of becoming more rational or acquiring decision-making skills. It has to do with vision, the way one looks at life. . . . It follows that one of the central tasks of moral education is to nourish the imagination with rich and powerful images found in stories, myths, poems, biography and drama. If we wish our children to grow up with a deep and adequate vision of life, we must provide a rich fund for them to draw on.[11]

Teachers are responsible for feeding their pupils' moral imagination, for ensuring that they truly encounter models of human excellence and frailty. Such figures should not simply be the focus of examination questions. Some of the things teachers can do to ensure students come to know these characters are

- ✦ assign students biographies and biographical sketches of great contributors to society.
- ✦ give students individual projects to report on the lives of significant, wholesome members of their family, community, religion, or ethnic group.
- ✦ display pictures of heroes (or writings about them) on school and classroom walls and bulletin boards. Make the study of these heroes part of the curriculum, regularly calling students' attention to them and their contributions.
- ✦ have students engage in role playing and dramatize crucial moments in the lives of great people.

✦ in social studies and history lessons, linger over the human factors involved: identify the negative and positive results that flow from human desires and actions. Do not leave students with the impression that foolish wars or cruel despots are simply the product of impersonal forces. This widespread view is another flawed intellectual attitude. Historian Richard Hunt has labeled it our "no-fault theory of history." In contrast, earlier societies preferred to emphasize, perhaps even overemphasize, the role of individual choice. A classic example of such an approach is Plutarch's *Parallel Lives of the Ancient Greeks and Noble Romans*. The book stresses the difference that human wisdom and determination can make in complex situations. Composed in the first century B.C., it is still engaging reading. Its emphasis on personal responsibility provides learners with strong motivation to strive towards self-control. The emphasis contrasts strongly with the personal irresponsibility transmitted by deterministic doctrines such as Marxism.

✦ in reading, stress "the heart of the matter." It is important to read literature for language and plot; however, the motivations and moral struggles of the characters also need to be highlighted and analyzed. Richard the Third's treachery should not be sacrificed in favor of Shakespeare's language. Nor should Huck Finn's ethical anguish over helping the slave Jim escape be lost to a study of Twain's symbolic use of the river or the steamboat's contribution to opening up the West. Teachers should try to bring these heroic and villainous actions into sharp relief for students, asking, "What has Huck done that you admire, that you would want to imitate?"

Everyday Heroes

The effort to surround students with heroes and heroines, and to help them acquire a sense of altruism, should not be confined to history and literature. Science, arts, and music classes should study the lives and contributions of great scientists and artists. The disciplined toil and persistence involved in creativity should be an integral part of the study of these fields.

The formal curriculum is not the only source of ethical models or moral stories. Teachers should not ignore events in the world around them. Each day brings reports of people doing heroic things: a bystander dives into a frozen river to save drowning passengers after an air disaster; an engineer persists in the face of repeated failure and finally develops an important safety device; a businesswoman gives up a lucrative career to work among the poor. There are also reports of villainous acts: A politician uses his prestige to hide the criminal behavior of a group of bankers, or a researcher distorts her data to justify a desired conclusion. We should always be careful about canonizing the living. Still, we should point out to the young that there are heroic people among us, such as ex-Vietnam P.O.W. James Stockdale and Rosa Parks. At a more proximate level, there are individuals in every community who work heroically for the good of others, for example, in business, service activities, or community affairs. These people and their works are legitimate subjects for examination by students. As William Damon has suggested in *The Moral Child*, perhaps these virtuous people can be encouraged to visit classrooms or attend school activities, telling their stories to pupils and being available for conversation—and, we hope, for emulation.

Alexander Pope said it best: "The proper study of mankind is man." There are heroes and heroines in every community. Imaginative administrators and teachers can find ways to weave these people into students' lives.

DOING THE GOOD

When asked, "How do you make someone virtuous?" Aristotle responded, "A man becomes kind by doing kind acts. He becomes brave by performing brave acts."[12] A curriculum that aims to form good students must give them occasions for moral action. However, our youth lack opportunities to become moral actors.

In an influential book, *Youth: Transition into Adulthood*, sociologist James Coleman described how the experience of youth in America has been radically altered.[13] The change was caused by many forces: by shifts in the means of production, the distribution of food and other goods, and the size and structure of the American family. The modern world has fundamentally revised the way we prepare children for adult life. Among the major changes is that young people have little to do with the economic survival of the family. Typical children no longer live on a farm or help their parents with a small business. They have little to contribute. Because of smaller families, there is less opportunity to be responsible for younger siblings. What responsibilities they have, such as making their bed, doing the dishes, and folding laundry, are not the kinds of tasks that help forge a sense of self-worth and competence. At the same time, today's young people exist in a world that urges them towards a self-focused mentality. They are surrounded by cultural forces vying to capture them as consumers of passive pleasures and luxuries. Many children become captives of such systems, unable to satisfy even the minimal expectations of home and school. They become, in effect, slaves to their pleasures.

Today's young people are caught up in a world of mediated sounds and pictures. Much of this world plays on their curiosity for the new and different. While they may "know" much more than their predecessors, their knowledge is eccentric. Coleman describes American youth as "information rich and experience poor." Certainly many young people learn self-discipline through academics and athletic programs, activities that stress the capacity to persist at difficult tasks and other virtues. But many students do not participate in such activities. Their physical and intellectual capabilities do not mesh with these particular endeavors. Because such activities are a source of failure, they avoid taking part.

Educators can provide experiences of fundamental importance to those youth who need to break out of their envelope of self-interest or escapism and develop as mature adults. Educators can give pupils opportunities and training to be moral actors by creating an appropriate mix of prosocial activities in the classroom. As for the use of schoolwide activities to foster such ends, chapter 3 provides a number of proposals. Educational gurus notwithstanding, not all students can be good scholars, aflame for new knowledge. More obliviously, not all students can become athletic stars. By contrast, the life of virtue, the acquisition of enduring habits, such as kindness and persistence, is open to and achievable by virtually all students.

Moral Action and the Democratic Schools Movement

There has been a good deal written about moral education being fostered in "democratic" schools and classrooms. John Dewey was an early proponent of such concerns. Certainly our schools should contribute to the maintenance of our democratic government and institutions. As stated earlier, we recognize that democracy, with its respect for individual rights and responsibilities, is a profoundly moral idea. Possibly in recognition of this fact, and of the need for schools to assist in the maintenance of democracy, a number of educators have begun what we call the Democratic Schools movement. Harvard psychologist Lawrence Kohlberg was notably associated with this movement.

Kohlberg and his followers did not believe educational democracy was simply an ideal for pupils to learn now and apply in the future. Instead, they thought it should be fully present in pupils' current lives:

> Democratic schools should be established. In such schools, pupils and faculty—everyone—has [sic] a *formally equal voice* [our emphasis] in making the rules. The validity of such rules are [sic] judged by their fairness to the interests of all involved. If the best learning is learning by doing, then students can best learn justice not only by discussing its claims in the abstract, but also by acting on its claims in the here and now of the school day.[14]

The precise characteristics of what a "democratic school" is varies from school to school and place to place. However, the core idea seems to be to give students—usually high school students—a direct experience in democracy. The movement involves students much more directly and gives them more authority than the traditional student council. In fact, democratic schools often allocate authority to students in areas that are usually reserved for adults in other schools. For instance, students in these schools participate directly in deciding school policies, such as the rules of discipline and the behavior code. Sometimes they have the majority vote in these matters. They have control of certain public funds to use as they decide. They receive petitions and requests from administrators, teachers, and other students, and they discharge those requests. Sometimes, such programs do not involve the entire school. Instead they are programs for special groups of pupils in otherwise traditional schools.

A *New York Times* article described one democratic public school. In the school, the students voted whether sex and knives should be prohibited at the forthcoming school picnic.[15] Fortunately, the prohibition forces won after lengthy debate. Presumably, if the vote had gone the other way, sex and knives would be licensed. One of the authors was incredulous about the report. As a result, he phoned the school to check the story's accuracy. He was told the story was true, that the incident had occurred under the school's former principal.

Probably very few American public schools have seriously applied these remarkable ideas. But there is evidence that the influence of such ideas extends beyond their precise number. When such a school innovation is carefully described in the *New York Times*, it has attained a considerable level of attention. And Professor Kohlberg, the founder of the movement, is one of the world's most frequently cited psychologists in professional literature. The practices in these schools have established an image of what "education for democracy" means, and few Americans are prepared to say they are against education for democracy. Thus, we are led to an anomalous impasse: either people are led to tolerate, or sympathize, with what are often dubious practices, or they feel guilty for opposing "democracy."

The principles underlying democratic schools are quite different from the basic governmental modes that have long prevailed in the U.S. We are a republic, a society where most government decisions are made by elected representatives of the people, not by direct popular vote. The plebiscite is not a typical form of American political action. (The legendary New England town meetings, where such direct democracy is practiced, have only affected minute numbers of American citizens for many decades.) Our country's founders deliberately selected a republican mode of government instead of a direct democracy for innumerable practical and theoretical reasons. Ironically, the educators and intellectuals who founded the democratic schools movement seem unfamiliar with our 200-year-old political traditions. In reality, the model of the school student council, where certain decisions are made by student representatives, chosen after election campaigns, is more like our republican system of government.

Actually, this prescribed direct experience in democratic self-government rarely meets even the theoretical requirements of a true democracy. Historically, democracy means an assembly of all the interested parties, each with a vote. But when votes are taken in democratic schools, no parents vote, though they clearly have a strong interest in what their children are licensed or required to do. No taxpayers vote, although they usually foot the bill for almost all school activities. Teachers often have a vote in these councils, but they are equal with students on a one-person-one-vote basis. Allegedly, the purpose is to give students real responsibility for moral action—to practice doing the good.

The movement is also seriously flawed because it continuously stresses the theme of student responsibility. But responsibility means accepting the consequences. If we break your window, our responsibility means we should pay for its repair. However, students will rarely have to pay money out of their pockets if something goes wrong due to their decisions. They will not have to pay the costs if someone gets stabbed on a picnic where they have voted to allow knives. That will be left up to taxpayers, the school board, or the injured pupil's family. Students will not be expelled if the policy they vote for proves unsound, although the principal allowing that policy may get fired. And so on. The talk about responsibility appears to be so much cant. It would seem that students in these democratic schools are given authority, while the responsibility remains with others. It is only play acting, and it is very unhealthy.

We do not question some of the impulses underlying the Democratic Schools movement: to prepare students for participation in civic life and give education more of a hands-on quality. Perhaps such experiments have done some good, for instance, teaching some individual students the skills and habits of public deliberation. However, we are skeptical. Our observations of these experiments in action and conversations with students who have participated in them lead us to conclude that, at best, they waste enormous amounts of valuable student time in labored discussions of the obvious. At worst, they give students a distorted perception of our political process and, even more importantly, what they, as students, should be about.

There is an old well-known truism that we must crawl before we can walk and walk before we can run. Another familiar and appropriate quotation is: "For everything there is a season and a time to every purpose under heaven."[16] The same is true for learning about democracy, and republican government. Schools are not, should not, and, indeed, cannot be either democracies or republics—just as there should not be democratic gas stations or democratic hospitals. The very nature of a school requires a hierarchy of knowledge and responsibilities. This hierarchy must be under the control of adults and accountable to representative external agencies that create and finance the school. In the classroom, the teacher must be the authority and have authority over students. Without this relationship, school quickly turns to chaos. The essential nature of the student is to be a learner, not a policymaker.

In the 1930s George Counts, a prominent academic, issued the challenge: "Dare the schools build a new social order?"[17] In effect, the book asked teachers to change America, by teaching new and different values to their pupils. It seems that, since that time, educators have been confusing education *for* democratic living with education *as* democratic living. Surely, one of the important subject matters of our schools is democratic, or republican, citizenship. However, this is learned in many ways, from the give-and-take of the playground and the Student Council to the careful study of the *Federalist Papers* and our Constitution. Not all education should necessarily be hands-on.

COOPERATIVE LEARNING: AN UNCERTAIN REMEDY

We have interviewed many teachers about their personal recommendations for transmitting prosocial learning. Probably the most frequent technique they recommend is cooperative learning—groups of pupils working together on academic assignments. Unfortunately, our experience makes us far less enthusiastic about this approach. Indeed, as now typically used, cooperative learning probably does more harm than good for pupils' character. And so the deficiencies—and benefits—of the approach require careful discussion.

Readers must first recognize that there are at least two forms of cooperative learning, although educators too frequently refer to the practice in an undifferentiated form. First, there are deliberately constructed cooperative learning packages designed for teaching particular curriculum materials, such as teaching part of sixth-grade math. One example is the carefully designed package of materials produced by the Center for the Study of Schools.[18]

Second, there are more diffuse packages and approaches. These materials are designed for general application, or adaptation, by teachers to diverse subjects. One of the authors has produced one such publication.[19] Vermette has also published a useful list of precautions.[20]

Either approach has its limits. Specific packages can be carefully designed, but they may cover only a fraction of the overall school curriculum. The more generalized materials may require teachers to engage in a considerable amount of adaptation or extrapolation. Furthermore, the principles applied in either of the two types of packages may be defective. Most such packages are labeled as "evaluated"; however, we hope that by this time readers will realize that the weight to be given to such evaluations is often problematic. The following discussion identifies ways readers can conduct their own evaluations—or design their own cooperative activities.

One of the authors has surveyed hundreds of graduate and undergraduate students, from about 1980 to now, about their personal experiences as students in cooperative learning. Respondents were asked whether and how they participated in cooperative learning in elementary and high schools. Since some graduated from high school only two or three years prior to the time of the survey, their replies fairly reflect current cooperative learning practices. Their replies indicate generally common experiences. Almost all the students, on some occasions during school, were grouped with other students to work cooperatively on academic projects. Many of these projects were brief—ranging from fifteen minutes to perhaps a few hours. These activities can be entirely legitimate education exercises, but it would be simplistic to suggest they encourage important prosocial conduct. The duration of most projects was too brief to supply the challenges necessary to stimulate profound learning. Such brief cooperative activities—especially as pupils mature and become capable of more elaborate exercises—are not very significant for character formation.

Many students also reported they were occasionally asked to participate in more elaborate cooperative projects with other pupils. The length of such projects ranged from several hours to several weeks. Assignments of this scope have the potential for encouraging the practice of significant prosocial skills. They can assist in the formation of good, or bad, character. Respondents who had substantial cooperative assignments were asked whether, and how, they were graded for their work on such projects. As we will see, this matter of grading is very important.

Some of the students were not graded on their cooperative work, but typically they were graded for their other academic work. Such contrasting grading policies have important effects. We can assume the students would probably dedicate little or no effort to the cooperative project. Logical students would assume that their teacher expected them to concentrate on their traditional academic subjects, where they could earn good or bad grades. In other words, without an allocated grade, or other vital form of evaluation and recognition, a time-consuming cooperative exercise is of no great importance for character formation.

Still other students reported their teachers gave elaborate group assignments and did grade their projects. In such cases, the teacher usually gave the whole project one grade, so that each cooperator received that same grade, which appeared on their report card, for their work. Such uniform grading is unsound. The students who were subjected to that process were often very critical of that cooperative learning practice. They frequently reported that, during the projects, the dedication and skills of team members were unequal. Often their groups included one or more freeloaders. These were pupils who consciously determined not to work very hard and assumed that other, responsible pupils would be pressured to do the work, while they would receive a high, although unearned, grade. Indeed, this expectation of freeloading was so common that the author's pupils regularly looked towards his forthcoming class, which would emphasize long-term group projects, with disfavor. They expected to be exploited by freeloaders once again, as had usually occurred in their earlier classes. In other words, many pupils' previous experience with significant in-school cooperative learning had been unhappy. It taught them to avoid substantial cooperative work.

Some other pupils reported other grading systems their teachers applied for longer cooperative projects. Without going into details, it seems most of these "solutions" were seriously flawed. The systems failed in diverse ways:

- ✦ They did not realistically accept the fact that there are or may be freeloaders, or seriously inept pupils (whom the able students see as an unfair burden).

- ✦ The teachers undertook the task of policing each group to maintain appropriate pressure. This is an extreme and unrealistic practice that actually shields pupils from the great learning experience in worthwhile cooperative activities of monitoring cooperation in their own group.

- ✦ Students in each group were given two separate grades: one for their individual efforts, and one uniform grade for the team's project. The individual-effort grade really reflected the teacher's assessment of each student's particular element of the whole project, for example, the student's chapter. However, the individual grades were the only ones entered on their report cards. This grading system would provide students with little incentive to engage in serious cooperative efforts. The system simply encouraged students to work hard on their isolated segments of the project, but not to care about the overall task assigned to the whole group.

- ✦ Students were explicitly or implicitly asked to monitor and pressure their own freeloaders. However, they were supplied with no effective tools for generating pressure. Of course they could not physically attack freeloaders. All they could do was practice social withdrawal. Freeloaders who were determined to be nasty and simply bully others throughout the project could get away with it. This was surely a disheartening lesson to teach all concerned. In some instances, the freeloaders comprised the majority of a group. They simply coerced the dedicated minority to do the bulk of the work.

The preceding general remarks about cooperative learning were tested in the first-hand experience of the other author, who regularly teaches a large, one-hundred-plus student education course. Among the education concepts studied is cooperative learning, which typically is extremely popular with these prospective teachers. The idea was so popular that, at the students' urging, the teacher designated a portion of the course, the development of a research paper, as a cooperative learning exercise. Initially students were extremely enthusiastic. They fully agreed to having 25% of their individual grades based on the teacher's evaluation of their group's collective research report. The experience was not an exact copy of an approved cooperative learning strategy; however, it conformed to many of the principles of that approach. The results were enormously disappointing, primarily to the more serious students who felt that they had to "carry" others in their group. Course morale was never lower. Convinced that the results came from his own inexperience, the instructor tried the cooperative learning strategy exercise for two more semesters. Each time the process was refined with modifications suggested by the students and agreed to by the teacher. The results were the same: frustrations, disappointment and lowered morale—and, undoubtedly, lowered formal learning.

The other author has developed, through prolonged application, a cooperative learning system that overcomes the foregoing objections to team assignments.[21] The system is a relatively elaborate simulation, a structured process that represents an attempt to replicate in the classroom the pressures that surround group cooperation in out-of-school life.

We will briefly describe this system. It is not the only way of solving the problems outlined, nor can it be mechanically applied to students in lower grades. Still, the system offers an example of how to attack the problem if we hope to encourage student cooperation in academic work.

At the beginning of the course, the instructor randomly divides students into teams of three to five students. During the course, all teams must complete two assigned writing projects. The projects, both done for grades, are the principal academic work for the course. The first project is relatively brief and serves as a practice exercise. The second is quite elaborate: the assignment is to find and describe in some detail a real operating school. Throughout the course, the pupils are instructed through lectures, exercises, and readings on how to conduct their research and write the necessary papers.

The instructor grades the papers for each of the two projects in toto. Each paper receives a numerical grade, for instance, 3.0 for a B grade; or 2.4 for a high C. Each team then determines the grades of its individual members by deciding how to subdivide the team's overall grade. For example, a four-member team with a B paper might decide to give each member a B, while another might subdivide the grades so there are two Bs, one C, and one A. Note that in the second case the total grade still averages B. In other words, the instructor decides the overall value of the work, and the team divides that grade among its members. Team members know who really did—or did not do—the work. No final paper is accepted unless a majority of team members have signed their assent, on the paper, to the proposed grade division. That division is expressed as proportions of 100%. If all members of a four-member team simply get B, that division is four grades of 25%, for a total of 100%. In the example when the four grades are two Bs, one C, and one A, the division would be 25%, 25%, 20%, and 30%, respectively.

After problems arose from the initial design, the simulation was altered in response. One problem was that the real workers are sometimes a minority of the team and may be exploited by freeloaders. Another was that most students need advice about how to handle the novel problems that arise during cooperative activities. In addition, we found there is insufficient time to hold all team meetings during class.

Our solutions to these problems deserve brief consideration, since the solutions themselves tell us much about the learning demands that serious prosocial conduct generates for team members. Students are given some freedom to switch teams on their own, after a short introductory phase. The instructor gives students generalized advice about cooperative work through lectures. The instructor also provides more focused counsel in a series of meetings with the teams and in one-to-one sessions with individual team members. Some team meetings occur during class time. This permits the instructor to observe and offer advice. Others occur out of the instructor's sight, to give students a chance to operate on their own. Finally, students are encouraged to arrange away-from-class meetings of their teams to overcome the problem of insufficient class time for meetings.

The consequences of the simulation are interesting. Many teams produce excellent papers, providing far richer descriptions than individual team members could do on their own. The instructor finds himself working more like a coach and less like a disengaged lecturer. All pupils agree that their interstudent contacts in the class are far more intense than in most other classes. A large majority of students say that such contacts are far richer and more gratifying. They are more likely to make friends as a result of the course. A few of the students, 5% to 10%, believe their interstudent contacts in the class are much worse than in typical classes. This is quite plausible. When human relationships become more intense, some are likely to change for the worse. The instructor is convinced that such dissatisfaction would diminish if the students could take similar courses over several semesters. The students who "erred" would be likely to correct their mistakes. However, it has not been practical to arrange such continuity.

In summary, the concept of cooperative learning is fine. However, if we want students to experience more elaborate cooperation, we must analyze the learning systems we design. It is no simple task to create a learning system that consistently operates in a wholesome manner. Many existing cooperative learning systems are probably teaching questionable skills and attitudes.

The Real Moral Action

Moral action is consciously doing the good. There can be heroic moral action, such as giving one's life for another; however, the occasions for moral action are usually rather ordinary. The schoolwide prosocial service programs we urged in chapter 3 should have counterparts in the classroom. Students should learn that helping other students and teachers is a normal part of classroom life. Fortunately, there exist unending opportunities for students to be of service and to do ordinary moral action in classrooms. Some examples are:

+ doing one's assignments as well and carefully as possible—being diligent
+ befriending a new or lonely student
+ working on a cooperative project with others, sharing what one knows and does not know
+ volunteering to help the teacher or other school staff, particularly when this action might expose one to ridicule
+ breaking up a fight or patching up a disagreement among classmates
+ not joining in when the class is taking advantage of a substitute teacher, or opposing such behavior as unfair
+ quietly helping another student who is having difficulty with an assignment
+ participating actively and well in school ceremonial events, such as saying the Pledge of Allegiance clearly and respectfully, or learning the school song and singing it well
+ performing simple, everyday acts, such as bending down to pick up a discarded paper in the main hall, even at the risk of being called a goody-goody—or worse

In conclusion, there are currently great pressures for the curriculum to cover more and more topics, such as environmental education and studies in pluralism, and include more and more goals, such as students' self-esteem and media literacy. One of the growing voices is for greater emphasis on moral education and character formation. We believe that, rather than representing a new voice, this emphasis amounts to a rediscovery of the curriculum's core intention.

Curriculum is the knowledge, skills, and attitudes we transmit and promote in school. The curriculum should aim to forge good students. Teachers and administrators should not look for special programs or imported panaceas to improve moral instruction. Instead, they can find their most potent instrument in the form and substance of their curriculum. Unfortunately, many educators have lost the habit of using the curriculum for this purpose. Therefore, we must look among ourselves to see how we can use what we have to help form good students.

Practices and Policies

1. In general, how aware are teachers of your school's hidden curriculum? List several ideas that seem to be promoted through the school's hidden curriculum. Do you think such ideas are good or bad?

2. Analyze your own classroom or have a colleague observe you for one or two class periods. Do you discover anything about your own hidden curriculum of which you were not aware? Is the hidden curriculum that is being promoted in your classroom consistent with your explicit curriculum and your perceived role as a moral educator?

3. Do teachers in your school have a common understanding of the most important goal in the school's formal curriculum? Are there goals in the formal curriculum that explicitly address morality and character? What are they? How could they be improved?

4. Consider the ethical ideals presented in this chapter. To what degree do you think these principles are directly and indirectly taught in your school or classroom?

5. List several activities or lessons currently being taught in your school that directly support any one of the ethical principles presented in this chapter. With some other teachers, list possible units or lessons in which these ethical principles could be infused.

6. With your students, identify and discuss the characteristics of heroic people. Each month, prominently display a picture of a hero or heroine and discuss that person's contribution to humanity. Depending on your grade level or subject, you could expand the concept of heroes and heroines to become a thematic unit for your class.

7. Are there service activities that you, other teachers, or the school as a whole could sponsor as part of the curriculum? For example, could you and your students, or you and members of a club or team that you monitor, take responsibility for picking up trash from the playground, "adopt" an elderly couple needing help with household chores, volunteer at a homeless shelter, or volunteer to clean up a local beach, park, or riverbank? For teachers with older adolescents, perhaps you could become involved in a blood drive. With several other teachers, list such projects in which you and your students could participate.

Notes and References

1. Moline, J. N. (1981). Classical ideas about moral education. *Character, 2*(8), 8.

2. Kozol, J. (1967). *Death at an early age*. Boston: Houghton Mifflin; Holt, J. (1967). *How children fail*. New York: Pitman; and Silberman, C. E. (1970). *Crisis in the classroom*. New York: Random House.

3. Lewis, C. S. (1947). *The abolition of man: How education develops man's sense of morality*. New York: Collier/Macmillan Books, p. 29.

4. Moline, ibid.

5. On the other hand, American humorous poet Ogden Nash wrote: "Hope that in the human breast does spring is fond of wine or beer, or anything designed to help a hope to spring."

6. Delattre, E. J. (1988). *Education and the public trust: The imperatives for common purposes.* Washington, DC: Ethics and Public Policy Center, p. 89.

7. Nord, W. A. (1991). Teaching and morality: The knowledge most worth having. In D. D. Dill & associates (Eds.), *What teachers need to know.* San Francisco: Jossey-Bass.

8. Bennett, W. (1977, August 15). Let's bring back heroes. *Newsweek.*

9. World Atlas. (1980–1989). Mahwah, NJ: Funk & Wagnalls.

10. Vitz, P. (1986). *Censorship: Evidence of bias in children's books.* Ann Arbor, MI: Servant.

11. Kilpatrick, W. K. (1985). *The emperor's new clothes: The naked truth about modern psychology.* Westchester, IL: Goodnews Press, p. 97.

12. Aristotle. (1941). Nicomachean ethics. In Richard McKeon (Ed.), *The basic works of Aristotle* (W. D. Ross, Trans.). New York: Random House, p. 953.

13. Coleman, J. S. (1974). *Youth: Transition to adulthood.* Chicago: University of Chicago Press.

14. Power, F. C., Higgins, A., & Kohlberg, L. (1989). *Lawrence Kohlberg's approach to moral education.* New York: Columbia University Press, pp. 7, 25.

15. Hand, D. (1989, April 9). Morality lessons? Hear, hear. *New York Times Special Report on Education*, p. 53.

16. Ecclesiastes, 3:2–3. *New American Bible.* New York: World Publishing.

17. Counts, G. S. (1932). *Dare the teachers of America build a new social order?* New York: John Day.

18. Center for the Study of Schools, Cooperative Learning Materials, Baltimore, MD; see also Slavin, R. (1990). *Cooperative learning.* Boston: Allyn & Bacon.

19. Wynne, E. A. (1995). *Cooperation-competition: An instructional strategy.* A Phi Delta Kappan Fastback, no. 378. Bloomington, IN: Phi Delta Kappa.

20. Vermette, P. (1994). The right start for cooperative learning. *The High School Journal*, 77(Feb–Mar), 255–368.

21. Wynne, E. A. (1976). Learning about cooperation and competition. *Educational Forum, 40,* 279–288.

CHAPTER 8

Fostering Community in Schools and Classrooms

. . . liturgy is not simply a function of religion but an inevitable feature of the life of the city. The Greeks were, I think, the first to define it . . . each citizen was assigned a portion of the material work of the city as his personal responsibility: the repair of so many feet of wall, for example, or the construction of so many yards of drainage facility. The word they used for this was leitourgia. They saw that community of life meant community in things, and that unless the citizens joined in the doing of the things, the city would not thrive. Each was to have his particular liturgy; but it was to be his as a member of the body politic, not on the basis of his private taste. As cities became larger and more complex, of course, it became unwieldy. But it is precisely the absence of visible liturgy that nowadays makes the common life less obvious to common men.

—Robert F. Capon[1]

Earlier, in chapter 2, we referred to the Great Tradition, which essentially focused on the moral aims of education. The Great Tradition envisaged children reared in a community, a social environment where relatively supportive, intimate, persisting, and predictable relationships prevailed among the inhabitants. America's history provides a striking example of the application of the Great Tradition. In 1620 the first English settlers in New England arrived in a wilderness. They quickly realized their children were being reared away from the routine supports typical of the English communities they had left. The settlers were appalled at the implications of their wilderness environment for their children's values. In 1647 they passed laws providing for systems of public education, "lest by degrees we sink into savagery and barbarism."

The settlers understood that New England lacked the communal structures prevailing in England. It became essential for them to make a deliberate effort to "invent" local communal forms. Without such forms, their children would not grow into vital adulthood.

COMMUNITY AND SCHOOL SPIRIT

Even in our own era many educators give high priority to the maintenance of community in and around schools. But they usually describe their efforts with the popular term *school spirit*, rather than the more academic term *community*. The two terms, however, have the same operational definitions, so we will apply them interchangeably. This matter of interchangeability is quite important; there is considerable literature on the development of community. We will tap this knowledge in our analysis of how to improve school spirit.

Many educators conceive of school spirit as a by-product of a school's successful athletic teams. Team success is often due to factors outside of school influence. One school may be lucky enough to have a good collection of athletes enrolled at one time. Another school's attendance area may tap some neighborhood where parents are especially interested in encouraging their children into athletics. Certain schools, elementary schools in many situations, for various reasons cannot participate in competitive athletics.

If athletic success is an important component of school spirit and yet partly beyond the control of educators, it may seem that school spirit is largely due—for better or worse—to unmanageable forces or random chance. This is incorrect. Although success in competitive athletics is not irrelevant to school spirit, there are innumerable other factors that also determine the quality of school spirit. The management of these other factors is largely in the hands of educators. To make wise decisions about how to foster school spirit, educators need a theory, a structured body of ideas about what to do and why.

A DEFINITION

First we will define what a community is. Then we can identify steps that schools can take to improve their levels of community to enrich school spirit. Elements of a community include:

- ✦ A community is a bounded environment, persisting over time.
- ✦ Its inhabitants share important common goals, articulated by significant rites and symbols.
- ✦ The inhabitants cooperate with one another and with certain external institutions to attain these goals.
- ✦ Frequently, such cooperation is managed by some system of benign hierarchy.
- ✦ In vital, large communities the members simultaneously belong to the larger group and various subcommunities. These subcommunities replicate, on a micro-scale, the essential factors of the larger community.

It will be profitable to dissect and analyze this definition. Our analysis will also identify concrete applications of relevant principles in school settings.

About Boundaries

Boundaries are means of keeping outsiders away from a community. Outsiders are persons or groups unsympathetic or at best neutral to the community's values. Boundaries, however defined, are critical to community. Indeed, without boundaries, there is no commonality. A randomly collected group of people are unlikely to form a community, since they will not have a common point of view about most complex issues.

Boundaries can exist around a school, or around certain programs, classes, or other activities in school. Much of the following discussion will focus on individual schools. Readers should also try to recognize ways the discussion applies to intraschool situations. Indeed, many contemporary efforts at school reform aim to create subschools and other kinds of minicommunities in schools. These efforts are directly concerned with the issues in this chapter. Unfortunately, the restructuring efforts often abort or fail precisely because the creators of these activities neglect to consider the principles that govern community life. Later in this chapter, we will explicitly consider the connections between such principles and inventions like minischools.

Some schools are situated in neighborhoods that are in disorder. It is important for such schools to establish boundaries that separate themselves from external disorder. They must control their doors to ensure that strangers with bad intentions and other exploiters cannot easily penetrate the school environment. If the school's tangible boundaries, its walls and doors, can be easily penetrated, the school's inhabitants will not feel safe. They will, quite understandably, withdraw from people they see in the building to protect themselves from danger.

One of the authors recalls visiting a school where all control of external boundaries had been lost. The administrators could not arrange for all the building's doors to be either closely monitored or securely locked. As a result, individual teachers each locked the door to their classroom to protect the class from the dangers in the halls. In such a situation, the level of community among classes was almost nil; they were too afraid to try to contact each other. The first step to fostering school spirit in such a school would be to regain control of the school's external doors to reestablish certain tangible boundaries.

Schools, especially if they are located in disordered neighborhoods, apply a variety of means to maintain tangible boundaries. They ensure that almost all doors are securely locked during the school day. They post guards and monitors where the active entrances can be observed. They require that visitors first go to the office and/or get security passes. They have bells that visitors must ring to be admitted. They maintain closed campuses to restrict pupil involvement with the neighborhood during the school day and cut down traffic into the school.

Another school-bounding device is the use of plastic I.D. cards containing a photo. These cards are typically provided for both faculty and students. Their use also has a semisymbolic nature: it implies recognition that, in larger schools, it is impossible for everyone to recognize everyone else. There must be a simple, immediate means of identification to separate community members from intruders. Hence, the cards serve as a form of boundary. Only community members have cards. In some schools, faculty and students are required to wear their cards at some visible place on their clothing. People walking by one another can then determine identity through observation, avoiding the need for monitors to ask for identification from each person.

It is obvious that I.D. cards work better if everyone wears them publicly. In many schools, however, the administrative and disciplinary problems involved in enforcing such a "wear a card" rule are too vexing. When the cards are not prominently displayed, they lose some of their efficiency. People are less safe, and the sense of community is weaker, partly because community members are not cooperating with a simple rule made in the interest of all.

Another symbolic boundary is sometimes applied, usually in private schools, when students wear uniforms. This practice has a variety of effects, but one is that it causes strangers in the school to be conspicuous. Since they are not dressed like students in the school, they clearly violate the school's boundaries. At this time there is increased interest in encouraging or compelling pupils to wear uniforms in some public schools. This development is an example of the revival of interest in traditional values.

Conceptual Boundaries

Schools or school programs can be surrounded by conceptual boundaries as well as physical ones. Such conceptual boundaries are extremely important. Essentially, they determine who is eligible to enroll in the school. They can be community-building devices. The boundaries may foster a sense of commonality among school members or encompass an extraordinarily disparate collection of pupils. A variety of concepts are applied, in both public and private schools, to define boundaries. Various schools, either by deliberation or coincidence, may restrict enrollment to

✦ children of families living in the immediate area of the school, which is the practice in most public neighborhood schools. Pupils share many common away-from-school experiences because they live in proximity of one another.

✦ children from a common ethnic group, who tend to share similar concerns and by coincidence or policy are served by a single neighborhood public school.

✦ children from the community (or one-school district) served by the school (common in some suburban or rural areas).

✦ children who have unique talents or interests, which a particular public school is specially designed to serve.

✦ children whose families enroll them in independent schools, where families who enroll their children may belong to a certain religion, pay a significant tuition, or display other common commitments.

These patterns of school-boundary definition are not free from criticism. For instance, at one time race was a criterion for school-boundary formation. We all know the injustices and controversies resulting from that practice.

Many forms of conceptual boundaries for schools have been under intellectual attack for having elitist implications. Despite these attacks, there is also a widespread tendency among members of all racial and intellectual groups to favor certain forms of boundaries. The boundaries enable group members to relax among their own kind. In schools, they play a role akin to that served by walls and doors which secure a family home. It has been cynically remarked that many opponents of school boundaries have ensured that their children are educated in schools "protected" by various boundaries. Even when such schools are racially integrated, measures are often taken to ensure that such integration does not generate a broadcast socioeconomic integration.

The conflict between open and closed boundaries will be perpetual. It involves certain emotional truisms. We need to mix with variegated groups to engage in certain forms of complex learnings and exchanges. On the other hand, such mixing is inevitably attended with various tensions since, by definition, these groups possess only diffuse common values. Again, we push for diversity to include in a group those who have been excluded. Sometimes, the intended results are achieved. Sometimes, as the excluded are included, they form support groups of their own and, after a certain point, even the supporters of diversity become uncomfortable. Community dissolution then recurs, in new and different forms.

Boundaries also persist because many institutions cannot operate unless certain levels of commonality prevail among members. If many adolescents in some neighborhood really do not like studying for school, it is hard for a school grounded on voluntary student cooperation to be academically effective. An experienced principal told one of the authors that the most difficult ethnic conflicts arise in urban high schools when there are two or more large student ethnic groups of nearly equal size. Each group may try to control the environment, as well as the other group. An enormous amount of adult energy is invested in moderating intergroup conflict in such schools. Conversely, when one group is clearly dominant, smaller groups can honorably accept a subordinate role. Everyone is then more relaxed, and academic learning proceeds more smoothly.

Boundaries may even take on a special importance when they concern children. Children are usually more emotionally vulnerable than adults and are less able to withdraw from distressing situations. Therefore, we might conclude that children are more in need of a coherent community—a strongly bounded environment—than typical adults. Ironically, just because children are relatively powerless, adults may use their power to apply policies to put children in noncommunal environments that most adults would reject. Sometimes, such noncommunal placements occur because the adults believe heterogeneity serves the interest of some larger cause.

Intellectual confusion sometimes arises when public non-neighborhood schools say they are open to all, but really apply implicit entrance criteria. These schools are offered as examples of open environments, but this assertion is inaccurate. Almost all open-enrollment public schools necessarily practice a form of discrimination. They favor families with the energy and initiative to carry out certain bureaucratic steps, such as collecting information, filing accurately completed forms by a certain time, and arranging interviews. These families may be rich, poor, or somewhere in the middle. Regardless of such differences, all applying families differ from families without the initiative. Thus, any public school with an application process, in contrast to the typical practice of drafting students, is defined by an important conceptual boundary. Once a school has an application process with any form of screening, it is extremely difficult to stop the school from choosing the cream: the most academically able students. As one principal of such a school frankly told us: "I do my best to select the most promising students from among many applicants for my school. Wouldn't you do the same?"

The basic issue is highly paradoxical. The absence of choice among schools and communities discriminates against families with the energy and judgment to make wise choices. They are often forced to send their children to schools they believe are unsatisfactory. Conversely, the existence of choice discriminates against families without the competence to make wise decisions or to make any decisions at all. We do not aim to propose some ultimate answer as to how inclusive or exclusive boundaries should be. We simply want readers to (a) recognize the tensions generated by urgent approaches from either perspective; (b) become more informed about how to handle particular personal or group conflicts; and

(c) increase consciousness of the hypocrisy sometimes prevailing around this issue, when policymakers assign children to noncommunal environments they would not accept for themselves or their own children or grandchildren.

Community and Charter or Magnet Schools

There is also the matter of special-purpose public schools that have diverse, selective entrance criteria. These are sometimes called magnet schools. A variant to the magnet school, the charter school, is also spreading in popularity.

A *charter school* is a publicly supported school, operating in a school district, but specially licensed (by the state or district) to bypass certain existing regulations or other constraints. A *magnet school* is a public school designed to attract and enroll students with specific and unique qualifications.

We have no doubt that some of such schools, with their particular boundaries, will persist. It is impossible to teach some subjects unless students have met certain rigorous academic criteria or demonstrated significant commitment. We have already considered some of these themes earlier in this chapter.

For a school of choice, educators should use its boundaries to intensify its level of community. The school must identify what particular values it stands for, such as making pupils diligent or having all members of the school display respect for one another. Families and prospective students should then be told, in writing and in clear, warm, attractive terms, what the school stands for. Families should be informed they are expected to help their child live up to the school's goals, for instance, by promptly responding to school requests for conferences and monitoring their child's homework. Parents should be warned that their child's continuance in school, in some sense, may depend on their willingness to display such engagement. We know of a public high school that even assigns an able staff member as part-time recruiter, equipped with an audiovisual display, literature, and other resources. The recruiter's program is available to pupils and families in the seventh grade in elementary schools that feed into the high school.

The process of screening should solicit commitment to the school's aims and discourage potential enrollees and families who are unsympathetic to those aims. Similar systems can be applied to recruit students into special, or bounded, programs in schools.

School Philosophies

In all schools—magnet or other types—educators can take many steps to enhance the vitality of their conceptual boundaries. Obviously, such steps can also have some bearing on their curriculum policies. Educators regularly remind the school's "inhabitants"—teachers, students, and families—what their community stands for. This uniqueness and clarity can be fostered by drafting and publicizing a strong, coherent statement of school philosophy. Even if students and their families have been drafted into the school, such clarity can persuade them to choose to accept the school's artfully stated principles. Of course, many school statements of philosophy are a medley of conflicting principles, pervaded with empty rhetoric. Our experience and research, however, have shown us other situations where public schools have adopted statements of philosophy or principles that are significant and distinctive.

As another identifying device, community members can be encouraged to recite pledges articulating the school's basic values. Such pledges can be recited along with the students' daily Pledge of Allegiance. Some idea of the power of such patterns can be seen in the Oath of the Ephebi, a pledge recited in about the second century B.C. by all male Athenian youths on their entry into adulthood:

> I will not disgrace the sacred weapons [I have just received], nor will I abandon the man next to me, no matter who he may be. I will bring aid to the rituals of the state and to the holy duties, both alone, and in company with many. Moreover my native commonwealth I will not transmit lessened, but larger and better than I have received it. I will obey those who are judging; and the established statutes I will obey, and whatever regulations the people shall enact unanimously. If anyone will attempt to destroy the statutes, I will not permit it, but repel such person. . . . [2]

The sum of the matter is that the forms of boundaries established for a school have much to do with its potential level of community.

In some situations, school administrators do not have much control over the conceptual boundaries that define their student body. However, it is often the case that the boundaries, conceptual or otherwise, are not as important as the symbolic weight with which they are invested. For instance, the principal and staff of a "plain vanilla" public school can create a sense of specialness through activities that distinguish the school from others, such as a community service program or an elementary school band. Even so, boundary definitions apply to other educational entities besides the entire school. Recall that our definition of community said that schools can and should have microcommunities, in classrooms, clubs, and so on. In our later discussion of microcommunities, we will see how such entities are critically affected by issues of boundary definition.

Persisting Over Time

Ideally, people should remain community members for a notable period of time. They need to have enough time to learn and apply common values. Community members should also be able to see that the community existed before they entered and will continue after they leave. If people are together only for brief periods of time or if they perceive their central values as being invented yesterday, their mutual coherence is diminished. After all, values invented yesterday may well be abandoned tomorrow.

It is harder to generate community feelings in schools with high levels of staff or student turnover, by definition. It is also harder in schools where the length of pupil enrollment is short, for example, two-year junior high schools, rather than K–8 schools or four-year high schools. Length of enrollment can also be an issue where one school encompasses two or more campuses. Sometimes this is done with freshmen and sophomores on one campus and juniors and seniors on another. In the eyes of many students in such settings, they spend two years in one school and two in a different one—not much time to put down roots.

Persistence also means the prevailing common values existed before the entry of the current students and will continue after them. The fact that we still honor the past gives a certain power to prevailing contemporary values. Persistence can also encourage current community members to more deliberately consider the values they create or revise. Persistence invites the question, "What do we want to transmit to the future?" The question can generate wholesome introspection.

There are different ways administrators can foster persistence through longer enrollment. Higher-level administrators and school boards can favor policies encouraging longer enrollment in particular schools, with one K–8 school preferred over two schools for grades K–5 and 6–8. Another step is to develop various incentives to lessen student, family, and faculty turnover. For example, one medium-sized district we know of has a policy of favoring staff promotions from within the district. The policy encourages able staff members to remain employed in the district; if they stay put, they have a reasonable chance of being promoted.

Listening to the Past, Speaking to the Future

Members of communities both listen to the past and speak to the future, and the effects are closely intermingled. They engage in these patterns because communities exist in time, with a past and a future. The two-thousand-year-old Ephebic Oath, for instance, talked of the initiates' obligations to the past and future. The community members' knowledge of these two time dimensions structure their current life patterns. Because community members know of their past, they (a) know of the successes and failures of the past; (b) have some gratitude for the benefits they are receiving due to sacrifices in the past; (c) have their present conduct shaped by such knowledge; (d) assume that their current lives in the community will form the past for some future community members; and (e) conduct themselves in the present with the expectation of such future surveillance and assessment.

Students listen to the past when

+ their school is filled with memorabilia from past classes, such as photos, trophies, and gifts from graduating classes.

+ the school observes important traditions inherited from the past.

+ the school's namesake—if one does or did exist—is conspicuously honored and the feats of that person are described in the school (e.g., a plaque or other display on an inside wall or a bust outside the building).

+ the school's graduates frequently return to the school to receive attention and offer gifts to their school, and the school honors any graduates who are deceased. (For example, one school sold pupils a calendar of activities. Each month featured a graduate with a photo and a short biography. The ages of these graduates ranged from twenty-one to fifty-seven.)

We recall a public high school where a graduate was posthumously awarded the Congressional Medal of Honor. The school mounted a plaque on a wall that displayed the commendation describing his heroism and a picture of the former student in military uniform. It seems likely that many American high schools have graduates who have been recognized publicly for acts of heroism. Schools should publicize the accomplishments of these graduates to enhance pride in the community.

Students speak to future classes when they

✦ carefully maintain, or constructively reshape, previous traditions. (In one southern school, Black pupils complained about a statue recognizing a White Confederate war hero. A school committee arranged for the erection of a second statue honoring a prominent local Black leader.)

✦ provide the school with significant, designated gifts, trophies, and decorations.

Sharing Common Goals

Community members must share common goals. To recall a famous statement made by Pilgrim leader John Winthrop, they "must rejoice in each other's success and mourn for each other's disappointments."

It is critical to realize that common goals are different from similar goals. In a boxing match, for example, the two opponents have similar goals: knocking out the other. But if one wins, the other loses. They would only have a common goal if they fought together to overcome a mutual opponent. Then if one won, the other would win too.

Sociologist James S. Coleman emphasized that, in many schools, students have similar goals, but not common goals. Most students are not better off because another student did well on an exam. The exam is akin to a prize fight, where the winning fighter transforms the other fighter into a loser. To elevate school or class spirit, administrators and faculty must identify and design more constructive activities that increase the number and intensity of common goals among school inhabitants. Then community members will care more about each other.

Interscholastic athletic competition is one classic means of achieving this bonding. Each competing team represents the whole school; the whole school feels better if the team wins and is distressed when it loses. Even the team members share similar feelings towards each other. Even second- and third-stringers gain some prestige if the team wins. But athletics is more than a means of stimulating school spirit. It can also serve as a metaphor for many nonathletic activities that can attain effects just as beneficial. The trick is to transform individual activities, which are often selfish in nature, into collective activities representative of the whole school. Then everyone gets some benefit from any individual success. Most people experience a special thrill when they achieve something that immediately benefits others. It is one thing to do well on a math exam and exceed your previous performance. It is another, possibly more significant, experience to do well in an activity when others desperately depend on your success.

There are many ways to structure activities to achieve this effect. Find nonathletic forms of interscholastic competition where school representatives can compete: band contests, debates, choral contests, spelling bees, dramatic contests, academic contests, and so on. Where such activities do not exist, work with other educators in your school or area to create them. Publicize the efforts of representatives from your school or class. Emphasize the link between their success and the school's prestige. Send them off with cheers, and welcome them home with celebration. One junior high school in a poor urban neighborhood won national attention for having a championship chess team. Pep rallies cheered them off to their contests. Outside the school was a large sign that read "Home of the Bad Bishops." The more such activities, the better. There will be more things for everyone to applaud, and more pupils lauded by their peers.

These patterns have important implications for the treatment of a school's academic successes. Of necessity, such successes will always have important individual elements. Still, there are ways to increase the collective benefits of individual academic success. Educators can emphasize that individual scholarships and other academic honors bring prestige to the whole school. They can devise contests that value schoolwide academic attainments, for instance, the school with the best average on the a certain exam. Each student's efforts can help raise the score, and everyone looks better if the average goes up.

We also want to comment on the matter of publicity. Large, well-budgeted schools often have a paid staff member whose primary responsibility is to get favorable coverage for the school in the community media. Even without such resources, a school can form an active publicity committee or enlist the help of some engaged faculty member who finds such work gratifying. Local publicity is an important means of building school spirit.

Significant Symbols and Rites

If we want pupils and faculty to learn to see the school as a community, we must sensitively apply profound forms of instruction. Ceremonies, symbols, and rites are among the most important kinds of instruction for this purpose. Such activities and forms of art can be repeated frequently and displayed conspicuously, have significant aesthetic content, and often involve body management.

Schools use a variety of symbolic forms to emphasize the nature of the school as a community. They use assemblies as rituals to communicate vital messages to students. In these assemblies students entertain each other, commemorate important occasions in school life, and relate to the external society. At a graduation ceremony, the graduates and remaining pupils say farewell to one another—this requires managing the ceremony so that graduates perform in some way before the remaining students. Each day students and their teachers may stand together and salute the flag.

Class gifts to the school may be clearly designated and scattered throughout the school as symbols of generosity and affection. Students may know and frequently sing the school song. There may be a school flag. Some public schools have school pledges that students often recite collectively. Banners commemorating school achievements may be created and hung in the building. After one school participated in contests where banners were not provided to winners, it found money to pay for having banners made and hung to memorialize the occasions.

Such patterns of symbolism and memorializing require adult ingenuity and application. We recall a high school principal who wanted his school to have a school song, an alma mater. He kept asking the music department to do the job, but nothing happened. Finally, he found someone in the community, paid that person $100 from his own pocket, and got the job done. Another principal had her school develop a faculty social committee. The committee made sure that all important public emotional events, happy and sad, in the lives of the faculty were properly demarcated.

Art can play an important part in community-building activities. Notable works of past or contemporary art can enrich the community: student actors can perform Shakespeare for the school; a choir can sing choral works; or the halls can be decorated with reproductions of important art works. In other cases, locally produced art, often designed and created by students, can serve the same purpose, such as decorating floats for homecoming or designing costumes for a masquerade. All great and enduring institutions have recognized the importance of mobilizing the enormous powers of art to enhance their vitality. A study of life in nineteenth-century English boarding schools quoted a visitor's remarks on pupils' singing at Harrow, one of such schools, during mealtime: "When you hear the great volume of fresh voices leap up as larks from the ground, and swell and rise, till the rafters seem to crack and shiver, then you seem to have discovered all the sources of emotion."[3]

Educators need to be aware of the role of pupil discipline in such matters. Many spirit-building activities require the faculty to bring together a large number of pupils and have them display decorum. Some schools cannot maintain discipline on such occasions. As a result, the gatherings do not occur, and the sense of community declines further. It is important for schools to work at maintaining discipline on public occasions. The problem is not pupil disorder, but the lack of adult skill and organization. Careful faculty planning for gatherings and, where necessary, practice drills for students, are undoubtedly the keys.

Cooperating With and Serving One Another

We have already emphasized many ways members of the school community should help and serve one another, through prosocial activities and cooperative learning projects. The community also includes faculty members. There are still some unique considerations to identify.

Cooperation includes having fun together. This may mean both adults and pupils being appropriately silly: a student-faculty volleyball game played before the whole school, a dress-silly day for everyone, a day for students to take turns being teachers and vice versa. Such occasions remind all community members of their common humanity and, incidentally, provide a significant test of school discipline. Indeed, they even provide students with a reason to maintain discipline. Unless there is good discipline, the school cannot plan lively activities when there is a risk of serious disorder. We know of one principal who makes the following announcement to students at the beginning of lively, interesting, and well-planned assemblies: "If you do not believe you can control yourself during this assembly, you are free, without criticism, to leave now and go to study hall. But if you choose to stay and then cannot show control, the consequences will be serious." No one leaves.

The implication of cooperating with and serving—in essence, caring for—one another is that community members are sensitive to one another's sorrows and joys. We have already mentioned the important role of a faculty social committee. In an organization as complex as a school, other concerns must also be kept in mind. For example, there should be ways of identifying, reorganizing, or supporting students who are experiencing joy or distress in their family lives, such as the birth of a sibling, a death or divorce, or a fire at home. Teachers should show appropriate engagement. In some cases, they should encourage students to respond with appropriate actions: throwing a party to celebrate a happy occasion, writing a card to express empathy, or attending a funeral. Students can also be encouraged to display solicitude to teachers. As an example, one school held a teacher appreciation week, during which the student council carried out "thank you" activities.

Some observers believe that many American adolescents are inarticulate. When real, this phenomenon is often due to a deficiency in adult instruction. We do not offer adolescents useful instruction and practice in responding to complex social situations. We can find an example of such instruction in a practice that is nearly obsolete. In earlier eras, adolescents, even in public schools, commonly attended classes in formal dancing. The participants learned more than dancing; they also learned proper social conduct. The aim was to transmit conventions that simplified public socialization in a complex situation, such as an adolescent's first dance. A school with a high level of community invents and transmits conventions that help students learn to display solicitude, partially remedying this deficiency.

THE NEED FOR HIERARCHY

Communities do things through various forms of cooperation among members. To get things done, community members consult one another and plan together. However, there must be some effective system of decision making and administration under the direction of one identified person. Otherwise members will engage in a frustrating and tedious pursuit of consensus, and nothing important will be settled. It is rare that a community can be born or persist without such a person. In the end, someone must have authority—a leader, boss, manager, or even coordinator, as long as the reality belies that ambiguous title. The person in authority must also be accountable. Although there may be drawbacks to such delegation, it is preferable to subjecting each decision to endless discussion or making the leader powerless to direct subordinates.

We believe these principles are obvious and make good sense. Yet they are opposed by advocates of the egalitarian tendencies that afflict education in our era. We have already discussed the deficiencies of these tendencies. We will simply note one irony. Many Americans decry the decline of community while they simultaneously resist the exercise of legitimate authority. Yet community must be grounded on such authority.

Microcommunities

Healthy human beings are embedded in communities that we might compare to concentric circles: their nuclear family, their extended family, their neighborhood, their city, their state and nation. Each successively larger circle serves a different function, helping members relate in more complex and abstract ways. Each smaller circle satisfies more profound and intimate needs. A typical school is too large a circle to meet all the emotional needs of students who inhabit it for long periods of time. There must be smaller circles within the school. These circles should replicate many of the generic characteristics of the school community: they should have boundaries, persist over time, have common goals, display symbols and practice rites, cooperate with and serve one another, and have a hierarchy.

These patterns are found in the traditional self-contained classrooms in many elementary schools. In some classrooms, there are further subcommunities, for instance, blocks of pupils grouped in rows or seated with their desks together to form a table. These are examples of what we prescribe when we talk of micro-communities.

The problem arises when pupils advance to departmentalized situations, where they pass through several different classes during the school day. In some schools, departmentalization begins in the fourth grade or earlier. Further, in passing, pupils may be grouped and regrouped, to bring the appropriate mix of capabilities together before the right teacher. This means that pupils in some junior high and high schools may share their classrooms with 200 different pupils and six teachers in one day. In four years this may total perhaps 500 different pupils and thirty different teachers, leaving little chance to develop microcommunities.

In typical junior high and middle schools, less interaction (less than typical in high schools) is the norm. American schools in general are too prone to shift students and teachers around to pursue academic instructional goals to the detriment of sound moral and emotional development. Many commentators, including Theodore Sizer, have voiced this criticism.[4] Even in foreign countries with greater academic pressure, there is less shifting of pupils or faculty. In Japanese high schools, for example, a teacher of a specific subject is assigned to a freshmen class. The teacher stays with the same students for four years as they progress through school to foster a sense of community. To the Japanese, it is more important for the math teacher and pupils to know one another than for the pupils to have four different teachers who each specialize in certain mathematical topics. The Japanese seem to be doing fine teaching math. In German schools, a different but relevant adaptation occurs. German students stay enrolled in the same class throughout high school. This class is called their *year group*. A student who flunks one subject does not stay with the class and simply drop down for the failed subject. Instead, the student is dropped down to the next lower class. All students in any year group take all their classes together. As students move through school, they come to know the others in their year group well.

Different formal and informal adaptations occur in American departmentalized schools to moderate the problems we have identified. Some pupils find vital micro-communities in sports, clubs, or other extracurricular activities. Some students take a focused academic program that develops a cohesive group of students under the direction of a limited number of faculty members. Other students make less satisfactory adaptations. They become part of groups or gangs without constructive adult monitoring. They may drift to, or beyond, the edge of trouble.

In many departmentalized schools, too many students are left without vital, constructive microcommunities. Most adults believe that academic learning should not be left to chance. Likewise, we believe that communal life in school should not be left to chance. Educators should establish systems that engage all students in significant microcommunities under adult monitoring. There are a variety of ways to achieve this goal, for example, each student must participate in at least one extracurricular activity. Here are two proposals, which may be used as alternatives or to complement one another.

The House System. The house system is one way of organizing social settings in schools. Houses, which are discrete, limited groups of students—50, 100, or 250—are each assigned to a specific area, with a boundary, in the school. Students regularly attend classes, eat, and study in this area. They take their classes from a small group of teachers, perhaps five or ten. Each house has a distinct identity in the school. Students may wear symbols identifying their particular houses. The teachers for each house work together as a team. Depending on the school's policies, houses can engage in other community-building practices.

Homerooms. Educators may use homerooms or divisions, as they are sometimes called, instead of the house system to serve the same purposes. Many departmentalized schools already have such units, where teachers regularly (daily?) make announcements to students, take attendance, and handle other school business. Too often, however, homerooms are not organized to serve the functions of the microcommunity concept properly. For instance, students in a homeroom may not stay together from one year to the next, or they may have a different homeroom teacher each year. Sometimes very little time is allocated to homeroom, preventing the possibility of much interaction. Educators sometimes deprecate the idea of vitalizing homerooms since, they believe, many homeroom teachers do not know what to do with their charges. The confusion is understandable; planning and leadership are needed to resolve this problem. Here are a few suggestions.

✦ Homeroom teachers, ideally, should teach their whole continuing class one academic subject each year.

✦ Homerooms should be assigned service responsibilities on behalf of the school, with the homeroom teacher overseeing the group. For example, one homeroom might organize a party for the whole school; another, help maintain the library; and a third, run the school's blood donation drive. School-wide contests can be held to identify the most helpful homerooms.

✦ Homeroom teachers should be expected to counsel their students and help correct their academic deficiencies; this might involve asking students in the homeroom to tutor one another.

✦ Homerooms should engage in intramural athletic or academic competitions.

✦ Homerooms might be composed of a mixed age group of pupils; under a monitor's supervision, the older pupils might counsel and tutor the younger ones. (We have seen one school using this system with excellent results.)

The point is that there's plenty to do in homerooms, if we choose to reorganize the way things are done. It is also true that, with the forms of organization that now often prevail, homeroom time is usually not well spent.

Practices and Policies

1. Some public schools, or programs within certain schools, have discretion in whom they enroll or recruit to enroll. If your school is in this situation, consult with others, including active parents, to consider whether steps should be taken to improve the clarity of the recruitment and enrollment process. As one educator in such a situation told us, "We enroll families, not students." But family enrollment cannot occur unless each family has a clear understanding of the significant policies and values of the school.

2. Does your school hold frequent, well-organized, enjoyable assemblies, often involving presentations by student groups? What steps, if any, should be taken to improve the school's assembly policies?

3. Should the school have a beautification committee? Its charge would be to devise and carry out activities to improve the appearance of the school's grounds, halls, library, floors, assembly hall, and public wall space.

4. What is the quality of the school's programs in music and art? Is student participation enthusiastic and widespread? Are the students' creations used to enliven the school's halls, ceremonial life, and other appropriate occasions?

5. Does the school have notable decorations or other memorabilia that provide students with reminders about the past life and traditions of the school?

6. If all or part of the school is departmentalized, to what extent does that program prevent each student from developing a powerful, adult-monitored base group in the school? What revisions, if any, are appropriate for the program?

7. Do or can the pupils and faculty of the school sing together? Develop a list of ten good songs that all students and faculty should learn, possibly as part of a music class, and sing together.

8. Design a community service project in which students provide service to some community group or agency.

9. Would your school have great support from the community if an organized community group suggested and helped initiate service activities that students could perform for the local community?

References

1. Capon, R. (1965). *Bed and board*. New York: Simon & Schuster, p. 94.

2. Botsford, G. W. (1965). *Hellenic civilization*. New York: Octagon, p. 478.

3. de Honey, J. R. (1977). *Tom Brown's universe*. New York: Quadrangle/New York Times Books, p. 139.

4. Sizer, T. (1984). *Horace's compromise: The dilemma of the American high school*. Boston: Houghton Mifflin.

CHAPTER 9

Leadership in Moral Schools

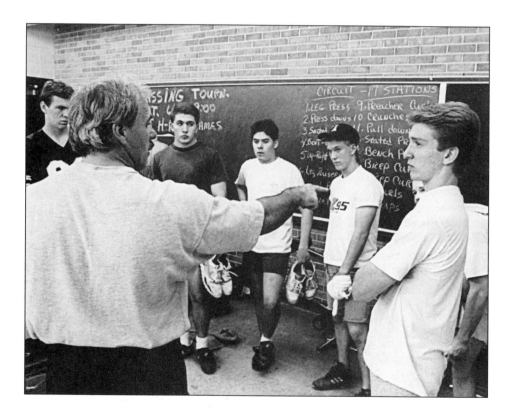

The intention to be effective in teaching, not to be incompetent, is more than simply a professional expectation implied by an employment contract; it is a positive, internalized psychological force pressing teachers. Teachers say they enter the profession because they want to have a positive influence on the lives of youth.

—Daniel C. Lortie[1]

If we assume a school is to transmit moral values to its pupils, then the school must conduct itself in a moral fashion. The concept of the morality of the school, rather than the morality of the teacher, is relatively novel. Most traditional authorities focus on the individual teacher as the moral transmitter. But, as we have indicated, the development of institutional schools has thrust new responsibilities on educators. We need to propose new concepts to meet this challenge. Many of the themes we have expressed in this book so far relate to the moral management of the school; they describe schoolwide policies necessary to generate moral learning. We have also identified other schoolwide policies that frustrate this learning. Apart from policies that impact pupils directly, many other school policies also affect pupils' moral learning in vital, although indirect, ways. Most of these policies involve the principal's management of staff relations: how faculty are hired and supervised, and how they are expected to work together. The principal usually implements such personnel practices.

This chapter will focus on the principal's role as a school leader. The concepts we will describe are not entirely original. We have derived them largely from the practices of able educators managing morally oriented public schools. But the practices have rarely been explicitly examined in terms of their moral efficacy.

At this time, considerable research focuses on the idea of effective schools. These schools generate higher levels of measured academic learning than other, similarly situated schools. Higher achievements are typically measured by better pupil scores on objective tests. From our study of the literature, it seems that such schools are, in many ways, like the moral schools we are proposing here. It may seem that we derive some of our recommendations from the effective schools literature. We are not concerned with establishing first rights on such insights. However, the fact is that the effective schools research and our moral school concerns have been moving along somewhat parallel lines. But the research on effective schools has not yet extended to carefully describing the moral environments of the schools under study. Perhaps further research will show the soundness of our contention about the two areas of study being somewhat similar.

What does the concept of the moral school mean? It means that public schools are agents of society. They are established and organized according to public statutes. They are supported by payments from taxpayers, some of whom are parents, others not. The ultimate morality for a school is for it to conduct itself according to the wishes of its "owners." Essentially, this means it should strive to be an efficient and diligent organization, teaching its pupils about character, academics, and discipline. It should be accountable within the organizational hierarchy established for it by society. It can transmit vital morality to pupils only if it meets this standard. Assume some educators strongly object to certain important priorities established by the society of voters and taxpayers who created the school and continue to support it. If these educators refuse to obey such injunctions and can see no way of reaching a compromise they can live with, then it is best for them to leave the school.

Discussion often centers more on school accountability to parents than on the school's organizational structure. But accountability to parents is often mere rhetoric. For instance, in one day, one high school teacher may teach children from 100 different families in four separate classes. And each family may relate to two to four different teachers. It is impossible that the diverse educational procedures that all such families desire, or that the different teachers apply, can satisfy everyone. There must be a process for shaping such complex patterns into a coherent whole. This requires compromise, deliberation, planning, delegation, and obedience. Thus, in practice, public schools are usually accountable to representative institutions designated to speak on behalf of individual families, taxpayers, and voters.

There are efforts underway to shift the focus of school control. Voucher plans imply that some schools should have greater accountability to parents, who may choose from various schools, which may hold different values or emphasize certain academic subjects. This shift may provide some educators with greater freedom to pursue employment in, or even design, schools with a set of values or an academic emphasis that appeals to certain families. Such changes potentially have many attractive characteristics. Voucher schools will still receive taxpayer support, merely via different mechanisms. Despite increased diversity, we assume that taxpayer-supported schools will be subject to many external controls. These controls, for better or worse, will inhibit principals' freedom of choice and surround schools with many demands beyond satisfying parents.

Discussions of school efficacy often center on the role of the principal. We share much of this concern. If one person in a school must be identified as critical to school efficacy, that person is the principal. However, the principal should not be seen as isolated from the sum total of school activities. In most activities, the principal acts through agents, such as teachers and other staff members. A key responsibility of principals is to ensure the school is staffed with highly competent and active staff members. Unless such broad-scale efficacy is achieved, any principal's assumed competency will go for naught. Furthermore, to foster morality, the principal must have a broadly gauged vision of the school's overall role. This book has described the elements of such a vision. This chapter focuses on the supervisory aspects of the principal's work.

BEING NIMMUKWALLAH

In the early nineteenth century the Duke of Wellington, a prominent English statesman and military leader, expressed his thoughts about personal responsibility with some poetic words. A friend asked him why he persisted in accepting politi-cal responsibilities, though he had long ago earned honorable retirement. Welling-ton's reply drew on his experience in military service in India as a youth:

> In India, the native troops said it was "becoming nimmukwallah." The term means,
> "I have eaten the King's salt." The eating of the King's salt was a ritual which signified
> the formal enrollment of recruits. By voluntarily taking the "gift" of the valuable salt,
> the recruit signified his willingness to repay the gift with loyal service. And I, too,
> am nimmukwallah.[2]

By "voluntarily taking" their jobs as educators—accepting the king's salt—school employees become *nimmukwallah*. They obligate themselves to try to carry out the wishes of their employers. Of course, those wishes are often ambiguous and contradictory, and there are inevitable issues of interpretation and extrapolation. Employees are licensed by circumstances to adapt and invent. When they must act on obscure directions, responsible educators are best advised to apply Wellington's dictum: to follow the difficult path of duty and hardi-hood, rather than to opt for cynicism or petulant resistance. If their conflicts with the status quo become too deep and important, such educators should exercise one of the precious freedoms available in a democratic society. They should seek employment elsewhere. Every day, we, the authors, as teachers, see many graduate students who have wisely chosen to exercise this right to learn new skills to pursue different work. Many other educators choose to teach in pri-vate schools that they find more congenial, even though the pay is typically lower than in public schools.

What policies should administrators follow to gratify the best aspirations of their employers?

The first step is to recognize that the issue of maintaining a moral environment in schools, public or private, extends below the top. It encompasses the rela-tionships among school faculty members and between faculty and pupils. Such relationships are critical to the success of pupils in learning character, academics, and discipline. Thus, we will consider how moral relationships among adults in schools can be formed and monitored. The clearest foundation for such rela-tionships is to simply recognize that school faculty are employees. By virtue of receiving a paycheck, they must be held accountable for establishing a moral environment. They, too, are nimmukwallah.

Next, administrators must carry out a system of supervision in the school. The system should ensure the school is meeting its responsibilities and that the employees are correctly doing their work.

For example, the work of faculty members necessarily involves many matters of judgment. As a result, there must be a process of coordination so that a vital exchange of ideas and new information occurs among faculty. In addition, chil-dren are uniquely vulnerable. Teachers have considerable authority over the lives of other people's children. Obviously, such power may be abused. A review system is necessary to prevent serious mistakes. Finally, adults need encourage-ment and praise from other adults as they carry out their employment; teachers need some structure to provide them with this support. All these themes relate intimately to the quality of the moral life of the school. The themes are encompassed under the concept of the moral school.

The matter of morality also touches on hierarchy. The acceptance of hierarchy has been an important theme pervading traditional values. Indeed, without appropriate hierarchy among the adults in a school, how can pupils learn to observe discipline? Vital hierarchy should not be equated with authoritarianism. In a moral environment, even people with authority should be subject to many constraints. Schools should have a framework for the exercise of temperate, legitimate authority over adults. People with authority must participate in polite but searching exchanges with their subordinates or team members. Without such discussions, superiors cannot obtain essential feedback, and they will inevitably commit serious errors. A school should have a well-conceived system of administration that will provide for the accountability of its leaders and faculty. The task of developing such a system is not insurmountable, but it involves numerous difficulties.

The topic of school-based management has received considerable professional attention. As with many other reforms, the term is vague and has different meanings to different people. For example, some interpret school-based management as meaning that the majority of issues concerned with managing a school should be settled on the job site, not determined by remote authorities. However, even if many decisions are to be settled on the job site, the question arises of which person in the school should have the final say. Some authorities imply that school-site decisions should be made through a highly consultative, semidemocratic process, with great emphasis on consensus. In many dictionaries, the definition of consensus "stresses attaining a high level of agreement or unanimity."[3] We believe such a stress on consensus is unwholesome and unrealistic. Too much time will be spent in consultation and, since a consensus often will not be attained, many necessary decisions will not be made. Such management policies will not provide the clarity and energy necessary to school efficacy or moral vigor.

Furthermore, when authority is too decentralized, it is difficult to enforce accountability. No one can really be held responsible for serious errors. A story collected by one of the authors illustrates this point:

The high school was in a disorderly neighborhood. Drug dealers infested the streets near the school. The students mixed among them when they went out for lunch recess or on breaks between classes. Some school staff members wanted to declare the school a closed campus. Students would have to stay in school throughout the whole school day. The declaration would not increase teachers' total work hours. However, it would affect the grouping of these hours. The teachers would give up their lunch period and go home earlier. The teachers' union contract required a majority vote of the teachers, by secret ballot, for the administration to make the change. The principal made such a proposal, and a vote was held. The closed-campus proposal was defeated by a ratio of 60 to 40. Explaining why the proposal lost, one teacher said she believed it was "because many of the newer, younger teachers believed the proposal deprived students of important personal rights."

Assume some citizen believes the school should have such a closed-campus policy. Or suppose a parent, whose child was hooked on drugs obtained during recess or injured in a drug-related fight while out on break, decides to sue the school for not having a closed campus. What school employees can be punished or criticized if the open-campus policy is held fundamentally unsound? The 60% of the teachers who voted against it?

If an unwise policy is adopted by a consensual or voting process, exactly who is responsible? In important institutions, there must be clear points of accountability, not merely an amorphous group of faculty members. Without focused responsibility, the clarity of decision making will be greatly impaired. We do not suggest that principals, as human beings, are necessarily wiser or more moral than individual teachers. Nor, in most circumstances, do we oppose strong faculty involvement in decision making. Our argument is that in education, the stakes are high. Some decisions, as in the preceding story, may even involve the pupils' immediate health and safety. There must be one person clearly in charge. There must be a system of accountability that is clearly defined and understood. Where such accountability is not practiced, the solution is not to further diffuse responsibility, but to clarify who is in charge. Many site-based management proposals lack this sort of clarity.

IDENTIFYING GOOD TEACHING

A school must establish criteria to define what kinds of faculty conduct are desired. After such criteria are established, employees will have clearer ideas of what is expected of them. Furthermore, the principal and other administrators can collect information to see whether employees are following the established criteria, working as they are supposed to. Employees who consistently violate the criteria can be compelled to leave. However, the matter of criteria is quite complex, especially when we recognize that the criteria should be partly related to moral concerns.

The first criterion is that teachers must be able to cause pupils to learn appropriate academic and character-related subject matter. This is the prime moral obligation of educators. The ability to cause desirable learning in pupils is so important that it may override almost any other teacher deficiencies. However, if adequate learning is not occurring, we must be able to provide teachers with constructive criticism. Beyond examining learning, we must identify particular traits and behaviors that are also relevant to teacher competency. The traits will enable us to offer advice to unsuccessful teachers.

In addition, teachers' specific traits are important because most learning effects on pupils result from a myriad of influences. The influences often include the efforts of several teachers. Assume we can recognize that desirable pupil learning has occurred. We often do not know which teachers are responsible for this success. Even if one teacher was clearly responsible, teachers have other important duties, such as cooperating with peers and administrators, that go beyond their immediate classes. Finally, when teachers are being hired, we often cannot obtain precise evidence of their previous formal teaching success, or they may be new teachers who have never taught.

In summary, we must often base the assessment of teachers on criteria separated from actual teaching outcomes. To apply such criteria, we will propose certain basic traits of good teachers. These traits relate to the general educational goals we have already articulated.

Desirable Traits

We will identify desirable traits in somewhat general language and then expand our definitions later. The following list presents ten traits in order of priority; this represents a considered hierarchy. Such a classification contains artificial elements. For example, it is often difficult to display one trait without displaying others. Our list has been subjected to extensive empirical analysis. Trained graduate students have conducted hundreds of interviews with practicing principals, asking them to identify desirable teacher traits and priorities among these traits. The priorities in the list are congruent with those indicated by the more experienced and thoughtful interviewees. Readers, whether they have supervisory experience or not, are free to justify their own alternatives, some of which may appear in the following list.

1. *Commitment*, or *dedication*. A willingness to work hard, accept extra responsibilities cheerfully, and try to do the job better. To walk the extra mile. This trait has some of the overtones of *nimmukwallah*.
2. *An adequate knowledge of the appropriate subject matter*. As many principals emphasized in the surveys, however, teachers can usually learn new or different subject matter as long as they have commitment.
3. *A liking for children and/or adolescents*.
4. *A good sense of humor*, but not one that is employed at the expense of others, particularly students.
5. *Being a good role model*, routinely displaying conduct we hope pupils will want to emulate and avoiding bad conduct.
6. *A set of principles of teaching and classroom management* that fit together logically.
7. *A commitment to the philosophic goals of the particular school*, if such goals have been identified. For example, if the school is sympathetic to tradition, the teacher should believe in the importance of character, academics, and discipline.
8. *The ability to work cooperatively with other adults*—peers, school administration, and parents—and accept significant supervision.
9. *Good communication skills*, being able to make oneself clearly understood and to understand others.
10. *Intelligence and imagination*. These are good traits, but perhaps rate below the preceding virtues. Clearly, a certain level of intelligence is required. However, if teachers are not committed to doing their job well, how valuable is their intelligence to their pupils?

Causing Pupil Learning

Once we have identified basic traits, we must translate them into observable conduct. Teachers can then know how they should act, and supervisors can know what behaviors to look for. We must apply the key measure: Are pupils learning? To find out, we have to search for signs of pupil learning in character, academics, and discipline.

How do we know that pupils are learning good character? We can see if they regularly display courtesy, good humor, and helpfulness. Are they frequently engaged in classroom and schoolwide activities where they display such conduct?

As for academics, do the students' different academic work products—oral recitations, projects, exercises, written exams, essays, writing activities, art—show significant application and learning of the subject matter? Are pupils learning at an appropriate pace? Is a relatively rigorous but fair grading system maintained? What are the pupils' grades on exams and report cards and scores on relevant standardized tests? Is there any way of comparing such outcomes with those attained by similar pupils in other classes or in previous years?

Regarding discipline, do students promptly and pleasantly obey their teacher? Do pupils generally maintain good order in classrooms and as they move throughout the school? Do they obey school and classroom rules? Does the class have many discipline incidents? Is the rate of student attendance high, and is the rate of tardiness low?

Teachers' supervisors can rarely afford to focus solely on direct measures of learning. We must also consider many indirect measures, largely related to the traits listed previously. We next identify specific teacher behaviors that should be associated with the desirable learning outcomes.

Translating Traits Into Observable Conduct

Observing human conduct is a subtle process that cannot be governed by formal rules. In other words, principals who are skilled observers must pay attention to indicators that may have little or no legal weight: the tone of someone's voice, a teacher's pattern of dress, or small factors in a person's demeanor. Such information will rarely, in itself, justify supervisory intervention. But it can provide clues about when and where further attention is appropriate. Principals are expected to be sensitive to matters such as child abuse by teachers, inadequate preparation for lessons, or alcohol or drug abuse. Such deficiencies are often deliberately concealed from other adults. They become apparent in very subtle ways. Without a system of identifying clues, a principal may not be able to sort out important indicators from the vast number of incidents that occur in a school.

Teachers show evidence of commitment and diligence by arriving at work promptly; being absent infrequently; coming to class well prepared; beginning instruction promptly and moving it along at a vigorous pace; being willing to accept extra assignments; being freely available to students, peers, and parents; and staying informed about professional developments in the school in particular and teaching in general.

Knowledge of subject matter may be apparent in a teacher's previous formal training; display of knowledge of pertinent information and skills; and active membership in an appropriate professional group.

Indicators of liking children and adolescents include a teacher's previous commitment to working with children, as in being a camp counselor, Sunday-school teacher, or scout leader; good relationships with pupils around the school; and a willingness to sponsor student activities.

A good sense of humor extends far beyond being able to tell a joke. It is being able to be silly when appropriate or turn ambiguous situations into tension-relieving, funny occasions.

Having a set of principles of teaching and classroom management means the teacher consistently applies and integrates different plans and policies—grading criteria, lesson plans, a system of examination, the amount and various forms of homework, policies for in-class discipline, and modes of instruction. Students, supervisors, and parents should not be constantly surprised by a teacher's unpredictable policies. If they are, they will likely see the policies as unfair.

Being committed to the school's philosophic goals means being knowledgeable about the school's philosophy; being able to identify its operational implications for teaching; and applying those implications in work.

Being able to work cooperatively with other adults requires tact, courtesy, knowledge of group processes, insight, determination, communication skills, and the ability to handle confrontation and accept appropriate hierarchy.

Having good communication skills means being able to communicate to, and receive communication from, groups and individuals, by speaking and listening (face-to-face or over the phone) and by writing and reading.

Teachers display imagination in education by using a variety of effective teaching modes and displaying ingenuity in devising incentives to encourage learning, as well as punishments to discourage misconduct.

Clues about intelligence are the teacher's ability to master new teaching material quickly; plan novel instructional arrangements; and work with other teachers in devising original policies and procedures.

Translating Role Modeling into Observable Conduct

Setting standards for observing evidence of teachers being good role models is a complex issue. One component of being a good role model is to be a diligent teacher, showing pupils that they should take work seriously. Another component is more complicated: a good role model should not be publicly connected with questionable conduct. Obviously, different people and different communities will have different opinions about what is questionable. We believe that being a role model implies that teachers have a larger obligation than simply observing the criminal law. Even if teachers are not breaking the law, they may still be poor role models. If certain public conduct persists after due warning, or if a first offense is flagrant, the school should dismiss the teacher.

In considering the following list of sensitive role-model issues, we believe it is important for readers to recognize the parameters of questionable conduct: being drunk in public; having an extramarital affair, especially with another teacher; teaching while conspicuously pregnant with an out-of-wedlock child; publicly avowing or advocating homosexuality; aggressively boasting about sexual conquests; appearing nude in a magazine; disorderly dress; engaging in conspicuously antipatriotic (even though legal) acts, such as publicly burning an American flag; smoking cigarettes on the school campus if such behavior is banned; or being a member of a racist organization.

Note that most of these acts are legal. We still believe that many public schools might remove teachers from their jobs for such conduct. An analogy in the workplace is that General Motors can fire its employees for going around advertising they believe Chevrolets are lousy cars—even though such opinions are legal. We do not propose to weigh the liability of teachers who commit any of these acts. Nor is it important where *we personally* would draw the line. Still, we believe most readers will agree that some forms of legal acts should make teachers subject to serious criticism and perhaps dismissal. Furthermore, we have urged that teaching extends far beyond academic instruction. If that principle is accepted, then public breaches of morality by teachers whom pupils respect can undermine the students' learning about morals, character, and discipline. Being a good citizen means more than merely obeying the law.

However, where supervisors or communities draw the line for dismissing teachers will vary by supervisor, by community, and by the age of pupils involved. Ultimately, we believe the values of pupils' parents should receive very great weight in such decisions.

Educators sometimes answer hypothetical questions about role-model issues with the qualification, "This conduct is okay, if it does not affect the person's teaching." Unfortunately, such an answer is excessively qualified. How can we know for certain when someone's teaching has been affected? That is a matter of definition. Consider the following scenario:

Mr. X is a teacher who is known publicly to be involved in an extramarital affair with Mrs. Y, another teacher. He still comes to work and applies himself to teaching. His pupils work quietly at their seats. However, many of his twelve-year-old students' minds are focusing on the ramifications of the episode, rather than on their work. Will Mrs. Y again spend the night at Mr. X's apartment? The question is, has Mr. X's conduct affected his teaching?

Publishing Criteria and Behaviors

After criteria and behaviors have been identified, they must be clearly disseminated to current and prospective faculty members. Many schools do this through a variety of informal means. It is better practice, especially in larger schools and those with high staff mobility, to communicate such standards formally. The process must rely on documents, such as job applications and evaluation forms, faculty handbooks, bulletins to staff, as well as oral communication in group gatherings and one-to-one meetings.

The aim of this formal communication is to (a) inform faculty and prospective employees what is expected; (b) explain why certain expectations are established;

(c) translate the criteria and behaviors into specific examples and requirements, applicable to immediate situations; and (d) invite faculty to apply their experience and perspectives to refining the monitoring process.

A large part of the work of a principal or other supervisor must be dedicated to such dissemination. There is always some employee turnover, and most new employees need education in these standards. Even experienced employees sometimes slip back into bad habits. Furthermore, new situations requiring reinterpretation of existing criteria are always arising; schools are dynamic environments.

Applying Criteria to Job Applicants

A key way for principals to ensure morally cohesive and efficient schools is to hire only competent job applicants, who are sympathetic to the schools' goals.

The applicant selection process is especially important in education. As is well known, it is extremely difficult to terminate incompetent teachers who have tenure. Even if teachers are terminated, they are almost always kept until the end of the year, leaving time to cause a lot of trouble. Furthermore, for reasons to be considered later, teachers have peculiarly large areas of independence compared to many other types of employees. A poor teacher has more freedom to cause harm than employees in many other jobs. Interviewers should use the multistep criteria we have outlined to assess job applicants and teachers who want to transfer from another school.

There are variations among schools and school districts as to the control individual principals have over their school's hiring or transfer-in process. Despite such variations, in many different districts strong and effective principals acquire more control over staff intake than less vigorous leaders. Regardless of a district's formal procedures, there is usually some room for principals—by hook or by crook—to assert influence. Better principals find ways.

Most principals, on being assigned to a school, inherit a staff. It is rare for a principal to hire or choose, all at once, a number of new teachers or teachers transferring from other schools. But many schools have turnover of active staff members, and the principal will have an opportunity to hire replacements. Furthermore, principals who have a strong vision of where they want the school to go will gradually encourage unsympathetic teachers to seek transfers or just leave. Over a few years, vigorous principals can create the opportunity to choose most of their staffs. But these principals need to know the characteristics a good staff should have. Otherwise, they will squander a precious opportunity.

Teacher applicants—whether new to teaching or applying from other schools—must be told orally and in writing what will be expected if they become employees. They should be invited to ask questions about the information. Some job applicants may be hungry for employment and so will try to disguise their real feelings. Other applicants, with a different motivation, will be more straightforward. Indeed, one of the challenges for interviewers is to identify an applicant's basic values. For various reasons, some applicants inevitably will try to hide their feelings—and take a job with reservations. But even these people will be more likely to apply the correct principles in their later work, if they are told during the application process what will be expected.

In many situations, it is appropriate for two or more staff members to participate in the screening. This is especially true in departmentalized schools, where teachers are more strongly subject-focused, and department chairs are expected to have special knowledge of such competencies. In any school, using more than one interviewer allows multiple perspectives on a candidate. This technique can also help candidates get a fuller picture of the spirit of the school, permitting them to make more informed decisions about where they want to work. In other words, the aim of screening is to avoid hiring unsuitable candidates. Certain candidates should be kept out by the process, and other candidates should be allowed to decide on their own whether the school is appropriate for them.

Applicants' past experience can be examined, through searching questions and careful listening, to see if they have previously satisfied some or all of the school's criteria. Helpful information can be gleaned from the application form; some districts even require applicants to submit brief essays or other expository documents. References should be carefully scanned and evaluated, often using phone calls for verification. If the applicant has significant prior teaching experience, skillful questioning and checking should eventually produce a portrait of previous performance. We know of principals who, when choosing teachers to be transferred in from other schools in their district, observe classes taught by the applicants in their current schools.

The point of entry is also important because it begins the socialization of new teachers into the school. The information in the interview should prepare new teachers to work more effectively in the school.

CHALLENGES SURROUNDING INFORMATION COLLECTION

Assume criteria for teacher performance have been established and translated into behavioral terms. Furthermore, suppose teachers all have been clearly informed what is expected, and why. Next, principals and other in-school supervisors must collect information to see whether teacher conduct meets the criteria. Administrators who do not engage in this practice will be unable to allocate praise or blame or to identify better practices and share them with others. At best, the school will stagnate; at worst, undesirable and even destructive practices may persist and spread.

The matter of collecting information about teachers is complex. Teachers usually work in individual classrooms, isolated from other adults. This isolation makes it difficult for principals to observe teacher behavior, compared to supervisors at many other work sites. The isolation also socializes teachers to working without regular observation. Research has demonstrated that such socialization makes many teachers uncomfortable with the forms of monitoring and observation typical in most adult work sites. For instance, many experienced teachers routinely see their supervisors in a highly critical light. By contrast, noneducation employees usually see supervisors in a more supportive perspective. For example, in many surveys of our own pupils—comprised of both teachers and noneducators—the noneducators usually have more favorable opinions about their supervisors than the teachers do. Some teachers say this contrast shows principals are unusually insensitive supervisors; other people might conclude that teachers are especially defensive employees. The matter of supervisors' insensitivity to the concerns of teachers is especially ironic. Due to state laws, probably more than 98% of all principals are former teachers. We would expect this would make school principals especially sympathetic to teachers.

None of this discussion about defensiveness in teachers is intended to belittle the general virtue of many teachers. However, as Willard Waller first demonstrated quite dramatically, the isolating effect of the self-contained classroom makes teachers especially prone to fear intrusion.[4]

One of the authors recalls interviewing an experienced teacher, who reported that no supervisor had visited her classroom during her 14 years of teaching. (This is the longest period of nonvisitation ever to come to the author's attention.) The author remarked that, under such circumstances, the teacher would be fearful if a threat of such a visit ever arose. But the teacher replied, "I would welcome such a visit." The author responded, "I believe in the sincerity of your remarks. However, the psychological probability is that, after 14 years of seclusion, the real prospect of a visit would trigger understandable fear and tension. Such fear and tension would complicate the task of the 'intruding' supervisor."

Waller described the process of teacher supervision as bordering on tragedy. He believed that teachers often fear the people who—usually with good intentions—want to help them. The supervisors, who began their efforts with good will, often became angry and frustrated because of such teacher fear and resentment, which they thought was unjustified. Because of such anger, the teachers' fears then seemed partly justified. And so on. A number of thoughtful books and articles have touched on such themes, calling this phenomenon "loneliness in school."

Supervision of teachers is also complicated by the matter of *span of control*. This term refers to the optimum number of subordinates whom a supervisor can monitor. Typical desired ratios range from 1:7 to 1:15. If the ratio exceeds this range, the supervisor's effectiveness may be spread too thin. For example, assume a supervisor must oversee twenty employees. It is unlikely that person can give twenty people adequate supervision, such as identifying their mistakes, providing them with deserved praise, encouraging communication among coworkers.

The optimum range for span of control is affected by many factors: the amount of discretion allocated among employees; the depth of their work experience; the levels of their prior training; the selectivity of the hiring process. The more routine the work, the greater the supervisor's span of control.

Most supervisory structures in education drastically violate the principles of span of control. For instance, it is not uncommon for a principal to have twenty-five or more subordinates. This means that, compared to most work environments and especially considering the sensitive nature of their work, teachers are grossly lacking in proper supervision. This probably also means that communication among adults in the school is poor, and teachers receive little on-the-job training and inadequate advice and support. None of these contentions are inconsistent with the prevailing research on teachers and teaching. Such factors generally handicap the evolution of collegiate supervisor-teacher relationships, regardless of the good intentions of the people involved.

In the short run, employees may be somewhat relieved that their supervisor is overextended. They are shielded from observation and possible criticism. In the long run, however, such employees may feel ignored, unsupported, and surrounded with disengaged colleagues. At the same time they may be fearful of serious supervision. Feelings of isolation, frustration, and anxiety are common among teachers.

COLLECTING INFORMATION

The basic principles about supervisors collecting information in education are simple. It is a matter of top priority for administration. It must be pursued energetically and ingeniously, and a great diversity of techniques must be applied. It will frequently be met with resistance. For instance, some teachers will consider their classrooms their personal property and be very defensive about supervisor's visits.

Sometimes, the matter of collecting information is contrasted with the supposed key role of the principal: instructional leadership. The phrase implies a principal directly counseling individual teachers about improving instructional techniques or otherwise directing instruction in a hands-on manner. Research has often deplored the fact that few principals spend much time on such activities. In general, our experience is congruent with these findings, especially in larger schools. However, we also believe that many excellent principals see the concept of instructional leadership in a far broader light. They think that improving instruction, or sustaining good instruction, depends on many factors beyond immediate principal-teacher interaction around instruction. Good instruction also depends on who is hired or not hired, what general instructions faculty are given, and how well discipline is monitored. It depends on the efficacy of teacher committees, the quality of school spirit, the standards established to identify good and poor teaching, and other factors. The narrow connotations sometimes attached to the phrase *instructional leadership* do not fairly characterize the realities of school administration.

We make the following recommendations knowing that conditions vary based on the size of the school involved. Some principals supervise as many as 200 teachers, and others, as few as fifteen. In large schools, tasks that are nominally assigned to principals are, or should be, delegated to other supervisors. We will regularly use the word *principal*, with the understanding that the actual tasks, in some schools, may properly be assigned to others.

It is important that principals often see and hear what happens in classrooms. Much of this information collecting is the by-product of activities such as dropping into a class in session for a quick chat with the teacher, walking down the hall and listening to the chatter in classrooms with their doors open, glancing into classrooms through the windows on their doors, or noticing the state of array or disarray in a temporarily vacant classroom. Many effective principals have told us that they "examine" ten to twenty classrooms on a typical day in the ways we have described.

Such examinations have many limitations, but their great strength is frequency. In a medium-sized school, each classroom may be examined in this way twenty to forty times a year. We know of principals in small schools who visit every classroom at least once every day. Large numbers of observations of many situations, even of brief duration, by a trained observer provide a rich base of information. Furthermore, such frequent contacts desensitize the pupils' perception of these visits as intrusion by the principal. Eventually, the visits become routine, and pupils, despite the principal's presence, continue their normal behavior.

Quick, drop-in visits should be supplemented by more prolonged, focused visits. The information obtained from drop-ins should be used to schedule more lengthy visits, for example, to classes with exceptional problems or novel strengths. Some visits should be completely unannounced, and some should be scheduled with deliberation: "This week I will be visiting classes in grades five and six." Some visits should occur at the request of teachers, who might ask the principal to observe and comment on some new technique or provide necessary advice.

During prolonged or drop-in visits, principals can observe a variety of matters: the state of pupil discipline; the level of pupil engagement; the tempo of instruction; the quality of the teacher's presentation and preparation; the teacher's engagement with pupils; the nature of materials posted throughout the room; the relationship between the instruction offered and the teacher's lesson plan; the quality of pupil learning evident in recitations and other performances; and the teacher's dress and demeanor. Such observations relate to criteria such as commitment, philosophic coherence, knowledge of subject, communication skills, good humor, and being a role model.

Principals can also collect information about staff performance by other means. Diverse methods are often necessary, due to the inherent problems of school supervision, for instance, the attenuated span of control and the comparative seclusion of teachers in classrooms. Information can be obtained through

- ✦ reading and skimming written reports and other data from and about teachers, e.g., reviewing lesson plans and grade books; pupils' report cards; pupils' test scores; samples of pupils' academic work made available to the principal; copies of notes sent to parents by teachers; teachers' and pupils' attendance and tardiness records; and records of pupil discipline incidents.

- ✦ observing teacher/pupil contacts outside the classroom, e.g., in the halls, assemblies, and play areas. Do mutual respect and good discipline prevail?

- ✦ frequently participating in small and large meetings with teachers to observe their demeanor and hear and consider their comments and suggestions.

- ✦ judiciously listening to remarks made by teachers, pupils, and parents.

- ✦ examining empty classrooms to observe cleanliness and the state of the bulletin boards.

- ✦ interviewing individual teachers about their work and plans and asking them to submit periodic written reports and other documents.

FOSTERING A COLLEGIATE SPIRIT AMONG TEACHERS

At most work sites, rank-and-file employees have important responsibilities for supervising one another. They help newcomers break in, share ideas about increasing their skills, and make plans to coordinate their efforts. This type of peer supervision is an especially important element of any vital profession. It should be pertinent in teaching, where aspirations for professionalism are frequently voiced.

Ironically, the level of peer supervision is much lower in teaching than in most work, even including production-line work. Peer supervision and support are lower because teachers work in isolated classrooms, cut off from one another. Furthermore, because their work schedules also often isolate them, they often lack occasions to cultivate peer engagement. Finally, many teaching responsibilities are assigned to individual teachers, rather than to groups or teams. Thus, unlike many other workers, they do not seem to have to cooperate to attain their goals.

Due to these factors, when teachers are provided time for peer interaction, their discourse often drifts into small talk. It does not focus on analyzing and improving teaching. It seems that, being ignorant of the specific details of one another's work, they are reluctant to "talk shop" in a focused way. Such discussion may disclose sharp divergences in principles, which could be very upsetting.

Well-managed schools strive to increase a true collegiate spirit among the staff. They often succeed. To attain this end, they may

- ✦ require teaching staff to participate frequently in small group meetings. Such groups are assigned definite, relevant, work-related responsibilities; are guided by agendas; and generate conclusions and minutes. The groups deal with matters such as curriculum, scheduling, various subject areas, publicity, safety, discipline, counseling, and coordinating the criteria to be applied in grading pupils' work. Principals and other administrators monitor committee activities, and their recommendations and decisions are taken seriously.

- ✦ structure school activities to facilitate social interaction among teachers. This might involve providing a faculty room with appropriate amenities or organizing a faculty social committee to plan and conduct a variety of engaging activities throughout the year.

Some principals, far from encouraging a collegiate spirit among the staff, see such cooperation as threatening their own status. As a result, they fail to stimulate a collegiate spirit or even take active steps to discourage it. But effective principals foster such cooperation and make sure it is directed at wholesome goals.

One commentator on this text asked our suggestions for teachers who work in schools where the principal is inept or even irresponsible as a leader. Obviously, there's no simple answer. For instance, many employees believe their supervisors are inept or even immoral—and those employees are sometimes objectively wrong. So our first reply is that one employee's opinion—or even the opinions of a number of irresponsible employees—can be in error. Our first counsel is to be patient and solicit the opinion of other wise people.

Next, we would be concerned with the nature of the irresponsible acts in question. There's only so much that subordinates can or should be expected to do, unless the conduct involved is directly criminal, as in a case of embezzlement. Then it may be a matter of going to legal authorities. Absent such overwhelming evidence, our counsel would turn to practical realities: Can the teacher get a transfer? Does the principal directly intervene in the teacher's work in significant ways? How strong and helpful is the union likely to be? In other words, as in handling many other life problems, aggrieved teachers may have to optimize the situation. Similarly, many competent principals, discovering themselves supervising inept teachers, have to make their situations as effective and functional as possible.

PROVIDING TEACHERS WITH FEEDBACK

After collecting information, a principal must provide feedback to the affected teachers in a useful form. Most often, the feedback will be brief, simple, oral praise. Sometimes praise will be written. Sometimes, the feedback will be a mixture of praise and constructive criticism, either written or oral. Other times, the feedback will be largely critical. When feedback is critical, it should be couched in constructive terms. What changes in behavior are necessary to attain the desired results? When the criticism is about complex matters, the principal should supplement written remarks with formal and informal discussion.

Designing an appropriate mix of praise and criticism for particular teachers can involve delicate questions. What rate of progress should one expect of new employees? When does it become relevant to begin developing a case against a teacher who is not performing according to the school's standards? There are no firm answers to such questions, but it is our impression that good principals often err on the side of formality. They regularly put their comments, often including sincere praise, in writing and place a copy in their personnel files. A fairly routine output of various documents evaluating a teacher will make these written comments seem less threatening to the teacher. If it becomes necessary to develop a record in a case of poor performance, the groundwork has been laid.

One principle about feedback is more easily settled. Employees should not be shielded from warnings or criticisms because the supervisor is afraid of a confrontation. Our impression is that the most common moral deficiency among principals is the reluctance to engage in such confrontations. Their reluctance is often portrayed as a form of charity or kindness. Certainly it is important that supervisors carefully consider their criticisms. But teacher defects can lead to serious deficiencies in pupil learning of academics or character. Good principals realize their first obligation is to the pupils under their charge.

MAINTAINING REWARDS AND SANCTIONS TO AFFECT TEACHER PERFORMANCE

Just as in the case of pupil learning, able principals strive to relate teacher performance to systems of rewards and sanctions. One obvious reward is the granting of tenure. Of course, the prevalence of tenure seriously undercuts a principal's power to provide additional sanctions or rewards. Still, it is our impression that too many principals use a teacher's tenure to avoid making controversial, but feasible, personnel decisions. In other words, many principals use the existence of tenure to excuse their failure to build a case to pressure poor teachers to either improve or be terminated. This is not to say that such cases can always be won. But too many principals fail to fight, even when they might win.

There are sanctions, however, beyond direct discharge. Skillful managers should be able to devise means of putting marginal employees—even those with tenure—under pressure to either improve or choose another field of employment. The precise tactics toward such ends vary from case to case, and they usually require courage and ingenuity. But the basic point is simple. A school is neither a site for early retirement while holding full-time employment, nor a base to sustain a second career in real estate or other entrepreneurial fields.

Good principals also work to invent various rewards and benefits for their more committed employees. The forms of such benefits differ among schools and districts, but they rarely include direct salary increases.

A very common and powerful reward is specific public praise. For instance, one of the authors has had contact with several teacher-recognition programs, which exist in different forms throughout the U.S. The winning teachers identified by such programs usually come from well-managed schools. Undoubtedly, this pattern occurs partly because strong, elaborately written recommendations from principals are invaluable in attaining such awards. Some principals do not want to go to that much trouble, and others lack the skills to produce persuasive recommendations. However, able principals know it is important to recognize dedicated service and put time into helping teachers win deserved awards. Even where efforts fail, the praised teachers appreciate the support.

THE PRINCIPAL AS ROLE MODEL

We must recognize the concept of the principal as a role model for teachers. If the principal tolerates shoddy performance from teachers, many teachers will act the same way toward students in their classrooms. If the principal strives to avoid difficult discussions with parents and teachers, teachers may learn from that behavior. If the principal has a poor attendance record or otherwise evinces disengagement, staff members may mimic those patterns. If the principal walks away from challenging pupil discipline situations, many teachers may apply the lesson being taught.

We are always teaching others by our conduct, especially when we are in a position of authority. The caution is that we sometimes teach the wrong things.

Practices and Policies

1. Can you identify any schools that are striving to be, or already are, moral schools? What characteristics cause you to reach this opinion? How near are they to attaining such a goal?

2. All principals, perhaps with some faculty assistance, must analyze their routines to see how and whether they can increase the frequency of some of the supervisory items on the checklist, e.g., frequency of classroom visits or regularly reviewing lesson plans. Should some of your principal's current responsibilities be delegated elsewhere? Which ones, and to whom? Should some of them be discontinued?

3. Should your principal seek any additional training or counsel to improve performance of supervisory activities?

Where and how can your principal obtain such help?

4. Are teachers now clearly informed of their work responsibilities? If the situation is now ambiguous, how can it be improved?

5. Does the district provide the principal with adequate discretion and information in hiring and transfer situations? Does the current process ensure that competent, well-informed applicants are chosen? If not, what improvements are needed?

6. Do faculty members now see most, or all, faculty meetings as productive? Are faculty members actively involved in the planning of most meetings? How can current meeting policies be improved?

References

1. Lortie, D. (1975). *Schoolteacher*. Chicago: University of Chicago Press, p. 97.

2. Longford, E. (1969). *Wellington: The years of the sword*. London: Weidenfels & Nicholson, p. 121.

3. *Webster's New Collegiate Dictionary*. (1973). Springfield, MA: G and C Merriam, p. 24.

4. Waller, W. (1932). *The sociology of teaching*. New York: Wiley.

CHAPTER 10

Using Ceremonies in Moral Schools

The historian Polybius (202–125 B.C.) described the Roman ceremony of honoring notable family members who were deceased. Masks of all such persons were kept in family homes. On important occasions, the masks were worn by citizens who were clothed in the robes of honor awarded to their predecessors. The masked images were carried through Rome on chariots, finally assembled at a prominent place, and seated on ivory thrones. Polybius said, "It is hard to imagine a more inspiring scene for a young man who aspires to win fame or practice virtue."[1]

Educational research has paid little attention to the role of ceremonies in schools. It has not provided educators with information about how to improve in-school ceremonial life. Ceremonies are an important means of emphasizing and transmitting moral values. Not all ceremonies communicate good moral values. Like books, ceremonies can communicate desirable or undesirable things. Books and ceremonies are morally neutral devices. Despite such neutrality, ceremonies are essential tools for transmitting good conduct and values in schools.

Educators should design and conduct school ceremonies to transmit and teach moral values. Many educators already conduct a variety of in-school ceremonies, such as assemblies, graduations, daily recitation of the Pledge of Allegiance, homecoming week, recognition banquets, and various forms of induction. Ceremonies can be conducted either in individual classrooms or for the whole school.

WHAT ARE CEREMONIES?

Ceremonies are reiterated, collective activities, occurring at determined times and locations. They often require participants to wear special garments, articulate or listen to certain formal words, assume prescribed postures, and give or receive gifts or tokens. Frequently, they involve honoring important symbols and displaying or performing significant works of art, such as music, paintings, or architecture. They are often accompanied by parties or other forms of good-spirited activities.

Ceremonies are important because of their teaching power. They encourage participants to adopt new values or practice current values with greater rigor. Ceremonies are public activities. Those who attend are properly impressed with values when large numbers of people display dramatic, conspicuous allegiance or respect to those values. Traditional ceremonies are, by definition, activities that have persisted. In part, they possess power because their persistence implies that they have been designed with considerable imagination and insight and that many previous generations have participated in such ceremonies.

Ceremonies always have certain formal elements. Some may also include cognitive appeals. The inauguration of a U.S. President, a traditional ceremony, includes an inaugural address. Abraham Lincoln composed the Gettysburg

Address for the consecration—another ceremony—of the war cemetery at Gettysburg. Much of the intellectual impact of such addresses is enhanced by the ceremonial elements of the occasions, for instance, the public gathering, the opening and closing activities, the site of the event. Many school assemblies can have important ceremonial elements.

Ceremonies are often the subject of controversy. Such conflict is, in fact, a sign of their psychological importance. Ceremonies incite conflict because they express values, and certainly not all people in a society or other environment share the same values. Some people object to certain ceremonies. Their real objection is not that a particular ceremony is meaningless; instead, they simply resist acceding to its particular meaning. There is a conflict of values.

Such ceremonial controversy occurred during the 1988 U.S. presidential campaign. The dispute was about reciting the Pledge of Allegiance in schools. One candidate, Governor Michael Dukakis of Massachusetts, said he did not approve of placing public school teachers under pressure to lead their classes in the pledge. The other candidate, Vice President George Bush, took a contrary position. Dukakis said that, while he loved America, he simply did not believe in forcing teachers to pledge their loyalty in this way. He also mentioned he believed Constitutional issues were involved. We believe it seems evident that, apart from consitutional interpretation, Dukakis, personally, did not believe in coerced salutes.

The two candidates differed about whether public employees, particularly teachers, should be compelled to show loyalty, regardless of their state of mind. The pledge was designed as a ceremony to compel schoolchildren—and perhaps their teachers—to show loyalty through public saluting. Dukakis did not believe in compelling people to profess public loyalty.

Elements of Ceremonies

Some readers may be similarly troubled by the concept of compulsion. However, school life is filled with compulsion. Students are compelled to come to school, study, and learn many things. Unless they want to be fired, teachers are compelled to arrive on time, file lesson plans, assign homework, complete periodic reports, and so on. All public, and many private, institutions apply forms of compulsion, though it may be seen as poor taste to stress the coercive elements of such occasions. The basic intellectual issue underlying the Dukakis-Bush debate over the pledge was not really whether compulsion, per se, is wrong in education. Instead, the question was, should we expand the compulsion already widely applied in schools to cover the pledge?

Compulsion is associated with many important ceremonies, often tacitly. The need for compulsion arises because certain people oppose the values underlying particular ceremonies. Some people may be uncomfortable accepting the formal obligations of marriage that they publicly profess in a wedding ceremony. Witnesses in court proceedings may resent having to publicly swear or affirm their truthfulness. Certainly anti-Hitler Germans felt uneasy giving the Nazi salute in public ceremonies.

Many ceremonies deliberately aim to stimulate people to publicly commit themselves to positions where they may have some uncertainty. For example, do I really want to stay married to this person "until death do us part?" Once people have made a public declaration by participating in a ceremony, they are less likely to reverse their commitment later.

Clearly, some compulsory ceremonies are so intrusive that they should be resisted by informed adults and not applied to young persons. But the question remains of how one should decide what ceremonies to resist, especially when the cost of dissent may be quite high. We cannot tell readers which ceremonies they or others should resist or assent to. The answers lie at the center of each person's moral and emotional being. There is also an enormous body of writings to assist explication. However, settling such ultimate questions is beyond the scope of this book. All we can offer is some very general guidelines. Many particular ceremonies have their moral pros and cons. Important communities rely on a mix of ceremonial volition and compulsion. All social life rests on a considerable foundation of compromise. Sometimes the cost of a particular compromise is so high as to be worth the pain of public dissent. Sometimes heroic dissenters, in the end, only motivate those in authority to create new and more elaborate systems of compulsion. Both heroes and demagogues have publicly resisted important ceremonies.

Ceremonies sometimes work better if participation is voluntary, such as choosing to take an oath of enrollment in an organization. Many scholars have concluded that people who take public positions are less likely to revoke their commitments later. Their public declaration increases their emotional investment in acting consistently with their declared positions. Furthermore, compulsion can help ceremonies teach because our own beliefs become strengthened when many others conspicuously share them—even when some of those who appear to share are secretly objecting.

None of this means that compulsion works perfectly. It remains a matter of probability. In general, people who take public positions on certain issues by participating in ceremonies are more likely to act on those positions than those who did not participate.

We believe it is also important to address the connection between ceremonies and religion. Almost all religions place considerable emphasis on ceremonies to communicate and intensify their members' beliefs. As we have noted, America is a relatively religious country, more so than other industrial nations. Thus, it is understandable why many important American ceremonies interweave religious and secular themes. For many participants, such interweaving increases the power of particular ceremonies. The president takes the oath of office with a hand on the Bible. The Pledge of Allegiance includes the phrase "one nation under God." Educators in public schools often find it difficult to design activities celebrating Christmas without religious content.

Undoubtedly, our current legal and philosophical attitudes about religion greatly complicate the design of in-school ceremonies. Everyday experience reveals that different public schools and communities draw the line on religious themes at various points. Even in communities that permit no possible religious entanglement, however, reasonably effective in-school secular ceremonies can usually be carried out.

A Multiplicity of Purposes

School ceremonies serve a multiplicity of purposes, and even individual ceremonies typically meet a variety of needs. Let us consider a high school graduation as a typical example.

Graduation can obviously have many ceremonial elements. The basic ceremony can be anticipated by various preliminary activities, such as a prom or a senior class breakfast. At the ceremony itself graduating pupils, and sometimes teachers, wear special garments and caps. A printed program is distributed, listing the names of the participants and some of the honors awarded. Adults in the audience are usually dressed up. Often, the graduates formally march into the site of the ceremony. Solemn music is played. Unique decorations may be displayed in the assembly place. Special dignitaries may be present to heighten the significance of the occasion. Typically each graduate's name is announced to the audience. One by one, graduates proceed to a stage and are presented with a formal document. A student representative may address the audience, symbolizing the students' advancement towards maturity. Graduates receive bouquets of flowers and other tokens from family and friends. Hugs are exchanged, and sometimes tears are shed. The graduation is often followed by elaborate family parties at the students' homes. Many high schools also enrich ceremonies with various local embellishments and traditions. The graduation reflects real changes in the status of the students: they will no longer attend their high school, and they may go away to college or cease school attendance entirely.

Graduation is actually a rite of passage; such rites are an important traditional form of ceremony common in many cultures. A rite of passage initiates the participants into a new status. It instructs both the initiates and their family and community. It teaches onlookers that the initiates are leaving one role and going on to a new and more responsible one. The rite of graduation also offers a reward to the graduates; they enjoy unqualified public praise and sympathetic attention. As a result, it stimulates the remaining students to anticipate and work toward, the happy day of their own graduation. Indeed, many students are very sensitive to the threat that, if they are irresponsible, they will be excluded from the public graduation ceremony.

Other rites of passage common in our society include weddings, induction into various organizations, and rites surrounding birth and death. In the case of birth and death rites, the focus of instruction is the audience, since the infant or the deceased person obviously cannot learn anything from the rite. Because of the rite, the audience is instructed about how to respond to a critical event—the birth or death of someone important to them.

The Heart of Ceremonies

Important ceremonies symbolize events and values that operate in the world.

They represent real tangible or structural relationships, or changes in such relationships. Where the underlying subject matter—the meat of the occasion—is not really important, the ceremony loses vitality. Conversely, where there is no ceremony (or a poorly organized one) to symbolize an important real event, that event may be misinterpreted. The heart, in effect, is missing.

The high school graduation ceremony has lost some vitality with the diminishing significance of school completion. We do not contend that completing school is a meaningless act, but that it has become a low priority for many students. In too many schools, most students know long in advance that they will graduate unless they die first or choose to drop out. There are few surprises. Many graduating students also know that, next fall, they will be sitting at another school desk in college. Furthermore, many other important indices of adulthood—attaining a driver's license, being allowed to vote—do not coincide with graduation. Patterns such as these have undermined the impact of high school graduation in many communities. In earlier eras, students might strive to finish high school and still fail, and far fewer graduates went to college. In those settings graduation marked a more dramatic passage.

Many contemporary patterns necessarily undermine the vitality of ceremonies. Still, many elements of school life invite greater ceremonial emphasis, including graduation. According to our research, schools that emphasize ceremonies transmit vital traditional values and increase the integrity of their educational programs.

Ceremonies in schools are not without cost. They require pupil and faculty time, not only for participation but often for rehearsal and planning. They take resources to manufacture apparatus and symbols and require talent and imagination—almost always scarce resources—to design activities well.

Still, most important and effective organizations have routinely used ceremonies to heighten individual and group commitment to important goals. In the case of schools, goals can include improving academic achievement, maintaining pupil discipline, improving pupil character, strengthening parent-school ties, improving attendance, and increasing school spirit.

CONCRETE EXAMPLES

We have studied two public schools—a high school and an elementary school—that provide rich examples of different forms of ceremonial life. We can draw two conclusions that apply to both schools, despite differences in the ages of the pupils.

First, each school emphasizes good pupil discipline in its ceremonial life. Discipline enables the faculty to bring large groups of pupils together, have them participate in novel and stimulating activities, and expect good conduct from them. Discipline is the product of determination, foresight, and planning. In the elementary school, planning often includes individual teachers conducting rehearsals for their classes to practice how they will enter and leave the assembly site or proceed to the stage. In the high school, planning often means developing a seating plan for teachers to place them strategically throughout the assembly hall. Pupils are also clearly warned about the serious consequences of individual misconduct. In a sense, the ceremonies are a public test of each school's discipline. Furthermore, the humor often generated by the occasions increases pupils' affection for the school.

Second, each school has faculty who work hard and enjoy their work, students who like being in the school, parents who are generally pleased, discipline that is excellent, and pupil test scores that are good.

The High School

The school had many assemblies to present awards and to provide other forms of recognition. The occasions demonstrated support for pupil achievements in academics, athletics, and school and community service.

In addition, all athletic teams and most major clubs had individual annual recognition banquets. At these banquets, notable achievements were recognized, and all group members received lavish praise in the presence of parents and faculty. Everyone was dressed formally. Rewards such as jackets, trophies, athletic letters, certificates, written reports of the accomplishments of the team and its members, and symbolic gifts to faculty members were distributed. Appropriate addresses were delivered. The school's booster clubs raised the funds for all the banquets. Instead of having one banquet for all athletic teams and significant clubs, the school allowed each team or club to have its own awards banquet, which considerably personalized each occasion. The school held more than twenty banquets a year.

The school understood the instructional value of ceremonies. For instance, each year it held two successive ceremonies to mark graduation, with slight formal distinctions. The first ceremony was the Senior Award Assembly. The awards were distributed before the entire student body, enabling students to see what opportunities for winning honors lay before them—if they applied themselves. Three days later a formal graduation was held before parents and family members. This process recognized that many ceremonies are designed largely to affect their audiences.

The school had many other forms of ceremonial activities: an elaborate homecoming week and pep rally, induction into the Honor Society, and farewell occasions for departing faculty members. A variety of dances and other well-managed, fun activities were held in conjunction with many ceremonies. Planners sought the advice and help of the Student Council and other student organizations in designing and carrying out many ceremonies.

The Elementary School

Many ceremonies were conducted in individual classrooms, for example, Christmas and other holiday parties for younger grades. Another was the daily recitation of the Pledge of Allegiance. Schoolwide expectations were concurrently established when a different member of the Student Council recited the pledge each day over the school's public address system. This practice signaled the prompt start of daily instruction. It also encouraged each class to recite its own pledge at the same time. In addition, many classroom teachers with skills or interest in music taught their pupils to sing patriotic songs after reciting the pledge.

Ceremonies almost always included fun elements appropriate to the pupils' ages. At Halloween, there was a costume contest in the auditorium, followed by a costume parade through the neighborhood. The parade also symbolized the opening of the school's attendance contest. In conjunction with ceremonial assemblies, dances for the seventh and eighth grades were held several times a year, usually toward the end of the school day. The school often enlisted help from parents to carry out such activities.

The various ethnic groups in the school were encouraged to perform different entertainments from their traditions as gifts to the whole school. Students in the audience were encouraged to applaud warmly. At the same time, the school placed such activities under an umbrella of quite emphatic American patriotism.

As part of their training in music, students learned to perform choral pieces for classes of the appropriate age or for the enjoyment of the whole school.

Since the neighborhood community had strong religious traditions, faculty members felt comfortable including expressly religious values in some of its assemblies. For instance, at the Christmas assembly some of the classes sang traditional carols with religious themes.

The annual graduation included several events. There was a "practice graduation" before the student body, except for seventh-graders who would attend the graduation itself. At the practice ceremony, graduates wore attractive street clothes, not their robes. They performed entertainment for the audience, just as they would later do for parents and families. Later that day there was a graduation dance in the gymnasium. Finally there was the official graduation ceremony, witnessed by parents and the seventh-grade students. Graduates wore robes and presented entertainment for the audience. All were invited to attend a reception after the graduation.

Assemblies were held to distribute awards for a variety of individual and group pupil achievements, and to emphasize the important role the Student Council played in the school.

Practices and Policies

1. Examine some or all of the following materials with other teachers in your school and discuss what you learned and/or can apply from the book or film. None of these materials cover exactly how to design a ceremony. But they describe and analyze ceremonies in many different environments and provide readers with concepts and insights to apply to their own situations.

Deal, Terrence, and Allan Kennedy. *Corporate Cultures.* Reading, MA: Addison-Wesley, 1982. A discussion of anthropological concepts applied to modern businesses.

Eisendstadt, S. N. *From Generation to Generation.* New York: Free Press, 1971. A classic describing the role of ceremonies in structuring relationships among groups of youths, and between adults and the young. Many implications for our current situation.

Gennep, Arnold. *Rites of Passage.* Chicago: University of Chicago Press. A seminal nineteenth-century work articulating the basic issues about rites of passage in a provocative and lucid style.

Lesko, Nancy. *Symbolizing Society.* New York: Falmer/Taylor, Francis, 1988. A study of ceremonies and values in a modern Catholic high school. Many insights applicable to public schools.

Wynne, Edward A. *Planning and Conducting Better Ceremonies in Schools.* Bloomington, IN: Phi Delta Kappa, 1990.

Triumph of the Will. A powerful and provocative 1934 film of an enormous Nazi party rally in Nuremburg, Germany. Available on commercial videotape. Seeing it gives one a new perspective on the power of ceremonies (whether used for good or bad ends).

2. Inventory the ceremonial life in your school or classroom. Describe the relationship between such activities and the school's or class's proclaimed purpose or goals. Are the existing ceremonies likely to stimulate appropriate emotions (e.g., dedication, good humor, community, and reflection) regarding goals?

3. Are some important school or class policies not now recognized in ceremonial form? What ceremonies should be invented or adapted to communicate such policies? What forms of ceremonial creation and redesign, if any, are necessary?

In speculating about ceremonial improvements, you might consider the following possibilities:

✦ Ceremonies marking the beginning and end of the school year. The beginning ceremony might be aimed at stimulating commitment and could invite pupils, faculty, and parents to identify significant personal and collective educational goals. (On such occasions, should pupils bring in flowers? Should they recite pledges? What special things should teachers do?) The end-of-the-year ceremony might help participants identify constructive educational goals for their summers, for example, to read ten books.

✦ Ceremonies to memorialize significant, deceased, recent, or past heroic figures or events.

✦ Public induction ceremonies for new principals or teachers.

✦ Commitment ceremonies, where students and faculty commit themselves to some important school or public-service activity.

✦ Gratitude ceremonies, to express thanks for significant services to the school or students, e.g., thanks to particular donors of gifts, to taxpayers in general, to parents, or to teachers.

4. Are the talents of faculty, students, and parents now properly mobilized to enrich ceremonial occasions? Remember, there are songs to be sung, costumes to be designed and made, food to be prepared and served, press releases and recitations to be written, posters to be constructed, instruments to be played, flags and banners to be designed and made, and schedules to be developed. There's room for everyone to make a unique contribution.

References

1. Polybius. (1979). *The rise of the Roman empire* (I. Scott-Kilvert, Trans.). New York: Penguin, p. 347.

CHAPTER 11

Sex and Character

The core problem facing our schools is a moral one. All the other problems derive from it. Hence, all the various attempts at school reform are unlikely to succeed unless character education is put at the top of the agenda. If students don't learn self-discipline and respect for others, they will continue to exploit each other sexually no matter how many health clinics and condom distribution plans are created.

—William Kilpatrick, *Why Johnny Can't Tell Right from Wrong*[1]

There is an important connection between character and what human beings learn about their personal sexual identities and how they learn it—the ways they conduct themselves in sex-related matters. Sexuality is an integral part of our humanity, and it is vital to the survival of the species. There is strong justification for making human sexuality an important part of the education we provide to the young. To keep our young ignorant of their true sexual nature is profoundly miseducative. They must be taught. Nevertheless, the topic can be a mine field. Perhaps the fact that the topic is so vast and so central to human existence helps explain why the subject of sex has been so highly charged and controversial throughout history. This situation notwithstanding, character-sensitive schools and educators must be alert to the implications of this significant and often complex topic.

First, we should recognize that people must learn how to express, and sometimes suppress, their sexuality. Human beings can act in many different ways regarding sex. Yet almost all these variations affect other people; sex acts are often social acts. The people involved, in order to cooperate, must have a mutual understanding—unless the relationship is founded on rape and assault. Even supposedly private sex-related choices, such as decisions about our clothing or vocabulary, can subject others to disturbing sexual stimulation. Due to such basic commonalities, all cultures strive to teach adolescents and children the forms of sexual expression and repression appropriate to their own society, sex and particular status, and the diverse occasions of life. Unless proper common values are transmitted, distressing confusion will arise around this strong and pervasive force.

Some societies allow certain forms of sex-related behavior that other societies constrain or prohibit. In some societies, it is acceptable for mature women to bare their breasts in public on certain occasions; in other societies, such conduct is taboo. Some cultures place notable constraints on contacts among unmarried males and females, such as insisting on chaperones or restricting certain activities on a single-sex basis. Such variations are exactly why children must learn the proper sexual behaviors of their culture.

THE INEVITABILITY OF SEX EDUCATION

Schools and teachers inevitably help children and adolescents learn about their sex roles. The relevant school policies may be decided by individual teachers and administrators, by people at a higher level, through general cultural norms, or via an amalgam of such forces. Some examples of sexual instruction include:

✦ The materials relating to sexuality presented in the formal curriculum—in literature, history, or biology—and the books available in the school library.

✦ The norms governing sex-related activities in and around the school and classrooms. Should there be single-sex activities? What are they? At what ages should they begin? Should there be single-sex schools? Should there be constraints on sexually provocative dress, makeup, or slogans on T-shirts? What is considered sexually provocative? Should pupils be required to wear relatively asexual uniforms, especially if all or most parents request such a practice? How closely should mixed-sex recreation, such as dances or overnight trips, be monitored by adults? Should there be constraints on sexually related language in and around school?

✦ The vigor that educators display—or fail to display—in enforcing school sex-related rules.

✦ The degree to which school employees, especially educators, are expected to provide pupils with wholesome sexual role models. What conduct is considered sexually wholesome or unwholesome?

✦ The consequences, if any, that the school applies to students who transgress defined norms of sexual behavior, e.g., an unmarried female student becoming pregnant, or a male student impregnating an unmarried female student, with or without her consent.

Obviously, schools inescapably do—and must—teach sexual values, whether the values they choose to teach are good or bad. Values are taught by many other social agencies, of course, such as families and religious organizations. Still, schools have a significant role to play. The questions inevitably arise: What sex-related values should be taught? And who shall decide?

As we have emphasized, the values transmitted in schools generally should be those preferred by the preponderance of the parents whose children attend the school. We deliberately use the word *generally*. It is possible that the values of the majority of parents in some locality may be so unusual or disruptive as to justify a state-supported school's refusal to honor their values. For example, suppose the parents in a public school community have an inordinate tolerance for out-of-wedlock births or adolescent promiscuity.[2] Such hostility toward local sexual norms is clearly a two-edged sword. The power to override the priorities of local parents can also be applied against protradition parents, for instance, parents who favor schools encouraging "patriarchal" sex role patterns. Parents who oppose locally favored sexual norms are often caught in a bind. If they decide to prohibit the transmission of these values, they put themselves and their children in cultural conflict with the rest of the school community. If they go along with policies and practices they oppose, they will not only fail their own parental ideals, but they may appear weak and ineffectual to their children.

This discussion about schools and sex-norms choices has obvious implications for the broader topics of school choice and the merits of educational systems that stress choice among different schools and in-school programs. Typically, parents desire their children to be in schools where the other students' patterns of values are similar to their own. Such patterns of family values enable schools to form focused communities. In the case of sexual values, in communities where relatively common patterns of sexual norms exist, schools should have confidence teaching and enforcing them. This topic has already been covered in some depth in this book. However, it is our belief that much of the smoldering discontent over vouchers and the search for alternative educational plans is fueled by the discontent of parents over the school's failure to uphold their norms and over the formal and informal sex education currently existing in our public schools.

Changing Sexual Values

Historically, sex has often been a subject of controversy. It generates powerful emotions, such as lust, love, and jealousy. Modes of sexual expression and diversity vary among individuals and among different cultures. As a result, sexual norms are never indefinitely stable. There is also a continuous progression of successive generations, each needing instruction, each capable of learning new and different means of sexual expression from what was previously typical.

In recent years, the pace of change in sexual convention has been further accelerated. A national survey provides evidence of this point. The survey asked adult respondents at what age they first engaged in vaginal sexual intercourse. The question was posed to a series of age groups.[3] The youngest were respondents aged twenty-five to twenty-nine; the oldest were fifty to fifty-nine. The average age of first intercourse for the youngest White cohort was 17.6; the equivalent age for the oldest cohort was a few months shy of 19 years of age. In summarizing this aspect of their study the authors wrote:

> There has been a steady decline in the age at first intercourse over the past four decades, and more young people experience intercourse in high school with more partners. Given the general ignorance of youths about sexuality and the lack of education in responsible sexual relations, it is not surprising that there has been an increase in risky sexual encounters among the young.[4]

The downward shift in the age of a first sexual experience by the youngest cohort is even more notable because people are now getting married at older ages than in the past. Thus, sexual involvement comes earlier than before, while marriage comes later. Although this study reports average or mean ages, the fact that among the youngest cohort the average age of first sexual experience was 17.4 years of age also means that there are still millions of adolescent virgins.

One important cause of such increased sexual expression in our era is our comparative affluence and better health. These benefits give us more time, privacy, and energy to dedicate to sexual expression than was available to most people in earlier generations.

Another cause is the development of our pervasive modern media, offering low-cost and engaging new—if simplistic—sources of sexual information and stimulation. The sources run from advertisements to situation comedies, from talk shows to the reports in the daily news. Many of these "sexual informants" earn their prominence (and high salaries) by publicizing the most outrageous activities they can imagine. Thus, we and our children are awash with sexual pseudoauthorities, from assorted guests on television and radio talk shows to tabloid newspapers on the reading rack in the supermarket checkout lane.

The forces of romantic egalitarianism—which we have thoroughly discussed—have also profoundly affected our sexual values. Those forces have undermined many previous distinctions and principles regarding sexual issues. In the egalitarian perspective, all forms of sexually related conduct are equally right. In other words, whenever sexual behavior is considered within an egalitarian institution, there is a strong tendency for such discussions to license many different forms of behavior. And many contemporary schools are relatively egalitarian.

The changes in sexual conduct are reflected in increasing rates of out-of-wedlock births as well as permissive attitudes toward sex portrayed in much of our literature and mass media, including print and visual forms. Ironically, at one time, a common complaint was that the media concealed or disguised the sexuality pervading human life. Today, the truth is that we find many examples of the contemporary media outrageously exaggerating the prevalence of illicit sex. Survey research, relying on anonymous replies, has consistently found levels of husband-wife sexual fidelity that are far higher than suggested by many contemporary TV soap operas and popular, or even serious, novels. A national survey reported that 79% of married persons queried reported they had been faithful to their mate for at least the last five years.[5]

These forms of titillation are enormously stimulating to many young people. They are understandably attracted by the fallacy that sex should be associated with permissiveness and painless novelty. Many writers, publishers, and dramatic producers also applaud such portrayals. After all, it enables them to attract customers and make money without displaying the imagination and discipline inherent in most significant art.

In the past two decades our public schools have assumed increasing responsibility for teaching pupils about the intimate elements of sexual expression. The format applied has essentially stressed sexuality without moral values. Recent research demonstrates the failure of sex education in our schools. The evidence is deep, wide, and obvious.[6]

Sex Education in a Moral Void

The formal approach that prevails in our schools is called comprehensive sex education. (We use the word *formal* because there is considerable evidence that many classroom teachers revise or moderate the more irrational components of that curriculum.) Currently, it is either mandated or supported in forty-seven states. Imported from Sweden some forty years ago, it has been strongly supported by the health education establishment for over twenty years. Like sex itself, its appeal is potent and seductive. We will describe what we believe are the major flaws in this approach.

First, advocates of comprehensive sex education start with a problem: those numbing statistics about sexual activity among the young, the soaring pregnancy rate and the increasing prevalence of sexually transmitted diseases (STDs) among teen-aged students. Those who support this approach are seemingly undaunted by each new year's report of a rise in teen-age pregnancy and new outbreaks of STDs. If anything, the righteous arguments of the advocates gain steam and volume: "Let us start earlier with longer, more realistic courses of instruction. And, remember, we're specialists. Children are suffering from an information deficit. Give us more freedom, and just get out of the way."

Second, comprehensive sex education proponents assert that schools should be scientific in their treatment of human sexuality, focusing on the facts. Translated, that means sex educators teach "what is" rather than "what ought." While schools feel empowered to tell students categorically that they ought not to smoke or drive drunk or eat fatty foods, in sex education judgmental "oughts" are out. Except, perhaps, for "unprotected sex"—the code words for not using condoms—the only major prohibition of the entire movement. On the other hand, their attention to unprotected sex would appear to give children the clear impression that, if not good, there is nothing particularly wrong with engaging in "safe sex," or sex using condoms.

Third, advocates urge that comprehensive sex education start in kindergarten and continue through the twelfth grade. Children—boys and girls together—need to learn how to talk with one another about sexual intercourse, genitalia, masturbation, birth control, sexual abuse, and a variety of other topics in a candid, matter-of-fact manner. This means starting young and keeping the conversation going. Only through science, the argument goes, can sex be freed of superstition, dangerous unfulfilled curiosity, and mystery.

Comprehensive Sex Education and the Evidence

Impaled by statistics and believing it is a "scientific approach" to the problem, our schools have put more and more effort into comprehensive sex education, devoting more and more of students' time to the subject. Available research data do not provide much support for this effort. One thorough review of such programs was conducted by Asta Kenney, an associate for policy development for the Allan Guttmacher Institute.[7] This institute is generally regarded as basically supportive of comprehensive sex education programs. The review concluded that "such programs, however, should not be regarded as panaceas . . . it is hard to know the results of such programs." Other evaluations of sex education programs have led to equivalent findings. The available evidence shows such programs have few or no positive effects—except teaching pupils certain facts about sex. However, there is little or no evidence that these efforts have any important effects on pupils' sex-related conduct, such as the likelihood of their having or avoiding pre-marital sexual intercourse before completing high school.

These findings should not surprise readers who recall our discussion of profound learning in chapter 2. We believe it is obvious that learning about our personal sexual conduct, and what to do and not to do, is profound. That earlier discussion emphasized that pervasive, frequently repeated activities, backed up by strong incentives or punishments, are needed to cause profound learning. Current sex-education classes typically lack such systems. We believe this is for the better, because it is questionable whether the subject matter in such classes is always good for pupils to learn. What should students learn about masturbation, abortion, homosexual sex, contraception, sexual techniques, massage, and other forms of sexual pleasure?

Some proponents of sex education programs recognize the inadequacies of sex-education activities that stress the acquisition of formal knowledge. These proponents contend that sex education can only be successful if the message is "delivered clearly, and in the language of intended listeners."[8] Perhaps such concepts underlie certain contemporary sex education programs in elementary schools. These "innovative" programs teach pupils by having them make clay models of male and female genitalia. They teach pupils about using contraceptives by encouraging them, in class, to practice covering cucumbers and bananas with condoms.

The Sexual Behavior of the Young

While this major effort to scientifically educate children about sexuality has been going on, there has been no real scientific evidence to suggest it has positive results. As it turns out, support for comprehensive sex education programs is not rational but ideological. As Barbara Dafoe White has stated:

> The absence of empirical support for comprehensive sex education does not, however, discomfort or deter its advocates. Up and down the sex-education ranks, from the Surgeon General . . . to local advocates, there has been little effort to make a reasoned case for comprehensive sex education. Challenged, the sex educators simply crank up their rhetoric: Criticize sex education, they say, and you contribute to the deaths of teen-agers from AIDS.[9]

There is other related evidence, however.[10] In spite of three decades of massive efforts to educate our children about their sexual nature and develop "healthy attitudes," we have witnessed during that same period a six-fold increase in out-of-wedlock births among teen-age girls. The rate has increased from 5% in 1960 to 30% in 1990. Currently, 70% of African-American babies are born to unmarried teen-agers. Our children are among the most sexually active in the civilized world. Twenty-five years ago, in 1970, 95% of fifteen-year-old girls in our nation and 68% of seventeen-year-old girls were virgins. In 1988, eighteen years later, the comparable percentages had decreased to 74% of fifteen-year-olds and 49% of seventeen-year-olds. In our country today, by age nineteen only 14% of boys and only 20% of girls are virgins. Instead of entering marriage and learning the secrets and joys of sex with their spouse, they come to their marriage beds sexually experienced, if not jaded. And woe to the partner who does not measure up.

Young people are entering marriage not only with sexual experience and high expectations, but with a range of sexually transmitted diseases from syphilis to herpes, from gonorrhea to the AIDS-linked HIV virus. On the other hand, increasing percentages of young Americans are choosing not to marry. From a sexual perspective, why should they? Thirty-five years ago, a young Elvis Presley was asked when was he going to get married. He brazenly answered with the quip, "Why buy a cow when you can get milk free through a picket fence?" Why make commitments and take on the responsibilities of marriage and a family when you can have no-fault sex for the asking? Why play by those old rules, when the Beautiful People—Donald Trump, Hugh Grant, Madonna, Pamela Anderson—and the top athletes—Earvin "Magic" Johnson, Wade Boggs, Wilt Chamberlain—featured daily in the media seem to be having it all?

In retrospect, it was foolish to think that comprehensive sex education could tame the tiger of youth's sexual passions by information alone. Giving children and adolescents facts about the varieties of sexual expression and offering mild suggestions about "responsible sexual choices" is more like whetting the tiger's appetite. It was naive to believe that instructing students about intercourse and "outercourse"—various forms of masturbation, massage, and assorted other forms of stimulation—would become something students could neatly file in their notebooks and bring out six or eight years later on their wedding night or when they had "established a significant relationship." It makes one suspicious that conceivers and promoters of comprehensive sex education were ever young. A hint may come from George Orwell, who once observed, "There are some things only an intellectual can believe. No ordinary person could be so foolish."

HOW DID WE GET THIS WAY?

For comprehensive sex education to have become so widespread and pervasive, it would appear that many ordinary people who are not specialists in sex education have gone along with its absurdities and excesses. Many teachers, school board members, administrators, and parents have stood on the curbside and watched this bandwagon movement take over the school. Like all too many educational questions, the answer to why this has happened is not readily available. However, it is worthy of speculation. Why have our schools changed, when they were once strongly supportive of an ordered relationship between young men and women, of sexual modesty, and of premarital chastity?

One conjecture goes back nearly thirty years to the advent of what was then referred to as the *sexual revolution*, a sharp change in social attitudes that began in the late 1960s. This was a period of intense questioning of social institutions and customs, brought about by many factors, including the civil rights struggle, the Vietnam War protest movement, and the emergence of the drug culture. Besides general cultural turmoil, sexual attitudes were greatly affected by the development of a birth-control pill and the belief that we were entering an era of liberated sexual practices, where openness and sexual freedom would reign. Formerly taboo, the sexual side of our nature became a staple topic of radio and television, from situation comedies to interview shows. Liberated from what was described as our uptight, middle-class hang-ups, we, like the cast of the era's emblematic play, *Hair*, would dance into the "Age of Aquarius." Previously reserved for limited situations and environments, the topic of sex went public and became a national obsession. For many, sexual fulfillment emerged as a chief criterion of success as a person. Old standards of sexual morality, along with old words, such as *chastity* and *modesty*, were ridiculed.

Our New Sexuality

The new sexuality, as some called these new attitudes, has had three particular effects on adults. First, it created vast business empires for pornography, which until recently was a mere cottage industry. It opened up a huge market for hard- and soft-core films, tapes, books, and magazines. It has been estimated that fully 40% of videotape rentals are hard-core pornography such as *Debbie Does Dallas*. What once was under-the-counter and hard-to-get is now front-and-center and in-your-face.

Second, the new sexual openness has fueled a greener-pastures syndrome. Many adults believed their marriages were keeping them from this new world and they were living a sexual half-life. Over recent decades, divorce statistics have skyrocketed, largely affected by these beliefs. Families have been shattered. According to 1990 figures, 36% of all American children lived apart from their natural, biological fathers, spawning what David Blankenhorn labeled "a culture of fatherlessness.[11]

Third, those who were merely spectators during the sexual revolution have lost their voice and have become, for all intents and purposes, a "Sexual Silent Majority." A recent study of American sexual attitudes and practices demonstrated that the great majority of Americans hold to traditional sexual behavior and standards.[12] Feeling generally out of step, with little support for their ideals, such as monogamous relationships and abstinence before marriage, their confidence in the correctness of their views has been deeply eroded. Long-cherished moral rules between the genders have been marginalized and represented as arbitrary lifestyle choices. On issues of sexuality, even parents who were strong and confident about impressing values on their children, such as honesty and responsibility, fell still. It has been the schools, however, where the silence has been most deafening.

The New Sexuality and the Schools

Prior to the advent of the new sexuality and its handmaiden, comprehensive sex education, teachers—without being self-conscious—conveyed a sex-is-for-grown-ups attitude. A teacher would look a sexually confused or at-risk student directly in the eye and caution, "Don't do it!" Cowed by the new sexuality, teachers are now quiet and leave such matters to a specialist, more than likely a specialist trained in comprehensive sex education. Further, many teachers have been warned in one education course after another not to impose their own values on their students. The results have been predictable. Unchecked and unchallenged, the sexual energies of the young have worn away the walls of decorum. Earlier policies about public displays of affection were quietly shelved. Hand-holding and kissing sprung up in halls and in classrooms. Necking and fondling followed. Verbal sexual overtures and groping—sometimes wanted, but often not—have become an everyday occurrence. Girls, and occasionally boys, who complain are asked, "Were there any witnesses?" or "What did you do to invite this treatment?" Students discovered copulating in halls, bathrooms, and parking lots are simply told their behavior is inappropriate in school, and they are directed to go back to class, with no punishment. In some high schools, boys form sex clubs, like California's infamous group who called themselves the Spur Posse, and compete to see who can "score" against the most girls.

Perhaps another factor in our failure to confront the young with moral arguments against engaging in sex is a desire to be accepted. Many adults, teachers included, do not want to be seen as old-fashioned or out-of-tune with what seem to be progressive and sophisticated views. Some might think, "Young people are so vital and so sexually free, who am I to tell them what they ought to do? Besides, I seem to have a lot of sexual hang-ups." Such attitudes are easy to acquire in our media-saturated world, where our sexual curiosities and appetites are continually whetted. A description like "sexually active" connotes vitality and freedom, making the many monogamous adults feel vaguely inert and out of step. Few adults have had the spine-strengthening experience of visiting a hospital AIDS ward and hearing the anguished regrets from the wasted bodies and lesioned mouths of misled sexual pace-setters. Nor is it likely they talked with fifteen-year-old girls who have had three abortions and twice attempted suicide. In light of such encounters, or even a careful reading of the newspapers, one might begin to suspect that what some call our prudish sexual hang-ups are a crucial part of the survival system of the human species.

The curriculum itself is no haven from the poisoned sexual atmosphere of many schools. Our school libraries and course curricula are awash with works that celebrate the new sexuality, from *Heather Has Two Mommies* in the early grades to Alice Walker's *The Color Purple* in the high schools. One of the authors was disturbed to learn that, in one month during the school year in which this book was written, his fifteen-year-old son was reading Philip Roth's *Goodbye, Columbus* in English class and was acting in the school's fall play, Ken Kesey's *One Flew Over the Cuckoo's Nest*. The pervasive sexual content encountered by the students was never commented on by the teachers. It seems the sixties are alive and well in the American high school. Instead of being protected environments for our children as they mature in mind and body, many of our schools and classrooms are places of lax sexual attitudes and behavior and of dubious and harmful information.

The Real Divorce: Sex Education and Character

The cause of our current plight is that schools have severed education and human sexuality from the school's traditional mission of character formation and moral education. The solution is to reconnect them. Historically, enduring societies have been intensely concerned with passing on reliable standards of right and wrong and the virtues and habits the young will need to function well as adults. Clearly this includes how the sexes relate to one another. Clearly, too, sex education becomes dangerous without a foundation of mutual respect, responsibility, and self-discipline.

Twenty-five years ago, American society convinced itself that it had no shared values and for the next few decades its attention wandered from the transmission of values to the young. The current climate of promiscuity and even date rape on our high school and college campuses, unstable marriages and abusive family life, and the explosion of sexually transmitted diseases are some of the results. But climates—libidinous and otherwise—can be changed. This has been possible in the past, and it can be in the future. Strong evidence of this comes from the distinguished historian Gertrude Himmelfarb's recent book, *The De-Moralization of Society: From Victorian Virtues to Modern Values.*[13] Her research shows clearly that not only can virtues be taught and promoted within a community, but they provide an environment of order and prosperity from which everyone benefits.

As we have suggested, there is evidence of the beginnings of a revival of attention to the teaching of civic values and morality in our country. Books of moral tales are on the best-seller lists. National magazines, such as *Time* and *Newsweek*, have featured cover stories on such traditional themes as virtue and shame. Education organizations, such as the American School Board Association and the Association for Supervision and Curriculum Development, are beginning the task of refocusing on the core moral values that unite us, once a primary task for public schools. As schools struggle to throw off their currently toxic sexual climate and recover their historic moral mission, it is crucial that the subject of human sexuality is not ignored.

The Moral Nature of Sex

Sexual intercourse is not simply a matter of so much erogenous friction, as it is often treated in current sex education courses. Nor is sexual activity merely a matter of personal taste and choice, as in deciding whether to listen to rock-'n-roll. Sex, by its very nature, is moral. Except for masturbation, sex is social. Sexual activity between two people means that one person's actions involve another person, a person with human dignity and with rights and specific responsibilities. Sex affects the body and mind, the physical and psychological well-being of both partners. It involves intimacy, power, and vulnerability. Sex should involve mutual giving and mutual taking. It has consequences, not the least of which is the possibility of bringing new life into the world. All cultures have seen sex as moral, carrying, as it does, the very source of their existence. Every enduring society has acknowledged this.

For whatever reasons that we have taught sex from a strictly biological, value-free perspective, we ought to turn back. We ought to reject this approach. Young people, who are typically curious about and confused by their own sexual awakening, recognize the moral nature of sex. They want to learn about sex in a moral context, which acknowledges the centrality of moral values, such as self-restraint, compassionate understanding of the other, and fidelity in sexual matters. Eunice Kennedy Shriver, who has been working with teen-aged mothers for several years, has stated:

> Over the years I have discovered that teen-agers would rather be given standards than contraceptives. . . . They are thirsting for someone to teach them . . . to tell them that for their own good and the good of society it is not wise for them to have sexual intercourse at 12, 13, 14, or 15 . . . sex at this age is not necessary for a caring relationship to develop and endure.[14]

And as a young male student at the California high school when the Spur Posse club was active stated: "They pass out condoms, teach sex education and pregnancy this and pregnancy that. But they don't teach us any rules."[15]

After a little reflection, most people agree that how we respond to our sexual passions and urges and how we live out our sexual lives are intrinsically moral matters. As we explained, sex both involves and affects others. It can lead to bringing new life into the world. It has not only strong personal consequences, but profound social ones, too. For example, our nation is currently struggling to pay an annual bill of twenty-five billion dollars to out-of-wedlock mothers for the care and feeding of their children. In essence, to educate young people about sex devoid of an ethical perspective is profoundly wrong. It is similar to encouraging children to play with loaded guns without alerting them to the dangerous consequences.

Sex provokes powerful forces in people, and especially in adolescents. History and literature, not to mention television soap operas, give regular testimony to how our passions can wreak havoc in our lives and the lives of those around us. An important part of being a sexually mature person is to be a person of character, a person who has enough self-control, along with a sense of responsibility and even courage, to deal with the demands of one's sexual nature. A true sex-education program must contribute to helping children acquire not only a moral compass, but also the enduring habits of good character.

Religion, Sex, and the Schools

Many advocates of comprehensive sex education use arguments concerning the separation of church and state and the pluralistic nature of religion in America to justify using an amoral approach in sex education in schools. And there is nothing quite like the topic of religion to paralyze public school educators. As Paul Vitz's research has demonstrated, our schools work hard to act as if religion simply is not there.[16]

As stated in chapter 1, the United States is widely recognized to be a nation of both distinctly religious people and distinctive religious traditions. Moral perspectives on sexuality are usually influenced by religious views. In fact, sexual morality has traditionally been intertwined with religious morality. However, our realization of our religious differences and our hesitancy to offend our fellow citizens have contributed to our current failure to address the moral nature of sexuality. Clearly, we differ on some sexual topics: abortion, forms of birth control, and gay sexual practices. These differences, however, are hardly justification for failing to acknowledge to children that sex involves important issues of right and wrong, issues on which their parents and church leaders can give them important guidance.

While some educators are truly hostile to religion, they are the exceptions. Most teachers and administrators, like the rest of our nation, are members of churches and think of themselves as religious. They have excluded religion and religious perspectives from our schools because of a perverted understanding of court rulings and a fear of offending the nonreligious and those of minority religions. Their thinking goes something like this: "Religions have a lot to say about sexual practices. Various religions have identified various behaviors as right or wrong. Therefore, for the secular, public schools to identify any sexual practices as right or wrong, good or bad, is inappropriate." The same logic would suggest that since various religions have identified various forms of violence—for example, unjust wars—as wrong, it is inappropriate for public schools to speak against any form of violence.

Faulty logic aside, no major religious denomination in our nation's very pluralistic patchwork of churches supports sexual activity among unmarried teen-agers. None disagree with what Jesse Jackson, the Baptist minister and liberal spokesman, calls "babies having babies." In spite of the fact that there is general consensus on these issues among religious groups, and between religious and nonreligious groups, our schools remain hesitant to teach in their moral context.

The Condom Solution

In the last few years media personalities and educators have often joined forces in vigorously promoting the use of condoms among the young. They justify their advocacy as both a moral and a practical solution to the issue of teen-age sexuality. Many school districts distribute condoms to students as young as fifth-graders and do so without parental consent. Much criticism has been directed at programs promoting the use of condoms. The criticism ranges from studies showing the high failure rate of condoms to discussions of the school's liability in a case where the school promotes condoms and later a student becomes pregnant or contracts a sexually transmitted disease. To us, a most telling criticism of condom distribution programs may be an observation of a New York City high school teacher who recently said, "My kids can't remember to bring a pencil to school. Do we really expect that, in the throes of passion, they are going to remember to fish out a condom and then use it properly? Come on! Get real!"

It is also relevant that, according to surveys, an important cause of adolescents' failure to use contraceptives is their desire to make sex an apparently romantic occasion, to associate the act with the appearance, or reality, of spontaneity or overwhelming affection.[17] Too much stress on being prepared or having practiced with condoms changes the tone of the occasion, making it seem highly contrived and manipulative.

The Traditional Wisdom of Parents

Sex educators may say to young people that using contraceptives is a form of caring or concern. But most adults know this is only a half-truth. Many parents would be troubled if a sixteen-year-old boy came around to go to a casual movie with their fourteen-year-old daughter and happened to drop a condom on the couch. They would probably be distressed because they believe that routinely having condoms ready at the age of sixteen implies a premature emphasis on sexuality. Presumably, many parents strive to prevent such premature development of sexual appetites in their adolescent children.

Most enduring cultures, striving to overcome the numerous hazards of premature sex, have opted for a different policy from allowing early sex as a routine occurrence. Such cultures stress that young adults should abstain from sexual intercourse until marriage. In other words, the adults in such cultures believe it is unrealistic to expect adolescents to manage early or premature sexual intercourse. There are not only problems over possible pregnancy and sexually transmitted disease. There are also the powerful emotional attractions unleashed by sexual intimacy.

To cite a simple literary instance, consider Shakespeare's *Romeo and Juliet*. True, the play is a fictional artistic creation. However, through many centuries, readers have responded to the vital perceptions underlying the play—especially its lyric and deep insights into the power and flaws of young love. As we noted in chapter 1, Shakespeare had obvious sympathy for his "star-crossed lovers." But it is also evident that neither of the tragic pair was blessed with notable common sense. Shakespeare implicitly recognized that only two teen-agers could be so foolish as to suddenly fall in love with the person most likely to destroy their happiness.

Things would have gone better for Romeo and Juliet if their two quarrelling families could have reconciled. But the Capulets and the Montagues had been engaged in a blood feud for decades. The idea that the families would suddenly make up to satisfy two moonstruck teen-agers is appealing, but not very realistic. Such an idea is exactly the sort of mistake young, naive persons can make. And that mistake led to a terrible outcome. Romeo's friend Mercutio is killed by Juliet's brother; Romeo then kills the brother; and then Romeo and Juliet each commit suicide due to misunderstandings arising in the tension-fraught environment.

Abstinence: The Dreaded "A" Word

The bankruptcy of so many schools' sex education programs is captured in their failure to advocate a strong and clear message of abstinence. The failure is couched in many of the twentieth century's most problematic clichés: "Who are we to impose our views on our children?" "We have to respect their right to choose." "Everybody's doing it, so it can't be all bad." It is curious that sex has been singled out for such special and vacillating treatment. Our schools do not permit smoking and are doctrinaire about its dangers. Without hesitation we discourage children from taking drugs and even driving without a seat belt. We disallow alcohol, preach against it, and tell young people at the very least to defer alcohol until they are old enough to handle it. Yet for some reason we cannot look our students in the eye and say, "Sex is serious, and you are much too young."

In our view, sex education programs should actively promote sexual abstinence among unmarried teen-agers. Sexual abstinence should be presented to the young as an ideal, the same way we present honesty to them as an ideal to be sought after. The self-control required for sexual abstinence can be an important part of character formation for a young person. It becomes even more valuable when associated, as it often is, with concern for the well-being of another person—for example, the potential for a young woman becoming pregnant or a young man or woman contracting a venereal disease.

Where does the ideal of sexual abstinence gain its authority? This is, of course, a legitimate question. The authority comes from the common experience and practice of wise people and successful societies. Good sexual attitudes and habits, such as abstinence, serve both the individual and the society. Except for the odd representative of the North American Man Boy Love Association and the occasional sexual adventurer, the overwhelming majority of Americans—liberal and conservative, religious and areligious, of all races—believe that it is unwise for high school students to be sexually active. They seem to know intuitively what researchers have found: that sexual activity is correlated with poor grades, dropping out of school, a weak self-concept, and, of course, premature parenthood.[18]

The most pernicious justification for not actively teaching abstinence is from people who say, "Well, they are going to have sex anyway, so we may as well equip them for 'safe sex.'" We are suspicious that those who use such arguments are not talking about their own children, but about "them"—those other children who are different by race or economic class or both. Those children apparently are seen as beyond the reach of reason or morality. "They" cannot fathom the emotional and physical consequences of sexual activity that begins at too young an age. "They" lack the capacity for gaining self-control and self-discipline. The best we can do is scare them about getting AIDS and other STDs, preach to them about "safe sex," and tell them about condoms. In fact, "they" are so disorganized, so short-sighted, and so limited, they cannot be trusted to go around the corner to the drug store to buy condoms that just might save their lives.

Whatever else this view may be—racist, classist—it represents a complete lack of faith in the potential of young people. At a minimum, it speaks to profoundly diminished views of education and human nature.

Not long ago, the noted essayist John Leo reported the results of a national poll commissioned by *Time* magazine. The poll found that two-thirds of all citizens surveyed want the schools to "urge teenagers not to have sexual intercourse" and that 76% of American adults old enough to have adolescent children consider it "morally wrong for [unmarried] teenagers to have sexual relations."[19] This being the case, it seems reasonable to propose that schools should criticize promiscuity and actively support sexual abstinence during adolescence. Rather than a value-free approach that advances condoms, abortion, and sexual experimentation, our schools should promote sex education, which not only has the support of the community, but also contributes to the development of character and moral maturity.

CONCLUSION

Human sexuality is one of those ultimately important issues in society that speak deeply to each individual as well as to the survival of a society. Comprehensive sex education slipped in the back door of the American schools when we were all a little startled by the new sexuality. It has contributed mightily to the toxic sexual environment in our schools, to unprecedented levels of promiscuity, and to rampant disease and unwanted pregnancy among our children. We need to reject comprehensive sex education and replace it with sex education programs grounded in character education.

The entire issue of how our schools treat sex education points to a larger problem: the school's loss of a clear sense of purpose. In the fourth century B.C., Socrates gave us a definition of education claiming that education should make us both smart and good. The aim of character education has always been to help the young know the good, love the good, and do the good. Character-centered sex education is not only what our children need; it also plays a key role in recapturing this lost mission of our schools.

Basic Principles

Since our children will, and should, come to know and understand human sexuality, it is in everyone's interest that they "get the story right." Although it would be comforting to be guided in this by empirically verified procedures, we must currently rely on good judgment and common sense about human nature to determine how to conduct sex education. We offer the following suggestions with the hope that they might contribute to sound school practices and policies.

First, sex education should always be taught within a moral—not necessarily religious—context. This does not mean that teachers should be heavily moralistic. But clearly the language of morality has a place in sex education. This topic should be discussed not simply in the language of science and the social sciences, but also in terms of ethics. As Eunice Kennedy Shriver[20] and Colleen Kelly Mast[21] have urged, teachers should ensure that sex is a matter of reflection and moral discourse, that biological knowledge and other issues are infused with discussion of ethical issues. There are "oughts" and "ought nots" that should be part of our understanding of human sexuality. Not all sexual practices or choices are equally good. The moral compass that students are developing should also be directed toward their sex lives. An individual's sexual behavior should be seen as a matter of character and considered in an ethical context. We fully realize that this is currently not the fashion in sex education, where the treatment of sex strives to be neutral on values and stripped of ethical implications. However, in the same way that our choice of an economic system is permeated with ethical considerations, and the manner in which we drive a car has moral considerations, so too is the way in which we live out our sexuality.

Second, neither the teacher nor the school should be the lone arbiter of what is taught on the topic of human sexuality. Schools continually get in trouble when they forget that children belong to their parents and that schools exist to teach what the community knows and believes to be correct. Sex education courses should not be used to separate the young from their family's sexual prejudices or to introduce them to what some might consider new and freer life styles.

If teachers feel unduly constrained, they should try to educate parents on their views and intentions. If they fail, they should probably find a more accommodating school community. If individual parents are uncomfortable with what their community has decided should be taught, then they should find another school for their children. There is a clear problem here, however. Allowance has to be made for those parents who object to the sexual messages and mores of the school. As it is now, the state compels parents under threat of prosecution to send their children to school. When parents' views are at odds with those of their community's public school, only those who can afford to do so may choose a different school to provide the education, moral or otherwise, they believe their children ought to have. Given the many sensitivities around this issue, it is imperative that public schools find common moral ground for sex education programs. We are confident that if this happens, the program that emerges will follow the direction we have outlined in this chapter.

Third, sex education should be treated honestly. The prevailing focus on simply teaching sexual techniques, individual options, and "safe sex" methods is incomplete, potentially harmful, and ultimately dishonest. As we have asserted throughout this chapter, sex is not like grammar or long division. Sex is strong stuff that can lead to great good or great sorrow in people's lives. Certainly students need to learn that sex contributes greatly to the joy and solidarity of a union. However, they also need to appreciate its dark potential: sexual abuse, especially of children; sexually transmitted diseases; the physical, psychological, and emotional risks of "safe sex" and "outercourse"; the contribution of sexual infidelity to the destruction of families; and the rippling consequences of out-of-wedlock births. At present, our schools feel justified and comfortable in teaching students the dangers to their well-being of alcohol, drugs, smoking, fatty foods, and even driving without a seat belt. Some serious caution about promiscuity and irresponsible sex is also warranted.

Fourth, sex education should teach students to see sexuality as an area of their lives that calls for the presence of virtues. They should be taught that their sexuality must be supported by self-control, a strong sense of responsibility, prudence, and, often, courage to withstand strong sexual desires. They should see that prudence, the careful consideration of consequences, is required in sexual matters. They should see that sexually involving another person, while personally satisfying, may be harmful to the other individual, that it can be, in effect, a serious breach of charity. They should be helped to realize that giving in to their carnal desires shows weakness and that chastity is a reflection of their strength. They should understand that to be sexually mature requires character. Students should also realize that learning to master their sexual nature is a means of developing character and preparing themselves for a deep, loving relationship as an adult.

Fifth, students need to know that sexual decisions require the use of their reason. As in all rational decisions, they should seek good counsel. Therefore, students should be urged to consult people with whom they have a special connection: their parents and relatives, a trusted minister or priest, a doctor or teacher, or some other adult they consider wise. They should come to realize that their sexual decisions are important, even life-threatening decisions and, therefore, they need the very best advice and help they can get.

Sixth, our schools should urge children to talk to their parents about the rightness and wrongness of sexual attitudes and practices. Potentially this topic could provide an important forum for parents to come together and share information with one another on how to talk with their children about these issues.

Seventh, public schools, while not teaching the consciously taught sexual views of a particular religion, should urge the young to investigate what their religion has to say about sexual behavior. It is constitutionally well established that to teach about religion as a source of knowing and guidance is not a violation of the separation of church and state.

Eighth, sex education should not be the sole province of health educators—or, for that matter, any one teacher. The question, What is sex, and what should we do with our sexuality?—like other great questions, such as What is human nature? or What is most worth knowing?—does not yield to easy answers. The nature of human sexuality has been the subject of reflection by philosophers, theologians, poets, novelists, sociologists, biologists, and even economists, to name only a few groups who have given systematic attention to this topic. In most American schools today the responsibility for sex education falls to health educators and sometimes physical educators. Their training tends to lean heavily on physiology and psychology. In most nonphysiological aspects of sexuality, they have looked to psychology for answers. Psychology is a relatively new discipline and one that has certainly enriched our understanding of human beings, and, indeed, of our sexual nature. On the other hand, psychology has spent much of its brief history lurching from one set of sexual verities to another. The academic excursion from Sigmund Freud to Carl Jung to Harry Stack Sullivan to B. F. Skinner to Carl Rogers to Dr. Ruth Westheimer should give pause to any health educator who leans heavily on this discipline for guidance.

Ninth, our schools should actively promote sexual abstinence among students. To provide information about sex without strongly promoting abstinence sends a dangerous message, a message that is provocative in the true sense of the word. Having raised students' curiosity, teachers send the message that students should make up their own minds. It is a denial of all that we know about the nature of children and human sexuality to seriously suggest that children should be on their own in such matters. In particular, students should come to realize that most teen-age sex is exploitative, and, to borrow from Hobbes' description of life, it is usually "nasty, brutish, and short." The victims of such sex, typically but not always young girls, are usually seduced and then abandoned, with very real emotional scars to take with them into adult life. In fact, we have an obligation to let students know that outside of marriage there is simply no safe sex.

Practices and Policies

1. Did you ever take a class or series of lessons formally covering sex education? What was its subject matter? How was it taught? What effect, if any, did it have on you?

2. Apart from formal sex education, did you ever have one or more teachers make remarks (or otherwise communicate to you) about a sexual matter? What were the contents of that message? What, if any, were its effects on you?

3. Do you know of a school where sex education is formally or informally taught? What are the contents of that instruction? Do you believe the instruction is constructive, or otherwise? Why or why not?

4. What role do you believe schools play in formal or informal sex education?

Notes and References

1. Kilpatrick, W. (1992). *Why Johnny can't tell right from wrong*. New York: Simon & Schuster.

2. The October 1995 *Atlantic Monthly* features an article on the rise of female genital circumcision in the United States resulting from the influx of recent immigrants from countries where this is considered the proper practice.

3. Laumann, E. O., Gagnon, J. H., Michael, R. T., & Michaels, S. (1994). *The social organization of sexuality*. Chicago: The University of Chicago Press.

4. Ibid., p. 347.

5. Ibid., p. 324–325.

6. Whitehead, B. D. (1994, October). The failure of sex education. *Atlantic Monthly*, p. 70.

7. Kenney, A. M. (1987). Teen pregnancy: An issue for schools. *Phi Delta Kappan, 68*(10), 728–736.

8. Bellingham, K., & Gilles, P. (1993). Evaluation of an AIDS program for young adults. *Journal of Epidemiology and Community Health, 47*(2), 134–138.

9. Whitehead, The failure of sex education, p. 70.

10. Ibid., pp. 70–73.

11. Blankenhorn, D. (1995). *Fatherless America: Confronting our most urgent social problem*. New York: Basic Books, p. 18.

12. Laumann et al., *The social organization of sexuality*, pp. 509–548.

13. Himmelfarb, Gertrude. (1995). *The demoralization of society: From Victorian virtues to modern values*. New York: Alfred E. Knopf.

14. Shriver, E. K. (1986, July 10). Teenage pregnancy: Something can be done. *Philadelphia Inquirer*, p. 7E.

15. Lickona, T., & Lickona, J. (1995). *Sex, Love, and You.* Notre Dame, IN: Ave Maria Press, pp. 25–26.

16. Vitz, P. C. (1986, Fall). The role of religion in public school textbooks. *Religion and Public Education*, p. 48–56.

17. Zabin, L. S., Stark, A. A., & Emerson, M. R. (1990). Reasons for delay in contraceptive clinic utilization. *Journal of Adolescent Health, 12*, 225.

18. U.S. Office of Education. (1987). *AIDS and the education of our children.* Washington, DC: Author, p. 14.

19. Leo, J. (1986, November 24). Sex and schools. *Time*, p. 321.

20. Shriver, Teenage pregnancy, p. 7E.

21. Mast, C. K. (1986). *Sex respect.* Bradley, IL: Respect.

CHAPTER 12

For-Character Schools
in Operation

Words alone never suffice for the inculcation of basic social values. The sense of anchorage which people are expected to develop must be driven deep and implanted with such permanence and fixity that it becomes almost a "physical" part of the individual.

—Yehudi A. Cohen, "Schools and Civilizational States"[1]

Some readers may naturally wonder: How will the principles explained in this book look when they are applied in a real school? In this chapter we will try to satisfy that reasonable question. We will describe the day-to-day operation of two public schools we studied that are noteworthy for their emphasis on pupil character. The descriptions can help readers by lending depth to our preceding discussion.

BACKGROUND OF THE STUDIES

Two character-oriented schools were identified and subjected to careful study by one of the authors. An elementary school was studied in the 1987–88 school year, and a high school was studied in 1990–91. We use the real names of the schools and their principals, who consented to the process.

Both schools are in the Chicago metropolitan area. For each school the study involved:

- ✦ more than 100 visits to the school over one school year
- ✦ frequent, unscheduled visits to the classrooms of five selected teachers
- ✦ monitoring of extracurricular activities, assemblies, staff and inservice meetings, and other meetings of adults either schoolwide or in subgroups
- ✦ numerous discussions with students, staff members, parents, and other adults
- ✦ collecting, reading, and analyzing of major documents and other writings composed and published within the school during the year, such as bulletins to staff, issues of the school newspaper, samples of students' papers and exams, materials posted in classroom and schoolwide bulletin boards, report cards, and discipline referrals

The studies were supplemented with thousands of unposed photos taken during the visits. All the photographs in this book were taken from that pool of photos. One study was published commercially, with more than 100 of these photos;[2] a report on the second study is still in manuscript form.[3]

The process of selecting the two schools for study is relevant. Between 1982 and 1987, three successive cycles of a For-Character school recognition program were conducted in the Chicago metropolitan area. The contest was open to all Chicago area public and private schools—about 2,000 schools. Three hundred schools chose to participate in one or more cycles of the contest. About sixty winners were finally designated.

We collected data to rank contesting schools using the criteria outlined in the School Assessment Checklist, which appears at the beginning of this book. We examined application forms, school documents, and written reports from site visitors to derive the data. The recognition system was designed to identify diverse categories of competitors and winners. For example, suburban public high schools in affluent communities were compared to others in similar settings, private schools were compared to other private schools, and so on. The process of classification helped to balance competition by ensuring that no single school or group of schools was favored due to special resources available in its community.

In other words, the two schools we selected were among sixty winners chosen from 300 competitors from a pool of 2,000 invitees. Among the winners, the two schools were targeted for observation because their principals and staffs were willing to be subjected to a relatively public study and the schools represent notably contrasting circumstances. While both have a strong character emphasis in their activities, we do not believe they are unique in their orientation. America is a vast country, with tens of thousands of schools. There is no reason to believe that our two subjects are so extraordinary as to surpass all other rivals. There are undoubtedly other equivalent schools in America, or even in the Chicago area. Some may even surpass the achievements of our two selected subjects.

One last qualification should be mentioned: there was little or no explicit reference to the word *character* in either school's daily activities. On the other hand, it will become evident that each school's faculties and administrators generally share a common vision of the school's goals. Readers will also find that those goals are entirely consonant with the for-character themes of this book. For instance, both schools emphasize encouraging many forms of prosocial conduct by and among pupils.

The "silence" about character in these two schools is understandable. As we have emphasized, there has been a notable and unfortunate decline in references to character as a goal of education. In effect, the word has been dropped from the vocabulary of many educators. Yet the particular practices associated with a character approach have persisted in many schools and classrooms. The practices have been sustained by a mix of instinct, recollection, and intuitive learning. However, the support of an explicit for-character vocabulary is a precious resource. Without such a vocabulary, the analysis and transmission of helpful practices is significantly handicapped. One aim of this book is to help educators revive, and possibly update, their for-character vocabulary. The matter is a little like the character Monsieur Jourdain in Moliere's *Bourgeois Gentleman*, who did not realize he had always been speaking prose. Likewise, too many educators fail to recognize that they have been striving, in their practices, to form pupils of good character.

THE TWO SCHOOLS

The Reilly Elementary School was a pre-K–8 public school. It was situated in a moderately low-income neighborhood in the city of Chicago. It had 750 pupils, including 50% who were White, many of Polish origin; 38%, Hispanic; and 7%, Black. About one-third of the pupils were born outside the continental U.S. More than half (57%) came from families entitled to free or reduced-price school lunches, almost twice the proportion of American pupils nationwide (30%) at the time of the study.

Oak Forest High School was situated in a comfortable, relatively stable, middle- to upper-middle-income suburb of Chicago. It enrolled 1,200 pupils, almost all White. Less than 10% of its pupils were entitled to free or reduced-price lunches. Of its graduates, 35% enrolled in four-year colleges, and another 25% attended community colleges. The average income of pupils' families ranged from $35,000 to $42,000. The most academically successful of its graduates attended the University of Illinois at Urbana, a well-regarded state university, and one or two might attend the University of Chicago or Northwestern University, both prestigious private universities.

The staffs of both schools—including its administrators—were relatively stable. Rosemary Culverwell had been principal at Reilly for more than ten years. She had been a librarian there for several years before becoming principal. Indeed, Mrs. Culverwell had the Chicago public schools in her blood: she was the third generation of her family to teach in Chicago public schools, and one of her daughters was now a beginning teacher in the same system. Ed Roberts, the Oak Forest principal, had been working in the Bremen School District, which includes Oak Forest and three other high schools, for more than twenty years.

HIRING STAFF

Both schools were regarded as good places to work—plum assignments. Experienced teachers in other schools in the systems figuratively stood in line in hopes of transferring into the schools. Both schools took full advantage of their appeal. The principals—and other staff members in the high school—carefully screened applicants for every position, including checking references. The screening especially aimed to identify the applicant's commitment, energy, and general intelligence. Applicants were also given a clear picture of the school's priorities so they could decide for themselves whether they wanted to work in a high-demand environment. Wherever possible, hiring choices were made among people who had worked in the school as substitute teachers or in temporary jobs. Hiring decisions could then be enhanced by first-hand observation.

The process of carefully bringing in new blood went beyond the formalities of hiring decisions. For example, one new teacher Mrs. Culverwell hired during the year of the study was assigned to a relatively difficult class. Mrs. Culverwell visited that classroom every day during the teacher's first two weeks on the job.

Some of the visits were quite brief. However, they provided the skilled and observant principal with a clear picture of how things were going. There was no suggestion Mrs. Culverwell had any uncertainties about the abilities of the new employee. She simply wanted to give the newcomer all possible help. According to an interview by the researcher, the new teacher regarded such frequent visits simply as a sign of strong administrative support.

Undoubtedly, another element on Mrs. Culverwell's agenda was a desire to condition new staff to accept frequent classroom visitations as routine. Character-oriented teachers provide pupils with support and constructive engagement. They avoid being defensive and expect to receive similar engagement from their own supervisors.

Unfortunately, not all teachers were so open to criticism and support. Mrs. Culverwell was having problems with a male teacher without tenure, who hoped to be recalled to the Reilly school the next year. She believed the teacher had not made good use of her constructive criticism. She was determined to do the required paperwork to transfer him from her school, possibly leading to his not being retained in the system. The School Board's procedure required one last face-to-face conference between Mrs. Culverwell and the teacher. Expecting that the conference might be stormy, Mrs. Culverwell arranged for one of the sturdy school maintenance men to stand outside her office during the meeting. Fortunately, no physical confrontation arose. After that, she needed to make one final classroom visit to complete the observation process. When she arrived at the classroom for her visit, she discovered her fears about the teacher's irrational conduct were justified. She could not enter the classroom, since the door was locked. Locking a door while class was in session violated school policy; undoubtedly, it was locked to frustrate her final visit. The principal devised a way to get around the problem. The next school morning, she waited outside the teacher's classroom as pupils filed into class. Then, before the door was closed, she quickly stepped in with the pupils. Once she was seated in the class, the teacher felt it was senseless to resist, so he left her alone while she completed the last necessary observation. By displaying courage and determination, Mrs. Culverwell was able to maintain discipline and integrity throughout the school.

ATHLETICS AND CHARACTER

Both schools were fully committed to use athletics to encourage prosocial conduct by pupils.

In Oak Forest, many pupils—over 40%—were involved in interscholastic sports, cheerleading, and similar activities. The school even used these activities as means to foster other desirable habits. All teams had prohibitions on team members' drug and alcohol use. Candidates for team membership were required to sign pledges of self-restraint. The pledges were also signed by parents during an evening meeting at the school. At that meeting, the significance of the pledges was explained to the pupils and their families. The school also talked up its scholar/athlete program for athletic team members who had noteworthy academic records and whose names were conspicuously displayed on a bulletin board.

Great stress was given to athletic competition. There were three separate athletic seasons: fall, winter, and spring. All the school's teams were in leagues, typically composed of schools of about the same enrollment, to permit balanced competition. Four or five separate sports or activities were scheduled for each season. For example, the winter season included basketball, swimming, gymnastics, and wrestling. There were often three levels of teams for each sport, such as freshman, junior varsity, and varsity. In many sports, there were also separate teams for both girls and boys. There were annual intraleague competitions. These led to the designation of winners in each league, plus winners in various interleague semifinals and finals contests. Exceptional individual players were designated for all-star honors in their positions at the intraleague, interleague, or state levels.

Over 600 good-quality, six-by-eight color photographs of previous winning teams and successful individual athletes were posted conspicuously on the school's walls. Each photo was accompanied by the team's or student's name and the feats being commemorated. It was not uncommon to see adult visitors to the school, pointing out to others, sometimes their own children, their own photo from years ago or the photo of a relative or friend. Obviously, the elaborate photo display had notable motivational power. The school's gym was also hung with banners, celebrating the league and state awards for first, second, and third place won by teams in previous years.

The researcher followed two teams, girls' volleyball and boys' swimming, by observing games and practices, interviewing coaches and players, and attending awards banquets. The students on these teams displayed enormous commitment to such activities. The coaches—usually faculty members, sometimes but not always in physical education—were skillful and adept motivators and relatively decent people. Throughout the swimming season, each swimmer had two practice sessions a day, the first at six o'clock in the morning. Swimming team members had only one day off practice over the twenty-day Christmas vacation. The assumption was that the players should improve their performance by practicing during a layoff. This contrasts with the assumption in most schools that students' athletic prowess will decline over long vacations. Most volleyball team members began playing competitive volleyball during sixth grade and played "club ball" every summer. At the first volleyball practice, the girls were tested, and publicly competed against each other, for jumping ability and sprinting speed.

The school had 21 different active booster clubs. Each club supported a different sport. The clubs were composed largely of parents of team members. The clubs encouraged audience attendance at meets, raised funds to provide a variety of goodies for team members, and organized the annual awards banquet at the end of the season. At these banquets, a vast medley of awards were presented for numerous achievements, for example, most improved player, best sportsman or sportswoman, and most valuable player.

The school used a medley of other motivators to excite team support and prestige, such as PA announcements, pep rallies, mention in the school newspaper, an elaborate and carefully trained group of cheerleaders, mention on announcement signs prominently posted on the highway passing the school, many different forms of sports jackets and athletic letters, conspicuous designation of a school athlete of the week, mention in local community papers, and displays of trophies in the school's hall and lobbies.

At Reilly, the athletic program was less elaborate, as in most elementary schools. Still, the school held outdoor recess in the school yard in all but the most severe weather. To provide space for play, the lower- and upper-level classes had recess at separate times. At the lower-grade recess, selected older pupils regularly served as monitors, taught the children games, and acted as referees.

The level of orderly, constructive, partly spontaneous play in the yard was notable, but understandable. We use the term *notable* because the children at Reilly differed from many contemporary American children who have not learned to organize or participate in simple competitive games. For those children, a relatively barren human environment inhibits such learning. Children have to learn how to play games; they are not born with such knowledge. In too many school yards, play consists of bored and disorderly aggression, because the students do not know how to play well and be good sports. We describe the play at Reilly as *understandable* because the school had deliberately made a series of decisions to encourage such play. These included arranging for the selection and training of pupil aides and directing teachers to send their children out to recess each day. The aides were supported by paraprofessional staff members, whose assignments also included generally monitoring play periods.

The Reilly staff members believed that such play was a desirable prosocial activity and that the help provided by the older student aides was a constructive form of learning and service.

Other steps were also taken to make use of the school's play policy. Since the pupils enjoyed recess, teachers had a convenient punishment available for pupils who had not done their homework or had committed other minor transgressions: they would have to stay inside during recess. Recess also provided a precious ten-minute break for teachers. The break was especially valuable since their closed-classroom schedule meant they would otherwise spend the whole school day—including lunch—supervising their classes.

The Reilly school used recess in another creative way. Each Friday was regularly declared an indoor recess day—recess was held in each classroom, as if the outside weather was inclement. Children played games or talked quietly with each other at their desks. During Friday recess, each classroom was supervised by a team of two eighth-grade pupils, supposedly on their own recess. Meanwhile the teachers adjourned to the cramped but neat teachers lounge for end-of-the-week coffee and pastry. During this unusual break, the aides patrolled the halls, in case any monitors needed help. However, our visitor never saw any signs of disorder during this period.

This Friday break dramatically demonstrated the school's excellent levels of prosocial conduct and pupil discipline. It also provided both teachers and pupils with incentives to keep up the good work.

PUPIL DISCIPLINE

Both schools recognized the need to combine healthy outlets for pupil energies, such as athletics, with vigorous suppression of disorder. The schools had clear, regularly updated, and comprehensive discipline codes, written in language appropriate for their pupils' ages. Copies were sent home to parents, and written receipts were signed and returned to teachers.

In the first week of each school year, the rules were specifically discussed with the students. At Oak Forest the discussions occurred in each student's first required gym class. These discussions were conducted by the school's two deans, who handled serious discipline matters. For each student, one academic class was also set aside for a one-period "rules review" conducted by the teacher. Some students, especially the seniors, treated the occasions with mild disdain. However, the point was made: students understood that Oak Forest took its rules and their enforcement rather seriously. It was also evident that the plea "Nobody ever told me!" would cut no ice with the deans.

At Reilly, the school held two separate opening assemblies: one for grades K–4, the other for 5–8. These divisions made allowances for the pupils' different comprehension levels. Mrs. Culverwell spoke at each assembly. Her remarks included clear statements about the importance that the school attached to pupils' attendance, being on time, and other forms of order.

Most teachers in the schools believed that it was appropriate to hold pupils to relatively high standards of conduct. Sometimes the consequences necessary to back up prohibitions came from the ingenuity and determination of individual teachers. For instance, in an interview with the researcher, a seventh-grade girl at Reilly said she thought Reilly was a good school compared to another public school she had attended. The interview continued:

Interviewer:	Why do you think Reilly is better?
Student:	Because, here, they make you learn.
Interviewer:	How do they make you learn?
Student:	In my old school, if you did not do your homework, nobody cared. Here, if you don't do your homework, the teachers yell at you. So you do your homework, and you learn.

The carefully timed use of shouting or "voice control," as one teacher called it, was a technique judiciously applied by some Reilly teachers. The interviewer eventually realized that being suddenly shouted at from close range (three to five feet) made unruly pupils noticeably uncomfortable and that others became anxious to avoid such criticism. The shouting also enabled the teacher simply to issue a rebuke and promptly get on with classroom activities, instead of having to send someone to the office or otherwise seriously interrupt class. Actually, the shouting, when done by adept teachers, was quite deliberate. It was not unlike the posturing of military drill sergeants, really a form of semidramatics—

an artificial display of displeasure. But it was also a significant, low-cost form of punishment.

At both schools teachers could generally expect the administration to back them up on discipline issues. At Oak Forest, teachers were empowered to simply issue detention to pupils for failure to do homework or other moderate violations. Detention and in-school suspensions were supervised by a responsible adult, who ensured that the time was served in an appropriately boring manner.

At Reilly the principal made it clear that any pupil guilty of breaking a criminal law—bringing weapons or drugs into school—would routinely be reported to the police. The police would come to the school in a squad car, pick up the violators, and take them to the police station, where they would be released to their parents. The principal realized that often such incidents were not actually entered in police records. However, she wanted her pupils on notice: they would have no special protection because of committing such crimes in a school.

EFFECTIVE STUDENT COUNCILS

Both schools had effective student councils. One reason for such efficacy was they were moderated by able teachers, people with energy, foresight, and imagination, who obviously liked working with pupils outside of formal classroom activities. Furthermore, the moderators expected to—and did—receive backing from the administration. The help was partly due to the administrators' sympathies, per se, for such activities and to the moderators' own efficacy.

Moderators at both schools were nicely able to tread a fine line between (a) failing to recognize the inherent limitations of council members because of their age and (b) the obverse deficiency, failing to help members learn to take on increasing responsibilities.

The Reilly council enlisted members from third to eighth grade. They largely undertook in-school responsibilities, where older members supervised younger ones in different service activities. These activities included making and posting signs advertising the school's science fair, planning in-class Easter parties for the school, and helping design a role for pupils during a teacher appreciation week.

At Oak Forest, council responsibilities were understandably more complex. Their council helped plan a quite elaborate school-spirit week, including a parade through town; conducted an in-school blood drive; and held a mock session of the Oak Forest town board in the board's meeting hall. During the month before that session, the council had several planning meetings for council members. Some of those meetings were briefed by adult members of the town board. The mayor, several board members, and some town employees observed all or parts of the final mock session. A reporter from a local paper also attended part of the session. After the session's end, the adults present came over and congratulated the council members. One of the employees remarked, half-jokingly, that the students seemed better prepared for their agenda than the Board members sometimes were.

In an interview with the researcher, the moderator for the Oak Forest council explained that such wholesome activities did not come about without foresight and planning. When the moderator took over her job, she received a charge to revitalize the then-moribund council. Its members enjoyed the mild prestige of membership, but the council's activities ranged from purposeless to nil. The moderator eventually got a bylaw passed, requiring council members to attend a minimum number of meetings or be dropped from membership. The election process was also revitalized, requiring candidates to get the signatures of two faculty members plus a specified number of students. The moderator encouraged teachers to recruit students with commitment to run for council and refuse to sign the petitions of less responsible students. Gradually, through this weeding-out process, a more dedicated group of council members evolved. The moderator also solicited funds from the school budget to send council members to leadership training classes. The training further increased the members' skills and raised the status of their activities. The council was now a relatively high-prestige school activity, partly thanks to the character displayed by the moderator.

ACADEMICS

Both schools treated academics seriously. Each school had an up-to-date honor roll posted near the main door.

At Oak Forest, where students were grouped in ability tracks, students from all tracks had an opportunity to make the honor roll. A grade in a lower-track class counted as much as one in an upper-track class. A disadvantage of such a system was that it might discourage some students who wanted to be on the honor roll from shifting toward upper-track classes. Students and their parents were closely involved in helping plan pupils' academic track assignments. Every effort was made to push students to their highest effective option. Pupils were shifted from one track level to another—either up or down—if the first assignment seemed inappropriate.

Reilly pupils, in their upper grades, had about one hour of homework a night—not bad by Chicago public school standards.

In the Oak Forest school, a survey of the eight classes we followed from all three tracks revealed that students whose homework time was in the 50th percentile did four hours of homework per week; students in the 75th percentile, six hours; and those in the 93rd percentile, ten or more hours. These homework data were just a little above the national average for high school seniors. The survey also asked students to estimate the academic demands of their particular class that we were observing on a regular basis. From three choices of responses, the distribution was: mild, 30%; fairly demanding, 60%; and very demanding, 10%. The class they perceived as most demanding was beginning algebra. Such ratings were congruent with the researcher's observations, although the pupils' overall ratings were disappointingly low, according to the researcher's taste.

Many Oak Forest teachers were quite familiar with the school's comparatively moderate demands. Such demands frustrated a number of teachers. However, they believed forces beyond the school were part of the cause for the situation. If the school's academic pressure became much higher, they believed more students might shift to lower tracks or drop out. This would upset too many parents. And so there was a sort of negotiated cap on the faculty's demands.

One of the most remarkable discoveries from the Oak Forest research was the notable contrast between (a) the dedication shown by many student athletes, and some club and student council members, and (b) the students' sometimes low levels of academic investment. This discovery affected our discussion of profound learning in chapter 2. In that discussion we tried to identify elements of the incentive system underlying the athletic activities and apply them to academics. The athletic motivation system relies on a complex mixture of team play, competition, volition, publicity, and colorful praise and criticism.

TEACHER SUPERVISION

Both schools gave strong emphasis to teacher support and supervision. We will report only on the practices at Reilly, where we observed greater emphasis on support and supervision.

Mrs. Culverwell, the Reilly principal, tried to get into five to ten classes a day, for even the briefest of visits. In addition to these visits, she also found many activities that kept her moving throughout the school halls. Many teachers kept their classroom doors open most of the school day. Windows on classroom doors were unblocked by posters or other obstructions.

Reilly also had a vital system of staff committees, and most teachers were on two committees. Most committees were quite active, meaning that committee members had frequent, regularly scheduled meetings that followed a standard format. A typical meeting began with a reading of the minutes from the last meeting; the members then considered an agenda, having provided Mrs. Culverwell with a copy in advance; information was exchanged, decisions were made, and responsibilities were allocated; and the meeting was then closed. Minutes were prepared and sent to the principal and committee members. Mrs. Culverwell could attend any such meetings she chose, but usually the teachers—as professionals—were left to work on their own. The committees dealt with: the policies for the three separate grade groups in the school (lower, intermediate, and upper), each with its own coordinator; providing counsel for troubled students; curriculum; arts; safety; hospitality; and the school's Spanish and Polish bilingual programs. One committee, largely composed of the chairs of the major committees, met regularly with Mrs. Culverwell and the school's assistant principal.

The committees kept teachers generally informed of one another's activities. As a result, the teachers supported and monitored each other. This process of structured engagement assisted Mrs. Culverwell's supervision. One experienced teacher, newly assigned to Reilly, told the researcher she was impressed by the school's committee activity. The interviewer asked, "But don't most schools have approximately similar committee structures?"

The teacher replied, "Well, yes, they probably do. But, in most schools, such committees rarely meet or decide anything. Here, they were expected to get things done. And they do."

Mrs. Culverwell had worked out an elaborate framework for annual teacher evaluation. The process involved a mixture of small-group and one-to-one sessions with teachers, each teacher's submission of goal-setting documents, a careful consideration of the test score patterns of each teacher's pupils, and Mrs. Culverwell's frequent examination of a variety of student work products, such as writing samples, art work, and typical written examinations.

These information-collecting activities were supplemented with one structured class observation visit by Mrs. Culverwell. The visit included an examination of the teacher's grade book, lesson plans, and diverse examples from students' portfolios. It culminated in the preparation of a written observation report by Mrs. Culverwell. For many faculty members, the evaluation cycle was largely a way of providing them with praise and constructive criticism for the good job they were already doing. And the last evaluation meeting usually wound up with Mrs. Culverwell asking the teacher, "How can I help you keep up your good work?"

However, the school did have a few problem teachers whose deficiencies were known to key staff members. Such teachers were subjected to a continuous evaluation process much more intense than the typical annual cycle. The process aimed to (a) prevent these teachers from significantly undermining the school's efficacy, (b) help them improve if possible, (c) persuade them to choose to leave Reilly if they do not improve, and (d) collect information to justify their dismissal, if necessary.

CREATING COLLECTIVE IDENTITIES

Both schools implicitly recognized the need to encourage students to develop bonds with others in a peer group working toward adult-defined goals. Such groups were vital tools for achieving good character formation.

At Oak Forest, most of such grouping occurred in voluntary activities through the school's teams and clubs. There were certainly deficiencies in this policy. Some pupils lacked athletic ability, and others lacked the protective instinct or initiative necessary to enlist in such activities. The school did not have a vital system of homerooms. Several staff members made remarks to the interviewer that such a system had sometimes been considered. Indeed, some staff believed the lack of homerooms was a significant deficiency in the otherwise highly supportive school.

At Reilly, things were different. Each class regarded itself as a unit, and their cohesion was encouraged in many ways. Students had lunch in their own classroom. Class members brought food up from the kitchen, distributed it, and cleaned up after lunch. Each class took a turn preparing and delivering its own entertainment (typically a song) to the school at periodic schoolwide assemblies.

A schoolwide attendance contest was another significant instance of fostering classwide cohesion. The contest worked as follows. Reilly was one of twenty-three elementary schools assigned to an administrative unit in the Chicago schools. Each year, that unit would run an interschool attendance contest. The aim was to see which of the schools attained the best pupil attendance level. At the time of our study Reilly had won the contest for three years in a row. The school gave the contest a relatively high priority. At the opening assemblies for the school year, names were announced of individuals and classes, as well as their teachers, who achieved the best attendance records the previous year. All were called to the stage to receive certificates, as they received the applause of the audience.

Furthermore, one of Reilly's faculty committees was the Attendance Committee. That committee met periodically to monitor the progress of the contest and make plans to improve the school's performance.

"Winning" was evinced by a large banner hung in the main hall, with the years of the school's victories conspicuously noted. The school also hoped to win the banner for the immediate year. The interaction between the attendance contest and intraclass and intraschool cohesion was significant.

To make the whole school an effective contestant, each class was identified as an independent competitive unit. In each class, each individual student also had a competitive—and cooperative—role.

Each student would strive to achieve perfect attendance for the month. All such achievers had their names posted for each successive month on the outside of their classroom doors. Every month, on a Friday afternoon during school time, the previous month's winners with perfect attendance were sent from class to see an "attendance movie"—a videotape of some appropriate popular film. There were two separate showings, to make allowances for the students' different age levels. At the end of the year, students with perfect attendance all year were guests at an ice cream party.

Each class also competed each month against the other classes in its grade block, so that three winning classes were designated. The winning classes had their names and attendance data posted near the banner. Finally, each month, Reilly's overall attendance record was tabulated, and displayed beside the data on the other twenty-two competing schools in their administrative unit.

These carefully planned activities caused a restructuring of students' attitudes towards attendance. For instance, one snowy winter day some of the school busses could not get through the snow. Thus, many students were absent. The researcher was observing a first-grade class. He noticed two girls—sisters—as they entered the room half an hour late, all bundled up. Other class members saw them and broke into spontaneous applause. Skillful questioning by the teacher brought out the girls' story. Due to the snow, their bus could not bring them to school. They went home and persuaded their uncle to drive them to school so they would not let their class down in the attendance contest. When the two entered the class, the pupils realized they had made a special effort. Their applause was a sign of praise and gratitude.

Teachers at Reilly used the contest to build class cohesion. The contest encouraged pupils to care about each other's absence or presence and gave them an incentive to try to help one another improve their attendance. It also served as a model of other kinds of team sharing that occurred in and around classes at the school.

CEREMONIES

Both schools recognized the important roles ceremonies could play in communicating appropriate values to pupils. Thus they held a variety of ceremonies and gave them significant attention.

Both schools conducted two-step graduation ceremonies. In the first ceremony the graduates paraded and received honors before the entire school, largely to motivate the succeeding graduating classes. The second event took place on a separate day in the presence of the graduates' families.

At Reilly, other ceremonies throughout the school year included: a Christmas pageant; an awards assembly; a series of assemblies where each class presented entertainment for the others; a memorial ceremony after the unexpected death of a popular mayor (this was organized on only a half-hour's notice, just after receiving notice of the school's sudden dismissal as part of the citywide mourning process); and an induction ceremony for newly elected members of the school's student council.

At Oak Forest, ceremonies included: an elaborate network of ceremonies and other activities related to a school-spirit week, including a lengthy parade; a variety of sports banquets for the different athletic teams; a noisy and enthusiastic pep rally for the football team before it went to the playoffs; the senior prom, of course; and a good-bye breakfast for the senior class.

Not surprisingly to the researcher, religion played a moderate but explicit role in some of these occasions. Reilly had two bilingual programs that enroll pupils from countries with rich religious traditions: Poland and Hispanic countries. At Christmas students in the Polish bilingual program, assisted by their teachers and some parents, conducted an elaborate ceremony. They paraded through the school's halls wearing beautiful traditional Polish costumes. As they paraded, they sang religious Christmas songs in Polish, while four of the paraders bore a model of a church on their shoulders. Many of the songs sung by other student groups at the school's popular Christmas festival—with many beaming parents present—were traditional religious Christmas carols.

At Oak Forest's ceremonies, religion sometimes also raised its head. At the graduation one pupil's father, who was a Protestant minister, delivered a brief, nondenominational benediction. On another occasion, the induction of students into the National Honor Society, a minister was the speaker and delivered an inspirational address.

Both schools recognized that keeping large numbers of pupils in a ceremonial setting for a period of time can create some challenges for maintaining order. They saw this real problem as something to be recognized and resolved, but not as a reason for avoiding ceremony.

One safeguard to avoid disorder was for the schools to ensure that their ceremonies were well-designed, with appropriate and realistic pacing. But other measures were also taken. Reilly teachers, especially those with younger pupils, spent time having their classes practice going quietly to and from an assembly. When appropriate, they practiced going en masse to the stage. Before an occasion that was particularly tempting to an upper-grade class, the researcher overheard a Reilly teacher say to her students: "I don't care if the whole auditorium explodes as you walk in. *You* will be quiet and respectful." And they were.

At Oak Forest, pupils were older, so there was increased potential for both good and bad. The previous year's pep rally—always a tempting occasion for disorder—had almost been blown apart by disruptive activities. At the peak of the rally's wild exuberance, several unidentified students threw rolls of toilet paper into the air. After that experience, the school made two basic decisions. The rally would be conducted as usual. As for disorder, precautions would be taken to ensure it did not recur.

An assistant principal had developed a lengthy security plan for the rally. The plan included about fifteen precautionary measures, such as removing all toilet paper rolls from pupils' washrooms a half hour before the rally began; assigning each teacher to sit or stand in a particular place in the gym where the rally was to be held; considering what teachers should be given what assignments; and establishing and staffing a detention room near the rally site so disorderly pupils could be easily removed and isolated. The plan was carefully analyzed by other administrators, revised, and put into effect.

The final rally was a beautiful example of structured chaos. Everyone had a great time—except for a few disappointed troublemakers and the assistant principal, who monitored the security plan throughout the whole occasion.

A CAN-DO ATTITUDE

During a casual chat with the researcher, the Reilly assistant principal told an informative story. The assistant principal mentioned that she once recruited her sister as an uncompensated tutor to try and "save" an especially troubled student. The interviewer mused to himself, "How does recruiting your sister to be a tutor fit into any job description?" Many other stories of a similar tenor came up in the research. The fact was that this type of commitment and a sense of adult personal responsibility pervaded these schools. The faculties taught character by first personifying it: "You—the students—should do as we say, because we—your teachers—do as we say."

The schools were pervaded with can-do attitudes. Not much time was spent reciting why certain things could not be done—using excuses such as inadequate funds, the union, or uncooperative parents. Instead, staff members tended to be pleased with what they were doing and were always pursuing ways to improve further. Undoubtedly, if pushed, they could identify external constraints that undermined their efforts. Both schools might easily devise good ways to spend more money. But the staffs assumed that the most important thing was for them to do the best they could, compared to wasting energies blaming remote scapegoats. They believed that if things were not working, they must first examine their own conduct—and then examine it again.

Practices and Policies

1. Identify a school you are familiar with. To what extent do staff members see themselves as responsible for their school's success or failure? In classrooms, to what extent do teachers see themselves as responsible for their pupils' learning? In either case, why?

2. From your own experience, can you think of examples where educators displayed courage or cowardice? Without mentioning names, what are the specific details?

3. Can you think of times when you saw an educator showing determination and commitment, or when you noticed a lack of determination and commitment?

Again without mentioning names, what are the specific details?

4. Did you ever participate in a significant educational ceremony? (Remember that even a small, repetitious ceremony may have notable cumulative effect, e.g., the flag salute.) If yes, what effects did it have on you? Why do you think it had these effects?

References

1. Cohen, Y. A. (1970). Schools and civilizational states. In Fischer, J. (Ed.), *The social sciences and the comparative study of educational systems*. Scranton, PA: International Textbook, p. 82.

2. Wynne, E. A. (1993). *A year in the life of an excellent elementary school*. Lancaster, PA: Technomics.

3. Wynne, E. A. (1994). *A year in the life of an excellent secondary school* [mimeo]. Chicago: University of Illinois College of Education.

CHAPTER 13

A Final Word

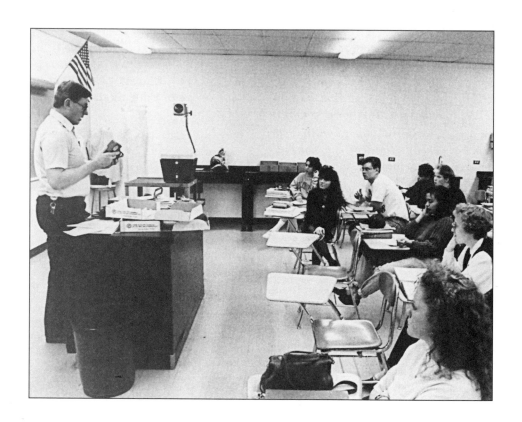

The Greek scholar Lucian (c. 120–200 A.D.) recited the following education principle: "Educators mimic farmers, who shelter and enclose their plants while they are small and young, so they may not be injured by the breezes; but when the stalk at last begins to thicken, they prune away the excessive growth and expose them to the winds to be shaken and tossed, in that way making them more fruitful."[1]

Many readers may find our proposals of interest, but may still be reluctant to adopt our whole package. This is understandable, and we believe it is appropriate. By this point, readers are informed enough to pick and choose among the proposals we have offered, relying on their own experience and values. Our closing remarks will stress the crucial role of sentimentality in shaping our current public and professional orientations regarding education.

There is an important contrast between *sentiment* and *sentimentality*, a contrast that may provide readers with novel and powerful insights. You can use these insights to assess the value of our preceding proposals, as well as the many other proposals for education reform.

SENTIMENT OVER SENTIMENTALITY

It may seem strange that a book on education reform concludes by discussing sentiment and sentimentality. We live in an era in which the paramount forces appear to be rationality and analysis. Achievements in science and industry have dramatically changed human life. Efficiency in transportation and communication have increased immensely during our lives. Important medical discoveries have continued a long-range trend of prolonging the human life span. Our comparative national affluence has enabled us to construct a complex and pervasive formal education system that provides pupils with steadily lengthening exposure to education. Computers are delivering on the promise to increase human productivity.

We recognize that there are frequent and recurrent public expressions of dissatisfaction with our times and circumstances. But, despite such objections, the data—such as we have just sketched—demonstrate that, in many ways, Americans have never had it better.

Most of these achievements were attained through the application of science, stressing logic and analysis. In a sense, such achievements are the outcomes of containing sentiment and emphasizing rationality. Inevitably, our record of scientific achievement has encouraged some citizens to approach education with an equivalent stress on rationality. For example, John Dewey stressed the application of the "scientific method" to education.

Ironically, sentiment is inevitably a paramount force in the operation of education. Parents' concerns over their children are a complex mass of sentiments.

Children, themselves, are volatile bundles of raw sentiment. And educators must be able to respond to—and often yield before—such powerful forces. Indeed, many able educators probably chose their profession partly due to their personal interest handling and expressing sentiment. The prevalence of sentiment in education is further stimulated by the remote goals often associated with education: the connection between the management of some elementary school classroom and the future adult lives of its pupils is certainly real, but also abstract and diffuse. Under these circumstances, education is necessarily—and inevitably and properly—strongly affected by sentiment. The problem arises when the necessary stress of sentiment drifts towards sentimentality. There is a crucial contrast between sentiment and sentimentality.

Sentiment simply means one is moved, or affected, by serious emotions, such as love, hate, fear, or pride. It is a truism that such emotions are inherent in healthy human life and are important motivators for human conduct. *Sentimentality* means the excessive cultivation of emotional stimulation, a predisposition to allow our emotions to ride roughshod over reason and experience, instead of cooperating with these critical forces. Sentimentality glories in the feckless, undisciplined expression of feelings. This weakness has especially affected education in our era. The affliction is partly due to the notable efficiency that science and rationality have displayed in many other fields of human endeavor. We often hear someone say, "If we can put a man on the moon, then why not—?" It is too distressing to contrast the important, but limited, triumphs of industry and science with the tragic limitations of human emotions and human existence. The contrast is especially dramatic in education, where we must stimulate and release emotion while simultaneously applying considerable rational thought. This is a demanding recipe.

THE DANGERS OF HAPPY-THINK

One friend put it to us simply: too many contemporary Americans have a special vulnerability to "happy-think." By this phrase we mean an inordinate, sentimental insistence on good feelings. Although the Declaration of Independence did laud the pursuit of happiness, we believe that few of its signers ever imagined that the right of pursuit implied the right to attainment.

The prevalence of happy-think does not mean afflicted people always think happy thoughts. However, they do assume that any disruption in happy-think is an unwarranted violation of personal liberty. As a result, in many quarters there is little patience with information or ideas about education that disrupt happy-think. Such intrusive reflections are considered taboo. When we repress upsetting information, however, we inevitably make things even worse. Conversely, in education many utopian and sentimental ideas are received with inordinate tolerance. This accounts for the short life of many fads in education.

As we have said, schools do and should involve our emotional life. In general, teachers should love children and the society in which they will live. Parents and children should be encouraged to like and love their schools. Despite such sentiments, our views are highly unsentimental. Many good things are now happening in education, and more good things can and should happen. However, we are obdurate foes of happy-think.

To quote the English philosopher Thomas Hobbes, "Man is the wolf to man." In other words, men and women have deep-seated, powerful instincts that often lead them to act against the best interests of their fellows. The recognition of such distressing potential in humans flies directly in the face of the premises of happy-think. One critical task for education is to moderate and redirect such threatening human capabilities.

These wolfish tendencies are often expressed by collective or institutional action. Indeed, even the romantic Jean-Jacques Rousseau recognized that capabilities for evil often existed in human institutions. Unlike Rousseau, however, we do not see men and women as innately good, and only their institutions as potential wolves. Instead, the selfish institutions that surround us, whether they are nations, businesses, unions, ethnic or religious organizations, professional associations, or public-interest groups, are not alien beings. They merely reflect the amalgamated aspirations of their members.

The matter is not entirely bleak. For example, economists have demonstrated that market economies are often able to harness such selfish drives to generate collective benefits.

Furthermore, selfish aspirations are not the sole motives for human action. Human misconduct often coexists with a remarkable medley of admirable and noble acts and motives. Despite this admixture, a disposition towards selfishness always will be an important part of human motivation. Serious, nonsentimental conceptions of education must include a clear recognition of this persisting proclivity.

These views are not novel. They would have been presumed by the authors of *The Federalist Papers*. They pervade the writings of Sigmund Freud and are most clearly expressed in his *Civilization and Its Discontents*. The concepts of hubris and tragedy are ancient. Such concepts recognize that overweening pride and significant flaws are inherent in human action. The theme of redemption, prevalent in many religions, provides another important insight. The theme suggests a widespread perception that human beings are strongly disposed to wrongdoing—and in need of being redeemed.

There is ample contemporary evidence to support such premises. America now has the largest, most costly, and most elaborate education system, ranging from preschool through college and graduate school, in human history. We possess a civilizing force of unprecedented scope. Yet, despite the breadth of this institution, many signs point to the continuing vitality of human selfishness. The dreary statistics about long-term increases in youth disorder are not news. Turning to other areas of social distress, we can identify increasing public concern with topics such as child and spouse abuse; declining commitments to parenting by adults; rising rates of divorce; pollution and global warming; and a variety of interethnic tensions. Whatever the specifics of such topics, the problems rest on a common theme: the human pursuit of narrow self-interest. Such selfishness may arise in small groups, such as parent-child or husband-wife relations. It may arise in conflicts between large institutions and groups, such as the tensions between conservationists and industrial developers and their customers.

Conflict, tension, envy, and disruption are inevitable concomitant elements of personal and group life. There will probably be persisting efforts to redirect such tendencies, and novel medical remedies or original academic courses that will try to extinguish these disorders. We can see improvement and even notable victories—and surely problems and failures. However, we wonder whether dramatic, all-out aspirations for change might just make matters worse.

From Its Beginnings

American education, from its beginnings to the present, has continuously been adapting, with necessarily mixed success, to the realities of our dynamic society. Adaptation has involved questions of ideology, interest-group conflict, resource allocation, and necessarily imperfect forecasting. If there is any special cause for increased distress in our era about education, it is the spread of sentimentality. Policies that would not bear serious intellectual consideration have attained excessive influence in education, due to their sentimental appeal. These policies support the prevalence of happy-think.

We have offered a variety of prescriptions for improving school and classroom management. These prescriptions have worked well for many teachers, and they can help other educators and their pupils. But we reject sentimentalism. Our prescriptions will work only if educators apply diligence and reflection. Furthermore, even with diligence and reflection, some pupils and their families will not respond adequately. Teaching can only be probabilistic. We must do our best, and pray our failures will be helped by other people and institutions.

References

1. Bowen, J. (1971). *A history of education: Vol. 1. The ancient world*. New York: St. Martins Press, p. 153.

100 Ways Educators Can Help Students Acquire Good Character

1. Hang pictures of heroes and heroines in classrooms and halls. With some of them, include appropriate explanatory text.

2. Institute a student-to-student tutoring program.

3. Promote schoolwide or intraclass service clubs with real missions to serve the school, class, or external community. Recognize excellent service where appropriate.

4. Ensure that recognition systems cover both character and academics.

5. Ensure that recognition systems recognize both excelling groups and individual pupils.

6. Recognize a variety of achievements, e.g., surpassing past personal achievements, surpassing other competitors, or meeting a predetermined goal—one that is absolute, rather than relative to other performances.

7. Create a written code of behavior for the classroom and the school. Distribute copies to parents, asking them to sign receipts for the copies and promise to help children comply.

8. Specify simple, fast, and unpleasant consequences for code violations.

9. Include a behavior reporting system on report cards. Monitor the system to ensure it is realistic and properly used.

10. Invite parents to observe and contribute to your classroom. Develop a structured format to assist participation.

11. Choose a personal motto, and let students know about it. Help the class develop its own motto.

12. Create and publicize a "virtue of the month," and award students who make the most progress towards that virtue.

13. Write, call, or visit parents to express praise for their child.

14. Lead by example. Leave a clean classroom for the next teacher and class. Have students help you with this. Pick up scraps of paper off the floor.

15. Impress on students that being a good student means far more than academic success.

16. Use posters, slogans, and announcements on the walls of classrooms and school hallways to stress virtues and achievements by individual students, groups of students, or others.

17. Have personal heroes, and tell your students who they are and why you choose them.

18. Prohibit students from being unkind or using others as scapegoats in the classroom.

19. Prohibit vulgar language in or around school. Explain to students it is a form of pollution.

20. Notify parents of student misbehavior via notes, phone calls, and visits to school.

21. If you engage in community or church service, let your pupils know, but do so in a low-key way.

22. Assign older students to help younger ones. Formalize such assignments with ceremonies.

23. Talk up the school's athletic teams and service activities with students, especially in high schools.

24. Consider sponsoring a club or team in your school.

25. Invite graduates of your high school or grade school to come back and talk about their experiences, especially successful ones, at the next stage of life.

26. Invite local adults to talk to students about how they have integrated character into their lives.

27. Explain to students the importance of listening, and help them learn how to do it.

28. Teach students to read media materials from a character perspective. Who are heroes, and villains? Why? What virtues are praised, or ignored?

29. Emphasize, from the first day of class, the importance of diligence and setting high goals.

30. Estimate the level of diligence that you demand of students in your class. Either informally or formally, compare your perceptions to those of the students.

31. Talk to students about why you are a teacher. Explain to them the responsibilities attached to the job.

32. Talk to students about empathy. Ask them how they think they would feel about certain things happening to them.

33. Teach students to write notes, such as get-well and thank-you notes.

34. When conflicts arise around the school or class, teach about discretion, tact, and privacy—and about discreetly informing appropriate adults of the conflict.

35. Read and discuss biographies of accomplished individuals. Identify and evaluate their character traits, yet encourage pupils to show some charity in assessing others.

36. Give students sufficient feedback when you evaluate their work. Teach them how to receive and solicit feedback. Talk to them about the virtues involved, e.g., courage, determination, ambition, prudence.

37. Frequently teach courtesy. Explain its power to students.

38. Encourage older pupils to involve themselves in local community affairs, e.g., engaging in politics or assuming helping roles in youth activities.

39. Don't be embarrassed to raise ethical issues with colleagues.

40. Bring up the acts of local or personal heroes and heroines in your classes.

41. Examine the school or classroom environment to identify more occasions for students to serve the school.

42. Does the school have an effective hospitality committee for the faculty?

43. Does the school have any "be foolish" occasions to be enjoyed by students

and faculty together? A volleyball game? A three-legged race?

44. If the school has ethnic diversity, does it have occasions to celebrate that diversity, such as when ethnic food dishes are brought in and shared or special ethnic virtues are displayed?

45. Encourage students to talk to their parents about their difficulties. Talk about how this is sometimes hard to do but usually wise.

46. Is your school or classroom appropriately symbolized? Is there a motto? A logo? Are they properly displayed? Are there school colors? Are they well-displayed?

47. Admit it when you make a mistake. Invite students to act the same way.

48. Thank students for bringing in media articles on moral and character issues. Talk them over in class.

49. Talk to students about their moral obligations to their parents and the taxpayers in the community.

50. Have students develop their own personal sayings or mottos. Display and discuss them.

51. Consider applying an honor system for various tests. Solicit the advice of colleagues who have successfully tried it.

52. Hold special collections for causes the students help identify.

53. Use cooperative learning, sometimes even in complex situations, applying the advice offered in this book.

54. Recommend that students keep journals. Establish, in advance, guidelines for privacy.

55. Develop clear guidelines—preferably written and appropriate for pupils' ages—regarding grading, homework, and late materials.

56. Read aloud a short (two-minute?) character-oriented story at the beginning or end of each school day.

57. Ensure that students conduct themselves in an orderly manner while watching athletic competitions.

58. Plan two separate graduation ceremonies: one for graduates' families, and an earlier one for the rest of the students so they can observe and be motivated by the ceremony.

59. Have a schoolwide homework policy, one that is applied by all teachers and broadcast to parents.

60. Informally poll students and parents to see how much student time really goes into homework.

61. Can people walking through school halls get a good idea of what is happening in classrooms? Are classroom doors usually open? Are there glass windows to see in classrooms from corridors? Is the principal frequently visible to students?

62. Is hiring carefully handled? Are references adequately checked?

63. Does the school know its expectations for new teachers? How are these expectations transmitted to potential employees? Is good character in faculty members an evident priority?

64. Does the school clearly explain its procharacter priorities to parents? Are they well-expressed in public documents?

65. Are teachers encouraged, expected, and required to send out monthly newsletters to parents?

66. Are there clear welcome signs, prominently placed immediately outside the school's main door?

67. In elementary schools, is recess held daily? Do older pupils help younger ones learn how to play?

68. Is courtesy effectively practiced by pupils during in-school meals or snacks?

69. Are students given preassembly drills, if maintaining order is a challenge?

70. Are the police automatically informed of all law violations in or around the school, even if only students are involved? Do students know of this policy? Does the school follow up on all cases referred to the police?

71. If the school has a rule maintaining a closed campus, is that rule effectively enforced?

72. If the school has a rule requiring students and faculty to wear ID cards, is that rule effectively enforced?

73. For pupils whose parents did not attend college, does the school have a deliberate program to elevate pupils' post-high school academic aspirations?

74. Is the student paper managed by an imaginative, procharacter faculty member? Is this reflected in the paper's editorial content?

75. Does the school or classroom have sufficient incentives for desirable group behavior, e.g., putting a marble into a large glass jar every time a student does a right act and then holding a party when the jar is filled, or having two or more competing in-class teams with separate jars?

76. Throughout the school year, have each class make its own contribution to the school's assemblies, e.g., perform a play or song.

77. Teach students a patriotic song to sing along with the flag salute.

78. Consider adopting a policy of requiring students to wear uniforms, if parents are sympathetic.

79. Solicit parents to coach athletic teams to represent the elementary school.

80. Have a school flag created, and display it.

81. Develop an activity through which students formally express gratitude to the taxpayers who support their education.

82. Have older students prepare pot-luck dinners for parents. The students should plan meals (with faculty help?), buy, prepare, and serve the food, present entertainment, and clean up.

83. Assign different classes or student groups the responsibility of keeping areas of the school or grounds clean. Post signs identifying such groups and their responsibilities.

84. Have students in self-contained classrooms take turns caring for class pets and taking them home over weekends. Be sure to get parents' approval in advance. Explain to them that living creatures need care.

85. Faculty members who sponsor clubs or teams should receive gratitude, plus supportive supervision.

86. Is the student council working well? What is the quality of its faculty advising?

87. Does the school have a lively alma mater? Do students know it? Is it sung fairly often?

88. Can students (and parents) organize a school garden? Post the names of persons or groups responsible.

89. Does, or should, the school have ceremonies marking the beginning and end of the school year? A farewell ceremony for leaving teachers?

90. Has the school any program to reach out to nursing homes, hospitals, and other helping institutions in the community?

91. Start a pen-pal correspondence.

92. In sports and games, emphasize good sportsmanship. Participation in sports should provide practice for life beyond sports. See that the athletic program keeps this in mind.

93. Ask librarians to develop and publicize lists of procharacter materials.

94. Analyze the school calendar of forthcoming activities. Does it give appropriate emphasis to procharacter activities?

95. Schedule time on the agendas of faculty and staff meetings for discussion of character issues.

96. Start a school scrapbook, and bring it out frequently to show to visitors and new families.

97. Organize thanks-giving gestures from students to nonteaching employees, e.g., lunchroom aides, bus drivers, janitors, classroom aides.

98. Compose a school pledge that students regularly recite.

99. Have a system for students to help welcome new students, especially transfers.

100. Adopt a practice of having a daily moment of silence before class, and advise students that they can use such time for prayer.

Index

Abolition of Man (Lewis), 146–47
Abstinence, sexual, 231–33, 235–36
Abuse of power, potential for, 44–45, 101–2, 191
Academics, 1, 75–84
  equality and, 76–78
  at for-character schools, 247–48
  incentives for excellence in, 78–80
  practices and policies on, 75
  principles of instruction, 59
  pupil grouping and, 82–84
  social promotion and, 80–82
Accountability, 190, 192–93
Adams, John, 139
Addison, Joseph, 148
Administrators. *See* Principals
Alcohol abuse, 9
Alexander, Lamar, 2
Allan Guttmacker Institute, 223
Altruism, 22–23
American culture, individualism in, 13–14, 150, 151
American Revolution, 150
American School Board Association, 228
Among School Children (Kidder), 109–10, 125
Anthropology, moral education and, 54, 138
Aristotle, 20, 33, 39
  on deferred gratification, 69
  on goals of education, 107
  on moral action, 161
Art as community-building activity, 183
Association for Supervision and Curriculum
    Development, 228
Athletics
  common goals and, 181
  at for-character schools, 242–44
  profound learning and, 48–51
  school spirit and, 173–74
At-risk children, 38

Attendance contests, 249–50

Bacon, Roger, 148
Bandura, Albert, 121
Barat, Sophie, 159
Barr, R., 83
Behavioral psychology, moral education and, 138
Bennett, William J., 2, 15, 157
Bias, Lenny, 130
Biehler, Robert, 121
Blankenhorn, David, 226
Bloom, Allan, 2, 113
Bloom, Benjamin, 13, 40
Body management, learning and, 41–42
Boundaries of school community
  conceptual, 176–78
  tangible, 174–75
Bowen, James, 77
Boyer, Ernest, 2
Brecht, Bertolt, 158
Buckley amendment and student privacy, 78
Burke, Edmund, 121
Bush, George, 210
Butler, Samuel, 123

California State Commission on Self-Esteem, 114
Capon, Robert F., 173
Cardinal virtues, 148
Ceremonies, 182, 208–16
  defined, 209–10
  elements of, 210–11
  examples of high school and elementary school,
    213–15
  at for-character schools, 250–52
  heart of, 212–13
  practices and policies on, 215–16
  purposes of, 212

Character, 1, 59–75, 139. *See also* For-character
    schools
  after-school paid employment and, 68–69
  curricula and school activities for teaching of, 62
  deferred gratification and, 69–75
  help for student acquisition of, 260–64
  incentives for development of, 67–68
  practices and policies on, 75
  principles of instruction, 59
  prosocial conduct and, 62–67
  sex education and, 233–36
  virtue comparison and, 60–61
Character Education (Yulish), 34
Character Education movement, 55
Charity, ethical ideal of, 148
Charter schools, 178
Cheating, rules against
  philosophical position toward, 18–19
  teacher diligence in enforcement of, 24–25
Children of Their Fathers (Read), 1
Cicero, 63
Civilization and Its Discontents (Freud), 37, 257
Classrooms, 106–19
  diligence in, 115–16
  ethos in, 109–13, 119
  moral action opportunities in, 169
  as moral environment, 107–9
  punishment in, 101–2
  rules in, 94–95
  self-esteem movement in, 113–15
  service opportunities in, 64
  student attitudes in, 116–18
Clinton, William, 15
Cognitive developmental moral education, 131,
    155
Cohen, Yehudi A., 33, 239
Coleman, James S., 59, 121, 161, 181
Coles, Robert, 127
Collective punishment, 103
Color Purple, The (Walker), 227
Combs, Arthur, 113
Community, 172–87
  boundaries of, 174–78
  charter or magnet schools and, 178
  common goals in, 181–82
  cooperation in, 183–84
  defined, 174
  at for-character schools, 249–50
  hierarchy in, 184
  microcommunities in, 185–87

  practices and policies on, 187
  rites and symbols of, 182–83
  school philosophies and, 178–79
  time as a factor of, 179–81
Comprehensive sex education, flaws in, 222–25
Condoms, 223, 230–31
Congressional Budget Office, 12
Consensus
  curriculum development and, 152–53
  leadership and, 192
Consequences, 45, 90–101
Consequentialism, 22
Consistency, 22, 23, 41
Constitution, U.S., 47
Cooperation and community, 183–84
Cooperative learning, 164–69
Corbett, William, 149
Counts, George, 164
Courage, prosocial conduct and, 67
Cox, Harvey, 145
Cremin, Lawrence, 25
Cultural literacy, 135
Cultural relativism, 131
Culverwell, Rosemary, 241–42, 245, 248–49
Curriculum, 142–71
  consensus on principles, handling failure of,
    152–53
  cooperative learning and, 164–69
  ethical ideals and, 147–49
  ethical thinking skills and, 153–55
  formal, 134
  heroes in, 155–59, 160–61
  moral action and, 161–64, 169
  moral content of, 146
  moral facts of life in, 146–47
  moral imagination development in, 159–60
  new sexuality and, 227
  null, 144–45
  practical roots of shared morality and, 149–52
  practices and policies on, 170
  as social wager, 145–46

Damon, William, 160
Deferred gratification
  concept of, 69–72
  in-school and in-classroom practice of, 72–75
Defining deviancy down, 11
Delattre, Edwin, 154
Democracy and Education (Dewey)
Democratic Schools movement, 162–64

De-Moralization of Society: From Victorian Virtues to Modern Values (Himmelfarb), 228
Desegregation, 153
Detention, 246
Dewey, John, 19, 22, 36, 42, 162, 255
Dilemma approach to moral education, 128–29
Diligence, 24–25, 48, 124
    as moral value, 7
    self-esteem and, 115–16
Direct guidance, defined, 126
Discipline, 1, 87–105
    breakdown, causes of, 89–91
    ceremonies and, 213–14
    defined, 87–88
    docility and, 133–34
    at for-character schools, 245–46
    public perception of, 11
    punishment and, 88–89, 97–105
    rules and, 88, 91–97
    student learning and, 12–13
Divorce, 226
Docility, defined, 133–34
Drebeen, R., 83
Drug use, 8, 9, 15
    Bobby Knight on, 130–31
Dukakis, Michael, 210
Durkheim, Emile, 8, 54
Duty, ethical ideal of, 148

Eagle Scouts, 54
Education, New York State Department of, 20
Education, U.S. Department of, 11, 75
Educational goals, 32–57, 107, 116. *See also*
        Academics; Character; Discipline
    authority and decisions on, 45–47
    Great Tradition of, 34–38
    happy-think and, 256–58
    learning theories and, 38–45
    practices and policies on, 56
    profound learning and, 47–56
    sentiment versus sentimentality in, 255–56
Educational research, moral education and,
        53–56
Educational Testing Services, 114
Education and the Public Trust (Delattre), 154
Education of Cyrus, The (Xenophon), 53
Educators. *See also* Principals; Teachers
    beliefs about moral values, 1–2
    philosophy and, 17–25
    reformers, relations with, 2–7

religion and, 25–28
    youth conduct and, 7–17
Emile (Rousseau), 42
Employment, character education and, 68–69
Enrollment restriction, school community and,
        176–78
Equality
    defined, 83–84
    Jefferson on, 77–78, 82
    learning declines and, 76–77
    learning incentives and, 78–80
    pupil grouping and, 82–84
    of sexual values, 222
    social promotion and, 80–82
Escalante, Jaime, 2, 110, 111, 125
Ethical ideals, 147–49
Ethnic conflicts, 177
Ethos, 109–16, 119
    in the classroom, 109–13
    diligence and, 115–16
    hidden curriculum and, 144
    self-esteem movement and, 113–15
Etzioni, Amitai, 107
Everhart, Robert, 114, 115
Extracurricular activities, later-life success and, 66

Fairness, 22, 102–3
Faith, ethical ideal of, 148
Family, 45–46
    American, changes in, 121–22
    as teaching entity, 107
Federalist Papers, The, 257
For-character school recognition program, 239–40
For-character schools
    academics in, 247–48
    athletics in, 242–44
    can-do attitudes in, 252
    ceremonies in, 250–52
    collective identities in, 249–50
    discipline in, 245–46
    hiring decisions in, 241–42
    qualifications for, 239–40
    teacher supervision in, 248–49
Formal curriculum, 143
Formal education, defined, 39
Fortitude, ethical ideal of, 148
Franklin, Benjamin, 148
French Revolution, 77
Freud, Sigmund, 37, 53, 257
Fullinwider, Robert, 108

Gallup Poll, 88
Geerz, Clifford, 3
German schools, 185
Goleman, Daniel, 13
Goodbye Columbus (Roth), 227
Gordon, Thomas, 113
Grading systems, 79, 165–68
Graduation ceremonies, 182, 212, 213, 251
Grant, Gerald, 95–96, 110–11
Great Tradition, 34–38
 community and, 173
 historical cyclicity and, 35–36
 intellectual rationale for, 36–38
 trait psychology and, 54–56
 undermined, 128–29
Greco-Roman tradition, ethical ideals of, 148
Green, Thomas, 125
Group cohesion, 149, 249–50
Group identity, learning and, 48
Grouping by ability, 82–84, 247
Guidance counselors, 126–27
Guild membership, 125
Gurr, Ted, 35

Habituation, 39, 60
Hackworth, David, 70
Hamlet (Shakespeare), 40, 42
Hansot, Elizabeth, 34
Happy-think, 256–58
Hard-case morality, 131–33
Hartschorne, H., 54, 56
Heather Has Two Mommies, 227
Herodotus, 43
Heroes
 community recognition of, 180–81
 in moral education curriculum, 155–59, 160–61
Hidden curriculum, 144
Hierarchy, need for, 184
Himmelfarb, Gertrude, 228
Hirsch, E. D., 135
Hirsch, E. J., 2
Hobbes, Thomas, 257
Holt, J., 144
Homerooms, 186–87, 249
Homework, 75–76, 247
Homicide, 7, 8, 9, 10
Honesty in sex education, 234
Honig, Bill, 2
Honor roll, 247

Hope, ethical ideal of, 148
Horace's Compromise (Sizer), 109
House system as microcommunity, 186
Hunt, Richard, 160

I.D. Cards, 175
Illegitimate births, 7, 8, 9, 10, 223, 224
Incentives
 for academic excellence, 78–80
 for character development, 67–68
 immediate and long range, 90–91
 for learning, 39–40
Individualism, American value of, 13–14, 150, 151
In loco parentis, 74, 126
Insight, learning and, 41
Institutes on Oratory (Quintilian), 33
Instructional leadership, 201. *See also* Principals
Interscholastic competition, nonathletic, 181–82
Intrinsic motivation, 22–23, 42–43
Invitational learning, 113
Inviting School Success (Purkey), 113

Jackson, Jesse, 230
Janissaries, 77
Japanese elementary schools, 80
Japanese high schools, 185
Jefferson, Thomas, 159
 on equality and education, 77–78, 82
 on government and discipline, 87
Jesuit education system, 79
Joplin Plan, 83
Judeo Christian tradition, ethical ideals of, 147–49
Justice, ethical ideal of, 148
Just Say No program, 15

Kean, Thomas, 2
Kenney, Asta, 223
Kesey, Ken, 227
Kidder, Tracy, 109–10, 125
Kilpatrick, William Kirk, 159, 219
Kirk, Russell, 20
Klapp, Orrin, 54
Knight, Bobby, 130–31
Kohlberg, Lawrence, 21, 53, 55, 131
 Democratic Schools movement and, 162, 163
Kohn, Alfie, 22
Kozol, Jonathan, 25, 144
Kramer, Rita, 113
Krathwohl, D., 40

Lanckton, Alice, 128
Leadership. *See* Principals
Learning
  continuous, in teachers, 124
  cooperative, 164–69
  defined, 38
  egalitarianism and declines in, 76–77
  idea of, as fun, 42–45
  incentives for, 39–40
  intensification of, 41–42
  invitational, 113
  levels of, 38–39
  observable, teacher evaluation and, 195
  profound, 40–41, 47–56
  skills for ethical thinking, 153–55
  teacher's dedication to students' success in,
    124–25
  youth conduct and declines in, 12–13
Learning-is-fun concept, 42–45
Leavis, F. R., 34
Leo, John, 232
Lerner, Barbara, 80
Letter grades versus percentages, 79
Le Vine, Robert, 43, 54
Lewis, C. S., 146–47
Liberal arts education, 135
Lincoln, Abraham, 7
Lithuanian-Americans, 51–52
Lortie, Daniel C., 189
Lucian, 255

MacIntyre, Alasdair, 20
Magnet schools, 178
Marine Corps boot camp, learning at, 41, 42
Masia, B., 40
Maslow, Abraham, 113, 114
Mast, Colleen Kelly, 233
Masty, Thomas, 148
Matthews, Jay, 110, 125
May, M. A., 54, 56
McLuhan, Marshall, 117
Meier, Deborah, 3
Memorization, teaching character and, 60
Microcommunities, 185–87
Minimum competency tests, 80–81
Misconduct, causes of, 89–91
Moline, Jon, 143
Moral action, curriculum and, 161–64, 169
Moral autonomy, 154

Moral Child, The (Damon), 160
Moral education. *See also* Academics; Character;
    Curriculum; Discipline
  classroom environment and, 107–9
  education research and, 53–56
  families and, 107, 121–22
  Great Tradition and, 34–38
  hard-case morality and, 131–33
  ineffectiveness in, 127–29
  philosophers and, 19–24
  preaching and, 129–31
  principles of, 59
  as priority, 138–39
  process of, 131
  religion and, 26–28
  sex education and, 228–29
  of teachers, 133–38
  teachers as direct source of, 126–27
  types of, 143–45
Moral facts of life, 146–47
Moral growth, theories of, 137–38
Moral imagination, development of, 159–60
Moral literacy, 135
Moral schools, 189–93. *See also* Ceremonies;
    Classrooms; Curriculum; For-character
    schools; Moral education; Principals;
    Teachers
Moral values, traditional, 33, 231. *See also*
    Academics; Character; Discipline
  America's shift toward, 15–16
  authority for teaching of, 45–47
  educators' beliefs about, 1–2
  erosion of consensus regarding, 134
  Great Tradition and, 34–38
More, Thomas, 33
Moynihan, Daniel, 11

Naked Public Square, The (Neuhaus), 28
National Assessment of Educational Progress,
    75
Natural consequences, 99
Nazi party, 46, 52
Neuhaus, Richard, 28
Newsweek, 228
Nimmukwallah service concept, 190–91, 194
Noddings, Nel, 60
Nonathletic competition, 181–82
Nord, Warren, 156
Null curriculum, 144–45

Oak Forest High School, 241
  academics at, 247–48
  athletics at, 242–44
  ceremonies at, 251–52
  collective identity at, 249
  discipline at, 245, 246
  student council in, 246–47
Oath of the Ephebi, 179, 180
Old Deluder Satan Act, 137
Oliver, Jose Garcia, 148
One Flew Over the Cuckoo's Nest (Kesey),
  227
On the Education of Children (Seneca), 87
Orwell, George, 225
Overt curriculum, 143

*Parallel Lives of the Ancient Greeks and Noble
  Romans* (Plutarch), 160
Partnership for Character Education, 16
Peer groups, moral advice of, 127
Percy, Walker, 122
Philosophy
  cheating and, 18–19
  educational reform and, 17–25, 137
  morals and, 19–24
  school's statement of, 178–79
  teacher diligence and, 24–25
Piaget, Jean, 53
Plato, 19, 20, 33, 54, 77
Pledge of Allegiance, 151, 179, 210
Pledges, school, 179, 182, 242
Pluralism, 37–38
Plutarch, 33, 160
Polybius, 209
Pope, Alexander, 148, 161
Powell, Arthur, 4
Power of teachers, 122
  potential abuse of, 44–45, 101–2, 191
Practices and policies
  on ceremonies, 215–16
  on character and academics, 75
  on classroom morals and ethos, 119
  on community, 187
  on curriculum development, 170
  on educational goals, 56
  in for-character schools, 252–53
  on principals and leadership, 206
  on sex education, 236
  on teachers as moral educators, 139–40
  on teaching discipline, 105
  on teaching values, 28–29

Praise
  for academic excellence, 78–79
  for prosocial conduct, 67–68
Preaching, moral education and, 129–31
Preliterate societies, 33
Principals, 1, 189, 190, 193–206
  communication of school standards by, 197–98
  desirable traits of teachers identified by, 194
  feedback to teachers from, 204
  at for-character schools, 241–42, 245, 248–49
  good teaching identified by, 193–94
  information collection by, 199–202
  observation of teachers as role models by, 196–97
  practices and policies on leadership and, 206
  pupil learning and, 195
  rewards and sanctions for teacher performance
    by, 205
  as role model for teachers, 205
  staff selection process and, 198–202
  teacher collegiality fostered by, 203–4
  translation of good teacher traits into observable
    conduct and, 195–96
Prisons, learning in, 41, 42
Professional teachers' groups, 125
Profound learning, 40–41, 47–56
  athletics and, 48–51
  educational research on, 53–56
  sexual conduct and, 224
  transformational education and, 51–53
Prosocial conduct, 62–68
  courage as outcome of, 67
  defined, 62
  discipline versus, 87–88
  incentives for, 67–68
  levels of, 68
  school service organizations and, 63–66
Protradition reforms, 15–16
  educators and, 2–7
  teacher diligence and, 24–25
Proximity, learning and, 41
Prudence, ethical ideal of, 148
Psychology, moral education and, 53–56, 235
Publicity, school spirit and, 182
Punishment, 45, 97–105, 244
  classroom policy for, 101–2
  collective versus individual, 103
  effective forms of, 97–99
  enforcement of, 103–4
  fairness of, 102–3
  learning and, 41
  natural versus constructed consequences, 99–101

need for, 87–89, 90
  principles for teachers regarding, 104–5
  rules under pressure and, 102–3
Purkey, William W., 113

Quintilian, 33

Ravitch, Diane, 2, 25
Read, Margaret, 1
Reagan, Nancy, 15
Reason, sexual decisions and, 235
Recess, 244
Recognition systems, 78–79
Reilly Elementary School
  academics at, 247
  can-do attitude at, 252
  ceremonies at, 250–51
  collective identity at, 249–50
  discipline at, 245–46
  hiring decisions at, 241–42
  recess at, 244
  student council in, 246
  teacher supervision at, 248–49
Religion
  ceremonies and, 211, 251
  prohibition in public schools, 27–28
  sex education and, 229–30, 235
  transmission of moral values and, 26–27
Republic (Plato), 77
Responsibilities, 1–2
  group, 103
  rules, rights and, 95–97, 111
Rewards, 41, 90. *See also* Ceremonies; Incentives
Rights of students, 95–97, 111
Rites of passage, 74–75, 212
Roberts, Ed, 241
Rogers, Carl, 113, 114
Role models
  heroes and, 157–59
  from history and literature, 62, 156–57
  principals as, 205
  teachers as, 1, 121–23, 196–97
Roman Republic, 45–46
Romeo and Juliet (Shakespeare), 11, 231
Roth, Philip, 227
Rousseau, Jean-Jacques, 42, 54, 55, 107, 257
Rules, 87–97
  against cheating, 18–19, 24–25
  classroom, 94–95
  guidelines for establishment of, 95
  need for, 87–89

rights, responsibilities and, 95–97, 111
  schoolwide, 91–93
  as teachers of civility, 91

Sarton, May, 159
Schlesinger, Arthur, Jr., 20, 36
Scholastic Aptitude Test (SAT), 12
School Assessment Checklist, 66, 240
School-based management, 192–93
School philosophy, statement of, 178–79
Schools and Civilizational States (Cohen), 239
School service organizations, 63–66
School song, 183
School spirit, sense of community and, 173–74
Scout Law, 60
Self-esteem movement, 113–16
Seneca, 87
Sentimentality
  in learning theories, 43
  sentiment versus, 255–56
Service organizations, 63–66
Sex education, 74
  abstinence as ideal in, 231–33
  character-centered, 233–36
  comprehensive, 222–25
  condom distribution and, 230–31
  inevitability of, 220–21
  moral education and, 228–29
  religion and, 229–30, 235
Sexually transmitted diseases (STDs), 223, 225
Sexual values, 218–37
  changes in, 221–22
  comprehensive sex education and, 222–25
  curriculum and, 227
  data on youth disorder and, 10–11
  inevitability of sex education and, 220–21
  moral nature of, 228–29
  new sexuality and, 226
  1960s revolution in, 225–26
  teachers and, 226–27
  traditional, 231
Shakespeare, William, 11, 40, 42, 231
Shanker, Albert, 2
Shopping mall high school, 4–6, 25
Shriver, Eunice Kennedy, 233
Shuttleworth, F. K., 54, 56
Silberman, C. E., 144
Simon, Sidney, 128
Sizer, Theodore, 3, 109, 185
Skinner, B. F., 21
Slavin, Robert, 83

Smoking, attitudes toward, 151–52
Social promotion, 80–82
Social Studies Syllabus Review Committee, 20
Social wager, curriculum as, 145–46
Sociology, moral education and, 54
Soviet Union, former, 46, 52, 145
Span of control, 200
Spender, Stephen, 159
Staff committees, 248–49
Stand And Deliver (film), 110
Status, learning and, 41
Student attitudes toward education, 116–18
Student councils, 246–47
Student handbooks, 95–96, 111
Students Against Drunk Driving (SADD), 71
Suicide, 7, 8–9, 10
Suspensions, 246
Swidler, Ann, 25

Taiwan, public schools in, 79–80
Tao, C. S. Lewis on, 146–47
Tardiness, 5–6, 90
Teacher education, 133–38
  moral literacy and, 135
  skills for teaching morality and, 135–37
  theories of moral growth and, 137–38
Teachers
  abusive power, potential for, 101–2
  collegiate spirit among, 203–4
  as craftspeople, 123–25
  criteria for conduct by, 193–94
  desirable traits in, 194, 195–96
  diligence in, 24–25
  education of, 133–38
  feedback for, 204
  moral ethos created by, 109–13
  moral schools concept and, 191
  principal as role model for, 205
  prosocial activities and, 65–66
  punishment by, 104–5
  pupil learning and, 195
  rewards and sanctions for, 205
  as role models, 1, 121–23, 196–97
  rules established by, 94–95
  selection and evaluation of, 198–202
  sex education and, 234
  sexual values and, 226–27
  students' attitudes, guidelines for changing, 118
  supervision at for-character schools, 248–49
Teaching, criteria for, 193–94
Temperance, ethical ideal of, 148
Tenure, 205

Theology, moral education and, 137
Time, 228, 232
Time
  as factor in building community, 179–81
  as factor in learning, 41, 47–48
Tracking by ability, 82–84, 247
Trait psychology, 54–56
Transformational education, 51–53
Troubled Crusade, The (Ravitch), 25
Turkish Empire, 77
Tyack, David, 34

Uniforms, 175

Values, traditional. *See* Moral values, traditional
Values clarification, 128, 131, 155
Values Education, Maryland State Commission on, 60
Vermette, P., 165
Virtues, 60, 148, 234–35
Vitz, Paul, 158, 229
Volition, learning and, 42
Voucher plans, 153, 190, 221

Walker, Alice, 227
Waller, Willard, 200
Wallpaper factor, 127
Washington, George, 148
Way of All Flesh, The (Butler), 123
White, Barbara Dafoe, 224
White, Merry, 43, 54
Whitehead, Alfred North, 157
Why Jonny Can't Tell Right from Wrong (Kilpatrick), 219
Wilson, James Q., 52
Winthrop, John, 181
World Atlas survey, 157–58
World We Created at Hamilton High, The (Grant), 110–11

Xenophon, 53

Youth: Transition into Adulthood (Coleman), 161
Youth conduct, 7–17
  decline in learning and, 12–13
  educational policies and, 15–17
  estimates of, 11–12
  meaning of decline in, 13–14
  measures of, 7–11
Yulish, S. M., 34

Zajac, Chris, 109–10, 111, 125